The Imperial Republic

BOOKS BY RAYMOND ARON

The Great Debate
The Century of Total War
The Dawn of Universal History
France: Steadfast and Changing
France: The New Republic
German Sociology
Introduction to the Philosophy of History
On War
The Opium of the Intellectuals
War and Industrial Society
Peace and War
Main Currents in Sociological Thought
Progress and Disillusion

THE
IMPERIAL
REPUBLIC

The United States and the World

1945–1973

RAYMOND ARON

Translated by Frank Jellinek

Prentice-Hall, Inc., Englewood Cliffs, New Jersey

The Imperial Republic, The United States and the World 1945–1973
by Raymond Aron, translated by Frank Jellinek
Copyright © 1974 by Raymond Aron
La République Impériale copyright Calmann Levy 1973
All rights reserved. No part of this book may be
reproduced in any form or by any means, except
for the inclusion of brief quotations in a review,
without permission in writing from the publisher.
Printed in the United States of America
Prentice-Hall International, Inc., London
Prentice-Hall of Australia, Pty. Ltd., Sydney
Prentice-Hall of Canada, Ltd., Toronto
Prentice-Hall of India Private Ltd., New Delhi
Prentice-Hall of Japan, Inc., Tokyo

10 9 8 7 6 5 4 3 2

Library of Congress Cataloging in Publication Data
Aron, Raymond.
 The imperial republic; the United States and the
world, 1945–1973.
 Translation of République impériale; les États-Unis
dans le monde, 1945–1972.
 1. United States—Foreign relations—1945–
 2. United States—Foreign economic relations.
 I. Title.
E744.A7613   327.73   74-1389
ISBN 0–13–451781–4

PREFACE TO THE AMERICAN EDITION

For some years I had been thinking of writing a critical essay on the foreign policy of the United States, and had arranged to complete the manuscript by January 1, 1973. I could not make up my mind which of the various possible approaches to the subject would be best. I could approach it by way of the United States' part in the shaping of the diplomatic system, and then, as the various topics arise, discuss the nation's part in forming the nuclear system, the monetary system, and the postwar trade system—that is, proceed in terms of subject matter. Or I could either identify the successive stages in the development of the foreign policy, or, conversely, stress its continuity and give a conspectus of the entire quarter-century, encompassing American paramountcy, containment, rivalry with the Soviet Union, and the cold war. This raised the further question of what prominence I ought to give to the debate initiated by those commentators who are known on the other side of the Atlantic as "revisionists," and who do not always realize that they are simply continuing a tradition of the American republic; for there were revisionists after each of the foreign wars waged by the American republic: those against Mexico, against Spain, and against Germany and Japan. The history of the War of Secession, too, has been revised time and again.

In the end, two events furnished me with the answer I had been seeking: the announcement of President Nixon's visit to Communist China and the devaluation of the dollar in August 1971. The first indicated a shift of direction in United States foreign policy, with an ideological significance even more important, perhaps, than its material consequences. The second fully illuminated the dualism of a great power's action—not so much the dualism of enemy-ally as the dualism of politics-economics. The above events provided a framework for a dual approach, and hence for the two parts of the book, the first being a study of the United States in the inter-state system and the second

vii

being an examination of the United States in the world market. The natural and necessary approach to the first part was chronological, but in the second, this method was applicable only to the tracing of the creation, expansion, and decay of the monetary system.

When I wrote *finis* to the last page of the French manuscript late in 1972, the outcome of the postwar era was clearly discernible: the United States' rapprochement with its enemies (the Soviet Union and Communist China), trade and monetary disputes with its European and Japanese allies, the narrowing of the gap between the wealth of the United States and that of its partner-rivals, the revolt of the Senate against the President's omnipotence, the massing of public opinion against the imperial burden, and the arraignment of those who had been responsible for the war in Vietnam.

Was President Nixon—the man responsible for prolonging the fighting for four more years, but also for negotiating the agreement with Hanoi without betraying Saigon—to be cast in the role of defendant or prosecutor? In January 1973 the career of this controversial figure, detested by the intellectual and political elites of the eastern seaboard for more than twenty years, reached its zenith. But his fall was to be swift and sudden.

At the time of the President's inauguration in January 1973 I had not anticipated that the French text of the book would need any significant revision for the American version. In the course of a single year no answer was likely to emerge to the questions on which the historical era and the book itself closed: Will the United States find a middle way between globalism and isolationism, between the pretension to make the dollar the pivot on which all currencies must turn and the temptation to resort to unbridled devaluation? These questions should therefore have still been valid in the spring of 1974. Events proved otherwise.

The Watergate affair and its ramifications are strengthening the Senate against a secretive and testy president. Even before 1973 the Senate, and especially the Foreign Relations Committee under Senator W. J. Fulbright, had, of course, frequently attacked the prerogatives which Richard Nixon had arrogated to himself in the conduct of diplomatic and military operations. Welcome as this revolt may be in some respects, Watergate is likely to secure for it a victory whose very completeness may well become a source of danger. Only yesterday the Senate had been incapable of performing its supervisory duties; will the President tomorrow be incapable of acting at all?

A foreigner is understandably reluctant to comment on an affair which has so many specifically American traits, not the least of which are the supremacy of the courts and the contrast between the cynicism of certain practices and a much paraded, yet perfectly genuine, respect for the law. Few sensible persons, it seems to me, would accuse the President himself of being cognizant of or ordering the break-in and bugging of the Democratic Party's headquarters. What his opponents and the bulk of the public do believe is that he has tried to "cover up" culpable behavior and prevent a "scandal." That the chief executive should try to cover members of his staff whose misdeeds have bespattered the presidency itself is normal enough, but it constitutes a crime when it amounts to obstructing the course of justice. And over and above the Watergate incident itself, further investigations have thrown light on various other matters of rather a different nature, such as the dubious use of public funds to furnish the President's private homes, the harassment of political opponents by the use of Federal agencies, and the general spread of wiretapping and taping conversations. It is not for me to determine whether Richard Nixon's behavior differs in kind from that of his predecessors (as his enemies claim) or whether it reveals the savagery of no-holds-barred competition in magnified and disproportionate form. The fact remains that the President's entourage was none too scrupulous (if I may venture a gross understatement) and that in a game of this sort it is the one who is caught in the act who takes the blame. Richard Nixon was not insensitive to the hatred he aroused in many journalists, intellectuals, and members of the Democratic Party. What was the point of using the methods of psychological warfare, spreading false rumors, sending emissaries into the opponents' camp, and resorting to other such puerile tricks to influence the choice of the Democratic candidate, or of stealing files from a psychiatrist's office, when, with the prestige of his pilgrimages for peace to Moscow and Peking and the imminent ending of the Vietnam War, his reelection was assured? The trials he is now undergoing, however agonizing they may seem to the impartial observer, are appropriate punishment for a strange misjudgment in the choice of his collaborators. Where a president is concerned, it is hard to draw the line between error and fault; to judge a president's advisers amounts to judging a president himself and appraising his perspicacity, if not his intentions.

A foreigner is in no position to carry the analysis further, nor should he. The Watergate affair is as specifically American as the Dreyfus affair was specifically French. One of Watergate's features is the presence in the White House of persons who are even less scrupulous in their methods than are their counterparts in most of the free European countries; but another, and far more important feature of the affair is the existence of a press freer and courts more independent than elsewhere. A Frenchman finds the public disclosure of the scandal even more characteristic of the United States than the scandal itself.

Everyone is of course free to take his own view of the affair; the essential point to grasp, however, is that President Nixon's authority is bound to be impaired to some degree and that the Senate is bound, temporarily at least, to exert more influence on United States foreign policy than it has since 1939, even if Secretary of State Henry Kissinger regains the trust of the elected legislature. Historically minded Europeans, however, cannot help harboring somewhat dubious memories of past senatorial interventions in American diplomacy, notably the refusal to ratify the Treaty of Versailles, the refusal to join the League of Nations, the enactment of the neutrality legislation of the Thirties, the onslaught by a section of the Senate against Harry Truman and Dean Acheson and in favor of Nationalist China, and the support for the House Committee on Un-American Activities; it was a senator who gave McCarthyism its name (though, to be fair, it was the Senate that censured and ruined him); and it was the Senate, too, that some fifteen years ago voted more funds for national defense than the President had requested and that is now trying to cut the defense appropriations.

What other conclusion can be drawn than that Senate and senators reflect in magnified form the swings of public opinion from one extreme to the other? Only yesterday China was an untouchable and any dissenter from this view was suspect of dealings with the enemy. Today anyone who compares the Soviet drive to step up its armaments with the American drive to economize on defense spending is regarded as a holdover from the cold war. One cannot help wondering at times whether the American republic will ever attain maturity and whether it will at length realize that power implies rights and duties—limited rights and permanent duties. In twenty-five years the United States has perhaps not yet learned what it took the European states centuries to grasp.

With this in mind, I feel that for once I can speak out forthrightly and assert that it is on Richard Nixon and Henry Kissinger that a European pins his hopes for a foreign policy governed by reason. The elected representatives of the American nation are swayed today by economic interests, both commercial and monetary, since public opinion does not cry out in fear of an enemy or call for a crusade against evil. It was in a somewhat similar period that Congress voted the Hawley-Smoot protective tariff. It is to the presidency rather than the Senate that Europeans look for an equitable policy. Similarly, it is on the presidency rather than the Senate that Europeans are counting to ensure that any withdrawal of the American troops back across the Atlantic is effected neither haphazardly nor without proper compensatory arrangements. Will the events of the fall of 1973 reverse the trend? The new war, or rather the fourth battle between Israel and the Arabs, has shown the limits of the so-called détente or rapprochement between the super-powers. Did Leonid Brezhnev really show the restraint—the favorite word of the Secretary of State—which was required by the spirit of the last agreement signed by the General Secretary of the Communist Party of the Soviet Union and the President of the United States in the spring of 1973? Put to the test, the Russian-American agreement perhaps contributed to maintaining communications, but not to preventing the threat of military action from either side. Collision rather than collusion was to be feared. The world was back, for a few hours, to brinkmanship, and peace again appeared precariously based on the common horror of the unthinkable disaster.

In 1956, the Atlantic Alliance almost fell apart when France and Great Britain, associated with Israel, used military force against Egypt after the nationalization of the Suez Canal. In 1973, at the crucial hour, when the United States had to supply Israel with sophisticated weapons and munitions to restore the balance, and when President Nixon and Henry Kissinger, thinking that the Soviet Union was about to send troops to the battlefield, put American forces throughout the world on an alert, the Europeans—with the exception of the Dutch and the Portuguese—refused to cooperate. They excluded themselves from any participation in the events, yet felt humiliated when excluded from the cease-fire and from the peace conference. More vulnerable to the oil embargo than the United States—they get 80%, and not 7%, of their oil from Arab countries—the European community was more eager to get along with the cartel of the oil producing nations than with the transatlantic ally.

For the past four years, after all, Henry Kissinger has devoted most of his time and skill to dealing with Moscow and Peking. About the Middle East, all the decisions (even the decision not to do anything) were taken in Washington, not in Paris or London. Why should the Europeans suddenly accept responsibility for a policy that had been conducted over their heads and would jeopardize their relations with the Arabs and their import of oil? Not a great-hearted attitude, to be sure, but any pupil of Metternich or Bismarck should hardly be surprised or irritated by such an interpretation of national interest. For a few days Henry Kissinger found himself alone, neither helped by Moscow nor supported by the Europeans.

The energy crisis—inevitable in any case—was merely precipitated by the war and will hurt the European Community far more than the United States. The relative strength of currencies may therefore be reversed again. The dollar may regain its power, and the Europeans discover the fragility of their prosperity. They have been drawing on external sources for the life blood of their economies. Similarly, the determinants of their role are largely external. On their eastern borders, they face the mighty Soviet empire; far away to the west lies their protector, still powerful but, as ever, not quite predictable.

Thus, 1973 was not the year of Europe. Rather, it was the year of the Arabs and of oil. But 1973 showed clearly that there is no way for the American republic to retreat from world responsibility. It illustrated, rather dramatically, one of the main ideas in this book: Just as the Imperial Republic must find a middle way between globalism and isolationism, so Henry Kissinger must now put as much emphasis on solidarity with allies as on dialogue with rivals. The difficulty lies in operating the policy rather than in conceiving it. Policy, like strategy, is an art in which everything depends on execution. Or, to quote Clausewitz rather than Napoleon: Everything about it is simple, but the simple is always difficult.

Raymond Aron

CONTENTS

Preface to the American Edition   vii

Introduction   xv

Prologue: The Insular Continent   xxiii

PART I

The United States in the Inter-State System: The Success and Failure of Paramountcy

Introduction   1

Chapter I: Assigning the Guilt: The Origins of the Cold War   9

Chapter II: The Two Crusades   43

Chapter III: Ascent and Descent   72

Chapter IV: Disciples of Metternich   110

Conclusion: Success or Failure?   148

PART II

The United States in the World Market: The Privileges and Constraints of a Dominant Economy

Introduction   159

Chapter I: Freedom of Persons or Freedom of Trade: The Economic Foundations of American Diplomacy   163

Chapter II: The Two Marshall Plans: The Round Trip of the Dollars   188

Chapter III: Aid or Counterrevolution: The United States and the Third World   220

Chapter IV: The Changing Forms of Imperialism   252

Conclusion: The End of Economic Sovereignties   286

Postscript: Between Imperial Diplomacy and Isolationism   297

Index   331

INTRODUCTION

Although contemporary history has at last come to be recognized as a valid university subject, academic scholars still deprecate it on the grounds that it smacks far too much of journalism; the contradiction between scholarship and journalism has yet to be resolved. How can one possibly write a book, whether analytical or narrative, on the external action[1] of the United States since 1945 unless one has a horde of assistants to process the vast mass of source material—newspapers, memoirs, books, interviews, and so on—spawned by every incidental event of the past twenty-five years? And there is the even greater problem of how to substantiate an interpretation of the protagonists' motives when not only are scores of the basic documents unavailable and the archives of most of the countries concerned still inaccessible, but the mass of uncheckable material presents an even worse hindrance than the gaps in the documentation.

The external action of the United States is a prime example of this contradiction, for it is both better known and less known than that of any other state.

Everyone will readily agree that the international stage has been dominated since 1945 by two major protagonists, the two great powers, the Big Two, the super-powers, the continent-states (whatever term the reader prefers). But these two, so akin yet at the same time so hostile, are by no means opposing counterparts, in the sense that they are not an open society and a closed society, an oligarchy wide open to in-

---

[1] In the notion of "external action" I include not merely diplomacy in the narrow sense, such as the decisions of the State Department, the Pentagon, and the CIA—what I have elsewhere called "diplomatico-strategic behavior" —but also the influence and the voluntary or involuntary pressure exerted on other countries by the United States just as much through what it *is* as through what it *does*, just as much through its multinational corporations as through its diplomats proper.

spection and an oligarchy lurking in the arcane depths of the Kremlin, a Washington capable of everything except silence and a Moscow where even the diplomatic corps' best source of information has at times been the newspapers.

Paradoxically, it might plausibly be argued that it is precisely the American diplomats'[2] all too lavish confessions of error and their consequent efforts at self-justification that make them totally elusive, whereas the Soviet diplomats are more prone to reveal themselves by their very silence. Paradox apart, the behavior of American diplomats is explicable only in terms of that of their Soviet counterparts. Any correct judgment of the diplomacy of deterrence as practiced by the United States would require a knowledge of the Soviet projects; for if deterrence is successful, how can we demonstrate that the rival power intended to do what it did not do? The memoirs of Mr. Khrushchev bear little resemblance to the books by Schlesinger, Sorensen, and other members of President Kennedy's entourage, all of them determined to relate their experience the moment they left the White House, having in their simultaneous role as advisers and memoir-writers an incomparable advantage over academic historians (an advantage whose cost only future historians will assess). As eyewitnesses and interpreters they describe history in the making as if it were history already made.

American action, which perpetually talks and is talked about, awakens echoes all over the world, giving rise to vehement discussion, more often hostile than favorable. The interest it arouses is far greater than that evoked by its rival's action. In Stalin's time the Soviet Union was a fascinating enigma; Khrushchev's era was marked by a picturesque medley of Marx and moujik that had a peculiar interest all its own. Brezhnev's Soviet Union lacks such interest, though we are probably wrong to be bored by it; for after all, to bring Czechoslovakia to heel in 1968–69 with practically no loss of life was a masterpiece of sorts. Stalin, the heavy-footed, with his frontier incidents and his witch trials, ultimately drove Marshal Tito to reconcile Marxism-Leninism with patriotism. There were no witch trials in Czechoslovakia (it was in "humanist" Cuba that a poet discovered in jail that his judges held the truth of the matter, and of his own accord decided to make his own self-criticism), but the reformers' abjuration was all the more degrading in that it was presented as voluntary. After a quarter of a century, the imperial technique of the men in the Kremlin displays its mastery by

---

[2] By the term "diplomats" I mean all those who are responsible for the foreign policy of states, not merely such professionals as ambassadors and State Department officials. "Diplomacy," then, denotes action by diplomats as understood in this very broad sense.

causing a minimum of outcry. One cannot say as much of the imperial technique of the men in Washington.

Because of the obstacles presented by overabundant, yet defective, documentation, the heterogeneous nature of the two super-powers whose rivalry dominates inter-state relations in the postwar period, and the violent emotions aroused by men and events that are still part of our present, or of a past in which we ourselves figured as both actors and spectators, no one can guarantee that any book he writes on such topics will be wholly impartial and scientific. Besides, I am not a professional historian by training nor do I have the necessary time or resources for exhaustive research. What I am presenting here is an *essay* or *sketch*, an essay which is intended to be a *critique*, not a *narrative*, of the external action of the United States.

Critical books on American diplomacy abound. The best of them have been written by Americans, and by and large I find that they follow two main lines of thought. One, that of the realist school, concentrates solely or almost solely on diplomatic-strategic behavior, questions the American perception of the inter-state system, and deals not so much with American diplomats' interpretation of the Soviet Union and its projects at any given moment as with the philosophy that American presidents from Wilson to Truman, from 1917 to 1947, have brought to bear on their duties. George Kennan has denounced the blend of legalistic and moralistic words and the impulsive and brutal deeds characteristic of American diplomacy at the turn of the century, from the war with Spain to the years preceding the Second World War. Henry Morgenthau has been the principal popularizer of the traditional philosophy, that of the European cabinets, the civilized Machiavellianism, the refusal to indulge in either the spirit of crusade or isolationism. The resulting lesson that the use of force is justified only when it serves the national interest amounts to the moral rejection of the moralistic, to the morality of realism.

Stanley Hoffmann, too, has fairly recently[3] expounded the arguments of the realist school with indefatigable patience and subtlety. The theme of the "Wilson syndrome," the swing between crusading and withdrawal into isolation, has now been relegated to the folklore of political science. More generally, Hoffmann tries to account for the external action of the United States both by the bureaucratic organization of the federal state and by a national style deriving from a systematic view or philosophy of inter-state relations.

---

[3] *Gulliver's Troubles, or the Setting of American Foreign Policy* (New York: McGraw-Hill Book Company, 1968).

The second school, which I shall call the "imperial America" school, is subdivided into a right and a left. The right—not very numerous—recognizes and applauds the imperial—not imperialist—role of the United States (George Liska's small book[4] contains one of the most perspicacious expositions of this view); the left—the "paramarxist"[5] school—sees the origin of American expansionism in the requirements of monopoly capitalism. Harry Magdoff's *The Age of Imperialism*[6] sets forth the facts and arguments on which the "paramarxist" interpretation of American diplomacy is based.

The "revisionists," that is to say, the historians who give an account of relations between the Soviet Union and the United States which differs totally from the way in which commentators interpreted them at the time or the way in which the Establishment presented them to the American people, do not form a school in the same sense as the realists or the paramarxists. While some of them (Williams[7]) use arguments of the paramarxist type to show the inevitability of American expansionism as the cause of the cold war, others try to delve into the hearts and minds of the decision-makers and reconstruct the intentions of the American diplomats dating from the atomic explosions at Hiroshima and Nagasaki (Ger Alperovitz[8]). Some of them revert to the Manichaeism of the cold war, but with the roles of the United States and the Soviet Union reversed.

This book, based as it is on a realist philosophy, is involved only indirectly or by implication in the disputes about moralism, revisionism, and even imperialism. Its main aim is to account for the diplomacy of the United States *as it was*. Like all diplomacy, it can be explained only within the system of inter-state relations to which the protagonist belongs. Since I have already described the main features of this system

---

[4] *Imperial America: the International Politics of Primacy* (Baltimore: Johns Hopkins Press, 1967).

[5] I am using the adjective "paramarxist" to denote historians who tend to find the key to United States diplomacy in economic notions or the requirements of the capitalist system. They are not, strictly speaking, Marxists; but neither was Marx when dealing with the foreign policy of Czarist Russia or capitalist Britain. In fact, Kolko (see page 179) and Magdoff seem to be based on Lenin rather than Marx, while Williams (see footnote 7) is more of a populist than a Marxist. Other critics classify them as members of the "New Left" school.

[6] *The Age of Imperialism: The Economics of United States Foreign Policy* (New York: Monthly Review Press, 1969).

[7] W. A. Williams, *The Tragedy of American Diplomacy*, 2nd ed. (New York: Dell Publishing Company, 1962).

[8] *Atomic Diplomacy, Hiroshima and Potsdam* (New York: Vintage Books, 1959).

in my *Paix et Guerre entre les Nations*,[9] I confine myself here to a summary analysis of the context within which the external action of the United States developed and is still developing. In the prologue I also remind the reader of what Europeans too often forget, the major trends in United States diplomacy from the thirteen colonies to continental union.

Taking this description of the past and the context as my point of departure, I try to criticize United States diplomacy during the twenty-eight-year period 1945–73 from the strategic, political, and moral standpoints. Where the diplomats openly declared their aim, did they achieve it? Does the result justify the accusation either of incompetence or of imperialism? Are we to credit Stanley Hoffmann's somewhat depressing picture of a Gulliver in a quagmire or Robert E. Osgood's statement, in his preface to Liska's book, that "American foreign policy in the first two decades of the cold war has been a striking success, judged by the normal standard of national security and power"?

Does not the reaction within the United States to a policy which had been "a striking success" only four years previously induce second thoughts about both the policy and its results? The imperial republic is trying to throw off its burden; once a missionary, it has lost the sense of mission; it is still capitalist, but its spoiled children no longer believe in money; it was puritan, but its cities abound in sex shops; it regards itself as scientific, yet mystical and nudist sects are rife; and the un-American activities hunted down by Senator Joseph McCarthy only twenty years ago are becoming, so to speak, the hallmark of good citizenship. *The New York Times* publishes secret official documents with a clear conscience and the virtual certainty of impunity.

My purpose here is neither to justify nor condemn the United States. I do, of course, point out from time to time the discrepancy between what was done and what should have (or could have) been done to attain the intended goals or to set immediate goals more consonant with the ultimate aspiration; but I have no intention of acting as the interpreter of the universal conscience. I detest the Stalinist tyranny imposed on a hundred million Europeans on the morrow of a war waged for the freedom of the peoples; but inter-state relations being what they are, within a heterogeneous system Stalin's desire to spread his regime as far as his armies had the power to do so is wholly consonant with customary practice. There is no need to saddle the United States with the responsibility

---

[9] Raymond Aron, *Peace and War: A Theory of International Relations*, trans. from the French by Richard Howard and Annette Baker Fox (Garden City, N.Y.: Doubleday & Company, 1967).

in order to find Stalin innocent, for Stalin never aspired to any angelic quality and could not have cared less for any such innocence.

Similarly, though practically no one any longer has doubts about the American diplomats' error in intervening in Vietnam, the effort to secure a non-Communist regime in Saigon is entirely congruent with postwar logic. If one of the two Germanies had instigated or supported a revolt in the other, outside opinion would have accused it of breaching the ground rules. It may be contended that people no longer accept these rules. That may well be so: The real source of moral revulsion lies rather in the disproportion of the means employed and concentrates on the losses inflicted on a people whom American arms were intended to protect.

This circumspection does not mean that I subscribe to a cynical interpretation of inter-state relations and that I accept considerations only of expediency or efficacy. Assessments of morality or political legitimacy fall into a complex and ill-defined category, on which some light will, I hope, be thrown by the findings set out in this essay. In the last analysis, any judgment about an external action is inseparable from a judgment about the internal system—that is, a state's institutions—and the imperial role appears beneficent or odious depending upon whether armies bring with them freedom or tyranny, economic development or stagnation, a modernizing or a reactionary elite. In the long view, it appears beneficent in one place, odious in another. In retrospect, historians attach more importance to this aspect of the diplomacy of great powers than to the consonance of any particular decision with international law.

In an attempt to remain as impartial as possible, I try to account for the external action of the United States as it was, not as the actors either intended or thought it to be. When they opposed the Anglo-French expedition to Suez, were President Eisenhower and John Foster Dulles intending to enforce respect for international law, to assert their authority over their allies, or to maintain good relations with the Third World? No one, not even the actors involved, can with certitude, unravel the elements of what was intended. But in practice everyone saw the fact that the two events—the Soviet suppression of the Hungarian Revolution and the American condemnation of the Anglo-French operation—happened simultaneously, as a strengthening of the hegemony of each of the two super-powers within its own sphere of inter-state relations. The reader may, if he is so inclined, substitute some other "reality" for this reality by applying some other pattern of interpretation. In the example I have chosen the strengthening of the two hegemonies, whether intended or not, remains a fact.

The sole justification for this book, which makes no claim to reveal

unpublished facts, will be the extent to which it displays, not total ob-
jectivity (which is perhaps a meaningless expression), but good faith. The
reader is not asked to endorse my own interpretations, but to try to discover the reasons for any disagreement he may feel regarding differences
in point of view or in political judgment. People who have acquired the
habit of thinking of the contemporary world in Manichaean terms—in
terms of the reduction of whole populations to slavery by monsters, or in
terms of capitalism, imperialism, or revisionism—may, of course, be outraged by a book that is not, in fact, concerned with grounds for outrage
and in which there are neither villains nor heroes.

Grounds for outrage abound in our time; the reader will pardon my
sparing use of a commodity of which the supply exceeds the demand.

PROLOGUE: THE INSULAR CONTINENT

Twenty-five years ago commentators were noting that for the first time in history a republic had risen to the first rank without ever aspiring to the glory of dominion. As the price of its victory it had to take half the world in charge, guarantee the security of Europeans too weakened to defend themselves unaided, and concern itself with whole areas of the globe that were on the point of lapsing into chaos.

This view or interpretation is not so certain today. When did the Romans become consciously aware of their mission *regere populos*? Do not some historians like to attribute their acquisition of the British Empire to a fit of absentmindedness? True, Roosevelt told Stalin (off the cuff, as he did in other instances) that the GIs would not remain in Europe for more than two years after hostilities ended. But, after all, the Roman legions evacuated Greece twice before they returned to stay. In 1973 American troops are still mounting guard on the demarcation line running through the Old Continent; how many Western Europeans, even among those who revile the war in Vietnam, really want them to go home?

General de Gaulle, with his special philosophical slant, discerned behind President Roosevelt's idealistic talk a will to power, all the more prone to assert itself because it was quite unconscious. Obsessed by their experience in the years following the First World War, Europeans, the man in the street and the statesman alike, feared American isolationism more than American imperialism. They had forgotten neither the United States' tardiness (from the European point of view) in intervening (1917, not 1914; 1941, not 1939) nor its refusal to ratify the Treaty of Versailles, nor the neutrality legislation voted by Congress in the Thirties to prevent what most legislators probably knew in their heart of hearts to be inevitable. They remembered, as well, the United States' swings between the crusading spirit (a world safe for democracy) and a withdrawal into isolation far from a corrupt world that refused to heed the American gospel.

We shall not for the time being choose between these two interpretations—which are perhaps more complementary than conflicting—but begin by reminding the reader of the obvious, though little appreciated, notion that the diplomatic history of the United States does not begin in 1917; it may well date back even before 1776 and the Declaration of Independence. The part played by the American colonists in the eighteenth-century wars between France and England—which ended in the destruction of New France, and twenty years later in the Treaty of Paris and the breach between the thirteen colonies and England—might well repay study.

The external action of the United States in the years 1917–39—or even 1898–1939—gives rise to a mistaken idea of what that action had been since 1783. Perhaps the years 1941–68 give an equally erroneous impression, and the present crisis set in motion by the war in Vietnam and the revulsion against the "burden of empire" may well be the precursor of yet another change of direction. In any event, the historian risks arriving at a false interpretation if he concentrates solely on the period 1914–39 or on the twentieth century alone. There is nothing more "traditional," more molded by the heritage of the past, than the diplomacy of a state, its perception of the world of international relations, and its conception of its role in that world. But, at the risk of shocking professional historians by an oversimplified classification, I shall divide the diplomatic history of the United States into three main periods: the first dating from 1783 to 1898, from the Treaty of Paris to the war with Spain; the second from 1899 to 1941 (or 1947); and the third, which begins with Pearl Harbor or the Truman Doctrine (March 1947), and which has perhaps been drawing toward its close during the past few years.

Why the contrast between the first two periods? Taken as a whole, each of them contrasts with the other *in essentials*. Whereas the movement of ideas and events from the end of the eighteenth century to the end of the nineteenth leads to a system devised and purposed by the Founding Fathers—a sovereign republic covering the greater part of North America, hence geopolitically insular—from the end of the nineteenth century onward the observer can discern neither the logic of the plot nor the aims of the actors. By the end of the last century the national purpose of the founders of the American republic had been achieved. Throughout the ensuing half-century the republic searched anew for a purpose and swung from one line of conduct to the other as whim dictated. The American diplomacy of today retains some of the habits it acquired during the first or the second of these periods.

By the Treaty of Paris in 1783 the thirteen colonies won international recognition of their independence; neither Vergennes nor the English negotiators were willing to grant the colonies sovereignty, either actual or potential, over the whole area of North America. European empires continued to exist to the north and south, the British and the Spanish. The territory of the nascent republic was bounded on all sides; navigation at the mouth of the Mississippi brought conflict with Spain, and the frontier to the north was ill-defined, gave rise to disputes with England, and was not finally fixed until around the middle of the next century.

Despite these initial weaknesses, the colonists had attained their goal: to occupy, populate, and exploit the territory of North America and to maintain a unified sovereignty over it in order to avoid the perpetual rivalries characteristic of power politics—the curse of Old Europe. The diplomacy of the thirteen colonies never experienced any serious setback throughout the century of expansion. It achieved its ends without waging any major war.

The colonies had no need to annex neighboring states in order to fulfill their ambitions; all that was necessary was to prevent their neighbors from becoming rivals. The issue was won by the end of the first third of the twentieth century, and Hegel acknowledged it:

> The free states of North America have no neighboring state with respect to which they are situated as European states are situated with respect to each other, that is to say a state which they must regard with distrust and against which they must maintain a standing army. Canada and Mexico do not inspire them with fear and England has learned from fifty years of experience that America is more useful to it free than subject.[1]

From that time on (1828), the disproportion of strength had reached the point of no return; for it precluded power politics under threat of the sword, even in the civilized form of the European tradition. An alliance between the Spanish and British empires or, later, between Mexico and Canada, to "contain" the expansion of the American republic was never conceivable—either between 1783 and the independence of Mexico, or between Mexican independence and the war of 1846.

The success of American diplomacy with regard to the neighbors of the United States—Spain (later Mexico), France, and England—was due less to any exceptional skill than to circumstances. During the first phase of the republic the tempest of the French Revolution drove the European

---

[1] Georg Wilhelm Hegel, *Die Vernunft in der Geschichte,* introduction to *Vorlesungen über die Philosophie der Weltgeschichte,* 5th ed. (Hamburg: Felix Meiner Verlag, 1955), p. 208.

states against each other. Washington was wise and energetic enough to restrain the enthusiasm of those colonists who wished, out of fellow-feeling, to join in on the side of France. In the brief War of 1812 the Americans were unable to attain their ultimate goal, the conquest of Canada. Their capital was occupied, the Capitol and the White House were burned; but successes at sea and Jackson's victory at New Orleans counterbalanced their defeats on land.

Meanwhile, in 1803 Napoleon sold the United States Louisiana—which had been restored to France by the Treaty of Amiens—for $15 million, and the expansion of the thirteen states had continued steadily (Kentucky in 1792, Tennessee in 1796, Ohio in 1803, Louisiana in 1812, Mississippi and Alabama in 1818 and 1819, Indiana and Illinois in 1816 and 1818, Missouri and Arkansas in 1819). Can this be called imperialism? The word is so fraught with associations nowadays and has such an ideological connotation that the neutral term "expansionism" is preferable. Many Americans even before independence did not doubt, in all good faith, that the whole continent was theirs by virtue of the right of occupancy (the Indians, as they saw it, were not occupying the land) and that they would establish upon it an empire or commonwealth such as the world had never seen. A speaker delivered himself in 1776 of the following:

> Empires have their zenith—and their descension to a dissolution. . . .
> The British Period is from the Year 1758, when they victoriously pursued their Enemies into every Quarter of the Globe. . . . The Almighty . . . has made choice of the present generation to erect the American Empire. . . . And thus has suddenly arisen in the World, a new Empire, stiled the United States of America. An Empire that as soon as started into Existence, attracts the Attention of the Rest of the Universe; and bids fair, by the blessing of God, to be the most glorious of any upon Record.[2]

In 1830 Alexis de Tocqueville, with his usual perspicacity, observed the causes and style of this irresistible movement:

> With their resources and their knowledge, the Europeans have made no delay in appropriating most of the advantages of the natives derived from the possession of the soil; they have settled among them, having taken over the land or bought it cheaply, and have ruined the Indians by a competition which the latter were in no sort

---

[2] R. W. Van Alstyne, *The Rising American Empire* (Oxford: Basil Blackwell, 1960), p. 1. The text quoted is by the Hon. William Henry Drayton, Esq., chief justice of South Carolina.

of position to face. Isolated within their own country, the Indians have come to form a little colony of unwelcome foreigners in the midst of a numerous and dominating people.[3]

Tocqueville sometimes expresses indignation; he always explains. He quotes Washington: "We are more enlightened and more powerful than the Indian nations; it behooves our honor to treat them with kindness, even generosity."[4] But he adds: "The noble and virtuous policy has not been followed." He attributes the Anglo-Americans' ascendancy to their superiority over the French as well as the Indians. He notes that at Vincennes, a small town founded by Frenchmen, "these Frenchmen were worthy people, but neither educated nor industrious" and almost all of them had disappeared. He concludes:

> The Americans, who were perhaps morally inferior to them, had an immense intellectual superiority. They were industrious, educated, rich, and accustomed to govern themselves. I myself have noticed in Canada, where the intellectual difference between the two races is very much less pronounced, that the English, being in control of trade and industry in the county of the French Canadians, are spreading on all sides and restricting the French within very narrow limits. In Louisiana, too, almost all commercial and industrial activity is concentrated in the hands of the Anglo-Americans.[5]

Tocqueville likewise saw how and why the migration of individuals opened the way to the republic's expansion.

> But the case of the province of Texas is even more striking; the state of Texas is of course a part of Mexico and serves as its frontier on the United States side. For some years the Anglo-Americans had been penetrating as individuals into that still-underdeveloped province, buying land, getting control of industry, and rapidly supplanting the original population. One can foresee that if Mexico does not hasten to halt this movement, Texas will soon be lost to her.[6]

In the very same year that *On Democracy in America* was published, the Americans of Texas, like the Americans of Florida in 1810, pro-

---

[3] *On Democracy in America*, I, 10, p. 334. [The translation of this and other passages from de Tocqueville is reproduced from that by George Lawrence, ed. J. P. Mayer (New York: Doubleday & Company, Anchor Books, 1969)].

[4] *Ibid.*

[5] *Ibid.*, p. 333, footnote 19.

[6] *Ibid.*

claimed their independence, defeated the Mexicans, and requested admission to the Union (which was not granted until 1844; the Senate accepted only after lengthy debates).

The style of expansion differed somewhat in the case of California. The colonists there were too few to revolt and claim possession. The Federal government first tried to negotiate the transfer of the province against compensation. The government of Mexico, which had not recognized the *fait accompli* in Texas, obstinately refused. By massing troops on the frontier it presented the United States with a pretext for a decisive war. Mexico, defeated and occupied, ceded to the United States all its territories north of the Rio Grande: New Mexico, California, and the southern region of the Rocky Mountains (Utah, Nevada, and Arizona). As was its custom, the United States paid for its territorial acquisitions in order to legitimize their military conquest. In 1818 President Monroe had similarly restored to the Spaniards the part of Florida conquered by General Jackson; the following year he purchased the two Floridas for $5 million. From the Louisiana Purchase from Napoleon ($15 million) to the purchase of Alaska from the Czar by Secretary of State Seward ($7 million), never did a state buy so much for so little.

Although this territorial expansion was quite certainly in line with the philosophical tenets of the republic's founders and the spontaneous action of its citizens, opinion was far from unanimous during the diplomatic crises caused by European events and the expansion of the Union. The origin of the War of 1812 was the blockade by the British navy and the violation of the rights of neutrals; the "war" party was drawn mainly from Westerners wishing to rectify the frontiers with the British possessions, from Southerners looking toward Florida, a possession of Spain, which was then allied with England, and from the "hawks" of the period who had not abandoned hopes of acquiring Canada. Even though the New England merchants were directly affected by the blockade, they tended to be "doves."

Nor did the war with Mexico command unanimous support; and it subsequently gave rise to serious debate. Was it not a war of conquest, just as unjustified as the practices of the predatory states of Old Europe? In other words, even as early as the first half of the period of Continental expansion the historian perceives certain traits characteristic of the external action of the United States to this day, such as the flare-up of public opinion (in 1792 and 1812), legalistic scruples, the swing between the will to power (or expansion) and an uneasy conscience, and a curious mixture of pragmatic and moralistic morality.

Washington's famous political testament, which is commonly interpreted as a refusal to become entangled in European quarrels or conclude permanent alliances, is likewise evidence of a specific way of thinking about international relations.

> Our detached and distant situation invites and enables us to pursue a different course. If we remain one people, under an efficient government, the period is not far off when we may defy material injury from external annoyance; when we may take such an attitude as will cause the neutrality we may at any time resolve upon to be scrupulously respected; when belligerent nations, under the impossibility of making acquisitions upon us, will not lightly hazard the giving us provocation; when we may choose peace or war, as our interest, guided by justice, may counsel. . . . It is our true policy to steer clear of permanent alliances with any portion of the foreign world; so far, I mean, as we are now at liberty to do it; for let me not be understood as capable of patronizing infidelity to existing engagements. I hold the maxim no less applicable to public than to private affairs, that honesty is always the best policy. I repeat it, therefore, let those engagements be observed in their genuine sense; but, in my opinion, it is unnecessary and would be unwise to extend them. Taking care always to keep ourselves, by suitable establishments, in a respectable defensive posture, we may safely trust to temporary alliances for extraordinary emergencies.[7]

And, in another context:

> The nation which indulges towards another an habitual hatred, or an habitual fondness, is in some degree a slave to its animosity or to its affection.[8]

Not to become entangled in disputes between European states was sensible advice for a young republic, protected as it was by its distance and by the wars in Europe. A presumed accord between interest and justice, honesty and the word as bond, is an optimistic ideology which does not preclude faith in what the men of the eighteenth century called the American Empire and those of the nineteenth Manifest Destiny.

Monroe's famous Declaration (message to Congress of December 2, 1829) expresses both anti-imperialism as Americans themselves conceive it and an imperial mission (as non-Americans see it) in the Western Hemisphere (a geographical concept devised by the Americans themselves, which established for them a sphere of responsibility or influence).

---

[7] Quoted in Marshall, *The Life of George Washington* (London, 1807), V, 776ff.

[8] *Ibid.*, p. 775.

The British cabinet had suggested joint action to President Monroe, but he preferred to act alone:

> The occasion has been judged proper for asserting as a principle in which the rights and interests of the United States are involved, that the American continents, by the free and independent condition which they have assumed and maintain, are henceforth not to be considered as subjects for future colonization by any European powers.[9]

The warning was addressed to the powers of the Holy Alliance, particularly France, which might have been tempted to intervene against the Latin American republics, whose independence the United States government had hastened to recognize.[10]

> But with the governments who have declared their independence and maintained it, and whose independence we have, on great consideration and on just principles, acknowledged, we could not view any interposition for the purpose of oppressing them, or controlling in any other manner their destiny, by any European power in any other light than as the manifestation of an unfriendly disposition toward the United States.

At that time the American republic had no means of imposing by armed force the decisions it solemnly promulgated to the entire world. It was the British navy that curbed any inclination that European states might have harbored to apply the principles of the Holy Alliance to the American continent. The statement of the Monroe Doctrine can nonetheless be construed, as it usually is, as the expression of the United States' political self-awareness. American statesmen have never seen any inconsistency between a rejection of European imperialism (or colonialism) and the special role or mission with which they invested their republic, a body that proclaimed itself the sole protector of the states on the American continent; it declared them its own preserve, an area set apart for freedom as conceived by the republic itself.

The consequence of the anti-imperialism that prompted the statement of the Monroe Doctrine and salved the conscience of the republic's lead-

---

[9] H. C. Allen, *The United States of America* (London: Ernest Benn, 1964), p. 114.

[10] The warning was also addressed to Czarist Russia, in the process of extending its dominions toward Oregon from Alaska, which it had owned since the eighteenth century. Cf. Franck L. Schoell, *Histoire des Etats-Unis* (Paris, 1965), p. 150.

ers was not simply to justify or dissimulate expansionism or the drive toward dominance, but acted as a brake on temptations to, or attempts at any annexations that did not concern territories adjacent to the Union and populated by Indians.

The westward drive did not, of course, stop at the Pacific coast. It was an American naval officer, Commodore Perry, who obtained the earliest concessions from Japan, leading the Empire of the Rising Sun into its extraordinary transformation, which, though with a disastrous interlude, achieved virtual miracles. The United States did not stand aside from the European onslaught on China, and it secured positions in the Pacific Isles as well. But anti-imperialism came to the fore whenever it appeared that the inhabitants of the territory concerned could not be assimilated or the territory itself was too distant to become an integral part of the Union.

After the purchase of Alaska[11] (proposed by Russia itself), the purchase of what are now the Virgin Islands ran into opposition from the Senate. The Upper House disavowed President Grant, whom it suspected of preparing to annex Santo Domingo by granting it loans, and refused a protectorate over Samoa, which Grant also wanted. It was the Senate again that refused to approve a trade treaty with Hawaii prepared by Seward because it seemed likely to lead to annexation. The Americans continued to establish themselves there nonetheless: a trade treaty in 1875; the cession of the base at Pearl Harbor in 1884; the revolt of the American residents in 1893, which forced the native Queen to abdicate. The independent republic of Hawaii applied for annexation to the United States. This time it was the President, Grover Cleveland, who refused. The island did not become a member of the Union until the mid-twentieth century.

Thus, the clash between the President and the Congress over foreign policy on the same grounds that also triggered off impassioned public debates dates back well before Wilson, the Treaty of Versailles, and the League of Nations. The President, responsible for the conduct of foreign affairs under the Constitution, did not hesitate to take action on his own initiative and carry on secret diplomacy. Similarly, the twofold attitude of expansionism and anti-imperialism, the urge to power and moralism, has been apparent since the earliest days of the republic. The break we observe between the first and second centuries in the history of the United States is due simply to the fact that the circumstances that made for a reconciliation of the two divergent trends no longer existed after

---

[11] Some leading politicians regarded this as a fresh opportunity to include Canada in the Union.

1898. The republic had changed more than the outlook of its citizens and statesmen.

At the close of the last century were the Americans to be content with their island, which they had barely begun to exploit? They decided otherwise, or circumstances made the decision for them. It may well be that the period 1898–1939 (or 1941) gives such an incoherent picture of the external action of the United States simply because the historian hesitates between the two forms in which that action found expression—that is to say, because the United States *could* not remain on the margin of universal history and did not *know how* to participate fully or determine what its role therein should be.

Was the war with Spain—the consequence of an unexplained incident (the explosion of the battleship *Maine* in Havana Harbor) hard on the heels of a revolt by the Cubans against Spanish rule and a domestic press campaign in the United States—a break with the anti-imperialist tradition? Or is it evidence of yet a further stage in Yankee expansion at the expense of the Spanish Empire or the Spanish-speaking peoples? Both explanations have been put forward; and each of them, I believe, contains a measure of truth. The Anglo-American sense of superiority over the Spaniards or Spanish-speaking peoples dates from long before 1898. A continuous current of feeling can be traced, without straining the facts, between the Mexican War in the middle of the century and the war with Spain at its end. There was a president—McKinley—who was all for peace, a proclamation of neutrality, a war party bound up closely with economic interests (the Cuban planters), but even more closely with ideological groups, followed by a mobilization of public opinion by a press loudly denouncing the horrors of Spanish repression, and finally an incident which swept the president away in its wake.

Once war had broken out, the imperial party, Theodore Roosevelt, and Admiral Dewey waged it for total victory, extending the field of operations to the Spanish possessions in the Pacific. The peace treaty which stripped Spain of the last shreds of its empire and gave the American republic sovereignty over the Philippines, Puerto Rico, and the island of Guam consequently ran into opposition from a section of the Senate and was ratified by only a narrow margin.

The annexation of the Philippines, a distant archipelago whose inhabitants could hardly constitute a state of the Union, was a deviation from the strict line of the American advance beyond its borders. Once freed from Spanish occupation, the Philippines proclaimed its independence; American troops were used to suppress the "rebellion," and the pacification lasted for some ten years, with great savagery on both sides.

Theodore Roosevelt himself was endorsing prevailing opinion when he regretted the annexation and acknowledged the error, despite his own share in its commission.

On the other hand, United States action in the Caribbean and Central America is evidence of a sort of compromise between rejection of European imperialism and awareness of special rights, or, alternatively, of a broad interpretation of the Monroe Doctrine. For instance, Theodore Roosevelt explicitly stated the case for the United States' special responsibilities:

> Chronic wrongdoing . . . may in America, as elsewhere, ultimately require intervention by some civilized nation, and in the Western Hemisphere the adherence of the United States to the Monroe Doctrine may force the United States, however reluctantly, in flagrant cases of such wrongdoing or impotence, to the exercise of an international police power.[12]

Cuba, the pretext for the war with Spain, became an independent republic, but the United States acquired a naval base at Guantanamo and, with the Platt Amendment, a permanent right of intervention to restore order or safeguard its interests. It engaged in gunboat diplomacy early in this century, just as the Europeans did at the same period, sometimes to secure the repayment of debts, sometimes to place in power a party or a president favorable to its interests. In Colombia it promoted the secession which finally resulted in the creation of the state of Panama. It speedily signed a treaty with the newly established state which gave the United States full sovereignty over a strip six miles wide across the isthmus in return for a cash indemnity. Although Theodore Roosevelt's successor put more faith in the dollar than in the Big Stick—as an instrument and as an end—he too landed two thousand Marines in Nicaragua to uphold a congenial president.

Until 1914 the external action of the United States—apart from the annexation of the Philippines—can still be fitted without too much strain into the old framework and logic of the original national purpose. The right to keep a watch on the Caribbean was simply an extension of the standard practice of territorial expansion. Regions bordering on the United States were part of its sphere of influence; without undue scruples or repugnance it engaged in the art of recruiting satellites within these zones, instigating revolts against uncooperative governments, even by the use of force when necessary. Otherwise, the United States had not made any choice between the consciousness of a global

---

12 Allen, *The United States*, p. 204.

role and the predominant interest in protecting trade and investment, between Theodore Roosevelt's idea of the greatness of America and Taft's concern with economic aims. An Asian power as a result of the war with Spain, it continued to turn its back on Europe. It was the First World War that induced the New World to intervene to redress the balance of the Old.

The interminable debate over the *causes* of the United States' entry into the war in 1917 involves one of those questions that do not call for a categorical answer and probably can never receive one. At the start, the President had proclaimed, as was traditional, the neutrality of the United States; and precisely as in 1796–1812, the belligerents had, in turn or together, disregarded the rights of neutrals and interfered with shipping on the high seas.[13] Great Britain was bombarded with notes of protest against a long-distance blockade intercepting neutral countries' freighters, while the Kaiser's Germany also received protests against losses of American lives in torpedoed vessels. Public opinion finally turned against the Central Powers—possibly because of revelations about the German ambassador's dubious activities, possibly because of the American bankers' loans to Great Britain and France, possibly because of the enduring solidarity between the English-speaking peoples, possibly for fear of a German hegemony over the continent and the decisive weakening of Great Britain, whose navy had safeguarded the security of the American republic. No one, I believe, can assess precisely what part each of these considerations played.[14] The important point for the understanding of what follows is, to my mind, that opinion was once again mobilized by an exalted, if cloudy, ideology and that the President himself *presented* and, to a large extent, *thought of* action by the United States as a rescue operation, one differing in essence from that of the Allied and Associated Powers.

This difference did exist in some respects. The United States did not and could not have any territorial ambitions in Europe (any more than Britain had had since the end of the Hundred Years' War). Hostility to European-style imperialism turned the United States away from colonial conquests. The peoples of the Old Continent were not mistaken, then, in their belief in American "disinterest" and the President's

---

[13] There had been an undeclared privateers' war between France and the United States from 1796 to 1798 and a declared war with Great Britain in 1812.

[14] I have never found the so-called realist interpretation—that the security of the United States would have been threatened by a victory of the Central Powers—wholly convincing. The common view, which has disregarded this point and has discussed intervention as a decision freely taken, is, I believe, closer to the truth.

"idealism," insofar as disinterest and idealism had any application to the issues at stake in the negotiations. The European statesmen viewed international relations in the light of the realism (or cynicism) of power politics and the requirements of the balance of power. Clemenceau feared the desire for revenge of a Germany only temporarily enfeebled, with human and economic resources far exceeding those of France. The American President's good intentions were no lasting guarantee against such a threat.

The Senate's rejection of the Treaty of Versailles, the refusal to join the League of Nations, and the withdrawal into isolationism, the whole of this oft-told tale, is, however, only a parenthesis or interlude in the destiny of the American republic. It hardly matters whether this parenthesis begins with the war with Spain, the annexation of the Philippines, or the intervention in 1917; the choice among them is probably purely arbitrary. What is essential, in my view, is to understand where the innovation lay. I would define it in two ways, which are in fact self-complementary: Having become the dominant power in the Western Hemisphere and the ranking power on a global scale, the United States enters world politics against its will. Henceforth it has to deal not with Indian tribes, not with a decadent Spanish Empire, not with a complacent or resigned British Empire, but with states that are determined to defend their own rights and interests. It does not enter the European international system whose corruption it has denounced, but the global system of which it becomes a full member and which has the same vices or even worse ones.

Taken as a whole, the external action of the United States during the period 1898–1940 is a unit only in its inconsistencies, its abrupt changes of front, its inability to choose a line of conduct and stick to it—in short, the rejection of the inter-state universe in the form it had taken throughout the ages yet whose rules the United States itself had unwittingly used for its own benefit and at the expense of first the French and then the English, the Indians, and the Spaniards. The Americans had never recognized the similarity between continental expansion and the imperialism of other states. Free of threatening neighbors, still with ample room to expand, toward the end of the century it came to the maturity predicted by Hegel:

> North America is still at the pioneering stage. Once the number of people going out to farm the land has ceased to grow, as in Europe, and once the outward migration to the land has died down and masses begin to return to urban industry and commerce and establish a compact system, only then will they feel the need for an organic state. . . . America is therefore the country of the

future in which the gravity of universal history will take the form
of antagonism, perhaps between North and South America. It is an
ideal country for all those who are weary of the bric-a-brac of Old
Europe. Napoleon is said to have remarked, "This old Europe
bores me." America should disclaim the soil over which universal
history has hitherto passed.[15]

In the half-century between the war with Spain—the end of an
empire whose remnants had been gathered up by the United States—and
the entry into war with Japan and Germany in December 1941, the
external action of the United States was guilty not of any will to
power, but of a failure to become aware of the role imposed upon it
by destiny. The outlawry of war by the Kellogg-Briand Pact is in the
same vein as the Wilsonian moralism and legalism against which
Kennan and Morgenthau protested so vigorously after 1945. Other
decisions evidence a similar rejection of the inter-state universe. In
peacetime the United States had no need of a large army because it
occupied a species of continental island. As soon as it came up against
Japanese ambitions in Asia and was threatened by aggression in the
Philippines, its former practice of waiting for the first shot before
raising an appropriately large-scale army became an anachronism.

The external action of the United States was equally shortsighted.
The low Underwood tariff introduced by Wilson in 1913 had been
replaced in 1922 by the Fordney-McCumber tariff raising the duties
on imports. In 1930, when the Depression had already set in, Congress
voted the even more protectionist Hawley-Smoot tariff. It did not—
or would not—realize, in spite of all the economists' warnings, that the
United States which had long been an importer of capital had become the creditor of the outside world as a result of the war. It is hard to
account for the incompatible decisions—in some sort amounting to
acts of omission—which demanded the payment of war debts, held to
be wholly separate from reparations, while simultaneously curbing
imports by high duties, except as a deliberate refusal to face realities.
It is equally hard to find a rational explanation for the neutrality
legislation voted by Congress in the Thirties to prevent a repetition
of the process that had led up to intervention in 1917. The Act of May
1939 prohibited all sales of war material and all loans to belligerents
and made it illegal for American citizens to travel in vessels of a state
which was at war. Any belligerent that wished to purchase nonprohibited
goods had to pay for them in cash and carry them in its own ships.
The Act, passed a year after Germany's annexation of Austria, en-

---

[15] Hegel, *Die Vernunft* . . . , pp. 209–10.

couraged the "aggressors," primarily Hitler's Germany, despite the violence of public opinion against them. It was consistent with the efforts of Franklin Roosevelt and American diplomacy to uphold the obsolete and hollow principle of the Open Door in China in order to resist the Japanese drive to expansion or conquest: Resistance by all means short of war seemed to be the stated American principle, devoid though it was of sense or, in any case, of common sense. Against a state like Japan only a miracle could have made quarantining the aggressor or loans to states that had been victims of aggression an effectual substitute for force. As if the United States itself had been able to avoid the use of force in the course of its brief history!

By voting additional funds for the navy, Congress was, as it were, expressing doubts about what it itself had done. It was seeking to forestall the inevitable. Its members may perhaps have hoped that France and Britain would manage to defeat the Third Reich, later to be allied with fascist Italy and Japan, without the aid of the United States. They would probably have acknowledged that, if need be, the United States would redress the balance of the Old World for the second time. If the conjunction of the neutrality legislation and moral support for the democracies had any effect on the course of events, it must have been to induce Hitler to press ahead of his program and launch his war before the hostility to the totalitarian regimes was translated into effective action. If the historian could with any plausibility credit the members of Congress with a super-Machiavellianism, he would adopt the explanation in which interpreters of British diplomacy have often indulged, namely that insular power rises in proportion as the continental powers exhaust themselves in "all-out" conflicts. A second European war made the United States' potential hegemony a reality. Europe achieved the objective at which it was blindly aiming by its discords, government by an American commission, as Paul Valéry put it. If the American republic's leaders had *intended* to extend to the Old Continent the hegemony they exercised over the Western Hemisphere, they would hardly have acted otherwise than they did.

Senators from Arizona or Wisconsin will certainly not be credited with such devious or foresighted designs. The insular power whose territory was sheltered from attack and which sent expeditionary forces to distant lands preserved—until 1945—the strange privilege of profiting politically from its errors. By its abstention, by spreading the illusion that it would continue to remain aloof from hostilities in Europe, by its inability to choose between compromise with Japan and a determination of which massive rearmament alone would have given convincing proof, the United States *historically* bears some of the responsibility for the outbreak of the twofold war in the Atlantic and the Pacific. The quarter-century of preeminence was the sanction—whether reward or punishment—of what everyone today calls an aberration in that a great power upset the system quite as much by its refusal to assume its due rank as by pride of primacy.

Twenty-five years later Europeans are once more beginning to fear this refusal after denouncing that pride.

The Imperial Republic

PART ONE

The United States in the Inter-State System:
The Success and Failure of Paramountcy

Introduction

The two wars of the twentieth century—combining to make up another thirty years' war—mark the tragic epilogue of the European era and the diplomatic system which had been characteristic of Europe since the end of the wars of religion.

> Christian Europe, except Russia (Russia was admitted to the Royal Almanach only in 1716), could long be regarded as a sort of Grand Republic divided into a number of states, some monarchical, others of a mixed complexion; the former aristocratic, the latter plebeian, but all of them thinking alike, all with a similar fundament of religion, even though it was divided into a number of sects, all of them with similar principles of public law and politics unknown to other parts of the world. It is owing to these principles that the European nations do not enslave their prisoners, respect their enemies' ambassadors, all subscribe to the pre-eminence and to certain rights of certain princes, such as the Emperor, the King and other lesser potentates, and, above all, that they concur in the wise policy of maintaining among themselves to the best of their ability an equal balance of power, constantly employing negotiations, even in the midst of war, while maintaining in each others' countries ambassadors or less honorable spies who are able to warn all Courts of the designs of any one Court and at once sound the alarm for Europe and safeguard the weakest against the invasions which the strongest power is always prepared to undertake.[1]

---

[1] Quoted by Jean Laloy, *Entre guerre et paix* (Paris, 1966). The passage is at the beginning of Chapter II of Voltaire's *Le Siècle de Louis XIV*.

Voltaire's much-quoted description identifies, in a neutral style only faintly tinged with irony, the specific features of the system of inter-state relations in Europe: the precautions against the hegemony of any one state (a similar idea is expressed in Montesquieu's terminology as *resistance to universal monarchy*), *a common basis of belief and practices* despite the diversity of institutions, *a civilized Machiavellianism* of statesmen who respect the principles of public law but suspect each other of sinister designs.

The European states did not accord the tribes or constituted states in Asia and Africa the privileges they allowed each other. The Euro-centered system treated as equals only those states outside Europe capable of imposing respect for their existence and their rights by force. Thus, Japan became a full member of the system of inter-state relations, possibly at the time of its defeat of China (1895), certainly by its victory over czarist Russia. The two Americas remained on the fringes of the system; the United States was part of it only from time to time.

World War I spelled the death of the Grand Republic described by Voltaire. It was waged on such an exorbitant scale and had unleashed such violent passions that the traditional practice of permanent negotia-tion could not possibly be restored. Russia, the last to be admitted to the Royal Almanach, quit the Republic in 1917, Hitler's Germany in 1933. The principal players of the diplomatic game no longer held any common basis of belief, no longer maintained a regular intercourse, and no longer respected identical principles. In 1814 and 1815 the Allies had imposed a change of regime upon France, but they were expelling a "usurper," the embodiment of a revolutionary idea, a glorious and defeated soldier of fortune. In 1918 the Allied and As-sociated Powers refused to treat with the legitimate heir of a royal and imperial family because they saddled him with the blame for the disaster.

The Europe of the Thirties no longer resembled the Europe of recent centuries, nor even that of the twenty-five years between the storming of the Bastille and the fall of Napoleon. There was no longer one "troublemaker," but two. The Third Reich appeared the greater im-mediate threat, as indeed it was. The Union of Soviet Socialist Re-publics remained hostile, mysterious, or at any rate alien to the Western democracies, which were compelled to concert with one of their enemies against the other in order to survive. Great Britain and France, paralyzed by conflicting alliances and by their scruples, resigned themselves to a fate which they could never master.

Hitler and Stalin led the dance of death. In 1939 they united to destroy the Polish army and to partition Poland once more. It was Hitler himself who tore up the pact with Stalin and made him Great

Britain's ally. It was Hitler, too, who, under the compulsion of Japanese aggression in the Pacific, declared war on the United States. When he killed himself in the Berlin bunker and the Third Reich apocalyptically collapsed, Europe no longer existed. It had become a chaos of rubble through which millions of deportees stumbled trying to find their way back to their native land. The meeting of John and Ivan, the American GI and the Russian soldier, on the Elbe, appears in our children's history books as a story-book happening symbolizing the rise of the states Toynbee calls peripheral and the irremediable decline of the nations which had produced the modern civilization which is now beginning to spread throughout the world.

With Germany crushed, and France and Britain among the victors, but exhausted—the former by defeat and occupation, the latter by its extraordinary efforts and the weight of victory—how could a balance be established within Europe? The fulcrum of the inter-state system was no longer the equilibrium between the nations of the Old Continent, and the United States became one of the system's permanent members, by necessity doomed to play the leading role.

At the same time, the old order in Asia and Africa was inevitably bound to disintegrate. Britain was solemnly committed to granting India its independence. No European empire in Asia would be able to hold out for long after the breakup of the British Empire. Without the Indian army Britain could not possibly maintain its positions in the Middle East. Stage by stage, the rot spread relentlessly to all the colonial and semicolonial possessions of the European nations, a process speeded by the official and shared anticolonialism of the Soviet Union and the United States.

It is within this framework that the main features of the inter-state system, in which the United States has played the leading role during the past twenty-five years find their origin. These features can be defined as follows:

Globalism: The United States has not been able or willing to confine its interventions to a single geographical area; it has formed organizations, even alliances, and signed pacts with dozens of states; nothing that happened, from the heart of Africa to the midst of Siberia, was alien to it.

Heterogeneity: The anti-Communist crusade was gradually replaced by *peaceful coexistence,* but, at the time of this writing, American aircraft were bombing Cambodia to prevent a Communist party coming to power in Phnom-Penh.

Revolutionary spirit: The retreat of the European powers has not caused popular turmoil to abate; neo-colonialism, a somewhat vague term for the economic influence or presence of the West, is as bitterly denounced as colonialism; the great American corporations are considered just as responsible for "domination" and "exploitation" as colonial officials formerly were; the more sincerely the Western powers denounce the gap between the wealth of some and the poverty of others, the more effectually they feed the resentment of the masses and the greater the justification they provide for revolt.

Bipolarity: In 1946 Europeans feared the drive of Soviet hordes to the Atlantic coast; in 1973 the Soviet Union possesses the whole apparatus of deterrence—ballistic missiles buried deep in silos or mounted on nuclear submarines—counterbalancing the comparable apparatus at the disposal of the United States.

The history of inter-state relations since 1945 is not simply that of the Russo-American rivalry. It may be that, in the near or distant future, the cold war will seem merely a postwar episode, more spectacular than important, as the implicit accord between Moscow and Washington grows stronger or develops into cooperation. For the observer in 1973 the best means of identifying the stages of American diplomacy is to look at the state of the relations between the two super-powers, for the simple reason that the policy-makers viewed their actions and the world itself, consciously at least, in relation to the Communist danger or threat. With this in mind, we can distinguish the following six periods:

1. *1941–45.* This first period is not, strictly speaking, germane to our subject. The United States enters the war against Japan and the Third Reich and makes the "strange alliance," as the American general stationed at Moscow in those years put it, with the Soviet Union. Roosevelt sets the immediate aim, the unconditional surrender of the hostile states after the destruction of their armed forces; haunted as he is by memories of the previous postwar period, his major desire for this one is to set up an international organization with both the Soviet Union and the United States as members (a resurrection of Wilson's League of Nations), thereby reducing as far as possible the danger of a return to isolationism. He dreams of a Russo-American triumvirate (together with Great Britain) or a condominium, while most of his advisers, and he himself much of the time, intend to remain faithful to Wilsonian legalism and universalism. These dreams do not hinder the forming of cynical agreements, or those entered into with a spirit of resignation, concerning the future frontiers of Poland and the price to be paid for the Soviet Union's entry into the war against Japan.

2. *1945–47.* This second phase, from the Potsdam Conference to the Truman Declaration of March 1947 and Molotov's withdrawal from the preparatory conference for the Marshall Plan in July 1947, is

characterized by the gradual shift from alliance to breach, the hesitation of the United States, and perhaps of the Soviet Union as well, between cooperation and hostility. Heads of state no longer meet, and the sovietization of Poland, Romania, and Bulgaria arouses uneasiness in some cases, indignation in others; moreover—and this is a major point—the division of Germany gradually becomes the main item on the agenda.

These two phases pose a single question, which is the theme of Chapter 1: *Was the breach inevitable?* The main burden of this critique will be strategic; in dealing with military and diplomatic decisions it will utilize the method of retrospective investigation which both Clausewitz and Weber considered legitimate and inevitable: what would have happened if . . .? The fact that no unassailable answers can be given does not preclude asking the question. The critique will also embody a moral element. Which of the two, the United States or the Soviet Union, bears the responsibility for the breach? Which of the two behaved in accordance with custom or equity? Which of them was aiming at objectives that the historian must approve?

3. *March (or July) 1947–March 1953.* These six years comprise the cold war proper; on both sides hostile propaganda reaches a paroxysm of virulence. In Eastern Europe the states liberated or occupied by the Red Army are brought into line with increasing rapidity; non-Communist democrats are ruthlessly eliminated. In Prague the Communist Party, holding the key positions, liquidates the surviving remnants of pluralist democracy. After the Yugoslav schism, all the satellite countries experience trials on the Moscow model. Slansky, Rajk, and Kostov are executed, Gomulka and Kadar are jailed and tortured. In 1949 the Chinese Communists establish themselves in the Forbidden City. In the West the Bonn Republic comes into being by a merger of the British, French, and American occupation zones. In 1949 the Atlantic Alliance in the form of a regular treaty joins together the United States and the portion of the Old Continent that is still free. In 1950 the campaign in Korea leads to American rearmament, the creation of NATO, and an invitation to Germany to participate in the common defense, and in Asia to a Sino-American conflict. The United States decides to back Chiang Kai-shek on Taiwan and the French operations in Indochina.

4. *March 1953–November 1958.* Stalin's death leads to the thaw and a new attitude toward the outside world on the part of the men in the Kremlin. But the organization of Europe in two military blocs continues. In 1955 the Federal Republic of Germany officially joins NATO, in the same year in which the Four Powers meet in Geneva. The cold war has slackened (the Korean armistice in 1953 and the Indochinese armistice

in 1954). Stalin's heirs look beyond Europe. The theater of confrontation widens. The 1956 crisis—the Hungarian revolt and the Anglo-French expedition to Suez—simultaneously almost disrupts the two blocs of allies, while revealing a measure of solidarity between the two super-powers.

These two phases, the subject of Chapter 2, call for a complex critique, the burden of which is suggested by my title, *The Two Crusades.* The historian can ask himself two questions, which, though apparently contradictory, are both well founded: Could not the United States have adopted an ultimately moderate and defensive strategy of containment, had there been no mobilization of moralism? Was not that mobilization in the last analysis a cover for the acceptance of the partition which Stalin had wanted and Truman rejected?

5. *November 1958–July 1963 (or November 1962).* Between Khrushchev's demand that Berlin should be made a free city and the Cuban missile crisis of October–November 1962 (or the signing of the Partial Test-Ban Treaty in July 1963) there occurs a curious and ambiguous phase, barely distinguishable from the previous one. Soviet diplomacy is seemingly playing two games at once, détente and the offensive. Khrushchev's aim is simultaneously a favorable arrangement in Berlin and perhaps a *modus vivendi* on a worldwide scale. Relations between the Soviet Union and Communist China continue to deteriorate (Moscow's denunciation of the agreement on nuclear cooperation in 1959, the withdrawal of the Soviet experts in 1960, and the bringing into the open of the Sino-Soviet dispute in 1963 at the very moment when the Western powers are signing the Partial Test-Ban Treaty in Moscow). The Cuban missile crisis in October–November 1962 marks the final point in Khrushchev's diplomacy. In 1963, at the time of Kennedy's death, the United States seems to have attained the zenith of its power. There are no longer two super-powers, but only one. In ten years, détente has led to American supremacy.

6. *1962 (or July 1963)–1969.* The Soviet Union does not resume direct confrontation with the United States, but gradually reduces the gap in ballistic weapons and naval forces. It, too, becomes a global power. The United States, at the very summit of its supremacy, gradually—perhaps irrevocably after 1963—commits itself to the war in Vietnam. For the first time, the American army enters into combat with guerrilla fighters supplied from outside and with regular units of the North Vietnamese army, which in many cases resort to guerrilla tactics. Militarily it wins most of the battles, but fails to win the war. United States and world opinion revolts against a Goliath unable to defeat a David, against the enormous military machine devastating a country which it pledged

itself to protect, and against the bombing of North Vietnam. Lyndon Johnson declines to stand for a second term, and Richard Nixon is elected by a narrow margin to wind up a war which is aggravating, if not creating, a real moral crisis (or crisis of civilization, the term preferred by the French).

The phases of American diplomacy coincide only roughly with the division into periods I have outlined above. Though John Foster Dulles's diplomacy falls within the period of détente, it continues to enforce the major principles of the spirit of crusade. Moreover, the disparity between the principal protagonists' projects and the results obtained, between intention and reality, appears strikingly evident time and again. After Stalin's death, American diplomatic policy-making goes through three successive stages: détente, with an unjustified fear of potential Soviet superiority;[2] Kennedy's presidency, with its dynamic policy, which, after the Bay of Pigs disaster, culminated in the Cuban missile crisis and the conscious awareness of world supremacy; and the Vietnam quagmire and concurrent revulsion against the imperial burden. In the ten years between 1953 and 1963 the American leaders gradually convince themselves in the light of successes that are spectacular rather than durable that they possess a supremacy, which has in fact been continuously eroded. In the few years from 1965 to 1969, the cost, the failure, and the horror of the Vietnam venture lead to self-examination. From détente to supremacy to revulsion: what William Henry Drayton called "zenith and descension" is described in Chapter 3, "Ascent and Descent."

Elected to end the Vietnam War, Richard Nixon, a former cold warrior, inaugurates a policy all his own, resumes relations with Peking, and concludes agreements with Moscow. Never was American public opinion so avid for moral purity, never have American policy-makers, the Nixon-Kissinger team, so assiduously practiced the European art of Machiavellian and moderate diplomacy—with the exception of the bombing strikes on North Vietnam, which were immoderate, to say the least. *Was Nixon becoming a disciple of Metternich?*

---

[2] A fear harbored by public opinion rather than by informed circles.

Chapter One

ASSIGNING THE GUILT:
THE ORIGINS OF THE COLD WAR

The expression "cold war," derived as it is from the jargon of journalists and politicians, eludes precise definition. Here I shall deal with three different constructions given to the term.

1. In his classic *Histoire de la guerre froide*[1] André Fontaine goes back as far as the Russian Revolution in 1917 and the military intervention by the Western states. He appears, therefore, to define the cold war as the basic and permanent hostility between the Soviet Union and the West consequent upon the nature of the Soviet regime and the capitalist or liberal states' fear of it, or even the global mission assumed by Marxism-Leninism and American democracy alike.

Fontaine himself, however, stresses the bipolar element in his observation that "no cold war would have come about had there not been in mid-century two, and only two, powers with large enough territory, large enough manpower, and sufficient confidence in the values of their creed and multiform armaments to dispute the mastery of the world, though neither of them could ever be wholly assured of its decisive superiority."[2]

If the cold war is defined as the rivalry for worldwide preponderance, it did not begin, between the United States and the Soviet Union at any rate, in 1917, but some time between 1941 and 1945.

Fontaine, then, places the emphasis (depending on the date) either on the bipolar element—that is, the rivalry between two states preeminent over other states by reason of their resources and will to

---

[1] André Fontaine, *Histoire de la guerre froide* (Paris: Fayard, 1965–67).
[2] *Ibid.*, I, 15.

9

power—or on the heterogeneity of the system—that is, the incompatibility between the Marxist-Leninist and liberal-capitalist ideologies. If the former is true, the cold war begins with the Russian Revolution in 1917; if the latter, with the ending of the Second World War and the collapse of the intermediate powers.

2.   The commonly held meaning of the cold war (or warlike peace) comes down, I think, to the idea that conflicts may become so virulent in time of peace that states employ against each other means normally or traditionally reserved for time of war. Professor Hans Morgenthau wrote that what distinguishes the cold war from the many hostile confrontations between states in the past are two factors: the *impossibility* for all concerned, given the interests at stake and the positions taken, to pursue conciliatory policies which through the instruments of give-and-take and compromise might have led to a settlement of the outstanding issues; and the consequent *necessity* for all concerned to protect and promote their interests through unilateral direct pressure on the opponent's will by all means available—diplomatic, military, economic, subversive— short of the actual use of force.[3] This definition reflects the commonest concept of the cold war, *war* because the diplomats were neither able nor willing to settle their disputes by negotiation, *cold* because they were neither able nor willing to settle them by force. What struck observers was the virulence of the propaganda, the severance or virtual severance of relations between the two opposing camps, and the seemingly implacable enmity which had become the style of intercourse between states in the absence of declared war.

3.   None of these definitions—struggle for worldwide preponderance, bipolarity of a heterogeneous system, the impossibility or rejection of both conciliation and settlement by force—enables us to distinguish precisely the periods of so-called cold war from the periods of peaceful coexistence, or, in other terms, between tension and détente. Negotiations by give-and-take have never prevented direct action and pressure on the opponent's will. Hobbes and Rousseau held that states have lived in a permanent state of war. The relative proportions of bargaining and pressure vary from one period to another. In this perspective—the one I tend to favor—there is a difference only of degree between "normal" inter-state relations, especially

---

[3] "Arguing about the Cold War," *Encounter*, May 1967.

in a bipolar and heterogeneous system, and the "cold war" phase. Between 1947 and 1953, however, owing to the conjunction of propaganda, the Berlin blockade, the Korean campaign, and rearmament by both sides, this difference of degree became such that, it seems to me, a special concept may legitimately be applied to the phase: cold war or warlike peace.

In this chapter I shall adopt the third definition; that is to say, I take cold war to mean the phase of extreme tension beginning as far back as the period of a war waged simultaneously rather than jointly against the Third Reich and becoming clearly evident in March 1947 with the Truman Doctrine or, a few months later, at the Paris conference to discuss the Marshall Plan for American aid.

The literature devoted to accounts or analyses of relationships among the Big Three—Stalin, Churchill, and Roosevelt—during the war is constantly accumulating. Therefore, I neither can, nor intend to produce any new fact or original interpretation. Furthermore, I am wholly at a loss to understand why certain American historians of the "revisionist" school are so eager to refute the traditional interpretation and demonstrate that the cold war could have been avoided or that the responsibility for it lies with the United States.

What does "avoid the cold war" mean? The phrase clearly suggests that events after the victory over the Third Reich could have taken some other course. What other course? Could the Big Three have maintained their alliance or have agreed on organizing Europe without engaging in an exchange of homeric insults? "Responsibility," too, is an ambiguous word; either it means causal responsibility, that is to say that a particular act or decision had necessarily, and to some extent predictably, to lead to a particular result or reaction on the part of the other party, or else it implies a political or moral responsibility, that is to say that a particular decision which led to consequences the historian considers culpable is held to be a fault rather than an error. I shall try to discover which connotations of *responsibility* apply in each specific case.

With the lapse of time the disintegration of the Grand Alliance now appears congruent with the ordinary course of inter-state relations. We need only recall Stalin's remark to Tito: "This war is not as in the past; whoever occupies a territory also imposes on it his own social system. Everyone imposes his own system as far as his army can reach. It cannot be otherwise."[4] If this was what Stalin believed—and there is little reason to doubt it—it does not make an examination of the origins (who started the dirty work?[5]) futile, but it limits its scope, because it suggests a prior answer to the two questions about responsibility, that is to say, that the partition of Europe was probably *inevitable* and that no one was to blame for it. Everyone involved behaved, individually, in a manner consistent with his historical philosophy, his ambitions, and his values— though, of course, this does not mean that the uncommitted observer must refrain from moral judgment.

1.

While the war was still being waged, no problem engaged the Big Three as totally nor was discussed at such length during their negotiations as that of Poland. In 1946–47 the major issues were Greece and Turkey, and later, and primarily, the future of Germany. For purposes of simplification it may be said that the moral breach came over Poland and the final breach over Germany, while the Greek crisis and the Soviet demands relating to Turkey led to the proclamation of the Truman Doctrine and the extension of the victors' rivalry beyond the frontiers of Europe.

The Germans had discovered the mass grave at Katyn (some ten thousand Polish officers murdered by the Soviet forces during the retreat in 1941)[6] on April 12, 1943. On April 16 the Polish government in exile in London demanded an investigation by the International Red Cross. On April 25 the Kremlin replied, blaming the Germans for the massacre, and used the Polish government's protest as a pretext for breaking off relations with it. At the conference at Teheran in November 1943 Roosevelt showed little interest in Poland's future and frontiers. He remained silent while Churchill and Stalin discussed them acrimoniously. Ever since his first meeting with Eden after Hitler's aggression Stalin had made no bones about the fact that he intended to keep the territories he had gained under

---

[4] Milovan Djilas, *Conversations with Stalin* (New York: Harcourt, Brace, and World, 1962), p. 144.

[5] The question who started does not, of course, exhaust the further question about causal responsibility or culpability.

[6] See J. K. Zawodny, *Massacre dans la forêt* (Paris: Stock, 1971).

the 1939 agreement with the Third Reich. Though this claim had not been recorded in the Anglo-Soviet treaty of alliance, Churchill was not unaware of Stalin's demands and considered it useless to oppose them. He accepted the demand for the Curzon Line as Poland's eastern frontier, with compensations to that country in the west at the expense of the German provinces that had once been Polish but had been Germanized.

When the Big Three met again at Yalta in February 1945, Stalin had already set up the Lublin Committee (July 23, 1944) and the Soviet armies were occupying Poland. The Secret Army's heroic rising in Warsaw had led to the city's total destruction. The Russians acted as they thought fit, and the Western Allies had no effective means of intervening. Churchill once more fought alone for Poland, no longer for its eastern frontier, which had been fixed at Teheran, but for the western frontiers and even more strongly for the composition of the government that was to take over the country when liberated. Great Britain and France had gone to war to honor their commitment to Poland; Poland was to emerge from the hostilities deprived of the territories occupied by the Red Army in 1939 extended westward to the line of the Oder-Neisse. Even worse, Poland seemed likely to lose its internal autonomy and to be subjected to a Soviet-type regime, with members of its government being chosen by Stalin from the survivors of the Communist Party, decimated in the Great Purges, together with some socialists. After lengthy discussions at Yalta, the Big Three agreed on an ambiguous formula: The government was to be reorganized into a fully representative government based on all democratic forces in Poland and including democratic Polish leaders living abroad. Roosevelt seems to have believed in the promise of free elections—"in about a month," Stalin had told him.[7] He had replied: "I want the election in Poland to be beyond question, like Caesar's wife."[8] According to a legend now beyond the possibility of evidential refutation, the Big Three decided at Yalta to divide up the world. To judge by all the evidence, Yalta was the summit of the Great Illusion rather than of the Grand Alliance. Roosevelt and Stalin

---

[7] Martin F. Herz, *The Beginnings of the Cold War* (Bloomington and London: Indiana University Press, 1966), p. 61.
[8] James F. Byrnes, *Speaking Frankly* (New York: Harper & Row, 1947), p. 33.

had indeed concluded a secret agreement whereby the Soviet Union would enter the war against Japan not more than three months after the war in Europe had terminated. The American President had assented to the territorial gains Stalin wanted at the expense of Finland (the province annexed in 1939), Romania (Bessarabia), and Germany (East Prussia). He hoped for cooperation among the Big Three, and in particular the Big Two, after the war.

Perhaps he even believed that the ambiguous agreement on Poland would be applied as the Western powers interpreted it, with genuinely free elections. A politician rather than a statesman by training, tinged both with greatness and pettiness, proud yet subject to human frailties, Roosevelt had a complex personality that defies easy definition. With all due reservations, it does seem that he did believe the terms of the agreement would be upheld. Harry Hopkins, one of the President's closest advisers, stated later: "We were absolutely certain that we had won the first great victory of the peace—and by 'we,' I mean all of us, the whole civilized human race."[9] Churchill himself displayed to the House of Commons a confidence which perhaps he did not really feel: "The impression I brought back from the Crimea, and from my other contacts, is that Marshal Stalin and the Soviet leaders wish to live in honourable friendship and equality with the Western democracies. I feel also that their word is their bond. I know of no government which stands to its obligations, even in its own despite, more solidly than the Russian Soviet government."[10] To General de Gaulle some months later he used quite different language: "When it is time to digest, the surfeited Russians will have their difficult moments. Then, perhaps, Saint Nicholas can bring back to life the poor children the ogre has put in the salting tub."[11]

Actually, everything goes to show that Stalin apparently continued to take the agreement with Churchill on "percentage influences" in October 1944 more seriously than the rhetoric of the

---

[9] Quoted in Robert E. Sherwood, *Roosevelt and Hopkins: An Intimate History* (New York: Harper & Row, 1948), p. 870.

[10] Winston S. Churchill, House of Commons, February 27, 1945, H. C. Deb. 5th ser., Vol. 408, col. 1283–84.

[11] Charles de Gaulle, *The War Memoirs of Charles de Gaulle*, III, "Salvation," 1944–46, trans. Richard Howard (New York: Simon and Schuster, 1960), p. 60.

final declaration at Teheran. Roosevelt's attitude toward the Anglo-Russian talks in Moscow had been ambiguous and he had even specified in advance that the British premier was not speaking for him,[12] but he refrained from openly expressing his opposition to the outcome of the bargaining between Stalin and Churchill, the details of which he may not have known. The percentage influences of the Soviet Union and Britain, designed primarily for the occupation stage only, and finally worked out by Eden and Molotov, were: Hungary 80–20, Romania 90–10, Bulgaria, 80–20, Yugoslavia 60–40, Greece 10–90. In theory this cynical agreement, indignantly denounced by Secretary of State Cordell Hull and never endorsed by Roosevelt, ceased to be valid as soon as the Big Three solemnly declared at Yalta:

> To foster the conditions in which the liberated people may exercise these rights, the three governments will jointly assist the people in any European liberated state or former Axis state in Europe where in their judgment conditions require (a) to establish conditions of internal peace; (b) to carry out emergency measures for the relief of distressed peoples; (c) to form interim governmental authorities broadly representative of all democratic elements in the population and pledged to the earliest possible establishment through free elections of governments responsible to the will of the people; and (d) to facilitate where necessary the holding of such elections.

Unfortunately, this declaration did not specify what would happen if the Big Three disagreed among themselves. The statement on the reorganization of the Lublin Committee was also somewhat ambiguous; Stalin may have understood it to mean that the men of the Lublin Committee would keep the majority and the preponderant power.

Events moved swiftly in Romania and Poland between the Yalta Conference and Roosevelt's death, and the agreement among the Big Three, proclaimed with such a flourish, had not the slightest effect on the Soviet authorities. Immediately after Yalta, Vyshinsky went to Bucharest and forced King Michael, under the threat of

---

12 Cf. Herz, *The Beginnings*, pp. 125–26. Cordell Hull was permanently and radically opposed to any "spheres of influence" diplomacy.

tank fire to dismiss Radescu, the prime minister, and appoint a fellow traveler, Petru Grozea, in his place. The joint decision to reorganize or enlarge the Lublin Committee was not immediately applied. The principal leaders of the Secret Army and the non-Communist Polish parties were invited to Moscow, where they were arrested and imprisoned. The rising of the Secret Army in Warsaw, ordered by the government-in-exile in London to prevent the Poles who had rallied to Moscow from seizing power, had, after a heroic battle,[13] ended in the elimination of the whole of the organized force which was not bound to the Communists. All of them, the officers murdered at Katyn, the Secret Army exterminated by the Germans because of an imprudent order from London, and the non-Communist Resistance leaders who were arrested, belonged to the old Poland, and all of them had to vanish from the scene if another Poland was to arise out of the grief and ruins.

On the basis of these facts, of which only the most salient have been mentioned here, for twenty-five years historians have been building up a case, some of them against Churchill (the Moscow agreement), some against Roosevelt, and some against Truman. Until recently most historians blamed Stalin for the breakup of the Grand Alliance. The revisionist school has been attracting fresh supporters for some ten years. After each of the wars waged by the United States—the Mexican War, the American Civil War, the intervention in 1917—a revisionist school has cast doubt upon the orthodox contemporary version of events, that of the protagonists themselves, and even more so on that of public opinion. The current growth in the revisionist trend is largely due to the political and moral revulsion against the diplomacy which led to the Vietnam War.

I shall not discuss in detail all the problems raised by the revisionists, since my basic concern here is to account for the way in which Roosevelt and Truman actually behaved during the decisive years between February 1945 (Yalta) and the spring of 1947 (the Truman Doctrine and later the Marshall Plan). It seems to me that

---

[13] Could the Soviet army have crossed the Vistula and come to the aid of the insurgents? Historians are not certain. In any case, Stalin refused for some weeks to grant the Western air forces facilities to parachute arms to them.

two questions are decisive: whether American policy changed under the new president after Roosevelt's death and any such changes are responsible—in the morally neutral sense of a determining cause—for the progressively increasing tension between East and West; and whether the error or fault was the British and American refusal to permit the Soviets to erect a bulwark to protect Eastern Europe. Some contend that this refusal was an "error," suggesting that the abandonment of the fiction of universalism was the only chance, and a real chance at that, of continuing the cooperation between the British and Americans with the Soviets; others contend that it was a "fault," meaning that the Soviets were demanding nothing to which they were not entitled and that the British and Americans were refusing them the legitimate extension of the sphere of socialist states out of shortsightedness or in order to meet the requirements of a capitalist economy.

2.

At Teheran, as at Yalta, Roosevelt had left to Churchill the thankless task of defending Poland's interests. At Teheran he was unwilling to commit himself because of the 1944 elections and the votes of American citizens of Polish origin. At Yalta he intervened to promote universalism, but acted only as an arbitrator or conciliator. Some remarks reported by his son Elliott (not an entirely reliable source) reflect his state of mind:

> Britain is on the decline, China—still in the eighteenth century. Russia—suspicious of us, and making us suspicious of her. America is the only great power that can make peace in the world stick.[14]

Roosevelt went on to define the function of the United States in the postwar world as follows:

> To integrate, in the future organization of the United Nations, the disparate views of the Empire-minded British and the Communist-minded Russians.[15]

---

[14] Elliott Roosevelt, *As He Saw It* (New York: Duell, Sloan and Pearce, 1946), p. 130.
[15] *Ibid.*, p. 207.

Some of the most lucid United States commentators, including Walter Lippmann himself, thought they could detect even in 1946 a power conflict between the Soviet Union and Great Britain, in which the United States should have no part.

Roosevelt was correct in his belief that the United States was the only great power capable of maintaining peace. The notion of keeping the balance equal or nearly equal between an empire which the British, defeated by their victory or constrained by their pledges and their own convictions, were about to dissolve, and Stalinist Communism on the point of sweeping over half Europe was, however, the aberration of a first-rate politician who was sadly lacking in historical background and was, in addition, badly informed. In Europe Churchill was not so much defending an empire as he was the requirements for a balance of power plus the very values advocated by the Americans.

Between 1941 and 1945 Roosevelt seems to have worked with two major considerations in mind, one relating to the war, the other to the postwar period, that is to say, the attainment of an unconditional surrender from Japan and the Third Reich, and the dissipation of Stalin's mistrust and the establishment of good relations with the Soviet leader in order to create the United Nations as an organization which would prevent both the United States from reverting to isolationism and the Soviet Union from withdrawing into its own concerns. Military pragmatism first, utopian vision later. Utopia did not rule out a new "manifest destiny" for the American republic.

Roosevelt became aware of the danger during the last weeks of his life, as the documentary evidence shows. The events in Romania and Poland and Churchill's urgent letters shook his confidence. The "strange alliance,"[16] he knew, would not be proof against a brutal sovietization of the countries liberated by the Red Army. On April 1 he sent Stalin a telegram stating that "a thinly disguised continuation of the present Warsaw government would be entirely unacceptable, and would cause our people to regard the Yalta agreement as a failure."[17] As Roosevelt saw it, Yalta was certainly still the symbol

---

16 The title of the book by the American general stationed at Moscow during the war: John R. Deane, *The Strange Alliance* (New York: The Viking Press, 1947).
17 Herz, *The Beginnings*, p. 90.

of the universalist concept, not that of the partition of Europe into spheres of influence. A few days later he died.

Could Roosevelt have continued the policy of cooperation with Stalin despite everything that stood in its way? No one can be sure of the answer. There is documentary evidence that approaching victory and the Soviets' behavior in Eastern Europe were pushing him toward a different position in the period between the Yalta Conference and his death. I myself believe that he would have altered the line of American diplomacy more rather than less rapidly than Truman. This, of course, is merely a presumption which cannot be finally demonstrated; but what can be demonstrated is that Truman's arrival in the White House did not lead to any interruption or revision of the external action of the United States.

Why is Truman held up to reproach? For his rudeness to Molotov on the way to San Francisco to attend the United Nations conference? Undoubtedly Truman spoke to the Soviet minister for foreign affairs in a tone that Roosevelt had never used; but Stalin never bothered about diplomatic periphrases in his letters to Churchill and Roosevelt. Furthermore, that heated conversation had no sequel. Late in May Truman, in order to symbolize the continuity of American diplomacy, sent Harry Hopkins (his predecessor's gray eminence) to Moscow to continue or restore Russo-American cooperation. As usual, the American envoy obtained a "concession" from Stalin without too much difficulty regarding the method of voting in the United Nations (the veto would not apply to procedural questions; the Security Council's right to raise a particular matter would be a procedural question, not a question of substance, and would not, therefore, be subject to veto from any of the five Permanent Members). Once again, most of the time was taken up by the Polish question. Once again, Stalin swore that he had not the slightest intention of sovietizing Poland, which was under a parliamentary regime. But he categorically refused to free the Resistance leaders ambushed in Moscow, promising only, as he had at Yalta, an enlargement of the Lublin Committee. He agreed to receive Mikolajczyk, who became vice-president of the council. The Americans did not obtain and no longer demanded that the elections for which provision had been made at Yalta should be held *before* the recognition of the Polish government (to all intents and purposes the Lublin Committee) and its admission to the United Nations. Eighteen months after his arrival, Mikolajczyk was fleeing abroad for his life. Truman, thus, was not acting any differently than Roosevelt, and he achieved similar results. He continued to take the United Nations Charter seriously, while Stalin raised legalistic objections and then withdrew them in order to give his interlocutors the impression that it had wrung concessions from him. In exchange he received the recognition of the *faits accomplis* in Poland and elsewhere in Eastern Europe, acts incompatible with the solemn pledges and commitments made to their allies by the British and Americans.

The abrupt ending of lend-lease on May 8, a few hours after the surrender of the Third Reich, raised a storm even in the United States because of the message (later cancelled) sent to the ships already at sea to return to port. Actually, this seems to have been simply the result of an automatic operation of the bureaucratic machinery set in motion by a strict legalistic interpretation. Hopkins assured Stalin that the United States had not had the slightest idea of using such means of pressure.

In the spring of 1945 Truman, a newcomer to world politics, followed the line traced out by Roosevelt, with the same growing uneasiness that his predecessor had felt shortly before his death. He refused, however, to be convinced by Churchill. Churchill begged the President not to evacuate immediately the portion of German territory which was to go to the Soviet forces in accordance with the mapping of the occupation zones. Truman stood fast; in exchange for the Western sectors of Berlin and Vienna and the establishment of an inter-allied commission for Austria, the American troops, followed by hundreds of thousands of refugees, evacuated Thuringia, Saxony, and Mecklenburg, so that Leipzig, Erfurt, and Weimar were left in what was to become the German Democratic Republic. Truman, therefore, continued up to the Potsdam Conference and beyond it to keep to the agreements concluded by his predecessor even while he blamed the Soviets for violating them.[18] One wonders who but an American professor could imagine that a Stalin was vexed or indignant at protests in words to cover up a surrender in deed.

---

[18] Stalin perhaps considered that he was not violating them, but interpreting the Yalta agreement on Poland in a different way. He was perhaps referring to the agreement with Churchill of October 1944.

Now comes the historic decision which has become the subject of a great debate—the decision in 1945 to drop the atom bombs on Hiroshima and Nagasaki.[19] Was this the end of the great war or the beginning of the cold war? A needless piece of cruelty to reduce the cost of victory or an attempt to intimidate the Soviet Union? These questions, which no one raised at the time (*Humanité* applauded the action), have assumed in retrospect a significance both moral and political. Inevitable or unnecessary? Aimed against Japan or the Soviet Union?

The answer can, I think, be fairly readily deduced from the existing documents. Let us look first at those facts which are definitely proven. American intelligence had broken the Japanese codes. The United States leaders were fully aware of the true situation; they knew that, with the Japanese fleet destroyed and the greater part of its merchant marine sent to the bottom, the government appointed by the Emperor and headed by Suzuki wanted an end to a war that was irremediably lost and had accordingly sent instructions to Sato, the Japanese ambassador at Moscow, to ask for Soviet mediation. Neither Tojo, the foreign minister, nor Sato in Moscow knew that their messages had been decoded in Washington on July 13, four days before the Potsdam Conference, nor that Truman and his advisers were perfectly well aware of the Emperor's anxiety for a speedy end to the war.[20]

That being so, why did the United States not open negotiations instead of dropping the atomic bombs? The oversimplified assertion that Japan was already defeated (which is true) and that dropping the bombs was therefore aimed at the Soviet Union is flawed by an evident contradiction. Why, in that case, had President Roosevelt asked for and received at Yalta in February 1945 the Soviet Union's pledge of aid, if Japan's situation was already desperate?[21] The com-

---

[19] Among the abundant literature produced by the event, the book by L. Giovannitti and F. Freed, *The Decision to Drop the Bomb* (New York: Coward-McCann, 1965) is, in my opinion, trustworthy, scrupulous, well-informed, and dispassionate.

[20] Giovannitti and Freed, *The Decision*, p. 148.

[21] It is an established fact that Roosevelt granted Stalin the advantages he demanded in return: the southern part of Sakhalin and the Kurile Islands, joint operation with the Chinese of the South Manchurian and Chinese-Eastern Railroads, restoration of the lease of Port Arthur, and the internationalization of the neighboring port of Dairen, with safeguards for the preeminent interests of the USSR. The price for Soviet intervention

plexity of the situation was due to the conjunction and interrelation of a number of factors:

1. In Japan, which had been indisputably defeated, the peace party had to conceal its intentions because the military party was holding out for continued resistance, remaining opposed both to unconditional surrender and even more strongly to a peace by conceding defeat.

2. In the United States the advocates of a negotiated peace did not venture overtly to condemn the formula of unconditional surrender or to state openly to Senate committees that the maintenance of the Emperor as an institution would prevent chaos and was consistent with a sound view of the United States' interests.

3. Within the administration the major topics of discussion were how severe the defeat inflicted on Japan should be, and what should be future relations with the Soviet Union in Europe and the Far East.

4. The atomic weapon, about which Truman had dropped a hint to Stalin during the Potsdam Conference, had been successfully tested on July 15. It became the best, possibly the sole, means of obtaining Japan's surrender (a) without invading the islands, which the generals believed would be very costly in human lives, and (b) without Soviet participation, which would deprive the United States of some of the spoils of a victory which it had in fact won by its own efforts alone.

If all these factors are borne in mind, it is at least probable, if not certain, that the decision to drop the two atomic bombs sprang almost of necessity from the circumstances. *Despite the bombs*, the Emperor had to struggle to the very last against the fighting determination, absurd and heroic as it was, of a section of the military party. The Japanese cities were being devastated by incendiary bombs; the number of casualties caused by the great raid on Tokyo was as terrible as that claimed by the atomic bombs. *If*, in order to gain the upper hand over the military, the peace party in Japan needed an unprecedentedly horrible event that would save the Army's face, and *if* the President of the United States, bound as he

---

was modestly veiled in the phrase, "the former rights of Russia violated by the treacherous attack of Japan in 1904 shall be restored." The Russian fleet had in fact been surprised and destroyed at Port Arthur in January 1905.

was by the principle of unconditional surrender, could not negotiate terms for peace, and lastly, *if* the choice came down to the alternative of either use of the atom bombs or invasion coupled with the Soviet Union's entry into the war, why should anyone be surprised or indignant? Truman and his advisers merely put into the indicative the three propositions expressed above in the conditional.

United States diplomacy did not, for all of this, become exemplary or rational. Five years later the United States was inviting the same Japan to rearm with the weapons that the victor had insisted it should renounce forever. American diplomacy itself had created a combination of circumstances which made resorting to the atom bombs almost inevitable by its demand for unconditional surrender, by its decision to "reform," "regenerate," and democratize Japan, by the timidity of certain leaders not devoid of acumen, and by crusading slogans which precluded negotiations, even of a secret nature. Added to this was the snap judgment of the government's military advisers based on the notion that only by an invasion could the objective consonant with the political end be obtained, as well as their encouragement of Roosevelt to invite Soviet collaboration and pay for it with concessions at China's expense.

Did Truman in the summer of 1945, after the successful test at Los Alamos, disturbed by the deterioration of Soviet-European relations, fear the Soviet intervention purchased by his predecessor? He was in any case eager to bring the war to an end as soon as possible. The decision to drop the atom bombs, *which the President of the United States would probably have taken solely for the purpose of helping or compelling the Emperor to surrender,* was in addition a first step toward the confrontation with the Soviet Union. President Truman did not inaugurate an "atomic diplomacy" because he wished or hoped to intimidate the Kremlin; rather, he wanted to finish off Japan as quickly and cheaply as possible in order to reduce the Soviet Union's share in the operations and to avoid the friction, already visible in Europe, among the victors.

How are the protagonists' intentions to be determined with any certainty? Which of the innumerable sources, written and oral, are to be trusted? How does one choose between contemporary documents and reminiscences written with hindsight? It seems probable that some prominent statesmen such as Churchill and Stimson did at some moment harbor the thought that the weapon of terror would give American diplomacy additional leverage against the Soviet Union. On the other hand, it can be demonstrated objectively that it is a juxtaposition of circumstances—the fact that the peace party headed by the Emperor did not yet hold the upper hand and that a governing team in Washington was enmeshed in the formula of unconditional surrender and divided on the crucial question of the Emperor—that makes the twofold tragedy of Hiroshima[22] and Nagasaki intelligible and logical, quite apart from any real or supposed intention to negotiate with the Soviet Union from a position of strength.

What can also be demonstrated is that there are no grounds for ascribing to President Truman during the ensuing years a diplomacy based on the threat of the atomic bomb. The American decision-making did not order a stock of bombs to be manufactured as speedily as possible. No sudden change either in tone or style between *before* and *after* is apparent either in Europe or in Asia. The Americans accepted the division of Korea into occupation zones just as they had accepted that of Germany. They assumed sole responsibility for the occupation of the Japanese islands,[23] the access to which they controlled after they alone had destroyed the enemy's fleet between 1941 and 1945 and reconquered the territories in the co-prosperity sphere. On the Old Continent it took two years for the British and Americans to realize the impossibility of a joint administration of Germany by the Allies in the crusade against Hitler. Furthermore, it was only after Great Britain, exhausted by victory, had divested itself of its imperial burden that Truman, in a solemn declaration in March 1947, pledged aid and support to nations threatened with subversion or Communist aggression The decision was fortunate in that it at last dispelled the illusion of a power struggle between Russia and Great Britian, with the United States acting as arbitrator. But the presidential message unfortunately distorted the nature of a necessary action, support for Greece and Turkey, by an inflated, hence deceptive rheoric; the anti-Com-

---

[22] Giovannitti and Freed's book shows that the scheme devised by some scientists for a demonstration in a New Mexico desert had been rejected in committee before it reached the President. Nor was a second decision taken on dropping the bomb on Nagasaki; that was due merely to the operation of the bureaucratic machinery.

[23] As they, together with the British, had assumed the responsibility for the occupation of Italy.

munist crusade remained purely *verbal*. United States' strategy not only in Europe but throughout the world remained purely defensive.

3.

Of greater interest, in my opinion, than the indictment of Truman are the accusations leveled against what some authors call the universalist concept of American presidents, the question of why they did not frankly accept Europe's partition into spheres of influence, as Churchill had seemed prepared to do in October 1944. The Red Army had carried the Soviet regime with it; Stalin used the same language as the Western powers, but did not interpret it in the same way. By protesting against Stalinist practices, the British and Americans created a climate of hostility and provoked the Soviet Union, but did nothing to better the lot of the nations to which they had assumed obligations without the means to fulfil them. This reasoning raises three questions: Was there *error* involved here because the consequences of this diplomacy were unfortunate in particular cases or in general? Was there a question of moral or political *fault* because the Western powers refused the Soviets what they were entitled to? And if there was fault or error, was there any way in which the British and American leaders could have avoided their commission, in view of their own ideas and the pressures upon them?

Let us first look at the matter in the terms of the realists who acquiesced in the spheres of influence: Stimson, the secretary of war, in Washington; and Churchill, at times at any rate, in London. The British and Americans alone negotiated the Italian surrender and gave the Soviet representative a place, not on the Armistice Control Commission, but only on the relatively inactive Inter-Allied Advisory Council, while the Soviets did not intervene on behalf of the Greek Communists when the British army fought them, and even refrained from protesting. Why not leave the Soviets to act as they chose in the countries which were geographically part of their sphere of security, responsibility, or influence? Did the British and Americans denounce Communist behavior? They did: but the Soviets, in line with their own philosophy of history, denounced the restoration or maintenance of the capitalist system just as bitterly. The Soviets, British, and Americans, acted in precisely the same way in the sense that each of them installed regimes akin to their own in their own spheres; and they consequently employed different men and different methods. *Symmetry* in terms of realistic diplomacy implied political *heterogeneity*. What was unfortunate, in this interpretation, was that Roosevelt, a universalist at least so far as others—and Europe in particular—were concerned, should have harbored the delusion that he had prevented the partition of the Old Continent. Had this partition been anticipated and tolerated in advance, it would not have fueled the fires of a fresh crusade with additional fury at having been duped.

This line of criticism convicts the British and Americans of error rather than fault. It is based on a philosophy in which realism degenerates into cynicism. Where the Western powers went wrong in this case, it holds, is that they did not totally ignore political heterogeneity and concern themselves solely with geographical or diplomatic symmetry. The British and Americans did not suppress the Communist Parties in France or Italy. They organized or ensured the organization of genuinely free elections there. In Eastern Europe the free elections in Czechoslovakia and Hungary did not give the Communist Party a majority. The Communists gradually eliminated men and parties suspect of hostility or qualified loyalty to the new order by using what were called in Hungary "salami tactics." If impotent protest was an error, what else *could* the Western leaders do but commit it? To put it in another way, could they prove false to their friends by averting their gaze?

American diplomacy took over from the British diplomats in 1946. No more than the British considered themselves hypocrites when protecting the freedom of European nations and the equilibrium of the Old World even while they gained an empire in Asia, were the American diplomats conscious of inconsistency in protesting against the sovietization of Eastern Europe even while remaining faithful to the Monroe Doctrine. This hypocrisy, if hypocrisy it be, is characteristic of the action of the insular power in preserving the nations of Europe from "universal monarchy" and embodying liberalism in its representative institutions. The Soviet armies carried with them the poverty and despotism of governments most of which had returned from abroad in their baggage trains. The revisionists who in 1970 compared Eastern Europe to the Caribbean (or even Latin America as a whole) displayed a lack of the realism which they postulated; for, in Europeans' eyes, sovietization in no way resembled the Yankee domination of an area about which they cared nothing in any case.

The height of absurdity is reached when the "error" of the American protests is represented as a "fault" because the United States allegedly refused the Soviet Union the legitimate fruits of a victory for which the Russian people had paid so dearly and because this refusal was due to the irresistible expansionary trend of capitalism. I shall revert later to the general problems of the economic-political aims of Washington's diplomacy. But when Truman in 1945 or 1946 demanded the application of the Yalta agreement on the Polish government and protested against the progressive sovietization of the Eastern European countries, he was acting in accordance with both American and European sentiment and the traditional imperatives of equilibrium.

It would have required nothing less than a twofold revision, of geopolitical perspective and of moral judgment, to resolve the contradiction between the realism of the partition of Europe and the heterogeneity of regimes and spheres of influence. The impossibility of a continental equilibrium assumed a significance other than it had had in the past because a global system was gradually replacing the European system. As soon as the Western Hemisphere became a member of the interstate system on the same footing as the Old Continent, the lack of an equilibrium within Europe, however much it was to be deprecated as regards the autonomy of Europe itself, did not preclude an equilibrium of another sort, based on confrontation and coexistence between a Soviet Union strengthened by the neighboring states converted to its form of socialism and Western Europe in conjunction with the United States. The sphere of influence stretching to the middle of Europe secured by the Soviet Union as a result of the war inevitably led to the emergence of a bipolar system embracing the Eurasian land mass as well as Europe itself. Or, at any rate, the system emerged as soon as the United States, abandoning the fiction of arbitrating between Moscow and London and realizing how weak Great Britain had become, did not refuse to take over the role which Britain was no longer strong enough to fill.

The ruthless methods of sovietization were due in part to the nature of the Soviet regime itself. In the case of Poland, the major stake in the dispute between the British and the Soviets, the Polish government in exile in London obstinately rejected the Curzon

Line, which made it easier for Stalin to set up the Lublin Committee with some show of reason and to complete what was begun by the Third Reich—the elimination of the ruling classes of the former Poland. Stalin was well aware that the Polish ruling class and the Polish nation at large had for years hated Russia quite as much as Communism. In granting the Kremlin the right to set up friendly governments in the adjacent countries while expressing wishes for free elections, the Western powers failed to appreciate the contradiction between that right and those wishes. Free elections would not have brought to power governments friendly to Moscow (at any rate not friendly in the sense in which Moscow understood friendship).

However, even if it be conceded that the Western powers committed an error (which they probably could not have avoided) in protesting against the Soviets' behavior in the liberated countries, this still does not clinch the realists' point. The Truman Doctrine was proclaimed in connection with Greece and Turkey, but the final breach between the Soviets and the British and Americans did not occur until June 1947 when Molotov walked out of the Paris conference called to discuss the Marshall Plan. In other words, although the Polish question poisoned relations among the Big Three, it was the German question that led to the final breach.

The Big Three had not spent much time discussing Germany's future at the conferences in 1943 and 1945. At Teheran, Churchill and Roosevelt had spoken of a possible dismemberment of the Reich, Churchill of separate treatment and appropriate punishment for Prussia, Roosevelt of autonomous regions. At Yalta the Three endorsed without discussion the mapping of the boundaries of the occupation zones proposed by the European Committee sitting in London. The French zone was put together from parts of the two other Western zones. With regard to the dismemberment of the Reich, Stalin reminded the others of what had been said at Teheran, and Roosevelt suggested that the problem should be turned over to a committee composed of the United States and USSR ambassadors in London, with Eden in the chair. There was no further talk of dismemberment after Stalin, without consulting anyone, announced immediately after the victory that the Soviet Union had no intention of destroying Germany.[24]

---

[24] According to Djilas, Stalin made this decision because he hoped to include the whole of Germany in his zone.

Unlike the Polish question, the German question did not become a cause of discord among the Allies until after the war had ended. Ultimately the British and Americans accepted both the new frontiers and the Communist regime for Poland. In Germany the heterogeneity of the two zones, despite diplomatic symmetry, was a constant source of dispute, because the Potsdam agreement vested the supreme authority in a Control Council composed of the four commanders-in-chief and because the general principles laid down for Germany's political and economic administration lent themselves to conflicting interpretations.

After the failure of the Four-Power Conference in Moscow early in 1947, the Western powers at last recognized that a joint administration of the whole of Germany was not feasible and that it was inevitable that there should be two units, one comprising the Soviet Occupation Zone, the other the three Western Zones, for an indefinite period. Actually, if we trace the chronology of events, the surprising thing is not the final deadlock, but the two years' hesitation in face of the unavoidable conclusion. The reforms—officially called conquests of socialism, the agrarian reform, and the nationalization of industry—had been set in operation by the occupation authorities as early as September 1945. That autumn those authorities encouraged the German Communists and socialists to merge in a single party, a fusion characteristic of the method of sovietization practiced in the other countries in Eastern Europe. The merger failed, or was not attempted, in Austria (which led me to believe at the time that the Soviets would end by evacuating the country). Karl Schumacher, who had emerged from a concentration camp physically exhausted, but with his will and moral strength intact, took over the leadership of those German socialists who opposed the merger. More than anyone else, more than the Americans, who in 1945 only vaguely grasped the significance of a "unified socialist party," it was he who frustrated the Communists' attempt to gain a stranglehold on the working-class parties in Berlin and West Germany and saved social democracy for the Federal Republic of Germany.

Meanwhile, the Russians were dismantling and transferring industrial machinery and materials. Despite Churchill's objections, Roosevelt had given consideration at Yalta to the figure (not finally approved) of $20 billion in reparations (including $10 billion for the Soviets). Agreement was reached at Potsdam on the following division: Each of the Allies would collect the reparations in its own zone by dismantling surplus industrial equipment, the surplus being fixed in accordance with the permitted ceiling of production. The Western powers would deliver 25 percent of the equipment dismantled in the West to the Russians to round up their share, 15 percent of this in exchange for foodstuffs supplied from the Soviet Zone. The following spring the Control Council reached agreement on the level of production not to be exceeded by Germany (e.g., 11.4 percent of the 1938 production of machine tools, 40 or 50 percent of mechanical engineering, 7.5 million tons of steel). Though the Morgenthau plan for "pastoralizing" Germany (which Roosevelt had taken seriously at first, but had dropped when all his advisers had objected to it) had been discarded by the British and Americans, and the French too, they had not yet recovered from the delusions of victors' spoils to be gained at the termination of the war. The Soviets refused to give any information on that what they were collecting in their zone and failed to deliver the food stuffs they had promised. In May 1946 General Clay stopped delivering industrial equipment to Russia until a joint program for exports and imports had been worked out for the whole of Germany. That program never saw the light of day. The French representative on the Control Council vetoed any establishment of a central administration for Germany as a whole. General de Gaulle was holding firm to his formula of "no Reich, return to the Germanies." He paved the way, not for the restoration of *the* Germanies, but for the birth of *two* German states.

Two separate entities already existed in the spring of 1947, and competition between Soviets and Americans for the favors of the German public had prompted speeches by both Molotov (July 10, 1946) and Byrnes (September 5, 1946). After the Soviet refusal at the 1947 Moscow conference to endorse the French demands relating to the Saar, Georges Bidault consented to join the French Zone to the bizone which the British and Americans had already decided to set up. It is hardly conceivable that the Western powers, having learned their lesson from experience of the sovietization of Eastern Europe, should not have determined to preserve the three Western zones in any case and to associate that fragment of Germany in the reconstruction which the American aid was intended to speed up.

By the time the breach had become final—early in July 1947, a few weeks before the Cominform was set up to replace the Comintern—the Western powers had signed peace treaties with the Soviet satellites and had thereby *de facto* accepted the sovietization of Poland, Romania, and Yugoslavia and the potential sovietization of Bulgaria and Hungary. Throughout Western Europe the economic situation was deteriorating. There was no prospect of a German treaty, so different had the two parts of the Reich already become and so greatly did the British and Americans fear the tactics of infiltration and subversion whereby the Communists gradually acquired total power. To this day I still consider, as I did twenty-five years ago, the offer of the Marshall Plan generous, enlightened, and effective. In retrospect, and in spite or because of the documents since published, I believe that the creation of the Federal Republic of Germany in 1948 was the best possible decision, justified not so much in itself as by the circumstances. Or rather, to put it more correctly, after the Soviet refusal to negotiate the terms for American aid, the Western powers (as they could thereafter be legitimately termed, since the French then ceased to go their own way and worked in concert with the other Western Allies) no longer had any choice; the immediate aim obviously and necessarily had become the economic recovery of non-Communist Europe, Germany included.

Did the Marshall Plan necessarily entail the declaration of cold war, as some revisionists of the "paramarxist" and populist schools maintain? The Plan was offered to the Soviet Union and the other Eastern European countries. To this day historians cannot fathom Stalin's reasons for deciding, after forty-eight hours' hesitation, to reject the offer in aggressive language after he had sent his foreign minister to Paris at the head of a large delegation. For some days the tone of the press of the Eastern European countries was thoroughly confused, as if it did not know what the master of the Kremlin wished and as if he was still hesitating between two courses. He finally refused this last opportunity to cooperate with the Western powers. The Czech ministers, headed by Communists, had unanimously declared in favor of the American secretary of state's proposal, but they now realized their true situation and the limits of their independence.

Why did Stalin make no attempt whatsover to join in, if only to frustrate the move, as most of the State Department's experts had predicted he would? Even now I am still inclined to accept the conventional interpretation, that the Soviet grasp on Eastern Europe was still too recent and too precarious for Stalin to accept the risk of keeping communications open between the West and the countries he was trying forcibly to integrate into a different system.

According to the Marxist-Leninist philosophy (the framework of Stalin's thinking), the United States' main objective was to secure outlets in Europe for fear of a crisis of overproduction.[25] In the official request for a $6 billion loan the Soviet *aide-mémorie* referred to statements made by American politicians "concerning the desirability of receiving extensive large Soviet orders for postwar and transition periods."[26] Deliberately blinkered as he was by his own propaganda and ideology, Stalin had necessarily to denounce the project as camouflage for economic imperialism. Besides, the offer of the Marshall Plan was a confirmation of the American desire to maintain a presence in Europe, a presence which, in Moscow's view, set limits to the expansion of Stalinist "socialism" and, by creating a pole of attraction, it may have compelled the Kremlin to harden its line. Whether Stalin sincerely suspected aggressive intentions behind the Marshall Plan or whether the reconstruction of Western Europe *objectively* imperiled the Soviet sphere is irrelevant. The distinction is perhaps meaningless to a Marxist-Leninist, since he always credits his enemies with intending the consequences of their actions.

The President and the secretary of state may well have feared rather than desired Soviet acceptance. By that time they no longer believed that agreement with Moscow on a joint administration of Germany was feasible. They wished to bar the way to Communism and to preserve the peoples, including the German people, from the temptations of despair. Dollars were indubitably used as a weapon against Communism and as an instrument in the policy of "containment." Since the instrument proved effective, its use cannot be said to have been an *error*. By what strange process of thought can the critics construe such usage as a *fault*?

All that they need do to produce this distorted interpretation is to substitute freedom of trade for the freedom of human beings and

---

[25] Molotov told Averell Harriman that the Soviet Union would be glad to help the United States avoid a crisis by accepting loans.
[26] Herz, *The Beginnings*, p. 169.

to equate the former with capitalism or imperialism. In the eyes of an author like W. A. Williams, for example, aid to the economic recovery of Europe forthwith becomes an integral part of dollar diplomacy and the Open Door policy, and consequently of the depravity inherent in external action whose purpose is the expansion of trade. Even within the frame of such an interpretation of history, to condemn *morally* or *politically* the unilateral transfer of billions of dollars from the United States to the European countries seems to me senseless. Even if the Soviet Union, because of poverty or the aggressive intentions it attributed to the leaders of the capitalist states, was constrained in 1947 to respond by isolating itself, this does not mean that Truman and Marshall committed an error or fault in provoking the Kremlin to furious response; for the response was in that case the price to be paid. Unless they regret that Stalinism was prevented from advancing to the Atlantic coast, the vast majority of Europeans still obstinately refuse to consider the price excessive.

There remains one further argument: the American offer was presented in the form least acceptable to the Soviets, with its suggestion for a list of requirements to be drawn up jointly and the suggestion for multilateral relations between the United States and Europe as a whole instead of bilateral relations between each state and the United States, the method preferred by the Kremlin. The Kremlin had reason to distrust American ulterior motives in view of the reception of earlier requests for loans.

The negotiations between the United States and the Soviet Union for a reconstruction loan, too complex to be recounted in detail here, began during the war. Eugene V. Rostow, who was responsible for lend-lease in the State Department from 1942 to 1944 as Dean Acheson's assistant (Assistant Secretary of State for Economic Affairs), has recently furnished precise information on the first phase of these talks.[27] Late in 1943 Mikoyan raised the question of an American postwar loan with Averell Harriman, the American ambassador at Moscow. *At that time,* Harriman replied that he was in favor of the

---

[27] In an article entitled "The Revisionists," later reprinted as a chapter in *Peace in the Balance, The Future of United States Foreign Policy* (New York: Simon and Schuster, 1972), Chap. 4, Rostow stresses the terms of the legislation setting up lend-lease, which bypassed the question of war debts and opened the way to future trade liberalization, Bretton Woods, GATT, the Kennedy Round, etc.

Soviet request and transmitted it to Washington. Rostow thought that section 3 (c) of the Lend-Lease Act might provide a legal basis for a postwar reconstruction loan. Under lend-lease the equipment required for reconstruction would have been ordered during the war and transferred after it. Rostow's idea was approved by the departments and by the President, and lengthy negotiations on the text of the projected agreement with the Soviet Union ensued, until a Soviet representative visited Acheson at the State Department late in 1944 and put an end to this first attempt at Russo-American postwar cooperation. Rostow concludes that the Kremlin changed its position during 1944. He adds that the Marshall Plan testified to a similar desire for cooperation and provided a further opportunity for it.

A great deal of water had, of course, flowed under the bridges of the Vistula and the Spree in the meantime; and Soviet requests for loans as well as the problems of lend-lease had given rise to misunderstandings and friction. Lend-Lease deliveries to the Soviet Union had reached $9.5 billion (29 percent of the total).[28] The Russian army was bearing the brunt of the war and Congress enthusiastically approved sending equipment to the fighters for liberty. After the discontinuance of the early talks on the use of lend-lease there was a formal request for a $6 billion reconstruction loan at $2\frac{1}{4}$ percent. The American reply hung fire. A new protocol under section 3 (c) of the Lend-Lease Act had to be negotiated, but negotiations bogged down on a seemingly petty dispute about the rate of interest, the Americans refusing to go below $2\frac{3}{8}$, the Soviets demanding 2 percent and proposing $2\frac{1}{4}$ for the contemplated $6 billion loan. The fourth protocol was signed at last in April 1945, but it covered only war material; the interest rate for industrial equipment was settled only on October 15, 1945, at $2\frac{3}{8}$ percent. Three-quarters of the equipment in the Soviet requests (about $1 billion) was never even manufactured. There were never any serious negotiations about the $6 billion loan.

The Russo-American tension relating to the Polish government in the months following the Yalta Conference, and later the disagreement about German reparations, were calculated to promote neither American receptivity nor Soviet insistence. Did the Marshall

---

[28] 14,700 aircraft, 7,000 tanks, 52,000 jeeps, 376,000 trucks, 11,000 railroad cars, 3,800,000 tires, 15 million pairs of boots, etc.

Plan come too late? Rostow does not think so; personally, I am inclined to think that Stalin had by then opted for a diplomacy that precluded cooperation, however slight, with the West. Rostow has the last word on one point which is indeed crucial. If the acceptance of an American loan meant economic domination of the Soviet Union by the United States, as some revisionists suggest, why then blame the United States for failing to grant a loan to the country which had suffered so much for the common victory?

4.

As I stated at the beginning of this chapter, I am simply unable to take the revisionist thesis very seriously. Even granting the symmetry between the sovietization of Eastern Europe and the democratization of Western Europe—and this is no problem within one particular system of interpretation, because all that is needed is to disregard the feelings of the people concerned and the way in which authority was exercised—could the Western powers have displayed even greater forbearance in their impotent protests? They did in fact acquiesce quickly enough; and the idea that Stalin could have been offended by anything Truman or Churchill said seems to me perfectly absurd. At Potsdam probably, certainly after the signing of the treaties with the Soviet satellites, Stalin had gained his minimum objective, the recognition of the governments he had set up in Eastern Europe.

Did the cold war begin between Yalta and Potsdam or between Potsdam and the proclamation of the Truman Doctrine in March 1947 or the Paris Conference in June 1947? The question cannot be answered exactly. Shortly after Yalta the Soviet authorities behaved, in the part of Europe occupied by the Red Army, without the slightest regard for British and American reactions. In particular, they took the first steps to sovietize East Germany, making the division of the former Reich, and hence the division of Europe as a whole, inevitable. Could the Western powers have employed some other form of diplomacy and thereby have brought such influence to bear on Stalin that he would have made concessions in order to maintain some degree of cooperation among the former allies? No one can answer this question categorically. No one can assert that Stalin had in mind beforehand a detailed plan fixing the bounds of the area to be subjected to his rule. Probably some of the men in the Kremlin, including Stalin himself, contemplated an agreement on Germany, provided they could thereby obtain partial control over the German economy as a whole, in the hope of ultimately acquiring complete control of it. From the great illusion in February 1945 to the breach in July 1947 the course of events unfolded in a fashion which is wholly consistent with any rivalry between powers, by action and reaction, challenge and reply.

What I still think probable is that in 1944–45 Stalin decided to place regimes modeled on his own and men dependent on himself in all the Eastern European countries to secure what some writers call a bulwark and others an *imperium*. Could he have contented himself with preponderantly Communist "friendly governments" without going so far as to bring them completely to heel? What does the *possibility* of some other policy mean? Stalin was not, of course, *compelled* by a superior force to resort to the ruthless methods that shocked and terrified Western Europeans. The first governments in Czechoslovakia and Hungary, the former with a Communist premier, the latter resulting from elections which had given an absolute majority to the party of the small peasants, would not have failed to fulfill their obligations to maintain a friendly attitude toward Moscow in what they did, if not in what they really felt. I still do not see that Stalin would have contented himself with any such half measure.

Why should he have meted out to the neighboring peoples any better treatment than he meted out to the Great Russian people who had emerged victors in the Patriotic War? The victory had been costly; the price was reflected in the state of the Soviet Union in 1945–46—a weakened economy, mass poverty, and a ruthless despotism. Had the Kremlin any alternative but force in order to maintain its domination? Did not Stalin have to apply the monopoly of power, the supreme and obsessive principle of Soviet practice, to the whole of the sphere he regarded as his own? The elimination of the persons and parties whose allegiance went to Western values and systems was inherent in the monopoly of power. A half measure such as the Czech government of 1945–48 proved fundamentally unsound in 1948, for new elections would have weakened the Communist Party. Could Moscow suffer such humiliation without losing face and playing false to its own principles? In other words, Stalinism created anti-Russian feeling precisely where it was not already deeply rooted in the past. Even if an English historian is right in thinking that Stalin was meditating a combination of a bulwark against and good relations with the West,[29] the peoples themselves rendered these two aims virtually incompatible; and it is hardly surprising that Stalin should have preferred the bulwark to cooperation with the West.

Even Stalin's hesitation has not been demonstrated. There are indications as early as 1945 of a reversion to the hard line, overt hostility to capitalism as such, fascism and liberal democracy being merely the same beast in other guises. Jacques Duclos published an article based on this ideological stance in *Cahiers du communisme*, while Molotov in his speech at the opening session of the United Nations accused the Western powers of complicity with Hitler. The program for economic growth, especially the expansion of heavy industry, prepared and proclaimed by Stalin immediately after the war, was justified by the parallel presentation of a renewal of the struggle against the capitalist world after the interlude of cooperation during the war.

In saddling the United States with *causal* responsibility for the cold war, or to put it differently, in accusing it of taking, unilaterally or first, the decisions that made the cold war probable or inevitable, the revisionists once more succumb to the national myth of American omnipotence. To postulate that Roosevelt or Truman would have managed to persuade Stalin by some other form of diplomacy to take some other attitude and to account for that attitude by the words or deeds of American presidents rather than by the interests of the USSR and the Communist philosophy is to attribute disproportionate power to the United States. In trying to demonstrate fault rather than error, the revisionists finally reverse the roles assigned to the two protagonists in the conventional version of the cold war.

And reversing the roles is simply the result of ideology. If a Marxist-Leninist posits an equivalence between power to the Communist Party and "freedom" and between the capitalist system and evil, American action is guilty of stopping or curbing the expansion of "freedom" and ensuring the survival of capitalism, and hence of evil, in a part of the Old Continent. This kind of playing with words

---

[29] William Hardy McNeill, *America, Britain and Russia, Their Cooperation and Conflict, 1941–1946* (London: Oxford University Press, 1953), pp. 406–8, quoted by Herz, *The Beginnings,* pp. 198–99.

is of no interest to anyone, even to genuine Marxist-Leninists, who would have acknowledged at the time, and at all events acknowledge today, that they were imposing their system on Eastern Europe regardless of the wishes of the people concerned, and would have legitimatized their actions by a philosophy of history.

American diplomats based their action between 1945 and 1947 on a twofold principle of legitimacy: free elections as a symbol and expression of the wishes of the peoples and a reversion to the traditional role of the insular power spontaneously opposed to universal monarchy (in Montesquieu's terminology) or to the unconditional domination of a *single* state over the European continent. It was evident to anyone viewing inter-state relations in accordance with the traditional, if not eternal, categories that the aim in 1946 and 1947 was to prevent the Soviet Union from filling the vacuum created by the disappearance of the Third Reich and the exhaustion of the theoretically victorious older nations. Criticism of the American action in Europe on the assumption that it derives from the "Open Door" ideology seems in the circumstances pointless, almost absurd. Naturally, non-Soviet Europe remains open to capital and trade; even Europeans who now impugn the monetary and trade system centered on the United States do not—unless they are Marxist-Leninists—regret the fact that Europe has remained "open." The reversal of roles—the United States as aggressor because of its social system—is a sign of the same oversimplification and the same arrogance as the version by American cold war extremists or the Stalinists, resultant upon setting oneself up as supreme judge of historical good and evil. Stalinism displayed enough brutal features at the time to excuse some of the excesses of Western propaganda. However horrible the Vietnam War may be, it does not excuse a reversion to a Manichaean outlook, merely substituting one devil for another.

Whether the revisionists denounce the United States simply as such or blame it for acts of commission or omission which, according to them, rightly exasperated Stalin and put an end to East-West cooperation, they overlook the part played by the Europeans themselves. Churchill first and Bevin after him, and the representatives of the other Western European states, begged the American diplomats to intervene before it was too late. The Americans protracted their efforts to reach agreement with the Soviets longer than the British wished. It was the Soviets' behavior in the territories they occupied, particularly in Germany, that gradually brought the responsible leaders in Washington to commit themselves alongside the British and to abandon the fiction that they were acting as arbitrators in a political rivalry between Communism and the British Empire, between two wills to power. Similarly, it was at the Europeans' request that the North Atlantic Treaty was signed, and at the Europeans' request, quite as much as at any suggestion from the Americans, that the man who had been in command of the crusade against the Third Reich returned to Europe as the commander of the armed forces of the North Atlantic Treaty Organization. If a United States military "protectorate" still exists in Europe twenty years later, it is because the Europeans themselves expressed an urgent wish for it.

The cold war—if this is what we are to call the breakup of the Alliance, the virulent outbreak of Communist and anti-Communist propaganda, the manifold incidents such as the Berlin blockade and the division of Europe into two zones with radically different regimes devoted to a war of homeric insults rather than a war to the death— the cold war in this sense seems to me due to a dialectic of history more potent, probably, than anything willed by diplomats.

Even if Stalin did not decide very early on, as early as 1944, to revert to the ideology of the two camps (the camp of peace and socialism and the camp of imperialism and war) and the "hard line" at home and abroad, and even if he counted on American aid for reconstruction or hoped for cooperation with the Western Allies until the end of 1946 or the Marshall Plan, the fact is that within the sphere he occupied he paid not the slightest regard to the Western powers' inevitable and legitimate reactions to the liquidation of their friends. The historian must, of course, credit Stalin with the fact that he made no protest against the British action in Greece and that the Communist parties in France and Italy displayed the moderation demanded by the doctrine of spheres of influence, which indeed, became over the years the implicit Party line, though long concealed by the clamor of cold war slogans.

The Western leaders could not have acquiesced indifferently in the partition, even had they wished, for three reasons: the Soviet's behavior beyond the demarcation line; Germany; and uncertainty about the Soviets' intention of setting limits to their expansion. On the morrow of a war waged for the people's liberation the British and Americans could not complacently accept the sovietization of

Eastern Europe, especially the fashion in which it was carried out. Even if they could not prevent its occurrence, such protest was part and parcel of the battle of ideas and propaganda. For the Soviet propaganda against the Marshall Plan and the economic reconstruction of Western Europe was unleashed as if Stalin no longer believed himself bound by the terms of the secret agreement of October 1944.

Two final observations: ought it to be said, all things considered, that events could not have occurred otherwise than they did? Basically, if this means the breakup of the Alliance and the partition of Europe, I am inclined to think that the answer is yes (though, of course, any such proposition can never be rigorously demonstrated). This does not mean that the fate of all the Eastern European states was predestined. If Finland had given way to despair or panic, how many historians would have argued that such was fate! Tito, too, showed that Stalin hesitated to resort to his armed forces and that he did not attempt to impose his sovereign will upon those who did not fear him. Even today I am none too sure that the fate of Czechoslovakia was sealed in advance, no more in 1948 than in 1938 or 1968.

The second observation has to do with the very concept of cold war. In Europe the two camps spontaneously made a rule of exercising caution. Truman preferred the technical triumph of supplying two million Berliners by air to a military convoy to force a blockade which was never officially proclaimed and was justified by the Russians by the need for repairs to roads and railroads. Despite the homeric insults, action by the Communist parties to bring economic life to a halt in Western Europe, the Stockholm campaign against the atom bomb, the question whether Stalin feared an American "aggression" (which I do not believe) or wished to conceal his real weakness by a show of aggressiveness, the fact remains that the period of intensive cold war which began in the spring of 1947 coincides with the partition of Europe rather than with any challenge to that partition. It was the Korean accident that gave it a military dimension and a global extension. By way of simplification, it might be said that the cold war served to obscure the United States' conversion from the universalist dream to the reality of spheres of influence.

Even if one does not revert to the commonly voiced criticism of Roosevelt's strategy and even if one endorses his advocates' basic argument that resistance to Communism would not have been possible had the American leaders not first done their utmost to bring the Soviet Union back into the community of nations, it is nevertheless easier to understand than to commend Roosevelt's diplomacy toward Stalin during the war years. Roosevelt was under no compulsion to devise the formula of unconditional surrender, which symbolizes a philosophy typical of the American tradition of first defeating the enemy's armed forces and then settling the political problems—as if those problems were not bound to be posited in terms differing with the way in which the enemy was defeated.

During the war all transactions among the Big Three were conducted as if Stalin held the trump cards, whereas in fact the United States, distant from the battlefield and with an industry working to full capacity for the first time since the Great Depression, was acquiring an overwhelming superiority over Great Britain—wholly dependent as it was on American aid, the longer the war lasted—and over the Soviet Union itself, which was making the heaviest sacrifices for the "common cause." It is true that Roosevelt and Churchill may have feared a separate Russo-German peace and suffered from a feeling of inferiority because of the Soviet Union's decisive share in the fighting. By the 1939 pact Stalin had tried to turn Hitler's aggression westward, but France's speedy defeat had reversed the position. Why should the British and Americans have felt themselves to blame for the results of Stalin's own miscalculation in signing the 1939 pact with Hitler?

Among the Big Three Stalin regularly prevailed because he knew what he wanted and how to get it. He traded concessions on the United Nations Charter for hard cash in the form of satellite territories and states. Roosevelt, paralyzed and near death, drove himself to make the long journey to the Crimea and, backed by almost unlimited resources, seemed more anxious to appease the despot than to support Churchill. Was his mixture of pragmatism and idealism perhaps a mask for a will to power? Yes, but even so, the conviction that it would be up to the United States to secure the peace is no justification for the diplomatic-strategic behavior of 1943–45—unless the American President is credited with prior acceptance of a Russo-American condominium based on the delimitation of spheres of influence. That Roosevelt may have had some sort of idea of a condominium of this sort, in which the United States would have held the first place, is possible. That he would have tolerated the fashion in which Stalin incorporated Eastern Europe in his sphere of power I can hardly believe. In the ensuing period American diplomacy gradually resigned itself to, or determined on, resistance or even hostility to the Soviet Union. But, with virtually one solitary exception, it never managed to divert Stalin from his ventures, merely raised barriers against them. Ulam[30] accounts for the Soviet retreat in Iran and the liquidation of the Soviet Republic of Azerbaijan by Churchill's Fulton speech; the clear expression of Anglo-American solidarity, he believes, impressed Stalin. This may be so, though the dates do not make for conclusive proof. Stalin had been afraid when faced with Hitler, and his behavior had betrayed his fear. Faced with Roosevelt or Truman he was never afraid, not because he was under any misapprehensions about American power, but because he despised what seemed to him a mixture of hypocrisy, weakness, and blindness. It is true that the Soviet Union had demobilized further than commentators said at the time; but the fact remains that the United States had brought the GIs back from the other side of the Atlantic and that the most powerful state in the world could barely defeat a satellite of the Soviet Union in 1950. Would diplomatic pressure have been effective without immediately available military resources? I can hardly think so.

After 1947 American diplomacy set itself a precisely formulated defensive aim. The Administration now knew what it wanted, and got it. Roosevelt did not hold the same view of the world of inter-state relations as Stalin. But Stalin modeled the world in accordance with his own philosophy. Truman accepted the idea that the world was as Stalin saw it or wished it. And this is a revision which marks the "finest hour" of American diplomacy in Europe. It was too radical a revision, since it led the very same diplomacy a few years later to conceive the world of inter-state relations more in terms of the schematic pattern of Stalinist propaganda than in terms of its complexity. Twenty years ago Roosevelt was criticized for misunderstanding the nature of the Soviet regime; today his successor is blamed for extending to the entire globe a containment that was called for in Europe.

---

[30] See A. B. Ulam, *The Rivals* (New York: the Viking Press, 1971).

Chapter Two

THE TWO CRUSADES

On March 11, 1947, Truman in an address to the Congress proclaimed to the world the doctrine which has borne his name ever since:

> I believe it must be the policy of the United States to support free peoples who are resisting attempted subjugation by armed minorities or by outside pressures. I believe that we must assist free peoples to work out their own destinies in their own way. I believe that our help should be primarily through economic and financial aid which is essential to economic stability and orderly political procedures.[1]

The message to Congress was intended as an introduction to a request for an appropriation of $250 million for Greece and $150 million for Turkey.

Though Stalin had refrained from protesting against British armed intervention in Greece in 1944–45, in 1947 the countries which had become socialist and were bound to the Soviet Union—Bulgaria, Yugoslavia, and Albania—were supporting and supplying the Greek guerrilla fighters under Communist military command against the royal government. Stalin, therefore, no longer felt himself bound by the October 1944 agreement—unless he held that it in no way obliged the Communist parties to remain quiescent or adopt a reformist line. The agreement only forbade him to intervene with military force in countries in which the government in power treated Communists in the same way as he treated liberals.

---

[1] *Public Papers of the Presidents of the United States: Harry S. Truman, 1947* (Washington, D.C.: Government Printing Office, 1963), pp. 178–79.

And he probably did not have the absolute authority over the Greek, and especially the Yugoslav, Communists (as Tito's secession in 1948 demonstrated) with which Western statesmen and commentators credited him at the time.

While George Kennan, reputedly the author of the policy of containment, did not disapprove of the content of the perfectly reasonable announcement that the United States was taking over from Great Britain and was going to the aid of Greece and Turkey, he did deplore its style and rhetoric. The Socialist Republic of Azerdaijan had been liquidated with far less fanfare. I am inclined to doubt, however, whether too much weight should be given to the announcement of March 1947. Turkey and Greece were a part of Europe, and the United States was acting as the insular power, taking the place of a Great Britain exhausted by its victory. The Americans were responding to an appeal from the Europeans and replacing Britain at its own request.

The major turning point was in fact the Marshall Plan so far as Europe was concerned, and, so far as the world was concerned, the Korean campaign, the consequences of which the historians of the new generation tend to underrate. Before the Korean campaign the United States' defense budget was about $15 billion. The American divisions in Japan and Germany resembled occupation forces rather than combat units. It was the North Korean army's crossing of the thirty-eighth parallel that set in motion a chain of events in Asia and Europe which is still running out its course today and has determined some of the main characteristics of the period 1950–72. It was in and after 1950 that the cold war assumed a military dimension and global extension and that the United States grew used to maintaining a vast military apparatus in peacetime for the first time in its history, and it was North Korea, backed by the two major Communist powers, that imposed upon the United States a limited war and a peace without victory. It was in Asia far more than in Europe that the American republic assumed the imperial burden which the war in Vietnam and the general public outcry it engendered are constraining it to reduce today.

1.

Though the events of June 1950 are well known in the main, some points are still obscure (only the Kremlin archives could throw light on them).[2] American diplomacy bears some of the responsibility for the North Korean aggression.[3] Dean Acheson's speech placing South Korea outside the American defense perimeter risked conveying a misleading message to the Kremlin, or at any rate a message liable to misleading interpretation. The withdrawal of the American garrison without any assurance of a balance between the armies of the two Koreas created a vacuum which the North Korean army could not resist the temptation to fill. Once this *political* responsibility is conceded, the President's decision stands up to the revisionists' test, for unless the Americans had intervened, Korea would have been unified under a Communist regime, and the republic, which was recognized by the United Nations which supervised its elections (North Korea refused to admit the United Nations' representatives), would have disappeared, a victim of aggression in the crudest sense of the term. The defeat would have been spectacular, for it would have discredited the American guarantee and intensified the climate of fear. In any appraisal of the pros and cons of intervention or abstention, the balance still inclines toward intervention.

On the other hand, the American policy-makers committed mistakes in the conduct of the campaign and perhaps in their interpretation of events and their rival's intentions. Early in January 1950 they were contemplating a recognition of the government of Communist China. The State Department had published a White Book severely criticizing the weaknesses of Chiang Kai-shek's government and hinting that the party defeated in the civil war might be abandoned. There can be no possible doubt that the United States surprised the Kremlin by fighting for Korea after refusing to fight for China. It probably surprised Mao Tse-tung as well by replying to the North Korean armies' advance by interposing the Seventh Fleet between the mainland and Formosa. At the same time, Truman and his advisers decided to send a mission to Indochina to assess the needs of the French expeditionary force and to step up the aid already granted. The diplomacy, worked out in forty-eight hours between June 25 and June 27, 1950, was seem-

---

[2] See note appended to this chapter, pp. 69–71.

[3] Responsibility in the causal sense, i.e., behavior which to some extent made probable an event which was neither desired nor inevitable. This implies there was error involved.

ingly based on the assumption that this was a single venture directed
from Moscow, with the participation of the Chinese regime. The
notion that the various Communist parties at that time were re-
ceiving and following similar instructions from Moscow was true,
or nearly so. The presentation of a worldwide conspiracy, its threads
woven in Moscow and stretching out throughout the world, was
never so close to reality as in the last years of Stalinism. Even in
1950, however, it did not entirely fit the facts. Mao Tse-tung's
negotiations in Moscow took several weeks. Ho Chi Minh, though
a loyal adherent of Moscow, was equally, perhaps primarily, a
Vietnamese patriot; in 1946 he would not have refused a temporary
arrangement with France.

Whether or not Washington believed that a general Communist
offensive in Asia would be the sequel to the North Korean aggression, it acted as if it did and inaugurated a policy which led
both to the quarantining of Communist China and to the prolongation of the first Vietnam War and the start of the second. The
decisions of June 1950 together with the vicissitudes of the operations of autumn 1950 are links in a chain of events the understanding of which is essential to a proper interpretation of American
diplomacy for the next twenty years.

It is considered improbable today that Mao Tse-tung instigated
the Korean campaign. The bulk of the Chinese armies was concentrated opposite Taiwan; the Korean army had been reorganized by
Soviet advisers and comprised units and officers who had fought
under the hammer and sickle. Stalin and Mao Tse-tung in Moscow
had probably discussed a possible move by Pyongyang, but China's
attitude before the American troops advanced to the Yalu was
definitely cautious. Stalin had ordered, or perhaps simply authorized, the North Korean venture (there was a movement in favor
of unification on both sides of the demarcation line). Besides, it
seemed to involve little danger and, if successful, considerable gains,
for the blow to American prestige would have been severe.

Historians are still debating Stalin's calculation and the reasons
why the Soviet representative withdrew from the United Nations,
officially in protest against the continued seating of Chiang Kai-
shek's representative. Were the Soviets already trying to prevent
what they were pretending to want? Did they hope to return after
a North Korean victory in order to save the face of the United States
and the United Nations? Even today historians have little to go

on but informed guesses. Whatever the truth, the American ambassador asked the men in its Kremlin to intervene with Pyongyang, an approach which seems to have reassured the Kremlin and encouraged it to permit the campaign to continue without interference. After the landing at Inchon and the destruction of the North Korean army, the American policy-makers made the decision, though not without hesitation, to cross the thirty-eighth parallel and try themselves to unify Korea by armed force. They did not take seriously the warning transmitted to them by Mao Tse-tung through Pannikar, the Indian ambassador. General MacArthur, too, refused to heed the warning of an initial and limited intervention by Chinese "volunteers" early in October. When he launched his great "end the war" offensive in late November, the "volunteers" attacked, en masse this time, cut to pieces the South Korean divisions holding the center, and compelled the Seventh Army to beat a hasty retreat.

Washington thus let slip several opportunities to gain a success. It might perhaps have succeeded in inducing Stalin to order the North Koreans to retire. By establishing themselves on the narrow strip of the peninsula north of Pyongyang, the Americans prevented Chinese intervention and gave South Korea a decisive advantage, while inflicting a resounding defeat on the Communist camp. Another opportunity for success appeared in the spring of 1951, when the Soviets suggested armistice talks and the Americans suspended their offensive.

These strategic mistakes (and who does not commit any?) concern us because they throw light on certain traits, less typical of American diplomacy than of the political system from which it derives. General MacArthur pursued his own policy without formally disobeying the orders of the President and his civilian and military advisers; he put pressure on his own chief, the President, by statements to the press and to members of Congress. He assured President Truman that China would not intervene. He reacted excessively, in words, to the intervention by the Chinese "volunteers." In Washington the secretary of state and the Chiefs-of-Staff Committee did not dare categorically forbid the final offensive nor categorically impose all the precautions (not to allow the American troops advance to the Yalu) which they themselves believed essential.

But the fact remains that at no time did President Truman and his advisers contemplate using nuclear weapons, despite the legends about Clement Attlee's dissuading them from it, and they accepted peace without victory within the frame of a limited war. If it had not been for General MacArthur's errors of judgment, they would in all probability have won a limited victory in late 1950. In this respect the Korean War marks a break with the American tradition of total victory and the fundamental difference between the treatment of war and peace. It was in 1950 that the United States resigned itself to the European practice of maintaining a large standing army, not merely a navy and air force. It was during the Korean campaign that it discovered in fact—and not without regrets and protests—that the practice of first destroying the enemy's armed forces, that is, winning a military victory, and then concerning itself with the political settlement was consistent neither with the logic of the relationship between the political direction and the military instrument nor with the requirements of a diplomacy with world-wide responsibilities. But it was also the Korean "accident" that enlarged the theater of the rivalry between the two super-powers and precipitated the formation in Europe of two military blocs, and in Asia the quarantining of Communist China.

2.

The Korean "accident"—I use this term because it seems very likely that the decision taken or tolerated in Moscow on the North Korean armies' crossing of the demarcation line was not part of a master plan—had two major sequels. The first of these was the beginning of rearmament in the United States and Europe.

At the time, discussion raged between the proponents and opponents of European, and especially German, rearmament, although the need for a certain amount of American rearmament was universally recognized. Looking back, all parties would, I think, acknowledge that rearmament led neither to the disastrous consequences feared by its opponents nor to the beneficial results anticipated by some of its proponents.

The United States had demobilized its army between 1945 and 1947 as rapidly as it had mobilized it. Whatever construction is placed on the Korean "aggression," the United States learned the first lessons essential for the exercise of its new function, that diplomacy in peacetime calls not only for potential resources but for troops immediately available. Pressure and implicit threat, which are an integral part of normal intercourse between rival states, remain ineffective and meaningless as long as their translation into action requires mobilization.

Did the "Kremlinologists" see the Korean accident as a crucial issue? Did they view it as the transition from one phase in the cold war—"short of war"—to another—"war not excluded"? Not to my knowledge. The President's advisers, at any rate those among them who were specialists in Soviet affairs, still believed that Stalin feared war quite as much as the United States did. Yet they recommended rearmament for two reasons: there was still some uncertainty about events, if not intentions, and in any case the United States had to accustom itself to its role as a great power. Neither atom bombs, which could not be used in a marginal conflict, nor the hundred million tons of steel which could be converted into shells and tanks furnished American diplomacy with the tools, no less traditional than contemporary, needed by a paramount state.

What remains today of the objections raised at the time? Stalin, some said, would not wait to strike until the United States had gathered its strength, an argument not only refuted by the course of events, but ill-founded from the start. On the morrow of June 25 the American leaders approached the Kremlin, not to tax it with instigating the "aggression," but to request its good offices. They therefore accepted from the outset the fiction of the Soviet Union's neutrality and its position as arbitrator. Once again, there is nothing to show that Stalin at that time was afraid, as he had been afraid of Hitler. He was concealing his country's poverty from foreign eyes, he was relentlessly pushing forward economic reconstruction, he was exploiting favorable opportunities in Europe and Asia, and he was taking advantage of every opening wherever he met with no resistance. It appears to me as if American diplomacy —save in a very few instances—failed to inspire Stalin with fear or even respect.

If rearmament perhaps had dangerous implications, they lay mainly in the domestic sphere. Tocqueville's classic observations on democracy's alternation between indifference to military matters and bellicosity was no longer valid:

> I have pointed out how in democracies in times of peace an army career is held in little honor and attracts few recruits.

Such public disapproval is a heavy discouragement to the army. . . . When a war has at length by its long continuance roused the whole community from their peacetime occupations and brought all their petty undertakings to ruin, it will happen that those very passions which once made them value peace so highly become directed into war. War, having destroyed every industry, in the end becomes itself the one great industry, and every eager and ambitious desire sprung from equality is focused on it.[4]

The cold war to some extent created within the United States the modern equivalent of what Tocqueville considered inevitable in wartime, the focusing of popular emotion on military affairs. There was, however, one major difference, in that arms' manufacture rather than the war itself became the great industry. The United States being what it is, the maintenance of a huge and permanently available combat force was bound to produce what President Eisenhower in his farewell address called the military-industrial complex.

Was the rearmament of the European countries, especially the Federal Republic of Germany, an absolute necessity? Once again, if the reason or justification for rearmament was the expectation of a Soviet drive to the Atlantic ports, the conclusion in retrospect would have to be that the policy-makers were wrong about Soviet intentions and that the precautions proved unnecessary. Some will reply that the precautions were unnecessary precisely because they had been taken. Though this answer cannot be dismissed out of hand (what might have happened if Stalin had lived a few years longer?), I shall not adopt it. I personally feel that the prerequisite for the economic and moral reconstruction of Europe was a climate of security and confidence, and this required a United States guarantee and the physical presence of American forces. The only way to secure this presence was through some sort of organization like NATO, and there was no reason why the European states should not be made to pay a contribution to the common defense. And how could the Federal Republic of Germany be allowed to enjoy the economic advantage of not having to pay its share of the burden of defense costs?

Those who opposed this diplomacy at the time will acknowledge

---

[4] Alexis de Tocqueville, *On Democracy in America*, II, 3, pp. 656–57.

that it did not lead to any of the disasters anticipated. The two alternative forms of diplomacy, which were not put to the test, do not seem to me to have acquired any greater credibility with the lapse of time. Western Europe could have declared itself neutral or nonaligned only by displaying a common will and coherence which it lacked in 1950 and has not yet acquired twenty years later. The Western Europe with neither nuclear nor conventional means of defense but relying on popular resistance against invasion, as suggested by George Kennan, simply did not exist in 1950. Even today, more than twenty years after General Eisenhower's arrival on the continent as the first Supreme Commander of NATO, it still seems to me that the *European* diplomacy of the Truman Administration from 1947 to 1952 was correct; by this I mean that it offered the best means by which to achieve its aims: the reduction of the risks of war to a minimum, the promotion of the recovery of Europe within a climate of security, and the paving of the way for the reconciliation, cooperation, and even unification of the former enemies.

A second observation is called for, and it is made in a purely noncontroversial spirit. Those who personally experienced the postwar years still have memories which the historians of the present generation should not disregard. Conditions during the latter years of Stalin's regime were what can only be properly described as dreadful. Anti-Stalinists, in France at any rate, were the more exasperated because among both their friends and their adversaries they came up against an extraordinary blindness. Philosophers of freedom went "part of the way" with a regime in which the only freedom that existed was freedom to acclaim the Father of the Peoples, and humanitarians sang his praises despite the Great Purge and despite atrocities, the evidence for which should have sufficed to convince any sane person. Admittedly, there was no necessary connection between the alternating phases of domestic tension and relaxation and the course of external action. Experts knew that and stated it publicly, and nonexperts occasionally accepted it as well. Analysis did not suffice wholly to dispel the impression of danger or unpredictability created by the atrocious behavior of Stalin himself.[5] Of course, from any rational point of view the West in gen-

---

[5] According to some Western experts, Stalin was preparing to alter his line in the direction of relaxation before his death. [See Marshall D. Schulman,

eral, and the Americans in particular, were wrong to answer Moscow's frenzied propaganda with crusading language. But, even apart from the American people's propensity to such language, excesses on one side almost inevitably generate excesses on the other. It would have been almost inconceivable to respond to the Communist diatribes and the accusations that the United States was waging germ warfare with reasoned arguments or the plea for accommodation between great powers.

A further criticism carries greater weight. There can be no doubt that the Marshall Plan, the Atlantic Alliance, and NATO were necessary till 1953. But after Stalin's death both politicians and the man in the street felt—and rightly so, I believe—that an abrupt change had taken place. Within a few weeks Stalin's successors had made lavish symbolic gestures of goodwill; they halted the propaganda against the United States' use of germ warfare, renounced the claim to the Turkish provinces of Kars and Ardahan raised by Stalin personally in conversations with Churchill as early as October 1944—at the same time as his demand for the revision of the Montreux Convention on the Black Sea Straits—and endorsed the appointment of a new secretary-general of the United Nations, a post which had fallen vacant with the ending of the term of office of the first incumbent, the Norwegian Trygvie Lie, whom the Soviets blamed for United Nations' participation in the Korean campaign. The remarkable verbal discipline imposed upon militants and intellectuals in Eastern Europe and self-imposed by converts to the new faith in the West crumbled at one stroke. As Lamartine put it: *"Un seul être nous manque et tout est dépeuplé"* ["One man is taken from us and all is unpeopled"]. The Boss died and the ice melted. The word "thaw," the title of a book by Ehrenburg, symbolized something of what actually happened and even more so the degree to which contemporaries felt that it had. But American diplomacy in Europe continued unchanged despite the thaw, with first hardly a sign of willingness to negotiate with Moscow to avert the rearmament of the Federal Republic of Germany, next the final hardening of two military blocs, with Dulles's threat of an

---

Stalin's Foreign Policy Reappraised (Cambridge: Harvard University Press, 1963).] According to other evidence and Stalin's conversations with Djilas, however, Stalin believed in a third world war, the final war between the two camps.

"agonizing reappraisal" if the French Assembly rejected the proposed European army, and finally with the Federal Republic's admission to NATO and the formation of the Bundeswehr.

Once again, none of the disastrous results that were feared and predicted by the opponents of this policy came to pass. The Soviet Union retorted by denouncing the Franco-Soviet and Anglo-Soviet treaties and setting up an organization similar to NATO, the Warsaw Pact, with an integrated general staff. Neither the denunciation of treaties which had to all intents become obsolete nor the official array of the Eastern European armies under Soviet command led to any noteworthy change in the situation.

On the other hand, what is still wide open to criticism is the inflexibility of Dulles's diplomacy and the virtual refusal to negotiate on German unification or any other subject, though the Four Powers did meet in Geneva in 1955 and though the spirit of Geneva was resoundingly evoked throughout the world. The major features of 1953–58 seem to me to be the crystallization of the two blocs in Europe and the Sino-American confrontation in Asia, despite the thaw and despite détente. The two symbolic crises, in 1956 in Europe and the Middle East and in 1958 in Asia concerning Quemoy and Matsu, brought into the light of day the partial understanding which was masked by the exchanges of invective between the two super-powers as well as the tensions within each of the two camps.

3.

In the absence of a knowledge of the arcane secrets of the Kremlin, historians still wonder about the chances of an East-West agreement on a unified and neutralized Germany in 1953. Did Beria contemplate, as his enemies charged after the event, sacrificing the German Democratic Republic to the hope of an understanding with the Western powers or to a fear of the disturbances that might be set off by Stalin's death? Though there are hints of a willingness to negotiate on Germany in 1953–54, one seeks in vain for evidence of Soviet assent to the concessions which would have been required if any such negotiation was to succeed. Would Stalin's successor have accepted genuinely free elections in a "democratic republic" at the risk of losing face and weakening their whole *imperium?* Would the Western powers have risked a confederation in which the German Democratic Republic would have kept its regime and the Communist Party its omnipotence? Once more, I cannot believe it, even after this lapse of time.

Nevertheless, critics are still entitled to blame American diplomacy for taking for granted the division of Germany and Europe after 1948. Perhaps Dean Acheson hoped to achieve a position of strength from which to negotiate in favorable circumstances. When the rearmament of the Federal Republic became a reality in 1955, the Soviet Union already had a nuclear armament, had exploded a hydrogen bomb, and was approaching the production targets for coal, steel, and electric power which were set by Stalin immediately after the war, and which he regarded as safety thresholds.[6] The strategy of liberation went no further than speeches or party platforms. Soon after his election Eisenhower, in order to appease Republicans who blamed Truman for his conduct of the war, gave Chiang Kai-shek permission to "reconquer" mainland China. This sort of offensive was hardly likely to set off Armageddon.

After 1955 there could be little doubt in Europe about the defensive aim of American diplomacy. The purely verbal rejection of the division of Germany, the nonrecognition of the German Democratic Republic, and the guarantee of the Western sectors of Berlin barely disguised the acceptance of the status quo. Was not to reject it in words only the best way to maintain it? In any case, what the Europeans feared at the time was not the defensive nature and caution of the United States' European diplomacy, but precisely the reverse, its rash decisions and irresponsible adventures. Neither the French nor the British nor the Germans denounced its ambiguity, the implicit agreement on the share-out covered up by the propaganda warfare. At most, Churchill, before suffering a stroke in 1963 and after Stalin's death, had had some inkling of the existence of an opportunity for negotiation with Moscow.

It was only in 1956, with the two simultaneous crises in central Europe and the Middle East, that Europeans became fully aware of their subordination to their own Big Brother and the price to be paid for the security ensured them by a power more powerful

---

[6] Cast iron, 50 million tons; steel, 60; coal, 500; petroleum, 60; these figures had been given in an electoral address in February 1946. The 1961 figures were 50.9, 70.7, 510, and 166, respectively.

than themselves. Reduced, not to essentials, but to the Europeans' realization of them, the combined event—Hungary and Suez—entailed two inevitable and incompatible alignments: while all the members of the Atlantic alliance were denouncing the Red Army's suppression of the Hungarian revolt, the United States in coalition with the Soviet Union was mobilizing the United Nations and the world's conscience in condemnation of the British and French. The action by the united Western powers remained purely verbal; the Soviet-American action against the British and French achieved what it set out to do.

There is no need to go into detail here about Dulles's relationships with Eden and the French ministers (Christian Pineau and Guy Mollet). I find it hard to believe that the American secretary of state foresaw and approved a scenario in which the British and French committed themselves and he, Dulles, called them to order and lectured them on their misdeeds. I did not think at the time, and I still do not think, that the Anglo-French enterprise had any chance of success or that its likely outcome would have been either a more compliant government in Egypt or an end to the revolt in Algeria. In any case, what sense was there in the anachronistic resort to gunboat diplomacy without American assent? Nevertheless, Dulles's behavior was as inept as it was infuriating. From the first day, in an elaborate maneuver to defuse the bomb, he set forth proposals which he failed to back, in the hope that the hotheads in London and Paris would gradually come to their senses and ultimately accept a compromise. But why, knowing as he did of the British and French military preparations, did he allow his opposite numbers to believe that he would tolerate the use of military force against Egypt?

Once again, the American leaders' language aggravated the crisis and laid them open to the accusation of hypocrisy. "There should not be two laws, one for our friends and another for our enemies," President Eisenhower said, wholly unconscious of the black humor implicit in his remark. For the law, if one may venture to say so, applied to the friend but not to the enemy, since the United Nations confined itself to laying that law down. President Eisenhower's famous remark was wholly in tune with public opinion in the United States. I remember a conversation with an eminent American judge some years later, during which he told me that he had felt an intense pride the day that the President had taken his stand against the British and French, a great day in American history because the President had placed respect for international law above friendship or interest. The interest sacrificed to law in 1956 was not an American interest; Europeans trained in skepticism by centuries of history recalled the creation, at Colombia's expense, of the sovereign state of Panama, which had presented the United States with the privileges and guarantees it needed for building the Panama Canal.

The French interpreted the "dual crisis" in the light of the "dual hegemony." At the very same moment, each of the two super-powers was, by an irony of history, restoring "order" within its own camp, with the consent rather than the connivance of the other. The Eastern European countries discovered the bounds within which destalinization would be tolerated; the British and French, the limits of their independence outside the area covered by the Atlantic Pact. Whether and how far the leaders in the Kremlin and the White House realized anyone else's view of the significance of the Soviet "victory" in Hungary and the Russo-American "joint victory" in the Middle East is irrelevant. The dual crisis left its mark on the European view of the world, most especially perhaps in France. In Britain it did not turn either Conservatives or Labour away from close alliance with the United States; but it does symbolize an important landmark, which may be described as *the end of illusion* or *the realization of hegemonic protection*. A protected state cannot lay claim to freedom of external military action. The nuclear *bipole* did not restore this freedom to the medium-sized powers which had once been great powers.

The double event in October-November 1956 was spectacular. By a combination of ineptitude and moralism American diplomacy humiliated allied and friendly nations; but on the main issue the governments in Paris and London were wrong. The Egyptians operated the Suez Canal perfectly well; it was closed to traffic only by Anglo-French action in 1956 and Israeli action after 1967. By that time the giant tankers were using the Cape route; the great engineering feat of the last century was no longer a vital stake in high policy. The British, it is true, had evacuated the canal zone only at American prompting; but the evacuation was nevertheless consistent with the logic of their own policy. Together with the Indian

Empire they had lost their army, and as soon as the world war ended they had accepted the necessity (in both senses) of decolonization.

Dulles's ineptitude or hypocrisy does not excuse the errors of judgment on the part of Paris and London. Basically, the French and British leaders had different aims in view, the former concerned with Algeria, the latter with the Suez Canal; they did not even know whether they intended to occupy the canal zone indefinitely or withdraw after setting up some other government in Cairo; unless Nasser collapsed suddenly (and even then, what would have happened next?), they had no reason to count upon United States' support or even tolerance. Furthermore, the timing was bound to exasperate President Eisenhower. Was he not likely to suspect the British and French of counting on the presidential elections to compel United States' neutrality or abstention?

Like its opposition to the British and French, the United States' inaction toward Europe does not in retrospect seem wholly unjustified. At the time of the Berlin blockade President Truman had held back from sending in an armed convoy (as proposed by Aneurin Bevan, the leftist Labour minister, among others). Historians have little doubt today that the Soviets would have let the convoy through and the blockade would have been forced in a few hours.

In other words, at the height of the cold war—1948—the American President, *with the approval of the European governments,* took no step that involved the slightest risk of armed confrontation with the Soviet Union. Stalin had concealed his weakness behind a façade of such aggressiveness that many Europeans, including General de Gaulle himself, believed in 1950–51 that war was at hand, and at no time, neither in 1948 nor in 1956, did the American President consider he was capable of forcing the Kremlin to retire in spite of the American superiority in economic and military resources. In 1956 the United States had the means to destroy its rival's cities while its own territory was still invulnerable, or nearly so. If President Eisenhower had sent even a symbolic detachment beyond the demarcation line, the European governments would have trembled and protested. They served, in a sense, as hostages, because they were not or did not believe they were capable of defending themselves against the Red Army. By adopting a defensive strategy, the government in Washington made a reality of the "dual hegemony," but did not betray its allies. It had used military force in Korea in reply to a *military* crossing of the demarcation line. It would have done the same if that line had been crossed in Europe.

Can and should this acceptance of the share-out be condemned? In retrospect it can be seen that American diplomacy after 1947 combined practical action consistent with the doctrine of spheres of influence with the use of universalist language. Criticism therefore swings between the indictment either of the action or of the language. The question is whether that diplomacy should, from 1946 on, have acquiesced in the sovietization of Eastern Europe, including one-third of Germany, or whether it should have used the language of the "rollback" at the time of Eisenhower's election in 1952, when the Soviet Union had set up regimes modeled on itself throughout its entire sphere of influence and "desovietization" would have caused it to lose face.

Without giving any categorical answer to these two questions, I would like to recall that the Europeans suffered from the share-out insofar as they were in favor of ridding themselves of the "dual hegemony," but were equally in favor of this defensive diplomacy and the respect for the demarcation line. They never wanted the Americans to risk trying to "liberate" those Europeans subjected to a Soviet-style regime and the supreme authority of the Kremlin. As to "liberation propaganda," deplorable as it was in arousing unfounded hopes in the other part of Europe, was it not necessary to counteract the Marxist-Leninist claim to represent the future with a Western claim to reflect the people's aspirations?

Disregarding the verbal exaggerations customary with American politicians and Congress, the aim of American diplomacy after late 1947 or spring 1948 was the reconstruction of Western Europe, military nonintervention beyond the Iron Curtain, and the refusal to accord moral or political recognition to the sovietization of Eastern Europe, East Germany in particular. The Western European governments never wished American diplomacy to take any risks to "liberate" Eastern Europe; in 1949–50 they endorsed this diplomacy, General de Gaulle included,[7] even though the General wanted France

---

[7] General de Gaulle later tried to reduce this dependence by better relations with the Soviet Union and the Eastern European countries.

to take a larger and more independent share in its own defense. This diplomacy involved *in fact* an element of "connivance" with the Soviet Union (military respect for the demarcation line). It entailed *in fact* what the Americans called "leadership" and General de Gaulle "hegemony" (which was in origin simply a term synonymous with military leadership). The United States policymakers achieved their aim in Europe; I am sure they never really expected that the trumpets of the Voice of America would flatten any walls.

Success, of course, creates as many problems as failure. The play of inter-state relations continued. As they began to lose their fear of Soviet aggression, the Europeans started balking at American leadership and the partition of Europe that rendered it inevitable. As the Soviet Union's nuclear arsenal grew and the United States began to seek direct intercourse with Moscow, America's European partners became worried or exasperated as they grew less sure of the efficacy of United States' deterrence and less inclined to acquiesce in agreements concluded over their heads. Before we go on to study American diplomacy after the success of containment, let us revert to the second sequel to the Korean "accident," American action in Asia.

4.

As we have already seen, President Truman and his advisers had feared possible Chinese intervention when the alleged United Nations forces had crossed the thirty-eighth parallel. Both the Chiefs-of-Staff Committee and Dean Acheson are known to have disapproved of the "end-the-war offensive" to the Yalu and to have followed its course with anxiety.[8] The sudden retreat of the Seventh Army, the United Nations General Assembly's condemnation of mainland China for aggression, the negotiations at Panmunjon dragging on from 1951 to 1953 followed by the armistice on a line near the thirty-eighth parallel, continued support for France in Indochina, the defeat at Dienbienphu, and the Geneva Conference are all stages in the crisis opened by a decision taken or tolerated in Moscow and culminating in an undeclared war between the United

---

[8] But the Committee had also warned against the landing at Inchon, which was a complete success.

States and Communist China. The Nationalist government which had taken refuge on Taiwan represented China in the United Nations. As soon as hostilities broke out in Korea, the United States invited Japan to take up again the arms which only a few years before it had been forbidden ever to possess again. The American government concluded mutual assistance pacts with the Philippines, Japan, South Korea, Formosa, Australia, and New Zealand. After Dienbienphu it sponsored the Southeast Asia collective defense treaty.[9]

Some form of intercourse never ceased, of course, despite the severance of diplomatic relations. An American envoy met with a representative of mainland China at Warsaw from time to time. Americans and Chinese from Peking met at Geneva in 1954[10] and again in 1958 in connection with Laos. But twice, in 1954 and 1958, when Chinese troops shelled Quemoy and Matsu and prepared to attack the Chinese Nationalists' outposts, the Seventh Fleet was put on the alert and protected Taiwan. During the 1960 Nixon-Kennedy election campaign these two small islands figured prominently in the first televised debate between the candidates.

It is hard to see the logic of this diplomacy. By supporting the Nationalist government defeated on the mainland, the United States was intervening in the final phase of a civil war after having abandoned any idea of determining its issue some years previously (rightly so, indeed, since it had no means of doing so). Undoubtedly, geopolitics accounts for this in part, for Taiwan is part of the belt of islands on which a maritime power installs its bases. The military argument furnished a justification rather than a motive. In any case, even though Communist China had acted as a satellite or ally of the Soviet Union in 1950, why focus the American people's fury upon it? Even if the expansion of Communist China or Chinese Communism was to be contained, why not establish the same kind of relations with the enemy in Asia as with the enemy in Europe? In point of fact, McCarthyism and the China Lobby hamstrung those responsible for American strategy, who were possibly bound by earlier decisions, for neither of the two Chinas

9 SEATO: United States, France, Great Britain, Australia, New Zealand, the Philippines, Thailand, and Pakistan.
10 Chou En-lai reported that Dulles refused to shake hands with him on this occasion.

would acknowledge the existence of any China but itself. Having opted for Nationalist China in 1950, American diplomacy did not find the way back to Peking for twenty years.

Did the men in the Kremlin want hostilities to drag on from 1950 to 1953 to prevent any contact between Communist China and the United States? Did they believe that it was to their advantage to keep their monopoly of relations with the leading representative of "imperialism"? Once more, we find ourselves spectators at a fight without knowing enough about the tactics of one of the fighters. If the Soviet leaders rejoiced in the shortsightedness of American policy, they must now be measuring the gap between its aims and its results. The United States' immediate goal should have been the disintegration of the Communist bloc, not in order to provoke a conflict between the Soviet Union and Communist China, but in order to restore a measure of elasticity to inter-state relations that would enable the states sovietized despite themselves to recover a measure of autonomy. Washington in fact hit a target at which it had not aimed. Diplomacy involves even more "friction" than military operations. By standing firm at the critical moments in 1954 and 1958, the United States contributed to the fissure in the unity of the Communist camp.

There is no need here to follow the stages in the Sino-Soviet conflict (the attempts that have been made to do so by the press of the two countries can only be considered to be a series of informed guesses). I shall confine myself to the known facts. Stalin really seems to have meant it when he told Roosevelt that Chiang Kai-shek would govern China for many years to come and that the hour of Communism had not yet struck. In any case, after Roosevelt's offers in return for entering the war against Japan, Stalin had willingly negotiated with T. V. Soong, the envoy from Chiang Kai-shek as head of the Nationalist government. It is true that after invading Manchuria the Soviet divisions handed over to Mao Tse-tung the arms they had captured from the Japanese, but according to Djilas, Stalin had in fact advised the Communists to reach a *modus vivendi* with the Nationalists. In the main, the Party owed its victory to its own efforts rather than to outside aid or Big Brother's contribution.

During his visit to Moscow in late 1949 and early 1950 Mao had to negotiate about the return of what Stalin had received at

Yalta from Roosevelt and Chiang Kai-shek. Having emerged from a time of troubles, Mao's China promptly asserted its national will. In accordance with immemorial custom, those who had obtained the Mandate of Heaven and had restored unity to the country and its strength to the central power were trying to recover what a weak central power had had to yield. Stalin, it seems, took some persuading before he assented to the requests of the leader of the brother party.

The Korean campaign created tension for the second time. At the time when the North Korean armies crossed the thirty-eighth parallel, the bulk of the Communist Chinese armies was concentrated opposite Taiwan, where Chiang Kai-shek, following the precedent of the Ming dynasty, had found a last refuge. Communist China's objective was apparently Taiwan rather than Seoul. Whatever Peking's share in the "aggression" of June 25, American policymakers tended to make no distinction between Moscow and Peking and to hold Moscow at least partly responsible for it. Only one further step need be taken—and some commentators leap to take it—to arrive at the assumption that Stalin's aim was the result which was in fact achieved, the raising of an impassable barrier of misunderstanding or hatred between Communist China and the United States.

The Chinese "volunteers" fought in Korea from late in 1950 to spring 1953, a few weeks after Stalin's death. Here again we do not know whether it was Stalin or Mao who rejected the armistice by demanding the forcible repatriation of all Chinese prisoners to the mainland. The delegates from Communist China made the decisive concession shortly after Stalin's death—which makes it at least probable that Stalin himself may have convinced the leaders of the brother party. If his successors succeeded in doing so, it is even more probable that he himself, as the head of world Communism, would have argued with success. Perhaps he saw no objection to an American army bogging down in an interminable war and a confrontation between Communist China and the United States, with the Soviet Union playing the part of *tertium gaudens,* an onlooker selling arms (to the Chinese) and keeping score of the rounds.

Admittedly, the Communist Chinese regime emerged from these three years of war consolidated, permanently established, and even with glory, since it had held its own against the greatest economic and military power in the world and had finally forced it to content itself with a draw. On the other hand, China had paid the cost of this struggle waged in the common interest, for Chiang Kai-shek survived on Taiwan, the Seventh Fleet made the Nationalist government's refuge impregnable, and the fury of American public opinion was turned against China even more virulently than against the Soviet Union; it was the Chinese, not the Russians, who had shed their blood. In North Korea the Chinese had strengthened their influence at the Russians' expense; the profit in prestige abroad and authority at home offset the material cost. The fact remains that Communist China, for the sake of warding off the twofold threat of direct confrontation between the Soviet Union and the United States and the collapse of North Korea, had had in late 1950, barely a year after the end of the Chinese civil war, to plunge into an adventure in which it assumed all the risks and gained only a fraction of the advantages. After 1953 the friendly feelings of Mao Tse-tung and his comrades toward Big Brother were no longer wholly unmixed despite their Marxist-Leninist convictions.

In 1954, and especially in 1958, it was the turn of the Chinese to try to achieve a goal of national interest, by driving the Nationalist troops from the islands of Quemoy and Matsu, a few miles offshore. They found themselves without support. In 1954 the United States evacuated the Tachen Islands; in return Eisenhower promised Chiang Kai-shek to help him defend Quemoy and Matsu and obtained the Senate's authorization to use military force for the purpose. After some weeks' uneasiness and alarming news in the American press, and after military preparations in the Straits, calm was restored. The Chinese leaders had perhaps never had any intention of trying for a military conquest of the islands (this seems probable) or perhaps they had yielded to the Kremlin's counsels of caution.

The Chinese artillery began shelling the islands of Quemoy and Matsu on the night of August 22-23, 1958. The military crisis continued for several weeks. Eisenhower and Dulles had never formally promised to intervene militarily to defend Quemoy and Matsu (the treaty of mutual assistance related only to Formosa and the Pescadores) nor had they undertaken to tolerate the military conquest of these two islets. Khrushchev, who was then engaged in negotiations with the United States in connection with the Middle East crisis,[11] left for Peking on July 31 either to justify his acceptance of a great power conference for a peaceful settlement or because of a Chinese proclamation (determination to liberate Taiwan) published after a military conference lasting from May 26 to July 27. Without going into details, the subsequent public controversy gives grounds for the belief that the Chinese and Russians blamed each other for their attitudes, the Chinese convinced that the Russians had refused to support them, the Russians that the Chinese had been trying to draw them into an adventure on the pretext that the United States was only a "paper tiger" (to which the Russians replied, "but with atomic teeth"). By standing firm, the American policymakers had once again not welded together the Sino-Soviet alliance, but rather brought out its divergences, or, to use the Marxist-Leninist term, its internal "contradictions": Moscow's indifference to Peking's national interests and a difference of opinion about the best strategy for dealing with the United States. By according different treatment to the two great powers of Communism, United States diplomacy—less by intention than by a dialectic unrecognized at the time—set off contrary and mutually incompatible reactions in Moscow and Peking.

There were manifold reasons for the breach between the two capitals; undoubtedly the atomic weapon was one of them. The Soviet Union had signed a treaty with Communist China in 1957 promising its aid to its ally's atomic program. It went back on its signature in 1959 after apparently demanding in 1958 some sort of joint command comparable to that exercised by the Soviet Union and the United States in Europe, each within its own sphere. Moscow recalled its technical experts in 1960 and abandoned the 183 industrial projects in course of execution.

How is the United States' Asian diplomacy to be construed? Territorially it may be compared with the diplomacy of containment. The United States entered into alliances with all the insular states, including Taiwan, and with the small mainland states, fragments of countries divided between a Communist and a non-Communist regime (Korea). This resemblance concealed a heterogeneity in depth.

---

[11] General Qassem's *coup-d'état* in Iraq which overthrew the pro-Western regime of the Hashemite monarchy.

In Europe the Western states had recovered a relative prosperity and stable governments after two or three years of American aid. Short of invasion by the Red Army, they had no need of external assistance to resist Communist penetration. The political and military role of the United States was confined to creating the conditions in which the Europeans were living in peace and constructing a system of cooperation or unity. Things were different in the Asian theater of operations.

By refusing the China of Mao Tse-tung the place which Roosevelt had promised the China of Chiang Kai-shek, the United States of Truman, Eisenhower, Kennedy, and Johnson was preventing the United Nations from achieving the universality which it was the settled American policy to secure. It supported on Taiwan the regime defeated on the mainland and denied itself, and forbade the West, normal relations with "one-quarter of mankind," as the press liked to put it.

Even worse, it failed, or apparently failed, to recognize that a diplomacy of containment which seemed to be the same in both cases was bound to require quite different methods. Since 1947 the non-Communist governments of Western Europe had taken it upon themselves to contain their own Communists. The United States had speeded recovery by the Marshall Plan and had created a context of military security, and the French and Italians had seen to the rest. In the early years of the cold war the authorities in the Philippines and Malaya had had to cope with internal guerrillas. In Malaya the British had prevailed by isolating the Chinese guerrilla fighters and granting independence to the moderate nationalists. In the Philippines, too, the guerrilla had been crushed. It was in Indochina that a mechanical application, so to speak, of the doctrine of containment involved American diplomacy in error after error. When Eisenhower and Dulles obtained the armistice in Korea following Stalin's death,[12] it did not occur to them to combine solutions for the two wars. To judge by the proceedings of the Geneva Conference in 1954, it is at least credible that Stalin's heirs, engaged as they were in a struggle for the succession yet still able to control the Communist bloc, would not have refused a compromise comparable to

---

[12] Perhaps the threat to use the atom bomb, transmitted, it is said, through the diplomatic channel, also had some influence.

that which followed the French defeat at Dienbienphu. In any case, why advise the French to continue the struggle in Indochina when the Americans themselves had acquiesced in a draw in Korea?

After refusing military intervention to save the French troops surrounded at Dienbienphu, American diplomacy went on to refuse to sign the Geneva agreements, though promising not to oppose their application. The refusal to recognize Communist China, found guilty of aggression by the United Nations, was extended to a refusal of normal relations with the new incarnation of evil.[13] In spite of the fact that it had long doubted whether the Chinese Communists were genuine Communists and after it had acquiesced, from 1946 to 1949, in the prospect of a victory by Mao Tse-tung, American diplomacy acted as if Communist China was henceforth the world's public enemy number one. The China experts do not seem ever to have endorsed either this interpretation or this attitude; but the China lobby and the anti-Communist obsession focused henceforth on Peking created an atmosphere in which even in late 1960 a candidate for the presidency of the United States had to declare his intentions with regard to Quemoy and Matsu. This diplomacy was a projection of the American people's passions, or rather the passions of active minorities which claimed to be speaking for the people as a whole.

These passions were, of course, to some degree understandable. The United States had fought Japan to defend China and maintain the integrity of the Middle Kingdom. Five years after its victory, General MacArthur suggested to Congress that China and Japan had changed sides and that China had come down on the wrong side, Japan on the right. The notions that states are never wholly on the side either of good or of evil, and that a change of regime may entail a reversal of alliances—the commonplace of European Machiavellianism—did not yet appear acceptable to those who claimed to express American public opinion, even if they were accepted by those responsible for American diplomacy.

The period whose major episodes have been recounted above may be regarded as either the end or the prolongation of the cold

---

[13] Communist China would not have refused normal relations in 1955. Chou En-lai made overtures at that time.

war. Stalinist diplomacy, with all its violence of method and speech, hardly extended beyond the European context. Even if it was responsible for the Korean aggression, it entrusted the Chinese with the thankless task of fighting the American divisions in the field. Arms were not sold to Egypt until 1955; Bulganin's and Khrushchev's travels are evidence of a different style, but also of intentions which had now expanded to encompass the entire globe.

The moderate judgment of American diplomacy commonly expressed by the liberals of the Eastern seaboard is based on considerations which have become common currency, to the effect that American diplomacy, relying on its successes in Europe, transferred to Asia the methods it had used on the Old Continent, that is, economic aid and a defense of demarcation lines however arbitrarily traced. Unfortunately, economic aid, so efficacious in reconstructing the economies of developed countries, was less effective for modernizing developing countries. Intervention, necessary in Korea because regular armies had crossed a demarcation line, was not effective against infiltration by guerrilla fighters, and even less so against a rebellion, especially if supplied from outside.

Before concluding that this view, held both by Europeans and by American liberals with their natural European orientation, is correct, I would like to recall a few facts and the sequence of events. Owing to its geographical position, the United States faces eastward as much as westward; it is a Pacific no less than an Atlantic power. *Its* war had been directed against Japan even more than against the Third Reich. Whereas it had taken over from Great Britain in Greece and Turkey in March 1947, in June 1950 it had taken over from Japan to bar the unification of Korea under a hostile government.

In Washington Dean Acheson pondered the intentions of the masters of the Kremlin and the masters of the Forbidden City. He did not rule out the possibility of further Soviet aggression. He considered it essential—and rightly so, I believe—to prove in action the worth of the American guarantee.

The strategic mistakes, committed by MacArthur rather than by Washington, prevented the limited victory which the United States might have won and obliged it to acquiesce in a draw. But the major consequence of these mistakes, the breach with China, proved in the long run beneficial (in terms of realistic diplomacy). Almost all commentators in the Fifties blame the American action for welding together the Sino-Soviet alliance. The American policy-makers usually replied that the United States could not exert any influence one way or the other on the relations between Moscow and Peking. By an irony of history, American action in fact caused the breach in the alliance. In 1971 President Nixon was at last able and astute enough to exploit that breach.

In a way, the attitude toward China adopted by the United States in 1958 with regard to Quemoy and Matsu was very similar to the Soviet Union's attitude with regard to the British and French in 1956. By resisting its rival's junior partner it caused a split in the other camp; for the Soviet Union wished neither to fight for the sole interests of its ally nor to risk a confrontation with the United States. Similarly, whenever they were not indulging in moralizing, the leaders in Washington told their French and British friends that they were not willing to alienate the Third World to protect national interests which did not coincide with their own. The more the great powers subordinated all other considerations to a concern to avoid internal conflict, the more disgruntled their allies became. The Atlantic Alliance resisted a split; not so the Sino-Soviet alliance.

To go back to 1960, the end of the Eisenhower-Dulles era: there were fewer than a thousand American advisers in Vietnam. Commentators denounced the "mania for pacts," Dulles's inflexibility, and especially the Eisenhower team's lack of drive. The first sputnik had shocked and astounded America. In response, the government, the Administration, and the universities launched out into vast projects to restore to the United States the supremacy which, if the Democratic opposition was to be believed, it had lost. In November 1958 Khrushchev delivered a sort of ultimatum: if there was no agreement on Berlin within six months, he would sign a peace treaty with the German Democratic Republic and the latter would assume responsibility for communications between West Berlin and the Federal Republic. The deadline had already been postponed, or even forgotten, by the time of Kennedy's election. In the meantime, the summit meeting in Paris had not been held because of the U-2 incident. What was worrying Europeans, American opinion, and the policy-makers in Washington was not Vietnam, but Berlin, Quemoy and Matsu, or the alleged missile gap. In retrospect one may very well say that the time bomb that caused the explosion in the Sixties had already been placed in position. Nevertheless, at the time of Dienbienphu the President's caution and objections from General Ridgway and the leading senators finally prevailed over the interventionist party, Admiral Radford, and Vice-President Nixon. In 1972 the survivors of the Kennedy clan joined the McGovern camp, being more sensitive to popular feeling than concerned with consistency. Twelve years earlier they had tried to awaken the sleeping giant; they had launched him on the conquest of the moon; and they had, too, their share of the responsibility for the misfortunes of Gulliver in the quagmire of the rice paddies of Vietnam.

Note to Page 45 As this book deals specifically with American diplomacy, the detailed investigation of Soviet diplomacy has had to be kept to a minimum. So far as the Korean war is concerned, Mme. Hélène Carrère d'Encausse has reviewed the major interpretations of its events in an article "Aux origines du conflit" in *Revue française de Science Politique*, December 1970, pp. 1182–99. The most rewarding account is by Allen S. Whiting, *China Crosses the Yalu: The Decision to Enter the Korean War* (Stanford, Ca.: Stanford University Press, 1968).

It seems probable that Mao Tse-tung, informed by the Russians and North Koreans of the projected military operation, had no major responsibility for starting the campaign. Mao stayed in Moscow from December 16, 1949, to March 4, 1950. There he signed a mutual assistance pact with the Soviet Union in case of attack by Japan or any country allied with it. He obtained concessions from Stalin (Port Arthur, Dairen, and the Chinese Eastern and South Manchurian railroads would come wholly under Chinese administration not later than 1952). The treaty differs from those concluded by Moscow with the other socialist states in that it refers to the principles of "equality, mutual interest, respect for national sovereignty, and nonintervention in domestic affairs."

The relations between China and North Korea, between both parties and states, were not close, and were difficult at times. A dispute about a dam on the Yalu had been settled with USSR mediation. The two governments had cooperated when Korean troops serving in the Chinese Liberation Army had been transferred to North Korea. Mao Tse-tung was not, therefore, in a position to decide alone on the North Korean operation or to impose it on Kim Il-song.

Furthermore, there was no American military activity on Taiwan at the time. Truman had stated on January 5, 1950, that he would not intervene in the civil war and would not supply Taiwan with military aid. Mao Tse-tung could, therefore, prepare for an invasion of this island without fear of American retaliation. The bulk of the Chinese army was facing Taiwan. In 1950, however, a Chinese army had been redeployed in the northeast before the Korean campaign began.

The essential point is, therefore, the relations between Moscow and Pyongyang. According to an article by Jungwon Alexander Kim ("Soviet Policy in North Korea" in *World Politics,* January 1970), the North Korean Communist Party in 1950 was still dominated by Soviet Koreans —i.e., Koreans who had taken refuge in the Soviet Union during the Japanese domination of Korea, many of whom had taken Soviet nationality and held key positions in the Party. Kim Il-song himself belonged to a group of Manchurian Koreans who had fought beside the Chinese Communists in the Thirties and had gone to the USSR in about 1940. As officers in the Russian Far Eastern Army they were less directly dependent on Moscow than the other group. The local Communists, or Yenan Koreans, at first formed a party of their own. They had fought beside the Chinese and were more popular than the Soviet emigrés. When the parties merged, one of their men (Kim Tu-bong) was at first the head of the Party, but in 1949 Kim Il-song became the general secretary of the unified party and the Soviet Koreans kept the upper hand in the leadership until the outbreak of the war. Since, in addition, the army had been reorganized by Soviet advisers, the conclusion is unavoidable that the decision to cross the thirty-eighth parallel could have been taken only with the assent of Moscow, if not at its prompting.

Mao Tse-tung did not wish to intervene; he sent many warnings before deciding on such action. The objective of any military operations he contemplated was Taiwan, Tibet, or the final pacification of southern China. Chinese policy during the first phase of the conflict did not go beyond moral support. When Malik, the Soviet representative, returned to the United Nations on August 1, he referred to the two governments of Korea, spoke of a civil war, and proposed that China should be invited to attend the United Nations. The United States rejected the return to the status quo ante bellum suggested by India and Great Britain. On August 20 Chou En-lai sent a telegram to the United Nations in support of Malik's proposal, which was finally rejected on September 6. On October 1 the South Korean troops crossed the thirty-eighth parallel, and on October 2 Chou informed Pannikar that China would go to war if American troops invaded the North. The Chinese had in the past concentrated their verbal attacks so vehemently on Taiwan and the island's liberation that Washington was neither convinced nor deterred, though the Chinese had mobilized their army close to the Korean border after this warning.

Why did Mao Tse-tung risk intervening when his regime was not yet stabilized and he had no means of replying to possible bombing by American aircraft? Communist China had ideological reasons and reasons of national interest against passive acceptance of a total victory by the United Nations, that is to say, the Americans. Just as a Korea unified under a Communist regime would constitute a threat to the American positions in Japan (the Americans acted precisely as the Japanese would have acted), so China, which had assumed the leadership of the peoples under capitalist oppression, would suffer a serious setback if the Pyongyang regime collapsed, yielding to Seoul the mastery of the whole of Korea. There is no reason for not thinking that Mao Tse-tung himself took the decision to intervene.

But he could only take that decision with Moscow's approval and aid. Stalin retained the key position for his own. This accounts for the Chinese invective against the Soviet Union when the breach between the two major Communist powers was consummated. The Chinese were fighting for themselves, but also for the common cause. The Soviets undoubtedly excused their abstention by the need to prevent the general conflict which might be set off by a clash between Russians and Americans. The real Soviet motives for launching or authorizing the initial action are still endlessly debatable.

The following possibilities seem to me unlikely: that Moscow did not *at least* authorize the aggression, or that Stalin sought a diversion or compensation for his check at Berlin (only a relative check in any case); for the Soviets continued the process of sovietizing the satellite countries (the essential Soviet goal in Europe). Commentators at the time tended to assume that Sino-Soviet relations were close and based on mutual trust, and they therefore took for granted the existence of a plan concocted jointly by Stalin and Mao during the latter's visit to Moscow. Nowadays they tend to interpret Sino-Soviet relations in 1950 in the light of the current conflict between them. That those relations were strained when Chinese and Russians had to acknowledge the failure of the Korean venture is true. Before the North Korean defeat did the Chinese and Russians together consider that the prospects were promising? Or did the Chinese, in the grip of *hubris*, draw Stalin into an adventure? Or, conversely, were they drawn in by the Russians? The third possibility now seems the most likely. It presents no difficulty save to those who refuse to admit that Stalin may have miscalculated. The prospects seemed good and promised great success at little cost. Events were to prove otherwise for all concerned.

Chapter Three

ASCENT AND DESCENT

Kennedy's entry into the White House inaugurated the most dynamic period of American postwar diplomacy, a period bestrewn with failures—the Bay of Pigs landing being the most obviously humiliating—and successes—the second Cuban crisis being the most brilliant. Viewed as a whole, the period culminated in 1963 in *apparent* world supremacy; yet hard on its heels came *spectacular* collapse, the rending of the fabric of American society caused by the Vietnam War. I stress the adjectives "apparent" and "spectacular" to show that a suspension of judgment is still necessary, since the objective elements of the situation did not in fact change very greatly between 1963 and 1972. We are not yet distant enough from the events to appreciate the true significance of this ascent and descent; however sensational the sudden changes of fortune may have seemed at the time, they may perhaps merit no more than a few paragraphs in the accounts given by historians of the future—unless, of course, they prove to be indicative of the destiny of the American republic and its incapacity to master the tendency to veer between crusading and withdrawal or to recognize and appreciate the constraints inherent in paramount power.

1.

During Nixon's election campaign in 1968 the survivors of the Kennedy team grouped themselves among the "doves." But in 1960 Kennedy had launched a call for New Frontiers; Eisenhower's United States was seen as the embodiment of middle-class complacency, with a low growth rate, a relatively high rate of unemployment, and a moderate diplomacy. Dulles had died; an American president welcomed Khrushchev visiting the United States. In 1960 the United States had intervened through the United Nations in the former Belgian Congo (opposing the secession of Katanga) to keep that vast territory together as a unit, and it had repudiated the notion of making Berlin a free city, though without rejecting outright all idea of negotiation.

Kennedy presented himself as a "doer"; he was trying to give the world a different image of the United States. He used the language of the cold war, or at any rate of confrontation, quite as much as that of détente. He surrounded himself with academics from the Rand Corporation and Harvard, who forced out the businessmen and lawyers that had formed the bulk of the presidential advisers during Eisenhower's, and even Truman's, terms. The conceptual system worked out by these academics and research workers was subtler than that of the generals and admirals. The general objective of American strategy was not changed, but those responsible for it had a clearer notion of the different levels at which Soviet-American rivalry operated: a military rivalry, both nuclear and conventional, and a politico-ideological rivalry whose results depended on factional struggles within states. Subversion and countersubversion were a sort of middle ground between the military and the political, containing an element of both.

The President's advisers, according to their own testimony, feared the open contempt of the chiefs of the armed forces and the professionals of the CIA for the "eggheads," intellectuals who knew nothing of the harsh necessities of the struggle for existence as waged among states. They wanted to be "tough"; and this was one element in Kennedy's consent to the Cuban refugees' expedition. At the last moment, when the chioce had to be made between disaster and sending in the fleet or the air force, the President decided for the former alternative, bringing down on his head simultaneous opprobrium for an unjustified act of aggression and inexcusable weakness. Would Eisenhower, who had authorized the preparations, have given the signal to go ahead? No one can say for certain. The establishment in the Caribbean of a regime which professed Marxism-Leninism was tantamount to an intrusion by the United States' rival into an area which United States policy-makers had always considered their own preserve; the attempt, organized by the CIA, to overthrow a revolutionary regime through its political opponents smacked both of earlier United States practice in Nicaragua and Panama, and of the resort to subversion (or countersubversion) which had succeeded more recently in Iran and Guatemala. How intelligent men could ever have believed that such an attempt would succeed in Cuba against Fidel Castro puzzles me to this day.[1]

President Kennedy's advisers, then, did not flinch from the more sordid and surreptitious aspects of power politics.[2] Their own contribution was, curiously enough, in the military sphere. They introduced into the Pentagon systems of reasoning which they called nuclear strategy, worked out in institutes and universities: The concept of a Russo-American agreement which suited the common interest of the two super-powers in order to reduce to a minimum the risks of a nuclear war which no one in his right mind could want.[3]

What came to be known as the McNamara doctrine—in which McNamara himself perhaps hardly believed—was based on a few simple ideas which I have discussed in detail elsewhere[4] and so will simply outline here. Each hydrogen bomb of a few megatons destroys a city. The inevitable consequence is a disproportion between the stake in any inter-state conflict (especially one between the Soviet Union and the United States) and the cost of nuclear war.[5] The great powers therefore aim, or should aim, primarily at nuclear non-war. The conviction that this common interest unites them more than divergency of local interests separates them induced the Kennedy team to do their utmost to seek an agreement with the Kremlin on the suspension of nuclear tests as a first stage in arms control. The partial Test-Ban Treaty was not signed until the summer of 1963, after the Cuban missile crisis in the autumn of 1962.

---

[1] I spent some time in Cuba in February 1961.
[2] The Pentagon Papers (New York: Bantam Books Inc., 1971) proves this.
[3] They also introduced the rationalization of budgetary options, the cost-efficiency system.
[4] See Aron, Le Grand Débat: Introduction à la stratégie nucléaire (Paris: Calmann-Lévy, 1963): trans. The Great Debate (Garden City, N.Y.: Doubleday & Company, 1965).
[5] Applied to total nuclear war the maxim of "Alain" (Professor Emile Chartier, the philosopher of the French Radical intellectuals of the 1920's and 1930's) that "none of the evils that one wishes to avoid by war is an evil as great as war itself" becomes true.

Did the Soviet leaders, Khrushchev in particular, share this conviction? During the first postwar phase, when the United States alone possessed a nuclear armament, Soviet propaganda had developed in two directions: depreciation of the atomic weapon which, according to Stalin, could only impress people with weak nerves, and the Stockholm appeal and mass action to prevent the enemy's use of the atomic weapon by mobilizing the moral revulsion of the masses.

During the second phase, after the Soviet Union had exploded a hydrogen bomb, the official language took a line midway between depreciation and menace. The Soviet Union would inflict merciless punishment on any aggressor. It possessed an atomic arsenal second to none. The launching of the first sputnik marked the beginning of a further phase. In 1957 Mao Tse-tung launched the slogan, "The east wind prevails over the west wind." At the time of the U-2 incident in 1960 Khrushchev brandished his nuclear weapons and tried, it seems, to terrify the United States' allies, if not the United States itself, by suggesting he might use these weapons of terror. In order to reach an agreement symbolizing an "alliance against war," each of the two super-powers would have to renounce the hope of deriving advantage from the threat suspended over the whole of mankind.

Within the Soviet Union the subject of nuclear war loomed as a major issue in the debates among Stalin's successors. Malenkov had already suggested that the atomic weapon had altered the prospects of the final struggle between the imperialist camp and the peace camp. Was it imperialism or civilization that nuclear war would destroy? Malenkov was inclined toward the latter possibility. Khrushchev took a similar line in his discussions with the Chinese some years later. He put matters in a nutshell when he stated: "The atom bomb recognizes no class distinctions." The responsible leaders in the United States probably did not have to convince their adversary-partners in the Kremlin of the need for Russo-American solidarity against the danger of nuclear war; neither camp had ever doubted it. But whether they all had an equal interest in admitting so publicly was something else again. Khrushchev could, until late in 1962 at least, stake the success of his policy on the inequality of fear or of the resistance to fear that might be incurred by a confrontation between countries in which public opinion exercises a constant and direct influence on rulers and countries in which a few decide in secret the fate of all. Or, to put it another way, nuclear weapons can always be of use in diplomacy. Khrushchev probably hoped to profit from them more than his rival could. Who would profit from atomic terror? By the early Sixties American diplomats must, it seems, have lost any illusions about the efficacy of "atomic diplomacy." What they feared was that the Soviets might now harbor such illusions and so imperil the entire world.

Khrushchev's illusions are accounted for in the behavior and words of America's politicians, journalists, and armed forces. The sputnik and the all-out production of Soviet missiles between 1958 and 1960 aroused indefinite speculations about relative strengths as measured in hydrogen bombs and missile-launching sites. The United States asked their allies for permission to install intermediate-range ballistic missiles in Europe, since it had no intercontinental missiles as yet. Turkey, Italy, and the United Kingdom acceded to the request, but in France the last government of the Fourth Republic refused it. Kennedy campaigned on the missile gap, whose existence was denied in private by the Pentagon experts and was not taken seriously by Eisenhower; curiously enough, the policy-makers did not, or perhaps did not wish to, dispel this haunting fear once and for all. Perhaps they attributed to the Soviet Union a production capacity it did not possess, or at any rate was not using at that time.

The Kennedy team made no further mention of the missile gap once they reached the White House, yet launched a huge program for the accelerated production of intercontinental missiles (the Minuteman program)[6] and completed the program for forty-one nuclear submarines, each armed with sixteen Polaris missiles. While Kennedy's diplomacy toward the Soviet Union was aiming at a dialogue, it was equally directed toward a "position of strength," the retention of a superiority which in the final analysis it had never lost.

The armaments program was not divorced from the inter-state system of the nuclear age. Officially, the initial doctrine of the American chiefs-of-staff, and even of the President himself, lived up to its description as the doctrine of massive retaliation. The autonomy of the Strategic Air Command, composed at that time of

---

[6] Over a thousand missiles (1,054, according to the official figures).

B-36 long-range bombers, symbolized the distinction between the supreme weapon and all others. The very doctrine for the weapon's use was unique—all-or-nothing—the choice between apocalypse or nonuse.

The academics and the research workers in the specialist institutes meditated during the Fifties on the lessons of the Korean campaign (the nuclear threat had neither deterred the North Koreans from aggression nor induced the Chinese to sue for peace) and on the consequences of reciprocal deterrence (which exists long before the rivals achieve equality).[7] These meditations led to technical results and a revised doctrine.

The B-36 bombers had long been concentrated on a few airfields. A considerable number of them had been damaged by a storm. As soon as the rival also has a strategic force, the need to shelter one's own force becomes obvious. The distinction in a hypothetical nuclear duel between the side that strikes first and the side that strikes second dictates the doctrine for its use and the target for selection. In the case of a first strike the hostile force is the logical target, provided that it is vulnerable. If a hostile force is invulnerable, there is no possible use for a nuclear weapon other than against the enemy's properties, resources, or cities; or, alternatively, the weapon presents the threat to destroy cities if the enemy commits an act of aggression from which the weapon is designed to deter him. Once the fiction of massive retaliation is discarded, the possibility arises of the selection not only of targets (weapons or cities) but of different intensities of response. The technicians had gradually succeeded in miniaturizing nuclear weapons to a point where the weakest of them had an explosive force comparable to that of the heaviest conventional weapon. At that point the analysts easily developed a whole set of schematic or typical duel situations: first strike capability (partial or total elimination of the adversary's nuclear armaments), second strike capability (where nuclear weapons are relatively invulnerable, hence a capability of inflicting unacceptable destruction on an adversary who had struck first), a diversity of possible responses (conventional, tactical nuclear, strategic nuclear, etc.), the risk of escalation from a limited conflict, and so on.

---

[7] Even at the time of United States' unilateral deterrence of the Soviet Union, defenseless Western Europe served as a hostage and thus made counterdeterrence possible.

From all these analyses the President's advisers had drawn conclusions suggested by their reasoning, but not necessarily positively demanded by it: 1. In a duel in which each of the adversaries has second strike capability, the threat of massive retaliation does not deter the adversary from a minor aggression; no one is going to believe that the United States would reply to the entry of troops from the German Democratic Republic into Berlin by launching ballistic missiles at cities in the Soviet Union, or even in East Germany. Therefore, the analysts around Kennedy reasoned, the right course in Europe is to step up conventional armaments in order to avoid being faced with the all-or-nothing alternative. 2. The implausibility of total nuclear war increases the probabilities of limited hostilities, or at any rate makes them less improbable. In order to prevent escalation the crisis must be "managed" by a single state, or in other words, by a single team grouped around a responsible leader, i.e., in practice the President of the United States. 3. Such management of the crisis becomes impossible if a number of states in a coalition possess nuclear armaments, especially where small and relatively vulnerable nuclear forces capable of use only against cities and only in a single strike are subject to a separate command independent of the authority of the supreme and responsible head of the coalition.

The logic of this doctrine entailed the establishment of three military instruments, each sufficiently effective not to require a transition to the level above it: one against subversion, another against a limited conventional aggression, and a third against nuclear blackmail or attack. In the early stages the Kennedy team did in fact substantially augment this threefold capability. In retrospect, the cult of the murdered President obscured the activist (to use an understatement) aspect of his military doctrine; the slogan "get America moving again" quite undoubtedly applied to the military program.

This philosophy, however rigorous it may seem, had some curious consequences. It caused the Kennedy team anxieties about the Berlin crisis that in retrospect seem exaggerated. West Berlin provided a prime example of a position which was locally indefensible and consequently safe so long as only one of the super-powers unilaterally suspended the nuclear threat over the other, but was imperiled once the party on the defensive had lost first strike capability. By schematic analysis the armchair strategist could readily show that the Soviet Union could always concentrate superior conventional forces at Berlin and that, since escalation to nuclear weapons was ruled out, the Western powers were beaten from the start on this field of operations. The late Sir Basil Liddell Hart, the greatest authority of this century on military topics, suggested an argument of this sort. Reasoning along these lines, some of Kennedy's entourage during the Cuban crisis feared a Soviet response in central Europe, where the Soviets had conventional superiority.

Late in 1962 or early in 1963 the United States had achieved a substantial margin of superiority over the Soviet Union, as the Kennedy team were well aware; they believed that they had the means both for limited conventional hostilities (two wars) and for effective action against subversion.[8] The professed nuclear doctrine created some tension with the European allies, but served the team well during the Cuban crisis; Khrushchev gave them an opportunity to gain a success and apply the other part of the doctrine (the explicit agreement between the super-powers faced with a risk of a nuclear war due to accident or escalation). A similar propensity to a dynamic policy led them to test the counterinsurgency technique in Laos and later in Vietnam. And the United States took a further stride down the road to what was to become the Vietnam tragedy.

Against Khrushchev the McNamara doctrine plus the American arsenal succeeded. Against Giap's little soldiers and against guerrilla fighters who carried their rice rations and arms on their own backs, it failed. Even in the nuclear age the human factor is still at times the decisive element for victory.

2.

By its logical implications rather than by deliberate intent the McNamara-Kennedy doctrine offered the Soviet Union a dialogue and kept its allies in line, at least where nuclear armaments were concerned.

The demand for larger conventional armaments disturbed the

---

[8] The official expression was "two and a half wars," i.e., two simultaneous wars, localized, but on a considerable scale, in Europe and Asia, plus counterinsurgency. This notion was derived from the doctrine of "flexible response."

Germans, and the criticism of small nuclear forces as "expensive, ineffective, and dangerous" annoyed the French. Who was wrong in the argument about the probable effect of increasing the conventional forces? Everyone and no one. At the time, I thought the American case more tenable logically, and I still do; for if a limited aggression is what the other side is contemplating, the threat of nuclear retaliation will not deter it. Everyone accepts this reasoning in the abstract. To conjure up "the rationality of the irrational" too often is unreasonable. To pretend that one is resolved to "proceed to extremes" at the slightest hostile gesture may, indeed, often succeed; but it takes only a *single* failure to bring disaster or call a bluff. All deterrence by nuclear threat contains an element of bluff. Yet the analysts quite rightly pointed out that one must also know what to do if the other side does not let itself be deterred.

What was not as clear as the analysts and presidential advisers believed, however, was how this reasoning applied to Europe. What was the message that the strengthening of the NATO forces conveyed to the men in the Kremlin? Did it give them the impression that the Western powers would not let themselves be brought to the point of the all-or-nothing alternative and that they were equipping themselves to cope with every threat at every level? Or did the Soviets take it as an indication that the United States, whose territory would not, this time, be spared the devastation of war, was no longer ensuring Western Europe the same protection as it had in the past? Did a preparation for limited wars in Europe increase their probability by reducing the risk of escalation? Or did it reduce their probability because they could be waged without escalation?

Even today I would still be reluctant to decide definitely between the two arguments; for only experience could settle the question— and fortunately these arguments have never been put to the test of events, the decisive, and the only decisive, test. Europeans necessarily inclined to one side, Americans to the other. The consequences of a so-called limited war would not have been limited so far as West Germany was concerned, for no part of the Federal Republic would have been spared the devastation of war. A doctrine that *seemed* to increase the risks of local hostilities in order to reduce the risks of hostilities in which the two super-powers would have been involved took care of the interests of the United States, not those of Europe. It virtually confirmed General de Gaulle's hypothesis of a Europe serving as a battlefield while the vast territories of the Soviet Union and the United States became in effect sanctuaries.

The hub of the controversy perhaps turned on the doctrine of the use of tactical atomic weapons. The proponents of the two conflicting theses agreed in recognizing that the simplest borderline, that which made the implicit understanding between the enemies far the easiest, lay between conventional and atomic weapons. So long as atomic weapons, even of small caliber, are not used, the intention not to transgress the bounds, not to cross the threshold of the irreparable, is inherent in the terrain. But to make this intention obvious surely weakens the efficacy of deterrence by nuclear threat, providing it also reduces the danger of escalation. Here at last emerged the relative order of priorities: whether to prevent any form of hostilities in Europe by deterrence or whether to reduce to a minimum the probability of escalation to extremes.

Everyone finally settled on the general notion that the alternative of capitulation or apocalypse should be avoided and that it was necessary to be equipped with means for proportionate response. At what moment should the danger of escalation as the automatic consequence of the use of tactical atomic weapons be created; or, to put it even more precisely, at what moment should it be announced that it will be created? The answer differs depending whether priority is accorded to the efficacy of nuclear deterrence or to precautions against escalation.

There were two drawbacks to the objections by McNamara and his advisers to France's atomic armament: in the first place, they made no difference and, in the second, they merely aggravated the mutual recriminations and the general bad temper. It seems extremely likely, judging by the Chinese strictures in later controversies, that the demands on their Chinese allies made by the men in the Kremlin were comparable to those made by the leaders in Washington on the Europeans; after promising their aid to the Chinese atomic program, the men in the Kremlin seem to have stipulated a system of single command equivalent to the centralized management of the nuclear armament, the only method acceptable to McNamara, described by Walter Lippmann in a striking image: If everyone is in the same car driving down a dangerous road, the Western Allies must trust the driver (the President of the United States) to take the requisite decisions at danger points.

It is not my intent to decide here whether General de Gaulle and the French government were right or wrong to devote a substantial portion of the military budget to manufacturing atomic weapons and their carriers (Mirage IV, and later, land-based or nuclear submarine-carried ballistic missiles). It is arguable that *within the current framework of the Atlantic Alliance* strengthening the conventional forces would have been a greater contribution to the common security than the additional margin of deterrence provided by a non-integrated force whose employment could not be foreseen by the other side. The French government looked to its own national interest, and the American case was not so cogently conclusive that leading United States officials could legitimately lecture the French government and tax it publicly with unreasonableness or irresponsibility. Was not the French government entitled to look beyond the end of a situation which had lasted since 1945 or 1949 and to give some thought to its security after the American forces withdrew from Europe? And who could possibly say for certain that a relatively vulnerable and undoubtedly weak "small force" was wholly ineffectual as a deterrent? Besides, inasmuch as deterrence by nuclear threat is based on fear, how was it possible to deny its efficacy and at the same time call it dangerous?

President Kennedy admired General de Gaulle. Following his visit to Paris and his conversation with the French president, he hoped that talks would be started on methods for a cooperation comparable to that still existing between Washington and London. Had he considered it, Kennedy would have seen nothing but profit in putting an end to the "special relationship" with the British government or even in making the relationship with Paris as close as possible to that with London. He did not, and could not, do so because General de Gaulle, on the point of winding up the Algerian war, was criticizing the Atlantic Alliance in 1961 only to justify a policy dictated by a radically different concept, which, unacceptable as it was to Kennedy, was prompted by an ambition harbored by the men of the Fourth Republic too, but abandoned by them under pressure of the cold war.

What General de Gaulle wanted was a diplomacy of independence; in other words, he did not wish France to appear as simply one among a number of members of an Atlantic coalition jointly liable for American action. The controversies on nuclear strategy and the organization of the Alliance were designed solely to dissimulate that objective. The word "independence" cropped up constantly in the French president's writings and speeches. As regards the management of its domestic affairs, the France of the Fifth Republic differed from that of the Fourth inasmuch as its government, sure of itself and its future, and possessing a surplus balance of payments, found it easier to ward off any attempts at foreign interference. But, by and large, from 1946 to 1958 the French governed themselves as they pleased; at the end of that period the Americans hardly felt that they need give moral or financial aid any longer to anti-Communist parties or trade unions.[9] From 1947 to 1952 the Americans had tended to disapprove of the *Rassemblement du peuple français* set up by General de Gaulle. Their share in the Gaullist movement's setback in the 1951 elections had, however, been comparatively slight.

As regards its foreign action the Fourth Republic had seemed dependent on the United States because it had been waging colonial wars and had labored under a deficit in its balance of payments. But French ministers up to 1950 sought American aid in Indochina more urgently than Washington encouraged them to fight on. It was only after 1950 and with the Korean campaign that the French war in Indochina definitely became an integral part of the campaign against the expansion of Communism. From 1950 to 1954 the French ministers depended on United States goodwill; nevertheless, neither in Indochina, nor even less so in North Africa, did they behave like clients or satellites of the United States. More than once Georges Bidault drew, or tried to draw, the United States further than it wished to go (the request for intervention to save Dienbienphu); in none of the three North African countries did any of the governments of the Fourth Republic act in accordance with Washington's wishes, except that of Mendès-France, who, however, also displayed a jealous concern for the national sovereignty.

In granting independence to Algeria, General de Gaulle fell in with Washington's wishes in recognizing the legitimacy of the Asian and African peoples' liberation movement. The events of the Second World War, far more than the anticolonialist ideology of the Soviets and Americans, had lent this movement a strength all the more irresistible in that the ex-imperial countries no longer believed in

---

[9] As they had done in the late Forties.

their mission, their right to rule, or the profit to be derived from ruling. By his style, his language, and his manner General de Gaulle gave the French and the world the impression that he alone made the decisions, whereas the governments of the Fourth Republic had appeared subservient even when they were rejecting West German rearmament and the ratification of the European Defense Community.

Lastly—and this was what General de Gaulle considered the essential point—France's diplomacy could not attain independence unless it dissociated itself from American diplomacy and, in consequence, from the Atlantic Alliance. The Alliance covered only a limited area. From time to time Gaullists emphasized this paradox and advocated a regional alliance to extend over the entire globe. In his letter to General Eisenhower in September 1958 General de Gaulle pretended to endorse a doctrine which in fact he rejected, and demanded a "triumvirate," though he certainly did not wish to obtain it. NATO had been set up in 1950 at the Europeans' own request, and the existence of a unified general staff in no way implied that the French forces would be under foreign command in peacetime. The Atlantic general staff exercised actual command only in case of war. General de Gaulle nevertheless attached historical significance to the successive decisions whereby he reduced France's military share in NATO and finally rejected the very principle of the integrated command while remaining within the Alliance. With considerable flourish he requested the United States to evacuate the bases in France occupied by its forces and set a deadline for the evacuation.

In point of fact, participation in NATO would not have prohibited any of General de Gaulle's diplomatic moves, any of his travels, or any of his trenchant declarations, nor would it have prevented him from distributing the military costs in accordance with his preferences or from building up a strategic force for deterrence. Independence, the highest form of political good, ruled out an organization which symbolized leadership by an ally and which encroached upon the traditional notion of sovereignty (by the presence of foreign troops on the national soil in peacetime, even though they were there by virtue of a freely negotiated agreement).

If this analysis is correct—and I do not think any Gaullist in good faith could seriously dispute it—Kennedy could not have had the slightest chance of converting someone whom he regarded as a historic figure and whom he would have been proud and happy to bring back into the Atlantic fold. The Kennedy team's dynamic policy, their nuclear strategic doctrines, and the survival of an urge toward confrontation with the Soviet Union made it inevitable that they would clash with de Gaulle. The Grand Design of the New Frontiersmen was incompatible with the Grand Design of the leader of Free France. General de Gaulle regarded Washington's goal— an Atlantic community comprising the European community, enlarged by the entry of Great Britain together with the United States —as tantamount to an even greater subordination of Europe to the United States and of all Europeans to the Anglo-Saxons. As to a combination of the Atlantic Grand Design and a dialogue with the Soviet Union (especially a nuclear dialogue), Kennedy's diplomacy, reduced to essentials, contrasted radically with the Gaullist diplomacy at two points: It curbed France's freedom to maneuver, the essence of independence, and it brought to bear the menace of a new version of what was symbolically called Yalta.

There is no reason to condemn either of the two diplomacies, Kennedy's or de Gaulle's. Some Frenchmen endorsed the American doctrines to some degree and there were some Gaullists in the United States. What concerns us here is the inevitable transformation of the most powerful ally into the leader and the reaction of the protected states to this hegemony (in the original meaning of the term). Most American policy-makers found the Gaullist concept hard to grasp, though it was wholly in accord with traditional practices, for a state's wish to have its hands free and not to be reduced to the rank of a protected state is part and parcel of the very essence of an independent diplomacy. Yet in late 1962 Kennedy renewed with Harold Macmillan the special nuclear relationship which President Eisenhower had in his heart regretted granting, and Kennedy was astonished and indeed shocked by the famous press conference in January 1963. He could not grasp the fact that the attempt to exclude France from the atomic club or to pose conditions for its admission (the integration of the French force in the Atlantic system) was bound to prompt the French president to reject the British government's application for admission to the Common Market. Once the United States had abandoned the Skybolt missile, Macmillan sought a substitute in an understanding with the President to support the reality (or fiction) of a semiautonomous nuclear force in the years to come.

The element of bureaucratic confusion and improvisation in these diplomatic maneuverings as disclosed by detailed study should not, of course, be disregarded. The secretary for defense abandoned Skybolt for budgetary reasons on the basis of cost-effective accounting, not in order to humiliate Britain nor to terminate the Anglo-American nuclear cooperation. To be consistent with his own doctrines, Kennedy should have stood firm and should not have concluded the Polaris agreement, much less attached to it an offer which, on the face of it, established an equality between France and Britain, but which was technically and politically unacceptable to General de Gaulle (technically because France would have had to abruptly alter its nuclear program, politically because the Anglo-American project seemed to entail integration in the American deterrence system). At Nassau Kennedy had to acquiesce in a decision dictated by the urge suddenly conceived during a tête-à-tête with Macmillan to preserve a special relationship with Great Britain, rather than by his general conception of policy.

General de Gaulle wholeheartedly supported Kennedy's action during the Berlin and Cuban missile crises.[10] He fully recognized the necessity for American deterrence and the containment of Communism by United States power. This balance alone enabled France to play its own game. Since the United States was obliged, in its own interest, to preserve this balance, France had no need to pay for the security it obtained free of charge. To line up with the "good Atlantic allies" was to sacrifice the political and moral advantages of playing a lone hand and appearing to the countries of the Third World as an uncommitted nation.

3.

In July 1963 the Kennedy team must certainly have felt that victory was theirs. In their first two years they had gone from disaster to disillusion. They had not only lost face over the Bay of Pigs

---

[10] In public he even took a stand against Kennedy's negotiations with the Russians. The French position on the action to be taken if a military crisis developed over Berlin has never been officially disclosed.

fiasco, but also, and primarily, lost their self-confidence. After the Vienna interview, at which Khrushchev had tried, not without some success, to intimidate the young President, the latter had sought every opportunity—in Laos and in Vietnam—not so much for revenge as to prove convincingly to his rival that he could stand firm. He must not appear weak, uncertain of himself, unconscious of his power. Meanwhile, the negotiations on the partial nuclear test ban, which had been dragging on since October 31, 1958, were still inconclusive. On August 29, 1961, the Soviets resumed testing without prior notice. A few months later the Americans carried out a series of tests of their own. It was not until October–November 1962 that the installation of Soviet missiles in Cuba gave Kennedy the opportunity for a spectacular, if not important, success and enabled him at last to achieve one of his objectives—that which he probably prized the most. In the last resort, dialogue with the Soviet Union meant more to him than the Atlantic community and its twin pillars.

So many books have been published on the Cuban missile crisis that there is no need to describe it in outline here.[11] I shall confine myself to a few observations which throw light on certain aspects of the American diplomacy. In the climate prevailing in 1962 no American president could have tolerated Cuba's conversion into a Soviet nuclear base. Any argument based on the similarity between the American bases in Turkey and a Soviet base in Cuba would have been indignantly rejected—legitimately so from the standpoint of power politics (why not compare Cuba with Finland?) rather than of international legality. On the committee set up specifically to consider the various options available and to make proposals to the President there were, as usual, advisers (in this particular case representatives of the armed forces) who recommended the immediate bombing of the Soviet bases. Once again, the President chose a moderate solution. During the negotiations he promised secretly[12] to withdraw the missiles in Turkey and undertook not to attack Cuba (an undertaking which, in point of fact, officially came to nothing since it was made conditional upon an inspection of the island, which Fidel Castro refused to permit). The Kennedy team

---

[11] See note on page 108.
[12] Through his brother, Robert.

felt that they had applied the doctrine, worked out by the analysts, of imposing one's will on the adversary by means of messages demonstrated by acts to be intended seriously (such as quarantining and military preparations on the mainland). The threat of violence between nuclear states was a substitute for actual violence. Clausewitz had written that war does not interrupt diplomatic intercourse. In the case in point, the latter seemed to act as a substitute for the former and to constitute virtually its equivalent—when the material and moral will to violence became evident to the adversary.

The doctrine of proportionate response and escalation had not been worked out with a view to a situation of the Cuban type, for the American analysts feared, whether as an assumption or as a received notion, an aggression coming from the opposing camp. Their thinking was based on a United States on the defensive and they were trying, in theory, to keep as many options as possible open between apocalypse and inaction. The vague and fairly commonplace idea of the progressive or proportionate application of force was still something of an innovation in the United States, inasmuch as it was at odds with the nation's temperament as expressed in its dealings with Indians and Spaniards in the nineteenth century and in the First and Second World Wars in the twentieth. The strategy that led to the peaceful and fortunate outcome of the Cuban crisis was based, in appearance at any rate, upon a similar idea. It was probably this that suggested to Thomas Schelling[13] the concept of "compellence" as a parallel to deterrence. This means imposing one's will on the other party, in one case *to deter him from doing* and in another *to compel him to do* (or to desist), a contrast between *defensive* and *offensive* which implies a somewhat ill-defined borderline area in inter-state relations. With respect to Cuba, was it "compellence" or "deterrence"? If the missiles had already been operational, the American strategy signified a counteroffensive designed to restore the status quo. If the installation of the missiles had not been completed as the official accounts confirm—the American strategy came close to deterrence, although the enterprise to be prevented had already begun. At any rate, the United States was at such a great advantage in the test of wills that its success is self-explanatory, the only difficulty being to determine the relative share of the various factors

---

[13] *Arms and Influence* (New Haven: Yale University Press, 1966).

involved. Did Khrushchev yield because of the United States' superiority in conventional weapons in the Caribbean or because of its general nuclear superiority? What was he trying to do? Deter the United States from an attack on the island, restore the nuclear balance disturbed by American superiority in intercontinental missiles, or force Kennedy to a global negotiation in favorable conditions with a view to a *modus vivendi?*

A number of points remain obscure. During a decisive period in October there had been no air reconnaissance of the western part of the island on which the missiles were installed. The interservice dispute—between the CIA and the air force—on the assignment of duties is said to have delayed the mission for several days. The American decision-makers must have known that the men in the Kremlin had not put their forces, strategic or other, in a state of alert. It is hard to conceive that any armed conflict between the Soviet Union over Cuba was at all likely. Cuba meant something to the American people, nothing at all to the people of the Soviet Union. Quite obviously, observers with a knowledge of the outcome can remain serene, whereas participants whose decisions are liable to affect the fate of tens of millions cannot. The fact remains, however, that the French[14] and the Europeans in general, with a few exceptions, do not seem to have shared the desperate anxiety of the Kennedy team and a large proportion of the American public.

Kennedy had won. Khrushchev had lost nothing *materially.* Had he lost face? Despite his plea in his defense—that he had obtained what he wanted: the American promise to abstain from aggression against Fidel Castro's Communist regime—the Chinese considered he had indeed lost face, and taxed him with both "strategic capitulationism" and "tactical adventurism." World opinion as a whole considered that the United States had gained a success. The debate is not yet closed. Was the Cuban crisis an episode without a sequel or a turning point in the postwar period?

Unlike Stalin, Khrushchev conducted a global diplomacy. It was he, according to Fidel Castro, who suggested that ballistic missiles should be installed in Cuba, off the Florida shores. Some of the military chiefs had recommended to the President an immediate air

---

[14] The French press as a whole was more favorable to the American strategy and less hysterical than the British.

strike on the bases; in that case, the men in the Kremlin would have had the choice between nuclear war (the least probable hypothesis), a military response in central Europe (a dangerous and therefore improbable eventuality), and impotent protest. They had thus taken a huge risk, barely intelligible even today. The installation could not be carried out unnoticed (U-2s were flying over the island) and even though Gromyko denied what Kennedy already knew, Khrushchev could hardly be under any illusion. What was he hoping for? That Kennedy would tolerate the bases? This does not seem to me wholly improbable, because of the lack of respect in which Khrushchev held him after the Bay of Pigs fiasco and the Vienna interview. He may well have thought that the missile bases would compel the President to negotiate, certainly on Berlin and possibly on other matters as well.

The ultimate consequences of the Cuban crisis of October-November 1962, apart from Khrushchev's disgrace (no one can tell exactly what part that setback played in it), were, if we follow the sequence of events, the final disposal of the November 1958 ultimatum on West Berlin and, barely a year later, the signature of the Moscow Partial Test-Ban Treaty, followed by the nonproliferation treaty four years afterward. It therefore seemed as if direct confrontation between the two super-powers had induced the leaders on both sides to make arrangements (such as the "hot line" between Moscow and Washington) and conclude agreements (on slowing down the armaments race and the nonproliferation treaty) symbolizing a common determination to do their utmost to eliminate the danger of an unthinkable war, the first war in history for which nations made preparations with the firm intention of never waging it.

Simultaneous with the Cuban missile crisis, an event on the other side of the world symbolized a new alignment of forces; in the Himalayas the Chinese troops inflicted a severe defeat on the Indian forces and then halted of their own accord and released their prisoners a few weeks later after subjecting them to a course of indoctrination. The Soviet press refrained from overtly supporting the Chinese cause. Soviet diplomacy and American diplomacy in Asia tended to converge where China was concerned.[15] At any rate, the fiction of a

---

[15] In the Bangladesh war in 1972 the United States took China's side against an India supported by the Soviet Union.

single Communist or Marxist-Leninist camp became incompatible with the actual behavior of the two great states, the two great continental empires in the traditional meaning of the term, which professed socialism.

By a further coincidence, the significance of which could hardly be overlooked, it was precisely in July 1963, the very moment at which the British and Americans were in Moscow to sign the Partial Test-Ban Treaty, that the Central Committees of the Chinese and Soviet Communist Parties published their correspondence on the ideological controversy and brought their disputes out into the open. The Western powers' quarantining of Mao's China had not, therefore, prevented a split in the socialist camp. Western observers wondered whether couching the dispute in ideological terms concealed or revealed its causes. While the Chinese taxed the Soviets with collusion with the United States, a regime embodying "capitalist" traits, the rejection of revolutionary militancy, and *embourgeoisement,* the Soviets accused the Chinese of adventurism, of trying to bypass the stages in the building of socialism and reach a higher stage of socialism in a single leap through their "communes," and of refusing to abide by the "unequal" treaties which fixed the frontiers between Russia and China. Did the Soviets suspect the Chinese of trying to draw them into an armed confrontation with the United States? After Nixon's visit to Peking in 1972 the commentator is inclined to feel that neither party had a valid case; each of them imputes to the other a "collusion" with imperialism which the facts of life make imperative for them both in certain circumstances and within certain limits.

It does not follow that the disagreements on the strategy to be adopted with regard to the United States did not contribute to driving the Russian and Chinese leaders further and further apart. The latter had never accepted the Kremlin's tutelage and had never slavishly imitated the Soviet model. The 1958 crisis (over Quemoy and Matsu), the withdrawal of the Soviet technicians and Soviet aid in 1960, and the 1963 agreement with the enemy against an ally (it was aimed at the Chinese and the French) gradually instilled a hatred of Khrushchev and Stalin's successors in one who had still been proclaiming that "the east wind prevails over the west wind" in 1957 and who had once been willing even to recognize Moscow as leader. Actually, the two great powers professing the same ideology had a further motive for disagreement; the difficulty of choosing a strategy was compounded by conflicting interpretations of a dogma. Once this dogma no longer bound them together, the divergences between their interests were aggravated. The Bolsheviks had retained the monopoly of revolutionary messianism together with unquestioned power within their own domain since 1917. In Stalin's time they had enforced a similar power over the Eastern European states. They neglected the art of compromise within their party, their empire, and their camp; and if there was no room for compromise, it logically followed that there could be no solution to the dispute. Russians and Chinese discovered that they had more to fear from each other than from the distant insular power; the two land empires had a common frontier thousands of miles long, and the border peoples, who were neither Russian nor Chinese, were fertile ground for subversion.

The enemy of my enemy is not always my friend. American diplomacy did not have to choose between the two Marxist-Leninist powers, both of them hostile to "imperialism" and the system and values of the West. What remains surprising, even in retrospect, is that the policy-makers in Washington made not the slightest change in their attitude toward China and their strategy in Vietnam. The Vietnam War and the Cultural Revolution retarded for some ten years the developments that were to be expected from the coincidence in time of a Soviet-American treaty and the public battle of slogans between Soviets and Chinese in July 1963.

When Lyndon Johnson replaced Kennedy in the White House after the latter's assassination, the United States was near the zenith of its prestige and power. Commentators, including the soberest among them, repeatedly wrote that there was now only one great power. The supremacy of the American republic asserted itself unchallenged in every sphere. Its military superiority was evident: In 1963 the United States had in its silos at least five times as many intercontinental missiles as the Soviet Union. The Seventh Fleet in the Pacific and the Sixth Fleet in the Mediterranean enforced the Pax Americana on the high seas. The growth of the American economy had speeded up between 1961 and 1965, and the United States had caught up in the race for the conquest of outer space. Science and technology had flourished remarkably after the sputnik alert. Authoritarian planning of the Soviet type had proved less and less suited to a complex industry. The predictions of Soviet triumph based on a comparison of growth rates had been discarded. Symbolically, the American farm surpluses coincided with the Soviet needs for imports due to low agricultural productivity. To paraphrase Lenin on electrification, socialism equaled the Soviets plus the American Middle West.

4.

Politicians are still only too well aware that "empires have their zenith and descension"; in 1972 President Nixon was advocating the virtues of the low profile. Between ascent and descent, supremacy and humiliation, there lies one outstanding event, the war in Vietnam, started by the French army in 1946 and taken over by the Americans in 1954 immediately after the Geneva agreements.

> The United States lost in Vietnam their finest title to fame, that of the champion of the right of peoples and individuals to self-determination. But it is not only abroad that its image has deteriorated. How many of the hundreds of thousands of well-fed and over-equipped young men who have been fighting in the rice paddies for a year against men, women, and sometimes children whose emaciation and reproachful gaze perpetually faced them with the question why they were there, have returned cynical, disgusted, drug-addicts, or at the very least disillusioned with the American dream on which they were raised? Nothing has been so instrumental in the profound crisis that has afflicted the United States for some years as Vietnam.[16]

Whether or not historians consider this judgment too severe, no one will question the Vietnam War's effect on the American people, and everyone, including most of the fiercest "hawks," will admit that the commitment to it was strategically and politically an *error;* for the spread of Communism to the whole of the Vietnam-Laos-Cambodia-Thailand region would have cost[17]—in every sense of the word, material and nonmaterial—less than the containment of North Vietnam at the expense of sending an expeditionary force of half a million men between 1965 and 1968 and then withdrawing them to

---

[16] André Fontaine, "Fin d'un grand rêve," *Le Monde,* May 13, 1972.

[17] Cost the United States, at any rate; some Vietnamese think otherwise.

the accompaniment of an intensification of the violence of the bombing. Two million tons of bombs were dropped on Germany during the Second World War, a million tons on Korea, and about six million on Indochina by the end of 1971. According to a study by academics at Cornell University published in November 1971, probably about half the annual tonnage of bombs fell on Laos (the Ho Chi Minh Trail). According to official Pentagon figures,[18] the tonnages were 2,865,806 from 1966 to 1968 and 2,916,997 from 1969 to August 1971. In 1972 the tonnage exceeded six million, more than half of it after Nixon's entry into the White House and the decision for "withdrawal." Once again, what concerns us here in trying to understand and criticize American diplomacy is not to try to demonstrate the "error," but to ask how the inconceivable came to pass.[19]

The first phase of the American commitment is a reminder of the evident change from anticolonialism to anti-Communism. Roosevelt, hostile as he was to French colonialism (which, according to him, treated Indochina as a milk cow), insisted on the occupation of the South by the British and the North by the Chinese. The expeditionary force fitted out for a final offensive against Japan succeeded in reestablishing French authority in the South after some fighting, but without negotiating an agreement with the nationalists. In the North the nationalists came to an agreement with the French; both sides wanted the withdrawal of the Chinese occupying forces. Ho Chi Minh did not reject membership in the French Union[20] and General Leclerc de Hautecloque deprecated any attempt at reconquest by force. The Vietminh, though under Communist command, could still be regarded as a party to negotiate with.

The war started on December 19, 1946, on Giap's initiative, but only after incidents (such as the bombardment of Haiphong) for which the French were largely responsible. At the time, the aim was not to contain the spread of Communism, but, as the French policymakers saw it at least, to preserve the sovereignty of France intact, or at any rate to find nationalist spokesmen more compliant than Ho Chi Minh and the Vietminh. After fruitless talks between the

---

18 *International Herald Tribune,* November 10, 1971.
19 *The Pentagon Papers* is an incomparable source for this.
20 *The Pentagon Papers* shows that he sent a number of letters to President Truman asking his aid in obtaining independence. Truman seems not to have replied.

French government's envoys and the head of the Vietnamese resistance, the policy-makers in Paris took the fatal decision to create the Associated States and, in the case of Vietnam, to conclude a treaty with Bao Dai, the former emperor of Annam. By that time, June 1949, Truman and Acheson had already decided to support the French "presence" in the area "as a guide and help to the three states in moving toward genuine independence within (for the present, at least) the French Union."[21] From this period dates the search, first by France backed by the United States and later directly by the United States, for Vietnamese rulers to whom "genuine independence" could be granted.

The refusal to treat with the Vietminh, originally dictated by France's wish to preserve something of its empire, assumed a different significance following the extension to Southeast Asia of the global philosophy drawn from the cold war in Europe and northern Asia. Acheson and Bevin would have liked the Asian states to recognize Bao Dai before they decided to do so themselves. They did not in fact take the decision until February 7, 1950, in response to the Soviet Union's recognition of the Vietminh (Mao Tse-tung, who had also recognized them, was then in Moscow). The Korean War was not the origin of the American commitment, but it did help to strengthen the American determination; the sending of an American mission was announced simultaneously with intervention in Korea and the protection of Taiwan. Between 1950 and 1954 (the Geneva Conference) American diplomacy assumed an increasing share (up to 80 percent of the total) of the cost of the war. The money was provided by the United States, the men by the French Union. The leaders in Paris and Washington were not waging the same war; the former were thinking primarily of the integrity of the French empire, though in the modified form of the French Union, whereas the latter were thinking only of containment and exerted continuous pressure to ensure that the Associated States should at last become fully and totally independent.

Georges Bidault considered that surrender in Asia would precipitate surrender in Africa. The new imperial edifice, the French Union, would not, he thought, survive the strain of the crumbling of a single of its pillars—a prophecy that had inherent in it the

---

[21] Dean Acheson, *Present at the Creation: My Years in the State Department* (New York: W. W. Norton & Company, 1969), pp. 671–72.

prerequisites for self-fulfillment. The North Africans in the French expeditionary force gained experience both of French weakness and of the potentialities of guerrilla warfare. The Americans were applying the doctrine of containment, thus rendering any negotiation with Ho Chi Minh impossible, a negotiation which General de Gaulle too had indignantly and contemptuously rejected in March 1949, even before the Korean campaign:

> The military situation in Indochina has been allowed gradually to deteriorate. But everything turns on that situation. I know well enough that some pitiable persons are trying, as they put it, to substitute policy for strength. But no policy, even and especially a policy of great generosity, has ever been effected by refusing to be strong. Some people advocate what they call the Ho Chi Minh solution in Indochina; this in fact means capitulation and, after fairly long-drawn-out formalities, the destruction of France's achievement in Indochina and of Indochina's own achievements, with its freedoms, its culture and its traditions.[22]

It is not true, therefore, that American diplomacy committed itself in Indochina and became progressively entangled there *inadvertently*, unless it is suggested that Truman and Acheson would have taken some other decision if they had foreseen the long-term consequences —a suggestion that is self-evident and meaningless. At the outset, about 1948–49, at first hesitantly so as not to upset the susceptibilities of France, an indispensable ally in Europe, and then resolutely, to prevent a nationalist party led by Communists from taking power, American diplomacy tried for an independent and non-Communist Vietnam, the first solution being Bao Dai. A continuous thread can indeed be traced, running from recourse to the former emperor of Annam to Vietnamization in 1969. Did the United States lose in Vietnam their finest title to fame, that of the champion of the right of peoples and individuals to self-determination, as André Fontaine wrote? If so, the French gave them the example; General de Gaulle and Marshal de Lattre de Tassigny also justified resistance in Vietnam by the domino theory, based on considerations of the balance of forces (where will Communism stop after the conquest of Indo-

---

[22] Press conference, March 1949.

china?) and indeed on the nature of the Communist regime itself.

From 1950 to 1954 American diplomacy under Eisenhower and Dulles held to the same line as it had under Truman and Acheson, fearing that the French might throw in the towel and be induced to make a deal. Dulles[23] failed to see any contradiction between the Korean cease-fire and the continuation of the war in Vietnam. He supported and financed the Navarre plan. After Dienbienphu the French, faced with the alternative between sending in conscripts and withdrawal, chose the latter. The American diplomats did not oppose the negotiations or the Geneva agreements,[24] but refused to take part in them. On July 21, 1954, they "took note of the different agreements concluded in Geneva and declared that the United States will refrain from the threat or the use of force to disturb them . . . and that it would view any renewal of the aggression in violation of the aforesaid agreements with great concern and as seriously threatening international peace and security." At the time of Dienbienphu in 1954 the American policy-makers had had two taboos facing them: Communist victory and a further land war in Asia. They had respected the second, but breached the first, a breach which was tolerable because the Vietminh[25] had obtained only half of the country; American diplomacy once again displayed its consistency by transferring to the Republic of Vietnam the financial support and military aid previously supplied to the Associated States through the French.

As the Americans saw it, by clinging to the last shreds of the imperial purple until 1954, the French were imperiling the cause which all the NATO governments had proclaimed common to all the states of the free world. Did the Americans themselves after 1954 play false to the ideal invoked by them in supporting Diem and, later, the generals who seized power, and finally President Thieu? In law, they could rely on the Southeast Asia Treaty of 1954.

The South Vietnamese and Americans violated the Geneva agreements—the Diem government at Saigon by persecuting the Commu-

---

[23] *The Pentagon Papers* reveals the pressures on the French government to prevent it from giving up the fight.
[24] Were the Vietminh leaders thwarted of a total victory just within their grasp, as is usually thought; or, as Khrushchev claims in his memoirs, were they agreeably surprised to get as much as they did, exhausted as they were? I do not find Khrushchev's version convincing.
[25] The Eisenhower inner circle seriously debated intervening well after the fall of Dienbienphu. See *The Pentagon Papers*, pp. 10–12.

nists, although the agreements had forbidden reprisals; the Americans by sabotage at Hanoi even before the entry of the Vietminh and by commando raids organized from the South. *The Pentagon Papers* shows that the CIA never ceased its clandestine activities against the People's Republic of North Vietnam.[26] For its part, the North Vietnamese regime conformed to the contemporary Communist model, which was hardly consonant with the liberal principles set out in the Geneva Final Act.

Who started up the war again? According to *The Pentagon Papers*, the Vietminh had taken most of its cadres and troops with it to the North, but had left in the South a skeletal apparatus, not very large in numbers but able to form the nucleus of an insurgency. From 1954 to 1958 the militants in the South received orders to confine themselves to political struggles. It was not so much the North as the repression conducted by the Diem government that determined the Communist cadres and militants threatened with destruction to recommence the armed struggle in about 1956–57. On the other hand, a decision was taken at the fifteenth session of the Central Committee of the Lao Dong (Communist Party) in May 1959[27] to supply and control the insurgent movement in the South until the unification of the two Vietnams. Infiltration into the South had never wholly ceased and was now stepped up. The Fourth Congress of the Lao Dong party, in 1960, openly proclaimed in its resolution that "the immediate task of the revolution in the South is to overthrow the clique in power in South Vietnam and to form a democratic and national coalition government in South Vietnam." Party cadres were notified of the resolution in the instructions dated January 26, 1961:

> In application of the decision of the Fourth Congress of the Lao Dong party, the National Liberation Front has been formed to unify the revolutionary struggle, to overthrow the American-

---

[26] *The Pentagon Papers*, pp. 54–99. Colonel Edward G. Lansdale (pp. 19–20) headed the earliest operations at Hanoi: the attempted destruction of a large printing establishment, the distribution of propaganda leaflets falsely attributed to the Vietminh and designed to cause panic, and the contamination of the bus company's oil supply "for wreckage of bus engines."

[27] Probably following the return of Le Duan, the former political commissar of the Southern Vietminh forces in 1951–52, from a secret mission to the South.

Diemist regime, and to set up a government of popular democratic union with a view to the peaceful unification of the country. Without the direction of the Lao Dong party the revolution for the liberation of the South will never succeed.

There is no doubt whatever that the Northern leaders took a decisive part in the organization and direction of the insurgency in the South after 1958–59. The Indian and Canadian members of the International Control Commission denounced the violation of the Geneva agreements in a report dated June 2, 1962: ". . . it is proved that armed and unarmed personnel, munitions, and equipment have been sent from the northern into the southern zone." However, these infiltrations by militants (of Southern origin in the first phase) would not have sufficed to start such a powerful rebellion so speedily had not a section of the masses in the South been alienated by the Saigon government's conduct.[28] The number of cadres, militants, and soldiers infiltrated rose from a few hundred in 1959 to 2,700 in 1960 and to over 6,000 in 1961, and increased massively in 1965 in response to the installation of the American expeditionary force. In short, neither the refusal to hold elections in 1956 nor even the persecution of the Communists in the South[29] (for how did the government at Hanoi treat dissidents and peasants who were adversely affected by the agrarian reform?) sufficed to condemn American diplomacy morally and politically. The three main reasons that finally rendered it odious were: 1. the conduct of the war itself, its inordinate violence and its disastrous effects on the very people whom it was, officially, the American intervention's purpose to defend; 2. American interference in the politics of a state which it was the Americans' task to protect; 3. the disparity between what the American forces did and what the American leaders said and between an interminable war and the new climate of inter-state relations.

An army always resembles the country from which it is raised and of which it is the expression. The United States military machine was as powerful as the industry that produced it. Nowhere else could soldiers have worn the armband symbolizing solidarity with the antiwar movement and yet not have refused to go to the front. Of these

---

[28] Between 50,000 and 100,000 persons had been put in prison camps in 1955 in the course of the campaign against the Communists.
[29] This persecution was obviously futile and self-defeating.

two expressions of American society—technology and the individual's right of dissent—the former was more visible in Vietnam than the latter. The military machine, with its B-52s, its hundreds of helicopters, its artillery barrages, and its bombing strikes and defoliation, pounded a people and polluted an environment. According to the official figures, defoliants had laid waste to about 9,000 square miles by the end of 1970; 13 million tons of high explosive in bombs and shells had been expended by the end of 1971. And all these lethal weapons were being used against a nation of only 17 million, the majority of them peasants. The disproportion of the means[30] discredited an end which was strategically as modest as American ends customarily are, the preservation of a non-Communist government in Saigon.

Seldom did the image of a David and a Goliath seem so symbolic as during this long-drawn-out trial of strength between huge machines and little men. Both sides perpetrated atrocities. During the first phase of the insurgency the Vietcong carried on a systematic campaign of murder against representatives of the Saigon government. When they occupied Hué during the Têt offensive in 1968, they ruthlessly massacred prominent citizens and officials; hundreds were found buried alive in mass graves. The American forces, too, committed atrocities (the highly publicized My Lai affair, for example). During the pacification of the Philippines early in the century there had also been atrocities in abundance, but radio and television did not yet exist and "natives" were not regarded by those who were taking up the White Man's burden as entirely human— "half devil and half child."

The strategy adopted heightened the inevitable effects of the American war machine. Between 1965 and 1968 General Westmoreland, commanding the expeditionary force, employed two main methods which required the minimum of cooperation by the Vietnamese themselves,[31] "punishing" North Vietnam to compel the leaders in Hanoi to give up the struggle, and concentrating the mili-

---

[30] *The Pentagon Papers* (p. 536) mentions "limited means" to achieve "excessive ends." Presidents never committed all the means demanded by their advisers. In any case, the end—a stable non-Communist regime in Saigon— proved unattainable. To call this "excessive" seems exaggerated. It was not so in itself, only in relation to the circumstances.
[31] And kept American troops away from the most densely populated areas.

tary effort in the sparsely populated areas immediately south of the eighteenth parallel in order to destroy as many North Vietnamese units as possible. Military and civil advisers had contemplated bombing North Vietnam to "punish" it for aiding the rebellion in the South long before President Johnson consented to it. This was nothing radically new, for the British had very often used bombing from the air against rebellious tribes in the Middle East. It did, however, represent something new in the context of the cold war or revolutionary wars in relation to the previous twenty years, because it violated the ground rules which the French had accepted in Indochina and Algeria and the Americans themselves had virtually established in Korea; Tunisia and Morocco had provided the Algerian guerrilla fighters with logistic bases, but neither the French land troops nor the French air force had attacked them. President Truman had not given his assent to the bombing of bases in Manchuria; and the Chinese had not hampered traffic between Korea and Japan any more than they had bombed the airfields on the Japanese islands. The American strategists were therefore reviving the ancient practice of "punishment"[32]—attacking the adversary's territory to weaken his morale even more than to destroy his resources—of which history provides innumerable examples (to recall Thucydides, for example, the Athenians, masters of the seas, and the Spartans, masters on land, went out each year to lay waste the enemy's country).

The American bombing failed to shatter the morale of the North Vietnamese leaders and people, just as area bombing had failed to break down the German people in 1942–45. North Vietnamese courage and ingenuity aroused the admiration of everyone, including the Americans. Life went on; factories, enterprises, and institutions were dispersed and continued to function. Despite their rivalry, both the Soviet Union and Communist China increased their aid. If the purpose of the bombing was to prevent infiltration into the South, its effects were limited at best, too limited to have a decisive effect on the course of operations in the South.

The same strategy of the progressive use of force, which had revealed one secret of the way to win a political victory at the least cost in lives during the Cuban crisis, led President Johnson and his advisers to take decisions which incurred odium, yet proved futile.

---

[32] Schelling, *Arms and Influence,* furnishes a theoretical basis for this.

With Cuba, threat had sufficed to force the adversary to retire; with Vietnam, millions of tons of bombs hardened the North Vietnamese will—as if to put armchair analysts on their guard against the dangers of schematic analysis. The schematic analysis of a duel between two nuclear powers applied approximately to the Cuban crisis, but not to the duel between the United States and North Vietnam. Between giants escalation is credible, but not between a giant and a dwarf. In any case, any man or people may prefer death to surrender. American opinion, so prone to technological reasoning, discovered to its astonishment and admiration the mystery and grandeur of human nature.[33]

While the bombers were "punishing" North Vietnam and armored divisions were harassing the troops infiltrated from the North, neither the government nor the army in the South were coming anywhere near the goal of a capacity to resist insurgency unaided. The Americans proclaimed to the world and to their own people that they were fighting to ensure South Vietnam the right freely to determine its destiny. But did South Vietnam even exist as a sovereign state? Who represented it? Who possessed legitimacy? What most struck readers ignorant of affairs of state and of the language of those responsible for them in *The Pentagon Papers* were the documents which threw light on the part that Ambassador Henry Cabot Lodge and the CIA had played in Diem's overthrow. The United States appeared to have manipulated conspiracies in its search for men who could be relied on to govern. It was not, of course, trying, like the French, to preserve the remnants of imperial authority; for it exercised it in fact. The less coherent the South Vietnam regime was and the less popular support it enjoyed, the less were the possibilities of winning the war and the less did the war seem justified. The French had discarded Bao Dai before the Geneva Conference and had given a chance to Diem, who had initially succeeded better than the most optimistic had hoped. In 1963 the Americans encouraged a generals' plot. Generals and *coups d'état* succeeded each other for several years. The political vacuum in Saigon was no proof that most of the South

---

[33] *All* intelligence reports had stated that bombing was futile as a means of compelling the North Vietnamese to capitulate. Only a few advisers had credited them. Moreover, according to the intelligence services, only massive and final bombing could have been materially effective. Progressive bombing simply enabled North Vietnam to adapt itself to this show of force.

Vietnamese were anxious to embrace the Northern regime, but it did cast doubt on the likelihood of victory and undermine the political and moral foundations of American intervention.

As the years and the horrors dragged on, the defense of South Vietnam, begun in the Forties, assumed an anachronistic and monstrous quality.

No one any longer contrasted a Communist camp united under the rod of the Kremlin with a free world united to preserve Western values. Beneath the confrontation of the two super-powers and the nuclear equilibrium, states with differing regimes renewed their ties and exchanged goods and diplomatic courtesies. From 1963 to 1968 while the war intensified in Vietnam, Europe was enjoying fair weather propitious to cooperation. Khrushchev's adventurism had received its deathblow with the Cuban missile crisis in late 1962. With the 1963 Moscow treaty and the Sino-Soviet dispute, Washington and Moscow had adopted a new style of dialogue. Against whom was containment directed? Against Communism as an absolute evil? Against the imperialism of North Vietnam? Against Chinese expansionism, of which North Vietnam was simply a tool?

From 1948 to 1968 American diplomacy once again displayed an extraordinary consistency; it confined itself to, but persisted in, barring Communist expansion to further countries. Once North Vietnam was "lost," the South had to be saved. On what grounds? An initial argument, the beforementioned domino theory, invented by the French and used by Marshal de Lattre de Tassigny, served for some fifteen years.[34] Where would the flood stop if the first dam burst? At the Suez Canal? At San Francisco? As late as 1961 Lyndon Johnson, then Vice President of the United States, reported on his return from a visit to Saigon: "We have to decide whether we are going to help these countries to the best of our ability or throw in the towel in the area and pull back our defenses to San Francisco." The notion sounds absurd when stated in this extreme form, but it does contain an element of truth, more today than in 1954. The American withdrawal and the collapse of the South Vietnam regime could lead to the triumph of the Communists in Laos and Cambodia and perhaps in Thailand. The prime minister of Singapore

---

[34] It is often used by policy-makers in classified documents in *The Pentagon Papers*.

predicted, though did not hope for, progress by the Communists in Malaysia and in his own city if the Americans withdrew.

A second argument emerged from the American morality, or at least philosophy, of international relations relating to the crossing of a demarcation line or resorting to force to alter the status quo. Civil war, not foreign war? The North Koreans, Soviets, and Chinese had talked of a civil war in 1950 when Malik had returned to his seat at the United Nations. Why should something which had not been tolerated in Korea be tolerated in Vietnam?

To counter the objection that containment was losing all meaning in the light of the Sino-Soviet dispute, some of Kennedy's and Johnson's advisers, notably Walter Rostow, developed an interpretation of contemporary history to which they pinned their faith. Lin Piao, the Chinese, and Ho Chi Minh, the North Vietnamese, they claimed, were the last prophets of revolutionary romanticism, and Vietnam was a decisive test of counterinsurgency, because if South Vietnam held out and won, the United States would have deterred the doctrinaires of the revolt of the countryside against the cities, the last proponents of Communist expansion by force, once and for all.

Whether or not the presidents or their advisers genuinely believed in these reasons or justifications, the war created its own logic. Vietnam's value grew with the growth of the commitment, since it questioned the credibility of the American guarantee. Truman and Eisenhower wanted containment, and the latter refused to send ground troops to fight in Asia. Kennedy did not want to lose the war, but he too was unwilling to send ground troops. Johnson, faced with the choice between losing the war and sending ground troops, took the latter course. But, like his predecessors, he was led astray by his services, although far less than has been claimed. Daniel Ellsberg, the person who passed the Pentagon archives to *The New York Times,* stated on the basis of documentary evidence that presidents always refused to "lose" Vietnam, but never wholly accepted the demands of their services. When the Chiefs-of-Staff Committee demanded 200,000 more men in 1968, Johnson rejected the demand because to satisfy the generals would have meant calling up the reserve, which he had always refused to do. He finally took the advice of Clark M. Clifford, McNamara's successor. After anxious deliberation, he chose instead to deescalate or halt the bombing and negotiate.

The pretexts for this decision—defense of the South Vietnamese and respect for international legality—rang false, even if some of the policy-makers themselves managed to believe in them. Obviously the Americans were not sacrificing so many thousands of GIs and so many billions of dollars for the sake of the South Vietnamese; they were refusing defeat, trying to preserve the value of their guarantee and their prestige as a great power, and attempting to prevent the spread of Communism to Indochina and Southeast Asia as a whole; the generals refused to accept the very notion that the humiliation of defeat or nonvictory could be inflicted upon them by little yellow men, among the poorest in the world, yet seemingly invincible. In 1968 no one any longer took interest in such questions as who had been the first to cross the demarcation line or who had been the first to violate the Geneva agreements. Against an expeditionary force of half a million men, the North Vietnamese and the Vietcong continued to represent the embodiment of nationalism, as Ho Chi Minh had against Bao Dai. The United States, despite themselves, played the part that the French had played fourteen years before.

What strikes a French reader of *The Pentagon Papers* time and again is the American policy-makers' tendency to half measures; Kennedy accepts an intensification of the clandestine warfare against the North in May 1961, refuses to send ground troops, and increases the number of American advisers to over 15,000, although historians cannot see exactly what were the meaning and efficacy of this augmented commitment.[35] In this respect the American style resembles that of the governments of the French Fourth Republic, despite all their differences. Perhaps it springs from the nature of democratic government in the absence of outstanding leaders.

Equally striking is the contrast between the accuracy of the analyses supplied by the intelligence services, especially the CIA, and the frequent errors of the civilian advisers, especially the academics. The CIA had foreseen that the bombing would harden the North Vietnamese leaders' will and would not prevent infiltration, and that increased aid to the North would be the response to any reinforcement of the American forces. President Johnson, before starting the air strikes, had transmitted a threatening message, virtually an ultimatum, through the Canadian member of the International Control

---

[35] *The Pentagon Papers,* p. 128.

Commission. This attempt at "compellence" had met with an in-flexible determination, which the intelligence experts, unlike the armchair theoreticians, had appraised at its true worth, and whose implications it had accurately predicted. Similarly, these experts had repeated over and over again to unheeding presidents and their ad-visers that the roots of the war and the key to success—assuming there was a key—lay in the South, not the North, or in other words, that it was essential for the United States to establish a government in Saigon capable of winning popular support and instilling in the South Vietnamese a will to independence against the Communist North.

George Ball, alone of Kennedy's and Johnson's chief advisers, ad-vocated disengagement and a negotiated acceptance of a coalition government in order to cut the losses and cover up defeat as far as possible. The Chiefs-of-Staff Committee, reticent in 1954 and realiz-ing that a South Vietnamese army first required a national govern-ment, finally joined the "hawks" in 1968. Whereas Robert McNamara had become progressively aware of past mistakes and of the military inefficacy of the bombing, the chiefs-of-staff and General Westmore-land still sought a "military victory" in the sense of the destruction of the Vietcong armed forces in the South. In spring 1968 Lyndon Johnson changed the strategy and renounced military victory—a meaningless objective from the start. Even if it could have been achieved, that objective provided no guarantee of the political goal, the survival of a non-Communist government in Saigon.

How in the final analysis can one conceive the inconceivable and render the disaster intelligible—this Sicilian-like expedition on a twentieth-century scale? First, by evoking *hubris*. The policy-makers in Washington refused to recognize the truth of the reports by the intelligence services, who, as early as 1949 and then again in 1954, stressed the link between nationalism and Communism in Vietnam and the extreme difficulty, if not impossibility, of arousing nation-alism in any other form. Second, there was a simpleminded trust in the efficacy of turning the techniques of subversion against the Communist enemy. A number of the President's advisers believed, like the French colonels in Algeria, that the technique of subversion and persuasion can be effective in any circumstances whatever. The commando operations ordered by Kennedy in May 1961 in response to infiltration and later repeated on a larger scale by Johnson[36] had nothing in common with the "parallel commands" of the rebellious generals in Algeria. Third, there was a *conviction*—genuine in many cases—that the United States would *jeopardize its role throughout the world if it accepted defeat anywhere,* a conviction strengthened by the course of events, a sort of self-fulfilling prophecy. And fourth, *a perhaps inevitable corruption of the men who conduct high policy* must be taken into consideration; good fathers, good husbands, good citizens in private life, they end up by "objectifying" situations and formulating "options," as if they were dealing with pawns on a chessboard or material in a factory. To give orders for such large-scale, cold-blooded bombing and then sleep at night requires a personality transformation, the need for which I do not deny; but I am puzzled by the ease with which it occurs in men whom I knew before they entered the realm of affairs.

The time is spring of 1968; Lyndon Johnson announces that he will not stand for reelection and begins deescalation. Richard Nixon, Kennedy's former competitor, is elected late that same year. Four years later André Fontaine wrote:

> To save a state which existed solely as a creature of the Americans, the United States changed its policy in Europe, disrupted its finances, devalued the dollar, looked on passively, without reacting, in spite of its most definite commitments, at the Egyptian challenge to Israel in 1967 and allowed Pakistan to be crushed in 1971 without raising a finger despite its alliance.[37]

The United States did not basically change its policy in Europe; if there was any change in that policy, it was in the right direction. The Vietnam War was partly responsible for the inflation, but the devaluation of the dollar had long been necessary. The Israelis replied to the Egyptian challenge and the United States reacted in the best possible way by deterring the Soviet Union from intervening.

---

[36] Johnson had failed to tell the Senate that South Vietnamese commando raids were being staged in the same area at the time when the American destroyers were attacked by North Vietnamese patrol boats in the Gulf of Tonkin.

[37] In *Le Monde,* May 14-15, 1972.

The United States had no alliance with Pakistan against India, and the independence of Bangladesh after the repression ordered by Marshal Yahia Khan was consonant with justice, with the circumstances, and, I am sure, with the real wishes of the commentator quoted above.

The fact remains that the Vietnam War tore apart and impaired the image of the American nation. No one, even in 1973, can foresee the long-term effects of that tragedy with certainty. Must one conclude, with André Fontaine, that "the Vietnam affair may well have played a part in the history of the United States comparable to that of the Suez expedition in the decline of France and Great Britain"? As I see it, the Suez expedition merely revealed, it did not cause, the decline of France and Great Britain, whereas the Vietnam War, which was not lost by the United States, served to illustrate the limitations of power, even the power of the paramount state.

Note to Page 87 A recent book on the Cuban crisis, Graham T. Allison's *Essence of Decision: Explaining the Cuban Missile Crisis* (Boston: Little, Brown and Company, 1971) should be read attentively by everyone interested in international relations. Allison uses all the relevant literature and gives an orderly presentation of the available information, while acknowledging the gaps in the documentation and the impossibility of knowing Khrushchev's real intentions. He makes use of three explanatory models: beginning with that of an individual actor who combines means toward an end, calculating the cost-benefit ratio, he goes on to correct such oversimplification by reference both to the theory of organizations and to the theory of political process. What occurred cannot be wholly accounted for by the reflections and decisions of an individual actor, who by definition is synonymous with the state; the way in which large organizations perceive situations and act on their perceptions must also be taken into account, as well as the conflicting arguments among the groups whom the President charges to present him with alternate forms of action.

The following are some of the more striking pieces of information and conclusions set out in the book: 1. Installing 48 MRBMs and 24 IRBMs in Cuba doubled the Soviet Union's first strike capability and therefore had a military significance, despite a view current in Europe, especially in France. 2. Although it is impossible to say with any certainty how such a hazardous decision was taken in Moscow, the fact that the ballistic missiles were controlled by a specialist section of the land forces gives a clue. Those responsible for the missile program at the time had installed 750 medium or intermediate-range missiles homed on targets in Europe and had neglected the production of intercontinental missiles; hence it would naturally occur to them to use the MRBMs and IRBMs to compensate for American superiority in intercontinental missiles. 3. The delay in informing President Kennedy of the presence of offensive weapons was due in part to bureaucratic friction, notably a decision not to order a U-2 flight over the western part of the island between September 19 and October 4 because the bases of ground-air missiles already observed suggested the possibility of a military incident, the destruction of the reconnaissance aircraft; disputes between the CIA and the air force delayed the U-2 flights still further, so that the decisive photos were not taken until the 14th and did not reach Kennedy's desk until the 16th. 4. One of the reasons that dissuaded the President from a surprise air strike on the bases was the air force's refusal to guarantee the destruction of *all* the missiles; they guaranteed only 80 percent destruction. 5. The Soviet decision to withdraw the missiles was taken under specific threat of forthcoming military action, in fact under compulsion of a secret but unquestionable ultimatum.

It seems to me that three points are still in doubt: 1. To what extent did the policy-makers in Moscow assess the risks they were taking? To what extent was an unflattering estimate of Kennedy one of the motivating forces in this piece of adventurism? 2. Until we have further documentation, we shall have to confine ourselves to speculation about the intentions and motives of Khrushchev and the various services involved in these decisions. Were they a response to the American intercontinental missile program or a test of the Kennedy team? Were they meant to protect Cuba, which the Soviets had never explicitly promised to defend against American aggression, or as an ostentatious provocation with a view to a negotiation? 3. Was the world on the brink of disaster, as the President and his advisers believed? Kennedy very nearly ordered an air strike on the missile bases; how would the men in the Kremlin have reacted to it?

Even today I still think it probable that bombing the bases would by no means have led to nuclear war, so unfavorable to the Soviets were the circumstances in which the crisis occurred. This assertion cannot, of course, be proved. It would probably be best to take to heart the lesson suggested by Allison, that there would be a better assurance that nuclear war will not come about if states were more like his model of a rational actor. President Kennedy had ordered the missiles in Turkey to be withdrawn several months earlier; they were still there at the time of the crisis.

Chapter Four

DISCIPLES OF METTERNICH

With President Nixon's visits to Peking and Moscow in 1971 and the admission of the People's Republic of China to the United Nations, an era in diplomatic history—the postwar rather than the cold war era—came to an end. On this all commentators agree. But that is as far as their agreement goes.

What share in this evolution is to be ascribed to the policy of the Nixon-Kissinger team? Is there indication here of a break with the policy of Nixon's four predecessors, Truman, Eisenhower, Kennedy, and Johnson, or merely a change of direction? Have aims changed with the change in methods and style? Just as Stalin made a world that conformed with the image of it produced by his ideology, will Nixon's "realism," framed in the school of Old Europe, shape the world of tomorrow?

For the first time in twenty-five years Americans and Europeans are openly using the word "isolationism"—wrongly, perhaps, at least if the term is used in the sense of the external behavior of the United States between 1921 and 1939. History does not repeat itself; the American republic can no longer withdraw into itself. It is nevertheless under no compulsion to continue the imperial role it has been playing for a quarter of a century. In an era in which North Vietnam and Israel are providing a concrete illustration of the autonomy of small powers, a global power can hardly be refused its modicum of autonomy.

A former cold warrior, narrowly defeated by Kennedy after eight years of the vice-presidency, Richard Nixon entered on a second term with the blessings of Chou En-lai and Brezhnev, Mrs. Golda Meir and President Georges Pompidou. In what direction will he guide the external action of a state which no longer identifies the fate of the West with its own, but remains the testing grounds for a mankind unsure of its destiny and the guaranteeing power both in Europe and Asia of a still precarious equilibrium?

1.

When Richard Nixon was installed in the White House early in 1969, the situation he inherited was far more serious than that bequeathed by Truman to Eisenhower. In both cases there was a common element, an unpopular and protracted war with no prospect of military victory. But there were vast differences, both locally and in the global system.

In Korea regular armies were confronting each other on a continuous front. The talks at Panmunjon were dragging on, Mao Tse-tung's plenipotentiaries refusing Chinese prisoners the choice of repatriation to Taiwan or the mainland. American opinion no longer supported the commitment of American draftees to a distant theater of operations in intermittent action which precluded any clear-cut decision. The age-old tradition of finishing off the job of war in order to return to business as usual made it imperative for the hero of the "crusade in Europe" to obtain a cease-fire in default of peace, an end to the fighting in default of victory.

President Eisenhower did not, of course, lack the means to achieve the objective dictated by circumstances at home and abroad. The United States had an overwhelming superiority over the Soviet Union both in industrial production and in nuclear weaponry. Was it Stalin or Mao who was obdurate in refusing the minor concession necessary and sufficient to stop the fighting? We do not know for certain. Stalin had more interest than Mao in prolonging a conflict which widened the gulf between Washington and Peking. But could Mao Tse-tung not have negotiated if he had really wished to do so? Be that as it may, Stalin disappeared from the scene two months after Eisenhower entered the White House. The cease-fire was concluded at Panmunjon a few weeks later; and Stalin's successors in the Kremlin engaged in more and more frequent symbolic acts, showing a change of style, if not a change of heart.

As compared with the Korean War, there were two basic differences with regard to the Vietnam War, even if both were justified by the same doctrine of respect for demarcation lines; in the summer of 1950 the Soviet representatives had contended that the Korean War was a civil war, and, in point of fact, the invasion had followed vain attempts by the North to instigate guerrilla warfare in the South. But no honest person had been able to deny the existence and legitimacy of the Seoul government and the army defending it. The North Koreans and the Soviets had used much the same terms—the Syngman Rhee clique, the puppets, the accomplices of imperialism— to assail the Seoul regime as the North Vietnamese used to assail the regime in Saigon. In 1950 they had convinced no one except their friends, then fairly numerous even in the West; now the impartial observer had his doubts. President Thieu was not regarded either by the Vietnamese or abroad as the embodiment of patriotism or nationalism, as Syngman Rhee had been. The Vietcong were the natural successors of the Vietminh who had fought the French for independence. Syngman Rhee had fought the Japanese all his life, whereas a number of the generals in South Vietnam had actually served in the French army. Anti-Communism and the fact that some of the people in the South had some reason to fear the ruthless regime in the North supported and in some degree legitimated the Saigon regime; but Saigon was not strong enough in itself to resist the combined onslaught of the insurgents, the North Vietnamese regulars, and worldwide "progressive" propaganda.

From the military standpoint, too, the differences were greater than the similarities. In the early phases the locally recruited Vietcong had undermined the Saigon regime and would probably have overthrown it if the United States had not committed an expeditionary force in 1965. North Vietnam had responded by stepping up its support of the rebels and infiltrating units of its regular army. The American expeditionary force had not lost a battle, but it had not won the war.

How was the war to be won? To revert to Clausewitz's terminology, the political end (*Zweck*) of the war waged by the United States was to preserve a non-Communist regime in Saigon. What military objective could encompass that end or supply its equivalent? To this question strategists, as we have seen,[1] had the choice of several answers. The first was to inflict such "punishment"—destruction and

---

[1] See pp. 100ff.

suffering—on the North Vietnamese that the leaders in Hanoi would give up the idea of supporting the insurgents in the South or would no longer be able to do so. The bombings were intended to serve both purposes; they achieved neither. The second answer was to "search and destroy" the North's regular units and the guerrilla warfare groups; this answer, too, was equally mistaken, because the expeditionary force had no chance of eliminating *all* the regular units or *all* the guerrilla groups. Partial successes brought them no nearer the goal. In a revolutionary war between guerrilla fighters and an existing government the guerrilla can succeed in winning simply by not losing. This is true when the existing government is identified with either a colonial power or a regime too weak to carry on the struggle alone. In the first case, opinion in the metropolitan country grows weary and finally turns toward the insurgents. American opinion grew weary, like French opinion at the time of the Algerian war, and began to question the legitimacy of, or even the practical justification for, the fighting.

This brings me to the third and only rational answer, that the appropriate military strategy was, and should have been, to strengthen the government and army in Saigon. Since the political purpose of the war, as seen from Washington, was the survival of a non-Communist South Vietnam, and since the expeditionary force could not stay there indefinitely, the main aim of intervention should have been to gain time enough to consolidate a government capable of maintaining order in South Vietnam and of resisting both the insurgency and any attack by North Vietnam. There is nothing to show that the United States was capable of achieving this purpose; this was not its aim—at least not its main aim—at any rate until early in 1969.

By putting an end to the bombing and agreeing to negotiate, President Johnson had made an irrevocable decision. His successor had to find a way out in order to heal the rift in the American nation and to recover a freedom of action restricted by entanglement in Vietnam. How was he to wind up the war "with honor"? What did "with honor" mean? From the American point of view, the North Vietnamese were fighting beyond the boundaries of their state and evacuation of the American ground troops required the withdrawal of Hanoi's troops in return. Neither Ho Chi Minh nor his comrades concurred in this view; they had vainly demanded from the French in 1945–46 the unity of Annam, Cochin China, and Tonkin. More-over, the "rebels" against the Saigon regime contemplated nego-tiating with it only on conditions that ensured their own supremacy and their enemies' final disappearance.[2] In Korea the cease-fire had at least ensured the Americans their minimum objective; but how were they to withdraw from Vietnam without accepting total defeat, even if that defeat was political rather than military?

President Nixon *could* have negotiated the withdrawal of the American troops with Hanoi if he had been indifferent to the future of the Saigon regime.[3] He could have accepted Hanoi's concept of a "coalition government." In fact, he refused a "shameful" winding up of the war. His aim was, indeed, both to win the war (or not to lose it) and to placate the American people.

Nixon inherited the Vietnam situation, an inheritance totally dif-ferent from that of Korea, at a time when the ratio of military forces was changing in the Soviet Union's favor, and domestic inflation, largely due to Vietnam, was weakening the dollar and reducing the apparent surplus in the balance of trade[4] year by year (it was not officially in deficit until 1971). Nixon's installation in the White House coincided with the moment of truth both within the Western world and with regard to the Soviet Union; the Europeans (especially the Germans) and Japanese had progressed faster, had narrowed their lag, and were coming forward as competitors of the United States in all markets, including the American. With the urgent task of finishing with Vietnam there was combined another longer-term and ill-defined task, that of restoring an international system in which the United States would not reign supreme and which, with-out ruling out a clash of interests or even disputes, would constitute, if not a balance comparable to that of the concert of Europe, at least relations of a traditional kind between all powers, including the revolutionary powers.

Nixon's policy lends itself to varied interpretations because of the

---

[2] This is, at least, what the American decision-makers said in private as well as in public. I am inclined to think that they were speaking the truth, though I cannot say so for certain.

[3] That would have been the price for freeing the American prisoners.

[4] I use the adjective "apparent" because the balance of trade had been adverse for several years if the purchases imposed by the tied loans are taken into account.

apparent contradiction between its two objectives, the refusal to lose the Vietnam War and the desire for normal relations with *all* states, including the Communist states. It is not that this refusal and this desire are basically contradictory; Henry Kissinger would most certainly argue that acceptance of a "humiliating" defeat would have deprived the United States of the authority without which retreat would have degenerated into rout. Retreat is a maneuver that requires both flexibility and moral strength. Nixon was foredoomed to a maneuver of this sort. The contradiction nevertheless visibly astounded commentators and the man on the street alike because the President's spokesmen announced (in April 1972) progress in the negotiations on strategic arms limitation at the very moment when television was showing the long files of Vietnamese refugees and the formidable armada concentrated in the Gulf of Tonkin.

Nixon's policy breaks *historically* with his predecessors' since it reflects an attempt at disengagement, and even a certain modesty, for the first time since 1947; neither Eisenhower nor Kennedy nor Johnson would have used the expression "low profile," which does not mean lowering one's guard, but guarding against *hubris*. Before examining the temporary significance and lasting impact of American disengagement, let us look at the brilliant strokes, the spectacular moves, and the general style of Nixon's diplomacy in 1969–72.

In concentrating his interest and action on a few key issues—Vietnam especially—and on relations with Moscow at the summit Nixon seems to me to have continued his predecessors' practice. The innovation appears primarily in method and organization.

What strikes observers both inside and outside the United States is the role of Henry Kissinger and his brain trust, or to express it differently, the replacement of the normal institutions provided for in the Constitution and subject to congressional control by an *ad hoc* organization brought into being by the President and manned by persons chosen by him and his adviser; in brief, a sort of royal council set above the department and secretary officially responsible for the conduct of diplomacy.

To my mind this apparent novelty is simply the accentuation of a trend which came to light with Kennedy's entry into the White House. Presidents, in their capacity as elected sovereigns, have always been free to choose their own general staff. At the time of the Great Depression Franklin Roosevelt had recruited a team of New

Deal intellectuals. During the war Harry Hopkins had played a far more important part in great affairs than Cordell Hull. There is a tradition of presidential confidentiality comparable to the king's confidence. The little prestige enjoyed by civil servants in a country in which the spoils system still survives and the President still appoints hundreds of petty officials on the day of his enthronement promotes the creation of "parallel bureaucracies." There is nothing to show that this trend is irreversible. Just as Dulles was Eisenhower's presidential adviser and secretary of state rolled into one, so Henry Kissinger will henceforth supplement his many tasks as a "gray eminence" with the responsibilities of the Department of State.[5]

Henry Kissinger, of course, has a great many functions which his predecessors, such as McGeorge Bundy and Walter W. Rostow, did not monopolize and perhaps did not carry out all at the same time. Kissinger reports to the President on the day-to-day key factors in the world situation; he sets forth the various possible decisions from among which the President will have to choose; in crises he chairs the special action group, just as he regularly presides over the National Security Council. As adviser on current events and the action called for, he must also direct or set in motion departmental action in accordance with the President's instructions, at any rate in serious situations. This still leaves him time for secret missions such as those to Peking and Moscow for pre-negotiation with Chou En-lai and Brezhnev and to Paris for negotiation with the North Vietnamese.

The apparatus responsible for carrying on the external action of the United States changes with the tenant of the White House. Thus the post now held by Kissinger can exist only if there is a president like Nixon. Kissinger came to the fore simply because he managed to establish curious ties with the suspicious and solitary Nixon and also because both of them had a possibly insoluble problem to solve, how to make a withdrawal "with honor" from Vietnam compatible with a worldwide diplomacy without a lofty cause, a devil to vanquish, or an angel to side with.

The Vietnam War troubled the Americans' conscience while exasperating the realists. Was the Saigon regime genuinely a member

---

[5] Will Kissinger be able to cope by himself with functions normally performed by two people? In any case, he is likely to suffer the fate of his predecessors at the State Department, constant harassment by Senate committees.

of the "free world"? Was dumping millions of tons of bombs on Vietnam the way to defend the free world? Why should Communism be contained when the two Marxist-Leninist states regard each other as the principal enemy and ideological allegiance no longer determines diplomatic alignments? Besides, when Nixon entered the White House, anti-Communism, far from providing a political or ethical foundation for the war, was itself emerging from the war discredited. By a sort of mental confusion or association, anti-Communism was becoming the principle of evil because it had led to evil, the horrors of Vietnam. Only one argument still held good, therefore: that the United States, being responsible for the global equilibrium, could not consent to a humiliation which would sap the trust of its allies and strip its promises and its pledged word of all credibility.

Nixon and Kissinger seem to have decided very early that the prerequisite for negotiation which the North Vietnamese and the Vietcong were demanding was the elimination of General Thieu's team, the only one capable of putting up some sort of resistance to a Communist takeover of the country. With this notion as his starting point, Nixon was driven to wage the war with a view to (political) victory and (military) withdrawal. If it proved able to survive, the Saigon government, and the United States with it, had won the war, in the genuine sense of a victory defined by the stake itself. But in order to make this strategy acceptable to the American people, the President had to undertake progressively to reduce the size of the expeditionary force and hence progressively to turn over to the South Vietnamese army the responsibility for fighting in the field. The concept of "Vietnamization" is exactly the same as that concocted by Dulles after the Korean War, a concept cynical if it means the Vietnamese killing each other for the benefit of the United States, acceptable if it is a means of transferring to a nation itself the responsibility for its own defense (would a European consider the "Europeanization" of the defense of Europe cynical or appropriate?).

The crises in Cambodia (1970) and Laos (1971) were the result of this strategy designed for political victory with the use of smaller military resources. No matter whether Prince Sihanouk was overthrown by the machinations of the CIA or by sections of the Khmer oligarchy opposed to him, this was a chance to strike at the Vietcong by invading the areas in Cambodia it was using as a refuge, a logistic base, and an assembly point. Nixon failed to resist the temptation, but the violence of the reaction on the campuses and in the country at large showed him the limitations on his freedom of action. The incursion into Laos by a South Vietnamese division in 1971 was motivated by a similar intention, to give the Saigon regime and its army time for reinforcement and to slow down the preparations for the North Vietnamese offensive, which in fact did not strike until April 1972, more than four years after the Têt offensive. By that time Nixon had practically no more troops in Vietnam able to take part in ground fighting.[6] He massed an armada in the Gulf of Tonkin, and the air force, taking off from bases in South Vietnam and Thailand and from aircraft carriers, was able to fly up to 600 missions daily.

At the beginning of the offensive Nixon could boast of achieving two results. The first of these was that the North's offensive took the form of classic warfare with divisions of Hanoi's regular army crossing the demilitarized zone, that is to say, the demarcation line. This was not a people's rising against "puppets," but a regular invasion, legitimate if it was granted that the leaders in Hanoi were entitled to forcibly impose their authority on the whole country, comparable to an aggression if the government in Saigon was seen as neither more nor less legal than that in Seoul or Hanoi. Since the North Vietnamese offensive looked like an act of aggression, the President recovered a margin of freedom of action—this was the second result. The universities remained calm (the students were no longer liable to the threat of the draft). The time chosen for the offensive, the interval between the President's visit to Peking and his approaching visit to Moscow while the evacuation of the American troops was entering its final stage, appeared to the bulk of Americans as conclusive proof that the North Vietnamese were aggressors by nature.

The timing of the North Vietnamese offensive caused a crisis in Washington simultaneous with the crisis in the field. It abruptly raised the question whether détente with two major Communist powers was incompatible with an "honorable" winding up of the Vietnam War. Nixon and Kissinger had quite evidently hoped that Russian and Chinese influence would be brought to bear in a way

---

[6] Two battalions, a few thousand men at most.

likely to promote their larger design. They were looking, of course, beyond the Vietnam War; in the perspective of the reconstruction and establishment of a global system, the war was downgraded to no more than a mere episode. Nevertheless, the North Vietnamese divisions' use of Russian arms and their early victories around Quang Tri faced Nixon's and Kissinger's entire strategy with a dilemma. Should they do their utmost to save the Saigon regime and so risk sacrificing the Moscow meeting or should they tolerate its collapse and so risk arriving in Moscow weakened and humiliated by the defeat of a government for which the United States had vainly expended so many lives and dollars?

In April 1971 the primary issue was once more the arbitrament of arms. In order to reconcile the clamor of domestic opinion with the requisites for nondefeat, Nixon's strategy required the withdrawal of the expeditionary force, a strengthening of the South Vietnamese army, and its support by the American fleet and air force. When the fall of Quang Tri and the rout of a South Vietnamese division led to fears of a military disaster, Nixon confronted the Kremlin with both a challenge and an appeal. Mining the North Vietnamese harbors could have no immediate effect on the outcome of the fighting. At the very worst, it gave Nixon a position of equality, if not strength, in the Moscow talks. At best, it might force the Politburo to choose between temporarily suspending the talks with Washington and putting greater pressure on the North Vietnamese to induce them to renounce total victory. Brezhnev chose a third solution, to receive Nixon as if nothing had happened.

Why should he have considered supplying the North Vietnamese with heavy weapons incompatible with the unwritten rules of the *modus vivendi* or détente between the super-powers when the United States had sent the South hundreds of thousands of men and was continuing to intervene with its fleet and air force? By deciding to mine the North Vietnam harbors on the eve of leaving for Moscow, Nixon was suggesting to Brezhnev three possible courses, two of them explicit and one implicit: to consider that each of the super-powers should respect the other's major interests; to regard the agreements shortly to be negotiated as more important than the fate of Vietnam or of any small power; or, third, to hold that a great power must not lose face, and hence that another great power must not seek to humiliate it directly or through an ally. Brezhnev probably accepted the first two propositions. Could he or would he heed the third?

The way in which Nixon responded to the crisis in April–May 1972—the North Vietnamese offensive equipped with Russian arms and the visit to Moscow with a view to concluding agreements— illustrates both his dual objective and his dual personality. The dual objective was to wind up the war "with honor" and to negotiate with Peking and Moscow without losing face. The dual personality was reflected in the wisdom of withdrawal and a low profile combined with an acceptance of risk and a firm stand, amounting, indeed, to bluffing to the limit in each crisis (the overthrow of Prince Sihanouk in Cambodia, the emplacement of Soviet batteries of SAM missiles as far forward as the Suez Canal, the use of a Cuban harbor by Soviet nuclear submarines, and the invasion of Jordan by Syrian tanks[7]). Nixon's opponents assert that the cold warrior showed through the mask of the prophet of "peace for a generation" and that he dropped more bombs on the three countries of Indochina on the pretext of withdrawal than Johnson had dropped to win the war. Leftist commentators speak of the Kissinger mystery, and wonder how a relatively unknown academic of German origins not devoid of either humor or humanity could sleep at night after giving orders that meant such indiscriminate slaughter. I have wondered about it myself; the only possible answer is that anyone to whom such a question occurs has not been born to become the Prince or even, perhaps, his Counsellor.

The visit to Peking symbolizes the style and substance of Nixon's policy. Nixon had probably been wanting to renew intercourse with Peking since early in 1969, or to put it more precisely, to rid the talks in Warsaw of the surreptitious flavor which doomed them to sterility. Once they had restrained the leftists after the sacking of the British Embassy and the clashes with the Soviet Union on the Ussuri in March 1969, the leaders of Communist China had been wanting to resume their place in the inter-state community. Of the three types of relations carried on by a Communist country— between state and state, between party and party, or between state

---

[7] These are the crises listed in the President's Report on foreign policy to the Congress as indications of a fresh period of confrontation before negotiations could go forward.

or party and a people or rebels—the leaders in Peking had to opt for relations between state and state. The ideology of the worldwide uprising of the countryside against the towns was disappearing, or at any rate no longer enjoyed the official sanction to which Lin Piao had set his name. The moderation in act[8] displayed in the main by the policy-makers in Peking was henceforth expressed in words and diplomatic approaches. In July 1971 President Nixon announced officially that he would go to Peking and that his adviser, Henry Kissinger, had already been there secretly to make the arrangements for the visit. The visit took place in March 1972.

Let us pause for a moment to examine the abovementioned *style* and *substance*. The style shows itself in the announcement of the visit to Peking without consulting or even informing the United States' allies in Asia beforehand, and the renewal of relations in the striking form of a visit by the President in person, received for an hour by Mao Tse-tung, the new emperor of the Middle Kingdom, and spending several hours in negotiation with Chou En-lai, the second most important personage of the regime. Is there any point in trying to determine to what extent these were the actions of the politician and statesman, of the candidate for a second term, or of the prophet of "peace for a generation"?

There can be no doubt that Nixon wished to dramatize his coup, thereby antagonizing the Japanese more than was strictly necessary. He was lacking in tact and in the delicacy to save the face of others, both essentials for a great power anxious to remain on the Asian stage. On the other hand, the visit to Peking, regarded by Asians as a humiliation—for the United States had quarantined Communist China and now its President was taking the initiative in rapprochement and asking for an invitation[9]—was the most spectacular, and possibly the only, way to symbolize to the whole world the inauguration of a new era. Nixon was neither able nor willing forthwith to reverse the policy which had culminated in the mutual security alliances and pacts between the United States and Taiwan and between Japan and Taiwan. Chou En-lai was neither able nor willing to pay

---

[8] Two noteworthy exceptions are the insistence on the return of *all* Chinese prisoners during the negotiations at Panmunjon and the bombardment of Quemoy and Matsu in 1958.

[9] Did Nixon ask for an invitation or did he merely agree to this way of presenting a prior agreement?

any price, whatever it might be, for the seat in the United Nations to which the government for twenty years in control of the Chinese mainland was entitled. Nixon and Chou En-lai could not, therefore, conclude any agreement of substantial importance in itself. The continuance of diplomatic relations with Taiwan precluded recognition of the Peking regime and the consequent opening of an embassy.

What then was the substance of the visit? When reduced to essentials, the balance sheet of the Peking meeting can be summed up roughly as follows: Communist China had emerged both from the cultural revolution and from isolation; following the fighting on the Ussuri and the concentration of Russian divisions on the frontier, the Soviet Union had become the primary enemy, for the time being at least, since it represented the looming threat of a preventive attack on the Chinese nuclear plants, if not actual invasion, at the very time when the United States was displaying signs of wishing to effect a partial and gradual withdrawal. The Communist Chinese leaders therefore found it logically consistent with their interest to consent to a visit by Nixon as a potential deterrent to a Soviet aggression, as the assurance of a seat at the United Nations, and as the foreshadowing of a new attitude on the part of Japan. For that matter, Communist China had already practiced a realistic diplomacy in Southeast Asia, despite Lin Piao's ideological messianism, by being on good terms with Pakistan and on bad ones with India.

For Nixon, on the threshold of an election year, this was an opportunity to turn his Democratic opponents' left flank, earn himself the name of a "fighter for peace," revive the American people's long-standing goodwill toward a distant and more or less mythical China, and provide the Soviets with an additional reason for dealing with him while at the same time he was giving the Americans a lesson in a diplomacy at once novel and traditional—novel because the Chinese and Americans had for twenty years been maintaining only intermittent intercourse through their ambassadors in Warsaw; traditional because, in accordance with the historical practice of Old Europe, intercourse between states involves no more than an acceptance of things as they are. The recognition of a state does not imply approval of its regime or its actions; Nixon, rather than breaking with the American practice of nonrecognition overnight, took the first step (the only step that counts) along the road to recognition.

He visited the capital of a state of whose existence the United States professed to know nothing.

The visit to Peking was a step down the road to Moscow: The negotiation with Peking was a start; the negotiation with Moscow was to set the final seal on the venture. For Chou En-lai the very fact that the conversation took place was the immediately essential point. For Brezhnev it was the agreement on strategic arms limitation and the final declaration on the rules of coexistence that symbolized the ending of the cold war and the dawn of a new era.

Ever since 1960 every president of the United States, Kennedy, Johnson, and Nixon, had sought to remove direct relations between the two super-powers from the scope of the hazards of local conflicts and inopportune interventions by the small powers. The American republic and the Soviet Union are still aiming at incompatible goals and are still opposed to one another as regards their world views and their ultimate aspirations. They are immediately concerned with broadening the areas of common interest, formalizing and establishing the implicit agreement, and perhaps deriving from it mutually acceptable settlements. Détente at the summit would at best be a means of pacifying local conflicts, or at least preventing their spread and escalation. The negotiation on strategic arms limitation (which was to culminate in a treaty during Nixon's visit to Moscow) was the sequel to the interminable negotiations on the nuclear test ban and nonproliferation, which, too, had culminated in treaties (the Partial Nuclear Test-Ban Treaty in Moscow in 1963 and the Nonproliferation Treaty, signed but not yet ratified by the principal parties concerned).

The conclusion of the SALT negotiations was a step forward in relation to the two preceding treaties. The Partial Nuclear Test-Ban and Nonproliferation Treaties chiefly disquiet states that are not members of the nuclear club or only minor members of it (China and France). Fixing the number of antimissile missiles or offensive missiles does not amount to a measure of disarmament, but to a deceleration of the armaments race[10] or a limitation of the arsenal which the two super-powers mutually agree they are entitled to

---

[10] Perhaps due to a shift from quantity to quality (MIRV—multiple independently-targeted reentry vehicles).

possess. This first limitation agreement had been made possible by American acceptance of the principle of equality and by the change in the ratio of nuclear forces (and conventional forces as well) in the Soviet Union's favor. It thereby illustrates both the continuity of Nixon's policy with his predecessors' and the emergence of new factors, relatively obscured by the President's rhetoric: the rise of the Soviet Union, a possible weakening of American determination, and the continuance of intercourse between the two super-powers as well as the continuance of confrontation, direct or through the intermediacy of allies, in various areas all over the world.

2.

More than seven months elapsed between Nixon's meeting with Brezhnev in Moscow and the signing of the agreement in Paris by Henry Kissinger and Le Duc Tho. The North Vietnamese offensive launched in April, in the interval between Nixon's visits to Peking and Moscow, continued for some weeks, but finally bogged down without achieving any of the ambitious objectives which General Giap had probably set for it: the striking of a mortal blow at the Saigon regime or, at the least, the seizing of a large town as capital for the Provisional Revolutionary Government (PRG). The offensive had nevertheless achieved the less ambitious aims of demonstrating to its two allies, the Chinese and the Russians, the independence of the government at Hanoi, reminding them that North Vietnam was its own master, and last but not least, reconstructing the administrative infrastructure which the South Vietnamese authorities had been able to destroy in some areas during the four years between the Têt offensive and the offensive of April 1972. In other words, the fighting in the spring of 1972 both showed that Hanoi had a power and an army in South Vietnam and sabotaged the pacification of the countryside.

The negotiations had seemed to be on the point of conclusion in October, for the American representative had suggested October 31 as the date for signing, though without formally promising to sign on that date. Talks were broken off and then resumed, but were deadlocked in December. President Nixon ordered heavy bombing of Hanoi and Haiphong by B-52s—causing over 1,200 civilian deaths, according to reports from Hanoi—and for the first time involving the loss of a substantial number of the giant bombers. (They became vulnerable owing to the altitude at which they had been ordered to fly.)

Did Nixon and Kissinger obtain on January 24, 1973, the peace "with honor" for which they had been seeking so indefatigably since January 1969? The President's critics—even before the Watergate scandal—were so bitter that they never used the phrase "with honor" without a tinge of indignation or irony. But honor in relations between states, now as in the past, is a somewhat dubious concept. Was France's signing of the armistice in June 1940 incompatible with honor? Was the British navy's attack on the French fleet at anchor at Mers-el-Kebir consistent with honor?

Perhaps it is better to avoid lofty but ambiguous words and look at the texts and listen to the persons concerned. Kissinger invariably, in private if not in public, presented the President's policy in the same terms, stating that while he was determined never to accept an agreement that would hand over power in Saigon to the Communists of the North and South, he was not claiming to guarantee the survival of a non-Communist government in South Vietnam forever. The symbol of what he was refusing was the coalition government, tantamount, as Kissinger saw it, to government by the PRG. The symbol of what he was demanding was the dissociation of the military settlement from the political settlement, first the cease-fire and only thereafter elections in the South to give its people an opportunity to exercise their right of self-determination.

A comparison of the seven-point proposals by the PRG (July 1, 1971), the revised peace plan of February 3, 1972, and even the PRG statement on September 11, 1972, with the cease-fire agreement of January 24, 1973, clearly shows that the Communist leaders did not press their extreme demands. The decisive change came with the proposals put forward by Le Duc Tho on October 8, 1972, which Henry Kissinger had immediately seen as very important indeed. According to the revised peace plan of February 3, 1972:

> Nguyen Van Thieu, and his machine of oppression and constraint, instruments of the U.S. "Vietnamization" policy, constitute the main obstacle to the settlement of the political problem in South Vietnam. Therefore, Nguyen Van Thieu must resign immediately [and] the Saigon administration must end its war-

like policy [and] disband at once its machine of oppression and constraint against the people.

The PRG statement of September 11, 1972, still included the following passage:

> [It is necessary] to achieve national concord. . . . To this end it is necessary to form in South Vietnam a provisional government of national concord with three equal segments to take charge of affairs in the period of transition and to organize truly free and democratic general elections.

Hanoi and the PRG finally resigned themselves or determined to treat with those whom they called "puppets" or "the clique in the service of the Americans"; they suspended the fighting without any assurance of achieving, in the short term at least, the objective they had been aiming at since December 1946, the unification of the three countries of Vietnam—Cochin China, Annam, and Tonkin—under a single, Communist-controlled government.

There is nothing to show, however, that they renounced it forever. President Thieu did not abdicate, but neither did the PRG troops, South Vietnamese irregulars, or North Vietnamese regulars (whose presence Le Duc Tho denies) give way. The cease-fire provided that each of the two parties in South Vietnam should remain in their positions. Whereas the 1954 agreement laid down that the Vietminh should regroup north of the eighteenth parallel and the non-Communists south of it, the 1973 agreement embodied what came to be known as the "leopard-spot" formula. The North Vietnamese and the Americans stipulated as the main peace terms the withdrawal of the American troops, the clearing of the mines from the harbors, and the freeing of the American prisoners held by the North Vietnamese. On the other hand, the agreement, despite all its detailed provisions, provided little help in forecasting how relations between "the two South Vietnamese parties" would be established, or even whether and when hostilities would cease. The second Vietnam War, the war in which the United States took the leading part, was drawing to a close in early 1973. In the new context, due to Nixon's policy and the Sino-Soviet dispute, the Vietnam War meant nothing to anyone—*except the Vietnamese themselves*. When left to themselves, would they discover the secret of compromise and peaceful coexistence?

Of the manifold questions which observers pondered and historians will ponder, some can be given an at least probable answer forthwith. The North Vietnamese, or at any rate a majority in the party Politburo, took the decision in the fall of 1972 to treat with President Nixon as soon as possible before his reelection (hence the insistence on the date October 31). The decision was logical in view of the world situation and the political and military position in the South; the North Vietnamese were forced to recognize that the Chinese and Soviets preferred rapprochement with Washington to total victory by their allies. By launching a general offensive in April 1972, they had given the American President an opportunity to strike a heavy blow, the mining of the harbors, from which Lyndon Johnson had always recoiled. The message implied by the inaction of Chou En-lai and Brezhnev was perfectly clear; the brutality of the American response and its toleration by the two major Communist powers spotlighted the virtual isolation of the North Vietnamese. This was equally true at the time of the bombing of Hanoi a few months later.

At the same time, while an analysis of the situation in the South held out little prospect of a decisive military victory, it did not preclude hope for a political victory sooner or later. The South Vietnamese army had reeled, had pulled itself together, and had at length stood firm. Having been reelected for four years, Richard Nixon could for a time still use his last weapon, the air force, to bolster up the Saigon government. By the January agreement Hanoi achieved its first objective, the withdrawal of the American troops, even if it had to postpone its real war aim, the unification of Vietnam (which, indeed, was recognized in principle by the Americans themselves).

I find Nixon's and Kissinger's decision equally comprehensible. I never had any doubt that they wished from the outset to extricate the United States from the quagmire and put an end to a war which outraged some by its horrors and others by its obvious absurdity. One question alone dominated the debate, namely whether the North Vietnamese were demanding the elimination of Thieu and his administration. According to the texts quoted above, they certainly were still doing so in 1972. Should Nixon have acceded to this demand?

Admittedly, the negotiators appointed by Johnson—Averell Harriman in particular—have claimed that they envisioned an agreement after Nixon entered the White House which approximated the one finally concluded. I find this difficult to believe. President Thieu had become the symbol of the decisive issue at stake, the nature of power in Saigon. Removing him meant dismantling the South Vietnamese administration and thereby handing everything over to the PRG. Can it be said that such total demolition would have been preferable to four more years of war? "Preferable" for hundreds of thousands, for millions of people, yes indeed. Preferable politically? That cannot be asserted, for the United States could not sever the ties binding it to Thieu and his fortunes; it could not do so morally or even materially (what means had it of compelling Thieu to resign?). Even if Vietnam is ultimately unified under a Communist government, such an outcome will not mean the same in the future as it would have meant if the Americans had imposed it on their allies or protégés by capitulating.

There can be no such evident answer to the question raised by the final events—the bombings of Hanoi and Haiphong in late December 1972. The nine-point agreement published by Hanoi in October left a great many questions unsettled. In point 1 the United States undertook to respect the independence, sovereignty, unity, and territorial integrity of Vietnam. In point 4 the North Vietnamese undertook that "the South Vietnamese people shall decide themselves the political future of South Vietnam through genuinely free and democratic general elections under international supervision." Point 5 went on to state: "The reunification of Vietnam shall be carried out step by step through peaceful means." How many of these points were to remain nothing more than empty clauses?

President Thieu's objections to some points of drafting in the agreements accounted for the American suggestion for further talks, which Kissinger believed at the time would last for only a few days. In his view, it was less a matter of amending the substance of the agreements than of clarifying various details. For lack of knowledge of the differences between the texts drafted in December 1972 and the texts signed in January 1973 historians will have to settle for probabilities for the time being.

According to the American negotiators, Le Duc Tho suddenly resumed the familiar obstructive tactics in December; points that had been definitely agreed were promptly reopened to discussion; as soon as one difficulty was overcome, another arose. In short, it seemed as if the faction in the Politburo opposed to compromise had temporarily prevailed in Hanoi and was taking advantage of demands by Kissinger or Saigon to revert to the hard line. According to the North Vietnamese, the Americans wished primarily to gain time to reinforce Saigon's military potential and then extort additional concessions by stepping up the bombing of cities in North Vietnam. The losses of B-52s and the worldwide wave of indignation aroused by the terror bombings recalled Nixon to reason.

It seems to me, however, that Kissinger obtained in January what he was aiming at in December, an indisputable distinction between the "national council of reconciliation and national concord" and a government, a vague reference to the demarcation line, and an enlarged international control commission. Vietnam's future—as Henry Kissinger knows better than anyone—does not depend on textual shades of meaning, forgotten within a matter of months, if not days. It may therefore be assumed that the Vietnamese negotiators, as Kissinger claimed, were acting in bad faith in December and playing on the differing meanings of terms in English and Vietnamese.

Be that as it may, there is still room for two interpretations of what transpired. The bombings of Hanoi and Haiphong either ensured the victory of the faction in the Politburo favoring peace or inflicted a punishment and a lesson for the future. Whether the more indulgent interpretation is accepted or not, the brutality of the means employed entailed a moral cost to the United States. But the balance sheet of the war was already weighted in that direction before this new explosion of violence, all the more intolerable to opinion in that it remained unintelligible.

In all fairness, however, I do not think that President Nixon and his adviser can be denied the merit of finding a way out of an apparently inextricable situation and avoiding both surrender and the indefinite continuance of hostilities, of not betraying the allies

chosen by their predecessors, and of fitting this operation into a re-
orientation of American diplomacy. Admittedly, the agreement of
January 1973 did not put an end to the fighting among the Vietnamese; Kissinger had to negotiate a further agreement in June
1973. The future of the non-Communist regime in Saigon is no
more assured today than it was in the past. The President's opponents could readily ask many more questions and level many
more criticisms against him. But could anyone have done better?
Southeast Asia is gradually being relegated to the minor place to
which it is entitled in the external action of the United States as a
whole. If Nixon and Kissinger could not convert into a victory a
war which was in any case already lost, they did succeed in winding
it up without disaster either in the field or at home.

3.

The originality of Nixon's and Kissinger's diplomacy relative to
American postwar diplomacy is due in the first place to the situation:
the desire for withdrawal, for disengagement, imposed by the state
of American opinion. It is due in the second place to the style,
changing with the personality of the President and his advisers.
And, thirdly, it is due to the combination of two objectives, local
and global, an "honorable" winding up of the Vietnam War and
"reasonable" intercourse at the summit. It is due, as well, to the
regime's major initiative, the visit to Peking. Does it also follow
from the philosophy of inter-state relations by which both the
Prince and his counsellor are motivated?

This philosophy is in the European, not the American, tradition.
Having come from Germany in the Thirties, Henry Kissinger was
to teach his adopted country some thirty years later the dubious
wisdom of Metternich or Bismarck. Admittedly, this is an oversimplification but one that perhaps does not basically falsify the
reality.

The influence of the gray eminence, the obscure, German-born
ex-professor, would be unaccountable unless both the President and
his adviser viewed the world through the same spectacles.

Even so, the contrast with the past should not be overexaggerated.
Every president of the United States, knowingly or not, has engaged
in *Realpolitik*. When Roosevelt "bought" Soviet intervention against

Japan by concessions at China's expense, he was acting in precisely the same way as statesmen do in all times and places and was discovering for himself the shady practices for which the Americans have never evolved a theory and of whose constraints and benefits they have remained unaware. Nixon, too, dissimulates and transfigures by his rhetoric the prosaic action in which he is engaged; on his return from Peking and Moscow he represented himself as a pilgrim of peace.

His predecessors—Kennedy and Johnson certainly, Eisenhower probably—likewise wished for a dialogue with Moscow and had made some moves in that direction. Why was Nixon fortunate enough to get further than they had? Primarily because he had the courage to go to Peking. For twenty years, from the Chinese intervention in Korea to the Sino-American negotiations in 1970–71, the United States had kept Communist China out of the United Nations and had communicated with it solely through intermittent meetings in Warsaw (at the ambassadorial level). This attitude on America's part did not prevent the split between the two major Communist powers; perhaps it even provoked it. The fact remains, however, that Nixon had the "Machiavellian" merit of breaking the taboo on China the untouchable, promoting the readmission of Peking to the great game of inter-state relations and giving the men in the Kremlin an additional reason for an understanding with Washington.

In Peking, as in Moscow, Nixon found interlocutors prepared to speak the language of reason and reality. The cultural revolution was a thing of the past. Chou En-lai had recovered control once Lin Piao had disappeared; the global revolution of country against town had descended with other myths into the limbo of history. In Moscow Brezhnev and his comrades resemble bureaucratic executives more than prophets. While they have achieved virtual military equality with the United States, they are well aware of their economic and technological inferiority. Russians and Chinese, therefore, are equally anxious for dialogue with the American President, the former for mainly economic reasons, the latter for fear of encirclement or even preventive attack by the Soviet Union.

Why did the Russo-American condominium of which Roosevelt had dreamed thirty years earlier fail after the war? Why did cold war replace cooperation? The revisionists blame Truman and the hypocrisy of universalism, others blame Stalin and his ruthless methods of sovietizing Eastern Europe. There is no need to choose between these two indictments; after Yalta the Americans neither prevented nor accepted the sovietization of Eastern Europe and part of the former territory of the Reich. Apart from a few spectacular episodes, the origin and significance of the cold war in Europe was the combination of protest and toleration—moral protest and de facto toleration. Today the ratification of the German-Soviet and German-Polish treaties has put the seal on the moral recognition of *faits accomplis* by the last state to protest against them. The dialogue between Nixon and Brezhnev does not involve the same risk of misconstruction as that between Stalin and Roosevelt, for the current two interlocutors understand one another better because they are more alike. Americans and Europeans, freed from illusions, no longer refuse the Soviets the right of armed intervention in a state of the socialist community.

Is it to be concluded that the philosophy of Roosevelt and Truman, of Nixon and Kissinger, has had less effect on their decisions than the situation itself as each side perceives it? There can be no doubt that Nixon was responding to the wishes of those who elected him by simultaneously seeking an accommodation with the Soviet Union—the past and present rival—and a limitation of the republic's foreign commitments. He nonetheless impresses both his supporters and his opponents as thinking and acting in a fashion—ultimately an un-American fashion—unlike that of his predecessors. The difficulty in analysis arises from the inscrutable dialectic of the men and the circumstances.

Nixon's and Kissinger's point of departure is certainly the idea that the world of inter-state relations normally and permanently involves collisions between the interests of states and hence conflicts. They believe neither in collective security nor in the rule of law; the inter-state system toward which they are moving would be the result of a balance between opposing forces rather than a community among states or peoples. Nothing is less like the Holy Alliance set up after 1815 than the dialogue between Nixon and Brezhnev or Chou En-lai, Brandt or Pompidou. The historian of Metternich has certainly not retained either the dogmatism or the rationalism of that intransigent defender of an empire doomed by the march of mind. The commentators who refer to the *Realpolitik* of European tradition define it as the substitution of the management of equilibrium for the gradual formation of a community and as the changing relationships among the actors, all of them jealous of their freedom of action and therefore little inclined to permanent alliances. Even if this be true, is the model to be the European cabinets or Washington's warnings against entangling alliances which paralyze action and drag a state into the quarrels of others? *For the time being,* neither of them.

The global system differs so greatly from the European system of the past few centuries that the same rules have a totally different meaning. The expanded scope of diplomacy, nuclear weapons, instantaneous communications, the diversity of regional situations, the disdain for civilized usage and the "traditional courtesies," all these and more preclude comparison of the operation of the European Republic of States described by Voltaire earlier in this essay with the operation of the United Nations or the practices of a jungle haunted by saurians, or *"monstres froids,"* as General de Gaulle described states, quoting Nietzsche. In the European Republic of the past, states akin to each other by proximity or culture formed temporary coalitions to prevent universal monarchy or the supremacy of a single power. The periods of disturbance occurred when the interrelation of domestic upheavals or religious or ideological schisms coincided with rivalries between states. The Holy Alliance in 1815 was based both on the restoration of the balance of military forces and on the attempt to fetter the "monster," the revolutionary idea with its train of conscription and war to the death. If Nixon and Kissinger want "a world restored," as the title of Kissinger's book puts it, what sort of a world do they want?

The global system is still bipolar from the military standpoint. Even now there are only two global powers, the Soviet Union and the United States, both of them fully decked out with arms, both of them present on every continent and every ocean. The Soviet Union not only has attained nuclear equality, but it is now supplementing its superiority in ground forces on the Old Continent with a modern fleet, which is growing stronger year by year.

It does not yet have aircraft carriers comparable to those of the American Sixth and Seventh Fleets. It still suffers from the drawbacks of a geopolitical situation less favorable than that of the United States. Can it be said that the equalization of military forces between the two global powers and the vulnerability of American territory are radically changing the structure and management of the global system and that these changes are in turn determining the style of the dialogue between Moscow and Washington?

I do not overlook these changes and their consequences. However, as I have shown in earlier chapters, those responsible for American diplomacy have always treated their rival circumspectly and have never tried to force it to a humiliating retreat. At times of crisis they have treated their allies more harshly than their enemies. The men in the Kremlin, for their part, have carefully calculated the risks they were taking, even during the two Berlin crises—with a single exception, the installation of ballistic missiles in Cuba. To date, the Soviet leaders seem to derive their strength from increasing self-assurance and, while asserting their claim to a status comparable to that of the United States, the status of a global power present at every turning point in history, they are behaving even less aggressively toward the enemy to which they are so ideologically akin.

If bipolarity—in the sense of the concentration of the military forces of two states which are far stronger than all other states—still exists, what is the multipolarity in the present system perceived by all commentators, a quarter of a century after the Truman Doctrine?

I can conceive of three different meanings for this term: 1. the relative autonomy of certain subsystems; 2. the Sino-Soviet rivalry, which is in some respects more virulent than the American-Soviet rivalry; 3. the manifold levels at which relations between states (and societies) are developing while military strength is not reflected in the equiproportionate strength of political power or moral influence.

The autonomy of certain subsystems is very clearly demonstrated in military conflicts between states in a particular area. In 1967 Israel, threatened by the blockade of the Gulf of Aqaba and the Egyptian divisions massed in Sinai, took the initiative in war, and in six days won a complete victory over its three neighbors, Egypt, Jordan, and Syria. The Soviet Union had armed Egypt and had close ties with Syria. Yet it only intervened in the United Nations to hasten the cease-fire,[11] to which Israel consented only after reaching all its objectives. The leaders of the two super-powers, who remained in touch during the week-long crisis, prevented one another from intervening directly. Owing to the isolation of the sub-system, Israel exerted its military superiority without restraint, in accordance with traditional practice.

The Indian subcontinent in 1971–72 provides another example of a crisis solved by military force by the locally strongest state. In 1970 Marshal Yahia Khan ordered free elections in the two provinces of Pakistan. The elections in the eastern province gave 167 seats out of 169 to the candidates of the Awami League, the party advocating autonomy, but not independence, for the province. After fruitless bargaining, Marshal Yahia Khan chose to use violence; Sheik Mujibur Rahman, the head of the Awami League, was jailed and the troops sent into East Bengal struck at the autonomists, politicians, intellectuals, teachers, and students. A few Awami League militants on the Indian frontier proclaimed the independence of Bangladesh. Millions of Bengalis fleeing from the excesses of the troops from the Punjab crossed the frontier into India and crowded into the refugee camps. Guerrilla warfare broke out in Bengal. The Indian authorities on the frontier gave material aid and moral support to the guerrilla fighters.

Here, too, the world situation enabled the locally strongest state to solve the crisis by military force. Marshal Yahia Khan's government, responsible both for the free elections and the refusal to accept their verdict, could not send reinforcements to the eastern province, separated from West Pakistan by more than 1,200 miles of Indian territory. India had, therefore, a superiority on the eastern front which ensured it an easy victory. Mrs. Gandhi had only to sign "a treaty in reverse" with the Soviet Union to be able to "conquer" or "liberate" the eastern province, shortly to become Bangladesh, without fear of Chinese intervention. Did Mrs. Gandhi's India infringe the United Nations Charter when its army crossed the frontier to bring help to an oppressed people? Undoubtedly.

---

[11] The Soviet delegation made things easier for the Israeli representatives in New York by at first demanding the withdrawal of the Israeli troops simultaneously with the cease-fire.

Would she have done better service to human beings if she had respected the Charter and had supplied the partisans for years? This is highly debatable. No matter how serious the express breach of the rule prohibiting resort to force of arms—although the hypocrisy of the aid to the guerrillas seems to me preferable on the whole to the frankness of a regular invasion—in this particular case I am unable to deplore Mrs. Gandhi's prompt solution.[12]

The solution gave rise to a curious alignment and even more curious arguments pro and con. Communist China had been in conflict with India since 1962 over the line of the frontier in the Himalayas (specialists disagree on the merits of the Indian and Chinese claims). On the other hand, it had cordial relations with the military regime in Pakistan. Peking's representative at the United Nations did not deny the Bengalis' claims and complaints, but argued against the interference of India and against the dismemberment of a sovereign state. The Soviet Union representative argued for the right of peoples to self-determination, the United States representative for respect for the Charter, suggesting that military action was hindering the political settlement then in course of negotiation. Here, again, as in the Middle East, it was possible to resort to regular armies, owing to the isolation of the battlefield and the superiority of one of the belligerents, since the outside powers were compelled to abstain by their distance, disagreement, and equilibrium.

These two subsystems, therefore, have certain characteristics in common: In the Middle East the Soviet Union and in the Indian subcontinent the United States could not prevent the victory of the locally strongest state, short of physical intervention. In the present global system no state any longer respects the rules of diplomatic courtesy under which small powers yielded either to the wishes of the great power to which they were allied or to those of the concert of great powers. On the other hand, the method of putting up a challenge is becoming current practice. The small powers resort to it in relation to the great powers, whether friends or foes—President Thieu in bargaining with the policy-makers in Washington, the Israeli government when faced with the Soviet Union. When the

---

[12] Though it was a flawed solution. The Bihari minority, hostile to the Bengalis or accused of collaborating with the Pakistani troops, were persecuted in turn. Bangladesh became an Indian protectorate and is still starving.

masters of the Kremlin received a desperate appeal from Nasser, they had to send fighter squadrons and batteries of anti-aircraft missiles to defend Egyptian territory against the Israeli air-force's long-distance raids; neither direct (dubiously credible) threats nor indirect messages through Washington would have deterred the Israeli government.

Did sending an aircraft carrier into the Bay of Bengal deter Mrs. Gandhi from supplementing her victory in the east by settling the Kashmir dispute by the same method? According to Nixon, yes; and the President attributed the cessation of hostilities to the Kremlin's good offices as much as to the movements of his own fleet. Is this a justification by hindsight of an unreasonable position? Probably, though no one can say so for certain. In any event, the essential fact is that Nixon could no more impose his will on Mrs. Gandhi, allied as she was to the Soviet Union, than Brezhnev could impose his on Mrs. Meir, assured as she was of American support. The mutual paralysis of the two super-powers, provided they are not physically engaged in a subsystem, once more calls for the arbitrament of arms and proves the truth of the old saw "Might is right."

The Indian subcontinent is in many respects quite a different matter from the Middle East. The super-powers could not care less about the fate of the Bengalis, or even about the power ratio between India and Pakistan. For years to come India will remain a regional power, not even a continental power, incapable of extending its power beyond the bounds of the subcontinent. In the Middle East, beneath the protracted conflict between Israel and its Arab neighbors, the great powers see a stake vital to both Japan and the United States, the vast oil reserves upon which both the Atlantic and the Pacific states will draw. They stand there alone, face to face, concurring in the avoidance of a clash, but incapable, despite Chinese accusations, of real collusion.

On the Indian subcontinent the United States, regardless of the strict letter of its guarantees and pledges, had never undertaken to fight India to preserve the integrity of Pakistan. Johnson had refrained from taking sides in the second war between India and Pakistan in 1965 and had apparently felt no bitterness over letting the Kremlin acquire the merit and prestige of Tashkent. Was Nixon carried away by his feelings with regard to the two protagonists,

Yahia Khan and Mrs. Gandhi? Did he feel that he had been duped by the latter? Or did he feel he had to pay a debt to the former for smoothing Kissinger's way to Peking? Was his aim to display an ostentatious respect for the United Nations Charter or an apparent agreement with Communist China? Did he wish to teach the rulers of India a lesson, convinced that they would not long hold against him a routine episode in power politics? With the information presently available no one can decide among these interpretations, not all of which are mutually incompatible.

What is of interest here in the attempt to find a precise meaning for multipolarity is where two rivalries, one continental, the other global, overlap in a subsystem—the Sino-Soviet rivalry, which is almost totally confined within the bounds of Asia for the time being; and the American-Soviet rivalry, which extends over the whole globe. At the supreme nuclear level the two global powers stand alone and unequaled, and for this reason and by virtue, too, of their air forces, fleets, and conventional armaments, they can intervene any-where—which, rather paradoxically, does not rule out the fact that one of them is becoming less and less tempted to do so, militarily at least, and the other has for the time being derived only meager benefits from its accession to the first rank.

The visits to Peking and Moscow, with the dual purpose of pro-moting the winding up of the Vietnam War and putting an end to an absurd situation, the nonintercourse between the Soviet Union's two main rivals, smack of *Realpolitik,* but also of good sense. There is no necessity to invoke Metternich, Talleyrand, or Bismarck, no reason even to stress the decay of ideologies, for the dispute between the Soviet Union and Communist China has ideological causes and aspects too. The schism within the world professing Marxism-Lenin-ism confirms historical experience by demonstrating the friendship among socialist states is no more proof against the erosion of time and the divergence of interests than the friendship among Christian states. Conflicting interpretations of a common creed can at least be used as a diplomatic weapon, even when they do not arouse inflam-matory passions.

The Korean campaign had, by accident or by Stalin's Machiavel-lian designs, disrupted the relations between Peking and Wash-ington. The Kremlin had retained a virtual monopoly on relations with the White House. The visit to Peking was the climax of Nixon's first term, because by a single coup he secured the advantage of intercourse with two states which were temporarily incapable of agreeing with one another, were, indeed, barely on speaking terms. As long as the Sino-Soviet conflict is, or seems to be, implacable, the United States, once rid of Vietnam, will be able to enjoy its turn to be the *tertius*, with full freedom of movement—a freedom, in point of fact, fully in accord with the teachings of the old diplomacy.

In Europe the justification for using the term multipolarity is not the Sino-Soviet split, but the multiple levels (transnational, international, military, economic, political, and ideological) at which relations between states and societies develop, without intercommunication between the levels and without the decisive influence of the nuclear level on the others. Stalin lowered an "iron curtain" in the middle of the Old Continent in the Forties and set up regimes in the Eastern European countries akin to his own, governed by men devoted to Marxism-Leninism, a number of them brought back in the foreigner's baggage train. In the West the elder nations, victorious or vanquished, all of them devastated or weakened, seemed to be spoils offered to the conqueror; only the American republic seemed able to raise a barrier against the tyrant's ambition and the spread of what Europeans called at the time the New Faith. So each of the two great powers surrounded itself with a bloc—the free world confronting oriental despotism—the nature of the domestic regime governing its diplomatic allegiance. In this sense, inter-state relations were dominated by ideology, each bloc being an equivalent of a Holy Alliance (an alliance of established powers against revolutionaries).

There were no such blocs outside Europe. Outside its own perimeter the Soviet Union never exercised unconditional authority over the countries which also professed Marxism-Leninism. Communist China did not accept the status of a satellite even between 1949 and 1953. The ideological kinship or affinity of regimes was a characteristic only of the two European blocs.[13] The states supported by the United States in Asia, the Middle East, and Latin America have hardly any characteristics in common except that they

---

[13] Even in Europe, with some qualifications (Portugal, and later Turkey and Greece).

are not governed by a monopolistic party professing Marxism-Leninism, and so there has never been a Soviet bloc or a Free World
bloc in Asia, Africa, or Latin America. When commentators refer
to the era of bipolarity, they mean it in a special sense. An extreme
interpretation of the doctrine of containment implied the refusal
by the United States to accept any loss whatever, territorial or
ideological; no state, however small, was to change its allegiance
or adopt Marxist-Leninist language. The consequence was that diplomats in Washington tended to assume responsibilities everywhere
and at all times, even where no specifically American interest was
involved.

In Europe or in regions outside the areas of Russo-American
confrontation Nixon's and Kissinger's policy is characterized by a
less imperious attitude toward its allies and toward the Third
World. The Gaullist veto on Britain's application to join the
Common Market in January 1963 irritated Kennedy and outraged
American opinion. Nixon was neither overtly hostile nor favorable to Britain's admission in 1971. Though undoubtedly favorable
officially, he refrained from exerting pressure on London or Paris.
In short, he was exercising his role as leader with greater discretion.
Although, consistent with his predecessors' example, he personally
retains the monopoly of nuclear negotiation and action, he keeps
his allies regularly informed. In this respect he is continuing a development started by Johnson, who had already abandoned Kennedy's grand designs.

The Congo crisis had led to American intervention through the
United Nations and to a Russo-American confrontation. The civil
war in Nigeria, on the other hand, was settled on the spot; though
the Soviets sent arms to the central government, there was no reaction
in Washington; the British were also sending arms. The decline of
globalism preceded Nixon's election; this was logically consistent and
was accelerated by the Vietnam tragedy.

Latin America and the Caribbean were other areas in which
Nixon's team did nothing strictly new. The innovation consisted
solely in a less active interest and less intolerance of revolutionary
regimes, even those prone to use socialist or even Marxist-Leninist
language. Washington apparently did not mobilize either the CIA
or its friends against the nationalist military government in Peru
or against Allende's experiment in Chile. It looked as if Nixon

were leaving the conduct of American action in Africa and Latin America to the State Department, and instructions from the White House were not spurring the professional diplomats to any initiative. The shift from activism to abstention can be viewed as a form of withdrawal.

4

In an interview with *Time* magazine (January 3, 1972) President Nixon said:

> We must remember the only time in the history of the world that we have had any extended periods of peace is when there has been balance of power. It is when one nation becomes infinitely more powerful in relation to its potential competitor that the danger of war arises. So I believe in a world in which the United States is powerful. I think it will be a safer world and a better world if we have a strong, healthy United States, Europe, Soviet Union, China, Japan, each balancing the other, not playing one against the other, an even balance.

A strange and even absurd definition of the ideal system for peace. Even if Europe between 1815 and 1914 comprised five major protagonists (Great Britain, France, Germany, Austria-Hungary, and Russia), there was no magic virtue in the number five. The European order of the Congress of Vienna was proof against the limited conflicts of the nineteenth century for a great many reasons which have nothing whatever to do with the number of principals. Moreover, the five actors listed by the President exist only in his imagination, or at least differ from each other in ways totally unlike those evident among the actors in the European system. They comprise two global powers; a great unarmed economic power (Japan); a continental power, poor but equipped with an embryonic nuclear force (China); and an ensemble of industrialized nations without a common government and without the ability or determination to assert itself abroad (Europe).

Furthermore, the major actors in the old European system constituted a system in the fullest sense, because each of them calculated the relation of strengths in the light of the strength of all the others. There is nothing similar in today's global system. Politically and strategically, the European nations, even if they were united, would keep out of Asian conflicts; similarly, Japan would keep out of European disputes. China exercises some influence owing to its prestige and ideology, and hopes to exercise it at least on the European countries of the socialist community. Chou En-lai privately encourages the Western Europeans to unite so that his chief enemy, the Soviet Union, may not be able to concentrate all its forces in the East. The evident fact stands out yet again: that there are only two super-powers, though this does not mean that the system is bipolar, at any rate if bipolarity means the formation of two blocs or two camps, each clustered around a global power. Japan, for lack of weapons, especially nuclear weapons, and Europe, for lack of unity and determination and because of its physical proximity to a global power, are still dependent on the American alliance and protection.

The notion of a pentagonal balance must make the Japanese even uneasier than the Europeans; for it implies a failure to make an explicit distinction between allies and adversaries. The refusal to make such a distinction would indeed mark a drastic break with American postwar diplomacy. If followed to its extreme conclusion, it would come to much the same thing as another famous remark, an expression, logical rather than cynical, of insular power as the guarantor of equilibrium: England has no allies, only interests.

President Nixon indeed repeated publicly over and over again that the United States would honor its alliances and would not sacrifice its allies to rapprochement with its enemies. But in that very same year, 1971, another event—the action on August 15—took Japanese and Europeans alike by surprise and highlighted the paradox that, since the world economy is divided into two markets—one socialist, the other capitalist—economic rivalries and disputes arise within each of these markets, and in consequence between allies. Romania's opposition to the decisions or planning of the Comecon illustrates the kind of disputes characteristic of the socialist community; debates about the international monetary system, about the causes of Japan's or Germany's trade surplus, about exchange rates, about discriminatory measures, and about overt or covert protectionism are developing with increasing bitterness between Europeans, Japanese, and Americans. The devaluation of the dollar, which in itself takes on historical significance—the moment of truth—on a par with the visit to Peking, raised technical economic altercations to the level of high policy. Indeed, how could the question not occur, first to the Japanese and then to the Europeans, as to whether at the very moment at which the enemies of the United States—China and the Soviet Union—became interlocutors and perhaps partners, the European Community and Japan became rivals and virtually adversaries within the world market. Was there not some reason to fear that the two alliances which had been the mainstay of American diplomacy since 1950, the alliances with Japan and with Western Europe, might fall into abeyance, victims simultaneously of détente with the enemies of the United States and tension with its allies?

In Asia, once the Vietnam War was wound up, the United States had the advantage of the *tertius,* of the global power present in the theater of operations, but likewise of the insular power, with its freedom of movement and freedom from ties. As long as Mao Tse-tung reigns in the Forbidden City, reconciliation between Peking and Moscow is not feasible, and the American diplomats do not need to play off one of the two major Communist powers against the other; they have recovered the room for maneuver of which they had been deprived by obsessive anti-Communism. Indeed, Chou En-lai may actually desire a residual United States presence in Southeast Asia to prevent China's encirclement by the network of ties woven by Soviet diplomacy. Soviet diplomacy, in turn, would be fulfilling an old dream of Stalin's, and indeed of Lenin himself, by obtaining credits and technology from the most advanced economy. As seen from Tokyo, however, Nixon's and Kissinger's action presents a major ambiguity; for over twenty years Washington was only too glad to take upon itself all of Japan's responsibilities, but now it wishes to delegate them. How far will this delegation go? What is to be Japan's role?

Naturally, Tanaka, the prime minister succeeding Sato, driven from office by the spectacular turn of events in 1971, followed the path laid open by Nixon and soon overtook him. Nixon could not break off diplomatic relations with Taiwan, but Tanaka abruptly did so without being asked. He too received economic offers from Moscow and Peking, the former much larger (the exploitation of Siberia) but with greater inherent involvement, the latter more modest to start with but with a considerable potential for growth. He is not bound to choose between them, though it is hard for him to stand strictly equidistant from Moscow and Peking.

What mainly worries policy-makers in Japan is how they stand with Washington, which brings up questions such as what is left of the military alliance, what course economic rivalry will take, and whether Nixon is differentiating between the empire of the Rising Sun and the empire of the Middle Kingdom, one an ally, the other a former enemy which continues to denounce imperialism, to support Prince Sihanouk, and to oppose clients or protégés of the United States. With the assurance of the American guarantee, can Japan project its power outward by economic means, with no weapons but conventional armaments and no ambition but to protect the areas in proximity to the islands? Asia for the Asians meant the withdrawal of the expeditionary force in Vietnam; what does it mean in Northeast Asia? Is Japan to recover its role as a great power *at the military level too,* or must it count on the United States' nuclear guarantee?

The situation and the questions are at once similar and different in Europe. The Soviet bloc still exists, in the precise sense that the men in the Kremlin still set the bounds to how much autonomy or ideological heresy they are prepared to tolerate; first Hungary and then Czechoslovakia had that brought home to them. Within the bounds set by the Kremlin, Romania displays its own personality in its diplomacy and Hungary in its internal administration. The United States has never exerted an authority in Western Europe comparable to that of Stalin and his successors in Eastern Europe.

The fact remains, however, that the recovery of the elder nations and the formation of the Common Market have gradually changed the relationships between Britain, France, and the Federal Republic of Germany, both among themselves and with the United States.

Each of the Western European countries has established ties with most of the Eastern European countries. General de Gaulle visited Poland and, evoking the traditional friendship between France and Poland, invited his hosts (vainly, as it turned out) to look beyond their immediate neighborhood, a discreet allusion to the socialist community to which Gomulka gave all his attention and allegiance. In cultural diplomacy and sports the Iron Curtain no longer exists; but there are still two distinct worlds; the Soviet Union still dictates doctrinal conformity and prohibits ideological coexistence. National administration and the partial integration of economies operate in ways that differ basically at either end of the Old Continent. Trade between the two blocs has continued to progress and is likely to do so in the future. The Soviet Union finds it to its interest to exchange raw materials and energy for fully tooled factories and manufactured goods, in many cases high-technology articles. The Western countries likewise consider it to their interest to promote such trade in the hope that interdependence will consolidate peace. The government of the Federal Republic of Germany, too, has some hope of infiltrating the German Democratic Republic (GDR) with ideas of democratic freedom. The rulers of the GDR reply with what they call *Abgrenzung:* In order that the German Democratic Republic shall continue to exist essentially as it is in a Europe permeated by the flow of goods and persons, it must harden the least physical of frontiers (*Grenzen*), the minds of men.

In a Europe still divided but apparently placated, in which the bluster of propaganda no longer resounds, what place does the United States now hold? What is to be its role in the coming decade?

Despite its geographical proximity to the community of socialist states, Western Europe belongs to the Atlantic bloc both economically and ideologically. The transnational currency is the dollar; the American conglomerates have a large number of subsidiaries there; its oil supplies are dependent on relations with the Middle Eastern producer countries, in which American companies have invested billions of dollars. Western Europe is continuously affected by American inflation, stock market movements, interest rates, and everything that happens on the other side of the Atlantic; no decision taken by the planners or Politburo in Moscow has an influence in any way comparable with that of the fluctuations in the American economic situation. There now exists a transnational economic society symbolized by the Eurodollar, which knows no frontiers, and in practice restricts state sovereignty and each state's ability to carry on an independent credit or monetary policy.

To put it in Marxist-Leninist terms, Western Europe is a member of one world market, the capitalist market, and Eastern Europe of another, the socialist market. The relations between these two markets or between state members of different markets are limited or marginal as compared with dealings within each of these markets.

Are the Western European states able and willing to establish closer ties with the other half of the Old Continent while remaining an integral part of the transnational Atlantic society? Undoubtedly they are. Can they have and do they want a Europe unified "from the Atlantic to the Urals"? Most certainly not. Politically, a Europe of this kind, without the United States and with the Soviet Union, would lead to what may be called a "Finlandization" of Europe,[14] the substitution of one protectorate for another—a protectorate which might well become intrusive in a way very different from America's.

Economically, trade with Eastern Europe can therefore supplement and enhance, but not replace, trade within the Atlantic, or capitalist, market. Politically, a Western Europe detached from the United States, or one in which the United States had ceased to take interest, would slide toward a subordination which would in the long run mean satellization, unless it made an effort at unity and determination of which it seems incapable.

Thus, the two decisive questions emerge: In Asia is the United States maintaining the alliance with Japan which prevents the Land of the Rising Sun from rearming and confirms the limited, but necessary, role of ideological kinship in diplomatic alignments? In Europe will the United States maintain a military presence that guarantees the compatibility of détente and security?

Nixon is contributing to the creation of a postwar world wholly unlike that of Metternich or Bismarck. Through Kissinger Nixon is, of course, borrowing from the wisdom of the European tradition. He accepts a certain degree of dissociation of inter-state relations from ideological conflicts, he does not dream either of crusades or of collective security, and he recognizes that conflicts of interest between states are quite normal. He does not hope for or count upon a global condominium, a strict delimitation of spheres of influence or bargaining at the summit to settle any and all crises, even those of secondary importance. The words most frequently used by those who drafted the President's Report on foreign affairs to the Congress are "restraint" and "self-restraint"—prudence and restraint, Aristotelian virtues of the political world made yet more imperative by the excess of armaments.

If this interpretation is correct what would remain of the skeptical

---

14 If the Western Europeans were in a position comparable to that of the Finns, I doubt that they would display a similar courage and preserve so large a part of their freedom.

wisdom of Old Europe in Nixon's and Kissinger's diplomacy save the rules of common sense, cynical at times, but—aside from the bombings of North Vietnam—cynical in a civilized fashion. There would be a nuclear equilibrium between the two global powers and relatively dissociated subsystems, in which the two global powers play various parts in conjunction with the regional and continental actors; each protects its own interests without disregarding the necessary respect for vital interests of the other. This has nothing in common with Metternich's dogmatic rigidity; the revolutionary monster is not fettered by a Holy Alliance of counterrevolutionaries. The revolutionary states renounce spreading their creed by violence and the United States renounces viewing every revolutionary movement of any sort as a menace.

Why, nevertheless, are there still nagging doubts? Will Nixon, or his successor, keep a flexible, moderate sense of proportion? If the American republic no longer finds itself facing an enemy devil, of what use are allies? Of what use are permanent ties? Why protect trade rivals, who show their ingratitude by invading the American market? How long will a business-minded republic tolerate the paradox of partners who are adversaries, partners in the diplomatic-strategic system and adversaries in economic competition? Will a dollar diplomacy take over from a crusading diplomacy?

The prospect that is really to be feared is a distorted interpretation by the Americans of Metternich's or Bismarck's form of *Realpolitik* or its identification with Washington's warning against entangling alliances.

Conclusion

SUCCESS OR FAILURE?

Let us look again at Robert Osgood's conclusion about American diplomacy in his preface to Liska's *Imperial America* (1967): "American foreign policy in the first two decades of the cold war has been a striking success, judged by the normal standard of national security and power." Would he have said this five years later? What remains of the grounds on which he based his conclusion that:

> . . . even though the world of the mid-Sixties bears no resemblance to America's ideals of international harmony, the United States has achieved its proximal goal of containing the expansion of Communist control. The moderation of Soviet policy, the loosening of the Soviet bloc in Eastern Europe, the disruption of the Sino-Soviet bloc, the frustration of Communist China's expansionist ambition, and the failure of either of the principal Communist states to extend their domain by exploiting revolution in the backward areas—these developments fulfill the most critical objectives of the policy of containment enunciated twenty years ago. The United States is now clearly the most powerful state in the world by any criterion; it is the only global power."

The last sentence, typical of what was being said in the years following the second Cuban crisis, has manifestly ceased to be true, even if it was true at the time of writing. The 1972 SALT agreement gave the Soviet Union de facto superiority in both megatonnage and the number of ballistic missiles. Even if superiority at the higher level has not changed sides, with the number of multiple independently-targeted reentry vehicles (MIRV) offsetting American in-

148

feriority in number of missiles and power of warheads, the Soviet Union has now achieved equality. At the same time, the Soviet Union is developing its fleet so fast that when it puts aircraft carriers into service, it will have become a global power in the full sense of the term, even though its geopolitical situation seems less favorable in many respects than that of the United States.

The United States has not, of course, lost its lead in production, productivity, technological innovation, and living standards. However virulent anti-Americanism may be in many parts of the world, though perhaps in words only, it is the American republic that still attracts emigrants, intellectuals, and scientists. Russia's bureaucratic despotism no longer exerts the strange fascination of Stalinism's demoniac aspect; it neither terrifies nor seduces. Brezhnev seems to be engaging once more in the imperial venture outside the Old Continent, with his will to power apparently intact, whereas the leaders of the American republic, lacking bipartisan consensus, are at odds with the senators who, jealous of their prerogatives which had fallen into abeyance, are restricting the President's freedom of action where he, as commander-in-chief, wants a free hand. Power in the inter-state system depends as much on will as on resources; Western Europe as an entity possesses the resources but not the will; France or Britain alone does not possess the resources. The question is whether the willpower of one of the two states capable of playing a worldwide imperial role is not slackening.

The last sentence in the quotation from Osgood might be rephrased to convey a more realistic proposition, namely that the United States after twenty-five years of paramountcy is still the most productive economy in the world, is still the leader in scientific and technological progress, but has not been able to prevent the Soviet Union from hoisting itself to an equal level of military power, even if the Kremlin is paying for this equality by devoting a larger proportion of its national product to defense. There was only one global power in 1947; today there are two.

Osgood's other observations still hold good within the philosophy he explicitly professes. The United States has achieved its proximal goal of containing the expansion of Communist control almost everywhere. Not all critics of American diplomacy, however, would agree that containment has been an unqualified success. The interventions in Guatemala in 1953 and Santo Domingo in 1965 succeeded, but are they respectable morally or politically? If the intervention in Vietnam succeeds, that is to say maintains a non-Communist government in Saigon, will it be said that American diplomacy has been a success in Southeast Asia? In order to bring a less partial judgment to bear on the significance of containment, at least two other criteria must be borne in mind: the means employed and the nature of the areas so preserved from Communism.

If the second criterion is applied, an initial crude but valid distinction immediately becomes evident, namely that success in Europe required neither limited war, counterrevolution, nor the CIA. Communism, the Communism of Brezhnev as much as that of Stalin, would mean an economic, political, and moral "regression" in Western Europe, a lowering of living standards as well as loss of freedom.[1] The term "regression" does not imply an evolutionary philosophy of history, but refers to the aspirations of nations and even of the doctrinaires in both camps. Marxist-Leninists do not, of course, intend to lower productivity; they lower it by using a crude method of planning. They want all power to the Party, but individually they are well aware that all power can be equated with individual freedom only by a dialectical play on words.

The "revisionist" critics cannot condemn American diplomacy in Europe without repudiating the values of American, and indeed of Western, civilization. On the Old Continent economic aid and the Marshall Plan merely speeded up reconstruction and enabled the nations to establish the institutions which were desired by the vast majority of their people. It is only possible to talk of the failure of success in this case insofar as the European economies have become rivals to the American economy commercially. This obviously applies to Japan as well.

What are the arguments for the prosecution? That the success was easy to come by because the Soviet Union never harbored the ambitions ascribed to it by the cold warriors. In point of fact, Soviet diplomacy also probably achieved its proximal, if not its maximum, goal in Europe, namely to ensure that the *faits accomplis* of 1945–46 were preserved and consolidated. Instead of asking, as

---

[1] I shall be dealing in Part II with the "paramarxist" contention that the Old Continent suffers from the drawbacks of a monetary and trade system dominated by the United States.

the revisionists do, the puerile question of who is to blame, it would be better to drop the expression "cold war" once and for all or to admit that in part it consisted merely of reciprocal abuse. The Americans and British could not tolerate the sovietization of Eastern Europe without protest. Even if Stalin did not fear military action by the Americans, he had to isolate his *imperium,* exclude Western influence from it and refuse to permit any comparison between sovietization and Marshallization.

This version may ultimately come to be accepted when the Kremlin archives are opened. For the present, let us merely conclude that once American diplomacy in Europe had taken over from British diplomacy, it combined prudence and the defensive with determination and efficiency. Some will blame it for acquiescing too rapidly in the partition of Europe; I do not think Americans or Europeans ever gave their leaders a chance to "liberate" the Eastern European countries by threat or negotiation. For the time being, the outcome of the rivalry has been compromises and accommodation. The continued existence of a divided Europe amounts rather to a draw, in which both of the rivals chalk up successes and failures, and spheres of influence are accepted though covered up by universalist chatter.

Other critics complain of the contrast between rhetorical excess and moderation in action. What was the use of crusading talk and transforming Uncle Joe into a new Hitler when the policy-makers in Washington never in fact took the liberation slogans seriously? This is another aspect of American diplomacy which has barely been touched on here. It is as if policy-makers, members of Congress, and journalists feel that it is essential at times to conjure up popular fury against absolute evil for fear that opinion may refuse to support a diplomatic action very much like that of other states in its acceptance of reality and a realistic approach. McCarthyism, verbal hysteria, and domestic controversy, especially within the political element, ultimately gave the world and the Americans themselves a distorted view of Americans. The "McCarthy terror" as imagined by some Europeans fortunately never existed; but the excesses of McCarthyism paved the way for the current excesses of revisionism.

The policy-makers in Washington were probably not basically motivated by the crusading spirit, but it was reflected in the way in which the doctrine of containment was generally applied. This generalization was due partly to the anti-Communist obsession (but the Soviet Union at that time represented the principal rival, and the United States logically opposed the expansion of Soviet power, though it was too long identified with the power of any Communist party whatever) and partly to the Korean campaign.

At that time—1950—the diplomats in Washington could not but attribute part of, if not the sole and entire, responsibility for the North Korean aggression to Stalin. European opinion was still dubious about the value of the American guarantee. It was preparing to judge the United States by its reaction to what appeared to be a direct challenge, the violation by a regular army of a demarcation line laid down by agreement between the two super-powers. What was unfortunate for the United States and the world was not that Truman and Acheson took the decision to intervene with military force, but that they likewise decided to intervene in China in the final stages of its civil war by interposing the Seventh Fleet between the mainland and Taiwan and to support the French more resolutely in Indochina. Those decisions in June 1950 engendered the entire United States diplomacy in Asia for the next twenty years, including the Vietnam tragedy. The strategic mistake committed by Truman, at MacArthur's instigation, leading to the entry of the Chinese "volunteers" into Korea, caused the breach between Peking and Washington, the quarantining of Mao Tse-tung's China, and the grim determination, shared by Truman, Eisenhower, Kennedy, and Johnson, to halt the spread of Communism in Asia.

Here, too, the policy-makers rapidly resigned themselves to the defensive in the area in which they were confronting, or believed they were confronting, their rival, even if only through one of its satellites. After the Seventh Army's defeat on the Yalu in the fall of 1950, Truman and Acheson accepted a de facto draw. They broke off the 1951 spring offensive as soon as negotiations started. It was probably Stalin who saw some advantage in prolonging hostilities, or at least let his then allies in the Forbidden City demand that all Chinese prisoners should be returned to the mainland (a demand which the Americans could not accept). In the end, American diplomacy acquiesced in the preservation of the demarcation line in

Korea, but continued to apply the doctrine of containment, by force of arms if need be, all the more resolutely.

By an irony of history the United States' Asian diplomacy, though unreasonable in itself, nevertheless brought more (short-term) advantages than disadvantages until 1962–63. It contributed to the disputes between Peking and Moscow and created the circumstances in which the national interests and strategic concepts of the two major Communist powers were likely to diverge or clash. The Sino-Soviet dispute was tantamount to an American success; is it to be credited to Washington's diplomacy, as Osgood does?

Once the disruption of the Soviet bloc had set in, traditional and conventional wisdom suggested the resumption of relations with Peking in order to restore the normal processes of intercourse between states. Diplomatic relations, wrote Clausewitz, are never interrupted even when armies confront each other. To refuse intercourse in time of peace makes even less sense. Perhaps Mao Tse-tung might not have agreed from 1963 to 1966 to talk with Washington before it abandoned its alliance with Taiwan. Perhaps Nixon and Kissinger simply had the luck to arrive after the fighting on the Ussuri and the cultural revolution, when Chou En-lai had come into his own. Even if this conjecture were confirmed later, the inflexibility of American policy-makers in Vietnam, one after another, reveals an aspect of the American style which is due neither to the "Wilson syndrome," nor to crusading rhetoric, nor to the contrast between words and deeds. Truman did not answer Ho Chi-minh's letters, Acheson felt it necessary to raise a barrier after the Communist victory in China and proclaim "no further." Dulles put pressure on the French government to continue fighting in Indochina. Eisenhower and Dulles took the decision to bolster up South Vietnam and to eliminate the remnants of French influence and at length discover a non-Communist Vietnamese nationalism. In Kennedy's view, according to books by his friends, the United States was already committed too far, and he was obliged to accept his inheritance; there were less than 1,000 American advisers in Vietnam in late 1960, and more than 15,000 by the time of the President's assassination. From among conflicting counsels he had chosen a half measure. While refraining from sending in ground troops for the moment, he substantially strengthened the American

military presence, without any clear definition of the function of
these combatant-advisers. Johnson felt more than ever bound by his
inheritance. American democracy showed in this tragedy the extraordinary and fatal consistency of which it is capable.

It is a consistency that does not rule out a reversal of the pro to
the con, the swing between extremes evidenced by the attitude first
toward the Soviet Union and then toward Communist China. Red
China was all the rage in American circles in 1971, as if twenty
years of quarantine had merely been an interlude which could be
ended by a few games of ping-pong. This kind of obstinacy in an
enterprise in which even success could never compensate for the
human cost, first to Vietnam and then to the United States itself,
throws some light on the defects of the American diplomatic system
as it operated for twenty years; for outside Europe containment
was not an unreasonable or culpable objective as such. If Europeans
like to think so, it is simply out of selfishness or Eurocentrism
rather than clear-sightedness. What is unreasonable, however, is to
construe containment as a sort of categorical imperative and the
coming to power of any Marxist-Leninist party whatever as a defeat.
Although the decision-makers in Washington acquiesced in the
Communists' coming to power in Indochina in 1965, they won a
victory there without intervening, perhaps indeed by reason of
their abstention. The refusal to be defeated coupled with the pre-
dilection of presidents for a middle-of-the-road stance, unbounded
confidence in the ability of the greatest power in the world to solve
any "problem" whatever, the application of abstract schemata without sufficient acquaintance with local conditions, undue violence
and excessive use of the military machine, all of these ways of thinking and acting appeared in their worst light throughout this period.
To try for a military victory by the "search and destroy" strategy[2]
instead of by helping the South Vietnamese army to defend itself
by its own efforts was absurd. The idea that Chinese expansion was
being contained by forbidding North Vietnam to unify Annam,
Cochin China, and Tonkin by force was absurd. The doctrine of a
decisive and final test which would show these last of the romantics
the futility of wars of national liberation was absurd. The supposi-

---

[2] In any case, an expedition northward would have provided a better
prospect.

tion that bombing the North would break the will of the North Vietnamese—a supposition for which all intelligence reports declared there was no basis—was absurd.

The American presidents' advisers, as General Maxwell Taylor now admits, knew nothing of Vietnam and the Vietnamese or of their past and traditions. They reasoned in the abstract, from models; they demanded a bag of gimmicks and gadgets for a counterinsurgency transferred, strangely enough, to the North and against the North, when at the time—1965—even stopping infiltration would not have sufficed to restore security in the countryside and the Saigon government's authority in the South.

Just as the policy-makers in Washington could not put themselves in the place of others—of the North Vietnamese, in whose eyes there were not two countries or states, but only one—so negotiation on arms control could not succeed so long as the disparity was such that Robert McNamara, the secretary of defense, stated that he favored attacking the adversary's forces, not his cities, simultaneously asserting that the United States temporarily had the means to apply this doctrine. Were the Soviets likely to accept such a situation?

The Russians profited by circumstances to attain parity of nuclear weapons and to approach naval parity and perhaps achieve it. In 1964 the Soviet Union had about a hundred intercontinental missiles, six or seven times fewer than the United States. The United States has not exceeded the 1967 total of 1,054; the Soviets passed beyond it in 1969. The SALT agreement signed in Moscow allowed the Soviet Union a 40 percent numerical superiority in intercontinental missiles (1,408 against 1,000) and in missile-launching submarines (62 against 44), a 33 percent superiority in the number of missiles launched from submarines (950 against 710), and three times as large a megatonnage. At present the Americans are still numerically superior in warheads (5,700 against 2,500). If the Soviets succeed in producing MIRV, they could easily surpass the United States in number of warheads, so much heavier are the loads that their permitted missiles can carry.

Their consent to this agreement, indeed, displays the Americans' inconsistency rather than their consistency. Perhaps equality at this level no longer is meaningful. Perhaps the concept of "assured destruction" is enough to keep the balance of terror stable without impairing the will of the weaker at a critical moment. The Moscow agreement on strategic arms limitation provides, as it were, a counterpart to American obduracy in Vietnam; massive retaliation, flexible response, and arms control mark the stages in American thinking, culminating in a treaty which the Senate would never have ratified before the Vietnam tragedy and the revulsion of American opinion. Osgood's phrase about the United States as the only global power has a somewhat anachronistic ring to it.

At this point in the analysis the irony of history may perhaps help us once more to find success in failure. After twenty-five years, containment in Europe has led not to the victory of one side or the other, but to accommodation; could the Western states have hoped for more, at any rate in the brief term of a single generation? Similarly, without the frustrations of the Vietnam War, would American diplomacy have had the courage to break with its inheritance and taken the road back to Peking? An Asian subsystem is obviously forming before our eyes, within which four states, the Soviet Union, Japan, the United States, and China, will establish complex relations. In southern Asia, India is coming to be numbered among the great powers, while Japan will take care, for some time at least, not to be one. The ubiquity of American diplomacy was due in part less to a will to power than to the suction of a vacuum. Failure becomes success because it induces withdrawal, teaches modesty, and prepares the way for an equilibrium among states.

History has not refuted the reasons on which Osgood based his judgment by the wave of a magic wand. The *guerrilleros* have not repeated Fidel Castro's exploit in any Latin American country. Governments, whether civilian or military, are becoming more and more nationalistic, and in some cases more and more anti-American, but none of them professes Marxism-Leninism. Allende's government in Chile did not abandon constitutional methods. In the Sixties, when the United States was hobbled by Vietnam, disturbances were rife within nations and violence became endemic in town and country in the wealthy as well as the poor countries. The Soviet world presented a façade of authority and order, if not law, to the outside world, but it no longer proffered the tidings of salvation to youth in quest of the absolute. Far less than it did twenty-five years ago does it stimulate the hopes of the disinherited and the faith of the revolutionaries. There is a new equilibrium in the inter-state system, and the messianism of conquest is less virulent; when George Kennan wrote his article on containment, was he opening up any other perspective?

As the paramount state, the United States has not ruled. It made strategic mistakes, as all strategists do, in Korea and Vietnam; it profited by its rival's mistakes in Yugoslavia and China, just as the Soviets cashed in on American mistakes. The American ambassador's support of Batista for years and its abrupt withdrawal enabled Fidel Castro to attain power. But Castro permitted the missile crisis, and his regime has degenerated into a mini-Stalinism, without the success of the Five-Year Plans, to such a degree as to deter other Latin Americans from following the same road. Washington's resumption of relations with Havana would suffice to deprive Fidelismo of the little prestige it still has; here is success through failure.

Before summing up, two questions must still be posed, one concerning the future, the other providing the main theme of the second part of this essay. To what end is the Soviet Union going to direct its military strength? Will the United States agree to play its necessary part in the inter-state system when the system calls for the traditional practices of European (or eternal) diplomacy without a crusading spirit and without exercising omnipotence?

American diplomacy succeeded in Europe not only because it contained Communism, but because it promoted economic progress and human liberty. The Bay of Pigs landing was a twofold failure, both political and moral; the intervention in Santo Domingo was both a military and a short-term political success, but the moral cost probably outweighed the benefit. Apart from these spectacular episodes, does the success of containment entail success or failure for other nations? When is it a success and when a failure? It all depends on the regime which succeeds in surviving, by itself or with American support.

PART TWO

The United States in the World Market:
The Privileges and Constraints of a Dominant Economy

Introduction

In the first part of this essay I have dealt with diplomacy in the broad but classical sense of relations between government and government (or state and state), including alliances, wars, crises, and military interventions. In essentials my examination of "diplomatico-strategic action" does not differ from that which those responsible for its conduct give (or gave at the time) in public or private. So long as they regarded the inter-state system as bipolar and the Soviet Union as their foremost rival, the notion of "containment" everywhere and at all times logically determined the end, if not the means.

American diplomacy undoubtedly passed through many different phases between the Yalta and Potsdam Conferences in 1945 and President Nixon's visit to Moscow in May 1972. But it remains intelligible throughout all its mutations once the Russo-American rivalry is interpreted as Washington appears to have interpreted it after 1947—as rivalry indeed, but directed toward at least reaching agreement on the ground rules and the basic principles for co-existence rather than toward renewing the wartime alliance against the Third Reich. No postwar or cold war president ever seriously contemplated translating the doctrine of "rollback" *into action*. The propaganda warfare obscured the de facto acceptance of the *faits accomplis* in postwar Eastern Europe. After 1960 nuclear weapons justified and confirmed a curious alliance between rivals against a common enemy, nuclear warfare itself. Russians and Americans mutually respected each others' vital interests. Rightly or wrongly, people gained an impression that the great powers were using the small powers to fight their battles by proxy.

This behavior by both sides was "rational" and consistent with one of the aspects of the bipolar system, which entails a death struggle between the two claimants either to universal empire or, after a fairly long period of limited conflicts, to the delimitation of spheres of influence and the emergence of new centers of power. At the time of writing, new centers of power have emerged, but the spheres of influence outside Europe are still no more clearly delimited than they were twenty-five years ago. On the contrary, the Soviet Union, having itself become a global power, with a fleet and combat forces present on every ocean and in every part of the globe, is perhaps presenting a challenge which the United States does not seem in the mood to accept.

This traditional aspect of inter-state relations, as I have noted in the introduction, is only one side of the coin. The suspension of dollar convertibility in August 1971 is as symbolic of the end of the postwar period as Nixon's pilgrimages to Moscow and Peking. The crisis of the international monetary system is quite as much an element in high policy as the Marshall Plan. And over and above this, the foreign subsidiaries of General Motors and IBM, though private persons in law, are to be seen as an integral part of the external action of the United States. The economic, ideological, and political relationships between persons and groups who are members of different spheres of sovereignty exert and at the same time are subject to too much influence in inter-state relations for specialists in diplomatic history to confine themselves to chanceries, ministries, conferences, treaties, the thunder of guns, and the rhetoric of peace.

I cannot within the confines of this essay examine the influence of American society in its entirety on the rest of the world. To simplify matters, let me say that each of the following chapters approaches much the same problem from different angles. Within the Atlantic Alliance the United States exercised hegemony in the true sense, what Americans themselves call "leadership." Within the framework of the inter-state system it enjoyed predominance because of its superior economic resources and military equipment. It made little use of this predominance to the detriment of the Soviet Union, but rather employed it to consolidate its own positions and to do its best to bar any transgression of a demarcation line.

Had this diplomacy, apparently directed toward order and stability, in fact some other aim in view? Were its causes other than they seemed? Were its military hegemony in the West and its global predominance serving some quite different purpose? Can the *reality* of American diplomacy, over and above the Korean and Vietnam wars, be deduced, as the Marxist and "paramarxist" revisionists deduce it, from the statistics for investment and trade and from the expansion of the network of the subsidiaries of the banks and conglomerates?

Chapter One

FREEDOM OF PERSONS OR FREEDOM
OF TRADE: THE ECONOMIC FOUNDATIONS
OF AMERICAN DIPLOMACY

The classic works on imperialism by J. A. Hobson, Rudolf Hilferding, W. Langer, and Lenin were published around the turn of this century and deal with Europe's colonial expansion in Africa toward the end of the preceding century and the apparent or real division of the world among the national capitalisms and the great joint-stock companies on the eve of the First World War. The debates did not turn on the actual expansion of the private companies or spheres of influence, for states made no secret of their conquests nor the companies of their investments. What historians were engaged with was the relationship between conflicts of economic interests, the seizure of sovereignty in Africa, and the explosion in 1914. The Marxist or "paramarxist" critics denounced the "exploitation" of the world by European and American capitalists and attributed the disaster in which Europe sacrificed millions of its sons and permanently lost its supremacy to the ruthless competition between the exploiters. By a kind of historical nemesis, Europe, they claimed, owed its riches and subsequent ruin to the avidity for profits of the monster called capitalism. Only the more unrealistic among them, even those who relied upon Marx, had persuaded themselves that national capitalists *could have* come to an agreement on an equitable distribution of profits, whereas a compromise of this sort would quite obviously have been better for Europeans, whether victors or vanquished, than a death struggle.

"Paramarxist" revisionism, or to put it another way perhaps, the paramarxist interpretation of American diplomacy, is now no longer expounded in pamphlets like Lenin's nor in learned treatises like Hobson's. The tomes by Claude Julien, W. A. Williams, Gabriel

Kolko, and Harry Magdoff do nevertheless outline a theory of American imperialism, in Lenin's sense of the term—that is to say, the necessary and inevitable expansion of capitalism or of industrial economies based on the private ownership of the means of production.

The theory of imperialism based on Lenin's interpretation as applied to the American diplomacy of 1945 onward has to take account of European decolonization and has consequently radically to dissociate the notions of colonialism and imperialism, as Magdoff does.[1] Imperialism does not disappear from the scene, however, if defined as the worldwide expansion of the banks and big corporations through direct foreign investment. For nobody, be he liberal or Marxist, pro- or anti-American, questions the facts; as the dominant economy, the United States holds a position in the capitalist world market comparable to that of Great Britain in the mid-nineteenth century. The dollar serves as a transnational currency. Subsidiaries of the great American corporations appear in every country in the world. The banks weave a network of branches throughout the area of the globe that is open to their transactions.

The debate turns substantially on three points: How far is the diplomatico-strategic behavior studied in Part I of this essay *determined* by the interests of the American economy? To what extent does the United States use its military supremacy to secure economic privileges? What, on balance, are the advantages and drawbacks of American supremacy to the other countries? These three questions cannot be treated in strict isolation. However, this chapter deals mainly with the first, and the following chapters will deal with the rest.

1.

At first glance, the economic interpretation of American diplomacy comes up against a decisive objection, that no national entity except the Soviet Union appears so nearly self-sufficient as the United States. The ratio of its foreign trade to its gross national product is very low: $43.5 billion for exports and $45.6 billion for imports as compared with a national product of over $1,000

---

[1] Harry Magdoff, *The Age of Imperialism: The Economics of United States Foreign Policy* (New York: Monthly Review Press, 1969), p. 39.

billion (in current dollars), or between 4 and 5 percent.[2] Even to-day Robert W. Tucker, a moderate advocate of a return to isolationism, uses these figures to show that there is nothing to prevent the United States from taking politico-military external action of a radically different nature, based on the ancient principle of "no entangling alliances."

The "paramarxists" reply to this argument by quoting other figures, which appear in practically identical form in all the various books mentioned above (Magdoff, Kolko, Julien).

So far as raw materials are concerned, the United States became a fairly large importer after 1940. Imports and exports of raw materials more or less balanced out in 1920–29; from 1940 to 1950 the United States was a net importer by about 5.4 percent; and from 1950 to 1960 this percentage rose to 12.8. Even though domestic reserves are not yet exhausted, the United States prefers to hoard them and procure its supplies abroad to guard against unforeseen contingencies. Though the aggregate percentage is relatively low, it rises appreciably in the case of certain ores; net imports as compared with domestic extraction are 43 percent for iron, 18 for copper, 131 for lead, 140 for zinc, and 638 for bauxite. The ratio of imports to consumption is high in the case of certain strategic materials: 24 percent for tungsten, 100 for columbium, 75 for nickel, 100 for chrome, 100 for cobalt.[3]

Other figures show the importance of foreign markets to American industry, an importance which is commonly underrated. To take manufactured goods alone, domestic sales in 1964 were $203 billion as against $20 billion for exports, or roughly 10 percent. If to the exports are added sales by foreign-based United States' firms, about $37 billion, the total comes to $57 billion, or about 25 percent of domestic sales of manufactured goods. Furthermore, total sales abroad—exports plus production by foreign-based American firms—are increasing faster than domestic sales. Taking 1950 as the base figure, the index for total foreign sales is 367 and for domestic sales 226.[4]

The uneven growth rates are readily accounted for by the higher

---

[2] Exports ($ billion): 42.770 (1971), 47.391 (1972); imports: 45.459 (1971), 54.355 (1972); GNP: 1,050 (1971), 1,152 (1972).
[3] Figures from Magdoff, *Age of Imperialism*, pp. 47–48 and 50–52.
[4] *Ibid.*, p. 180.

rate of profit from foreign investment. Between 1950 and 1965 total profits from investments abroad rose from $2.1 billion to $7.8 billion (in 1965), while the profits (after tax) of domestic non-financial corporations rose only from $21.7 billion to $36.1 billion, or in other words, they multiplied more than 3.5 times in the one case and by slightly more than 70 percent in the other.[5] For many reasons, the tax system in particular, the average return on a dollar invested abroad was higher than that on a dollar invested at home.

Another set of statistics combining exports and Federal government purchases (most of them connected with defense and consequently with foreign policy) clinches the case. In almost all industries the proportion of total production accounted for by exports and Federal purchases averages between 20 and 25 percent—22.6 for iron and steel, 22.4 for nonferrous heavy industry, 44.7 for nonferrous ore extraction, 45.5 for radio, television, and communications equipment, 45.5 for electronic components and accessories[6] Industry, in the narrow sense of manufacturing, depends, therefore, to a large extent on foreign markets and government purchases.

If we look back for a moment at these three sets of statistics, we can see that the United States has become a net importer of primary commodities,[7] though it still exports some commodities, especially foodstuffs. The United States unquestionably consumes a volume of raw materials entirely disproportionate to the ratio of its population to world population: "With 6 percent of the world's population the United States consumes 33 percent of the world production of bauxite, 40 percent of the nickel, 13 percent of the manganese, 36 percent of the tungsten, asbestos and copper, 41 percent of the tin, 23 percent of the zinc, 14 percent of the iron and lead, 28 percent of the potassium, and 50 percent of the coffee." The Japanese and Europeans have far less raw materials in their subsoil; nevertheless they do not conduct a militant American-style diplomacy. The volume of raw materials consumed depends on the degree of industrialization. The underdeveloped countries at present dread a reduction in consumption, and there-

---

[5] *Ibid.*, p. 183.
[6] *Ibid.*, p. 188.
[7] It is also a net importer of energy.

fore in raw materials purchases, in consequence of an economic recession. They are not yet contemplating the consequences of an absolute scarcity of nonrenewable resources. So that when Claude Julien observes that "the disparity in technology and management methods is real, but infinitely less than the disparity between the ability of the United States and other countries to exploit the whole world's raw materials for its profit,"[8] he is falsifying the data of the problem. Nobody denies that industry, and therefore the consumption of raw materials, are unevenly distributed. The uneven consumption of raw materials is the result of uneven industrialization, not the other way around.

The dependence of certain branches of industry on markets abroad is the obvious corollary of the American economy's dependence on raw materials. It is easy enough for Julien to give a list of the industries in which exports account for a large proportion of the production, such as 24 percent for machine tools, 23 percent for oil-drilling equipment, 36 percent for sewing machines, and so on.[9] Every country in the Western world is equally dependent in this respect. What conclusion does this lead to? Certainly not the conclusion drawn by Julien that "if deprived of their markets abroad, these branches of industry would have to reduce production by 15 to 30 percent or even more, and the effects of this reduction would affect the whole of industry." This implies that production factors are nonmobile and nonsubstitutable—which is nonsense. What conclusion would this sort of reasoning lead to in the case of a survey of the economic situation in Germany or Japan? As a component of the world economy, the American economy could not isolate itself without experiencing considerable disturbance, though it would be less serious than that which Japan or Germany would undergo in similar circumstances.

There remains the last argument, or rather the last and the most important fact, that of United States' direct investment throughout the world and the network of its industrial and banking subsidiaries in Europe, Asia, and America. The United States was certainly an importer of capital until the First World War. Even in 1950 the book value of American investments abroad did not

---

[8] *L'Empire américain* (Paris: Grasset, 1968), p. 223.
[9] *Ibid.*, p. 222.

yet amount to as much as $12 billion, when the national product was $284 billion. The volume of American investment has increased considerably in the past twenty years and its distribution has changed. The total book value as estimated by the *Survey of Current Business* (October 1971) was about $78 billion, including $24.5 billion in Western Europe, $22.8 billion in Canada, $1.5 billion in Japan, and $14.7 billion in Latin America; that is to say, Canada's share had remained stable at about 30 percent, Latin America's had fallen from about 40 percent in 1950 to under 20 percent in 1970, while Europe's had more than doubled.

What had happened? In the early phase American investment had gone mainly to countries in the Western Hemisphere, which had seemed the normal area for expansion, and capital had been invested preferentially in the primary sector. Since 1960 the big American corporations have continued to invest in mines and oil fields in Canada and the Middle East but also, and primarily, in manufacturing industry in Western Europe, both in the free trade area and the Common Market.

The figures illustrate an equally incontrovertible fact, one stressed by Julien. In the past fifteen years the book value of American investments in Europe increased from year to year with the reinvestment of a large proportion of the profits and an influx of new capital. Moreover, the value of repatriated profits was regularly lower than the combined value of the reinvested profits and additional investment. In Latin America the ratio was inverse. There the proportion of profits repatriated was regularly higher than the ratio of investments to the total.[10] The developing countries, particularly those in Latin America, have suffered the consequences of this reversal, which is certainly incompatible with the aims officially pursued by the United States government. Repatriating profits aggravates the poorer countries' balance of payments difficulties, while reinvesting profits enhances the value of the American subsidiaries in Europe. But no third alternative to repatriation or reinvestment exists. Both courses give rise to a great deal of adverse criticism. There would be far less of it if only the position were reversed so that the poorer countries enjoyed the benefits of

---

[10] Christian Goux and Jean-François Landeau, *Le Péril américain* (Paris: Calmann-Levy, 1971), pp. 30ff.

reinvestment and the repatriation of profits was confined to the relatively wealthier countries.

2.

The salient features in the past twenty-five years—the brief span of American predominance—have been the dissolution of the colonial empires built up by the European countries, the diplomacy of "containment," and the expansion of American banks and conglomerates. Historians will not contend that there was necessarily a chain of cause and effect between American predominance and the dissolution of the European empires, or at any rate assign more than a partial responsibility to that predominance. It was the weakening of metropolitan countries, the march of ideas, and the anticolonialism of the Marxist-Leninist countries that created the context in which the Europeans' withdrawal became inevitable. Winston Churchill said that he did not wish to preside over the dissolution of the British Empire, and the electors took him at his word. Franklin Roosevelt displayed a more determined hostility to the British than to the Soviet empire; whether he meant to or not, he served Great Britain's lasting interests very well by inducing it solemnly to pledge independence to India. How much bloodshed would have been avoided had he managed to induce General de Gaulle to make a similar pledge to Indochina or had the leader of Free France undertaken that commitment himself!

What link, then, is to be detected between American predominance, the diplomacy of containment, and the expansion of the big corporations? American predominance was based on economic superiority (the highest per capita product in the world), technological and scientific superiority (nuclear weapons, ballistic missiles, and science-based industries), and military superiority, itself the product of the first two. The size of the national product enabled the United States to maintain naval and air supremacy without inflicting hardships on its citizens or appreciably slowing down the rise in the standard of living (at least until 1965).

It was the United States' economic, technological, and military supremacy as defined above that *made possible* the diplomacy of containment simultaneously with the expansion of the banks and conglomerates—a conclusion, in point of fact, virtually self-evident. The diplomacy of containment required the military and economic resources resulting from supremacy or predominance, while the prerequisite for external investment was some kind of superiority, without which the banks and conglomerates would not have found it worthwhile to set up subsidiaries or buy up European firms.

To my mind, this raises a number of questions: 1. Was the purpose of containment the expansion of capital or, conversely, was the latter used to promote the former? 2. Would other countries have tolerated the expansion of American capitalism and capital unless the United States had enjoyed military superiority? 3. Was the expansion of American capital dictated by an internal necessity of the American economy? The answers to these questions are neither obvious nor easy. The historical movements thus distinguished for the purposes of analysis are not *logically* implicit in each other, but they are interrelated and they extend over one and the same period. No one can distinguish precisely what in inter-state relations and international economic relations is due to military supremacy or to economic superiority. It is, however, possible and necessary to dispel some of the mythologies and demonologies in which they have been enveloped.

Let me first come back to, and dispose of, the argument about raw materials to which I alluded above and to which so much space is given in Claude Julien's book. I should remind the reader of a point which no Frenchman or any other European should forget, that while the Americans consume more raw materials per capita than any other people, the Europeans and Japanese import more than they consume. To take only the most instructive example: the big American oil companies have acquired a leading position in the Middle East, Iran, Saudi Arabia, and the Emirates of the Persian Gulf, and have to some extent driven out the British companies. But the prosperity of Europe to an even greater extent depends on the oil under the sands on which Arab peoples live than that of the United States. Access to the richest fields in the world, those in the Middle East, will be a vital matter to Europe for some twenty years to come, while the main issue for the United States was profit, at any rate until 1970.

The Japanese and Europeans base their prosperity on the consumption of raw materials purchased abroad and converted into

manufactured goods; they sell some of these goods abroad in order
to obtain the foreign currency they need for buying raw materials.
Japanese and Europeans buy and sell with no intent of conquest
or wish to garrison distant parts of the earth. Why should the
United States alone among the industrialized countries have to
mount guard on the thirty-eighth parallel in Korea and the corner
of the Potsdamerstrasse in Berlin? Claude Julien should ponder
the implications of his argument. One of two things must hold
good: Either military supremacy alone enables the industrialized
countries of the West to buy the raw materials which they cannot
do without—and in that case, the American cold war extremists
are right in their belief that the United States is defending the
entire West in arms and that Europeans must assume their share,
financially at least, in this essential and common task—or producers
are glad to sell their raw materials to the industrialized countries—
which is what appearances provisionally confirm;[11] and in that
case, the United States has no need of a thousand Minuteman
missiles and a dozen aircraft carriers to purchase abroad a portion,
and still a comparatively small portion at that even now, of the
raw materials for processing by its industries.

The doctrine of living space became very fashionable between
the Wars, especially in the Thirties in consequence of the Great
Depression. Hitler's diplomacy invoked the imperatives of *Lebensraum* and Japanese diplomacy harbored ambitions for a Greater
East Asia Co-Prosperity Sphere. The contrary doctrine—that there
is no need for colonies and no need for military hegemony in order to grow and grow rich—confirmed by the examples of the
Netherlands, the Federal Republic of Germany, Japan, and France
—is unanimously or almost unanimously endorsed. If this is true
for the vanquished or the secondary powers, why should it be false
for the dominant state (unless, once again, the secondary powers
misconstrue the essential role of the dominant state)?

The reference to access to raw materials which appears in the
Atlantic Charter can have two different implications. As a result
of the world crisis and the disintegration of the international economy, some countries feared that they might not have the foreign

---

[11] I deliberately say "appearances" rather than "reality" and add "provisionally." I revert later to some complications of the problem.

currency they needed for buying raw materials. This fear lent some sort of rationality to the Hitlerian and Japanese doctrines of *Lebensraum* and the Co-Prosperity Sphere; the enlargement of the sphere of sovereignty, virtual sovereignty or the monetary unit area, would reduce dependence on outside sources. The remarkable growth in international trade in the past twenty-five years has led to a radical revision of thinking and policies; European and Japanese do their utmost to buy raw materials wherever they are cheapest. The Americans might do likewise without resorting to their proconsuls or the CIA.

Others interpret access to raw materials to mean freedom to purchase and the consequent obligation on producers not to refuse to sell. Apart from conceivable but exceptional cases (such as a monopoly-type agreement among all producers of certain products which consumers cannot do without, as when the oil-producer countries blackmail higher prices out of the Europeans or Japanese), the refusal to sell is only likely to be a danger at some future date when a real scarcity of nonrenewable resources actually sets in. What critics have quite properly denounced in the past twenty-five years was the oversupply of some primary commodities with the consequent fall in their prices relative to the price of manufactures, or in other words, a deterioration in the terms of trade for many developing countries.

Is there any merit in the further argument put forward by Claude Julien and the American "paramarxists" to the effect that "American prosperity is largely based on the cheap exploitation of the Third World's natural resources and the repatriation to the United States of profits drawn from the underdeveloped countries"?[12] The United States already had the highest per capita product and standard of living at the time when it was a net exporter of primary commodities and a net debtor (not net creditor) relative to the rest of the world, that is, just before World War I.

Let us restrict ourselves for the moment to the question of raw materials and their prices; regardless of whether the latter are held to be fair or not (fair in relation to what criterion?), they are not the major cause of American prosperity, for the simple reason that raw materials account for only a fairly small proportion (10 to 15

---

[12] Julien, *L'Empire américain,* p. 386.

percent at most) of the national product. The most telling criticism against the industrialized countries is based on precisely the opposite argument, that they could pay considerably more for primary commodities without impairing their prosperity. There can be no doubt that the United States profited in the nineteenth century from the abundant supply of land and raw materials available to a sparse population. The ratio between land and man stimulated economy of labor and accumulation of capital, resulting in a large added value per worker. Despite its natural resources the Soviet Union has not achieved a comparable productivity per person employed. All Claude Julien's half-truths and basic errors culminate in the following passage, a model of confusion and muddleheadedness:

> It is not true that, as Senator Fulbright proposes, America can renounce its empire and "utilize" its huge resources to give the world an example of an affluent civilization. In order to preserve this affluence it must, on the contrary, keep its access to the immense resources of the entire world, the major(!) part of which it consumes to gratify 6 percent of the world's population. America does not yet realize that the American Dream is dead. It could be resuscitated only by abandoning empire. And abandoning empire does not mean renouncing some abstract will to power. It means renouncing the copper, bauxite, nickel, chromite, manganese, tin, lead, and other mines which America is exploiting all over the world in order to make the American way of life an inimitable example. To abandon empire would be to deprive America of its status as a privileged consumer in order to achieve a more equitable distribution of the raw materials consumed throughout the world.[13]

What does "renounce its empire" mean? Julien nowhere defines this empire precisely, but transmogrifies it into a sort of Beast of the Apocalypse, failing to make any distinction between direct investment, military bases, economic or intellectual influence, and CIA intrigues. Of course the United States, like the other industrialized countries of the West, though in their case to a lesser

---

[13] *Ibid.*, p. 386.

degree, needs to "keep its access to the resources of the entire world." It would not lose this access if the American corporations exploiting the copper and lead mines in Latin America were nationalized; the nationalized corporation replacing the American conglomerate's subsidiary does not refuse to sell, and often does not even get better prices. The loss of repatriated profits does not seriously affect the American economy as a whole, or even, in most cases, the conglomerate, which is insured by the Federal government against nationalization. The uneven consumption of raw materials is due to the uneven distribution of industry, and hence of wealth. Would a "renunciation of empire" change this distribution?

The real question, which goes much further than this purple passage in a pamphlet for consumption by Leftists only, turns on the relationship between military supremacy and capitalist expansion, or to put it more precisely, between the diplomacy of containment and capitalist expansion. Is what the United States is defending the free world or a world open to a free economy? The question need only be put in these terms to see how hard it is to answer it categorically one way or the other.

If the policy-makers in Washington set out deliberately to create an international context favorable to the expansion of their economy, their general aim would be to limit the areas closed to their goods and capital. When a Marxist-Leninist party comes to power, the usual result, at least initially, is that trade with capitalist countries falls off, foreign investment is prohibited, and bureaucratic regulation replaces the free market. The motives of American diplomacy are economic where its action is designed to prevent a Marxist-Leninist party from coming to power. But then its motives are also political or strategic, because once a Marxist-Leninist party is master of the state, it tends to take sides against the United States and the Western and capitalist countries. So long as the rivalry between the two super-powers was total—each of them carrying with it a form of organization, a way of life, and an ideology of its own—the two aims could not be totally dissociated. Within the bipolar system prevailing during the past twenty-five years the United States has defined its national interest not in the restrictive sense—the physical security of its people and the stability of its institutions—but in the broad sense—securing a milieu favorable to its ideas, goods, and investments.[14]

On the basis of this definition, free world and world with a free economy tend to merge into one another. Not that the United States has invariably protected countries with liberal institutions nor that it has not at times protected despotic regimes in order to checkmate Marxist-Leninist parties. What stands in the way of a decision between the two propositions—containment for the benefit of capitalist expansion or priority to containment over economic interests—is, *in a total perspective,* the fact that the ultimate aim deliberately chosen by American diplomacy was to set bounds to the area of sovietized countries, without, at least until recently, distinguishing among a Communist regime, hostility to the United States, and alignment with the anti-imperialist camp. An anti-Sovietism of this sort found quite as much justification in the logic of the political and ideological competition between the two superpowers as in the logic of capitalist expansion.

How, then, are we to choose between these two logics? Certainly not by quoting statements by politicians who use arguments calculated to convince the Senate committees they are addressing and language which does not reveal what is at the back of their minds. I can therefore see only two ways to try to dissociate, in part at least, the economic purpose from the diplomatico-strategic purpose in the external action of the United States: To examine the specific cases in which the facts enable at least a probable distinction to be drawn and to analyze the factors within American society itself which determine its diplomacy.

3.

The paleo-imperialism of the European states combined the glory of empire with the profits derived from its exploitation; the neo-imperialism of the United States, if imperialism it be, has no need to replace the rulers of independent states with its own administrators. Quite the reverse; it rejects a costly responsibility inconsistent with the spirit of the age and economic sense.

---

[14] The reader is at liberty to choose the order he thinks most appropriate for the sequence of "ideas," "goods," and "investments."

Thinking along these lines, it would be quite easy to present American anticolonialism as a devious form of imperialism (or at least of will to power), for a world without frontiers is a situation in which the strongest capitalism prevails. Only a weak capitalism keeps special preserves of its own and tries to keep out its rivals by hoisting its flag on public buildings. The dominant economy, British in the nineteenth century, American in the twentieth, normally banks on the market and free trade, and at all events on the most-favored-nation clause.[15]

This sort of interpretation of American anticolonialism gives ample rein to Hegel's theory of the Cunning of Reason, *Die List der Vernunft*. It perceives by hindsight an economic rationality which was not perceived at the time by those engaged in the action. American anticolonialism seems to me to derive from an ideological tradition, a conventional view of the nation's history. Roosevelt did not conceal, either in private or at times even in public, his hostility to the British empire in India and the French empire, especially in the Far East. It took some time in Washington for the fear of Communism to prevail over dislike of French colonialism in Indochina. American leaders, from Roosevelt to Johnson by way of Truman and Kennedy, were not thinking about the expansion of trade or capital investment when they advised or forced their allies to grant independence to India, Indonesia, Indochina, and Algeria; thus they could act with a clear conscience. It was a fact too that the new states, even India, represented, at least in the short run, only a meager addition to the world market; the transition from British sovereignty to independence did not appreciably change the terms for the purchase or sale of goods or even the opportunities for direct investment.

If an economic interpretation of decolonization is really insisted on, it is better not to concentrate on the motives of American diplomacy, but to view the historical developments as a whole, the disappearance of all the European empires in Asia and Africa within a single generation. The proximate cause was obviously the Second World War and the economic, military, and moral decline of the metropolitan countries. But at the same time the facts proved that

---

[15] The case of the United States, in the twentieth century at least, shows how complex the problem is. American opinion's conversion to free trade is recent and precarious.

the liberals were right (for how long is arguable); sovereignty as practiced by the Europeans no longer paid. Henceforth it entailed obligations of which the Western powers wished to rid themselves and which they could only with difficulty fulfill. Westerners and non-Westerners became conscious of the disparity between standards of living and the simultaneous existence of peoples whose per capita income was less than $100 and peoples with an income of $4,000. However misleading the unwarranted precision of such comparisons, the international organizations talk in such terms and deduced from these figures the imperative need for development. In the past, the rulers' consciences were tranquil if they used their power to fulfill their elementary duties of keeping order and the peace, directly or through traditional chiefs, to extract raw materials and sell manufactured goods, and to educate a limited elite in the Western manner to carry on the administration to educate in the future. Depending on circumstances or the metropolitan country, the colonizers prided themselves either on respecting traditional cultures or, conversely, on leading the natives out into the enlightenment of civilization. They built the infrastructure of what the twentieth century calls development, such as roads, railways, and schools. They calculated neither the national product nor per capita income; no universal conscience held them accountable. By an irony of history or a hidden logic, the super-powers' anticolonialism precipitated the Europeans' retirement at the very time when they could no longer elude the conditions attaching to sovereignty and were prepared to spend more than they had in the past on developing their possessions. American anticolonialism, as an integral part of the American republic's national conscience, was consonant with the exigencies of the postwar economy and coincided with *both* the true interest of the European nations and the claims of the native peoples, or of the minorities vocal on their behalf.

In this first instance economic logic harmonizes, it seems to me, with the American view of the world; once the occupation of the land, the expulsion of the Indians, and the conquest of the Spanish and later the Mexican provinces had been forgotten, the independence of the thirteen colonies and the creation of the Commonwealth made the United States "the first new nation."

The instance of the Marshall Plan, a quite different matter, does lend itself to a strictly economic interpretation, but this interpretation lacks probability. In the phase of reconstruction immediately after the war the Marshall Plan and the needs of the European economies aggravated inflationary tensions. Since the grants or loans to the Western European countries were financed out of taxes, the Federal government could have spent at home the sums it raised from private incomes. A "surplus production" in the absolute sense has never been readily incorporated in any scheme of economic system; quite certainly no responsible decision-maker in Washington in 1947–48 feared a production surplus in any branch of industry or a surplus of capital in search of remunerative employment. The purchasing power neutralized in wartime and inherited from it created a surplus of aggregate demand.

Molotov, as a good Marxist, may have believed that a loan to the Soviet Union would help the American economy to operate at full capacity and counter unemployment. European propaganda against the Marshall Plan used the same kind of argument, with the additional argument that the grants or loans were a cover for an attempted "colonization" (whatever that meant). But *in point of fact* direct investments in Europe by the American corporations did not go hand in hand with the Marshall Plan, but started to flourish only in 1955 and onward, that is to say several years later, attracted primarily by the acceleration of European growth and the prospect of the Common Market. The objectives which the framers of the Marshall Plan set themselves were the rehabilitation of the ruined countries and the reconstruction of the European economies with a view to containing Communism and reducing the dangers of domestic subversion.[16] Naturally, containment, a legitimate and reasonable political objective, itself coincided with the economic objective, since an extension of the Communist regimes in Europe would have led to a shrinkage of the area of capitalist or liberal economy open to American-type transactions.

In certain specific cases the United States subordinated commercial considerations to political or political-military reasons of state. Although the conditions for trading with countries with a Soviet system are not the same as those for trading with the free world,

---

[16] I refrain from mentioning the purely human desire to help the Europeans widespread among the bulk of ordinary Americans; I assume as a matter of principle that policy-makers in all countries do not harbor such sentiments.

trade nevertheless continued. Since the thaw after Stalin's death the Western European countries have sought outlets for their manufactures in Eastern Europe far more eagerly than the United States has. Americans showed no visible desire to trade with the Soviet Union until Nixon initiated a new policy; it was the United States that imposed an embargo on so-called military and strategic exports, and it, too, quarantined trade with Communist China. American industry had aided the "building of socialism" with its capital and technology at the same time of the first Soviet Five Year Plan. Many heads of corporations would not hesitate to sell the Soviet Union the latest model of computer tomorrow, some of them because they take no interest in politics, others because they share the conviction of an "Americanized paramarxism" or "rejuvenated liberalism," that trade is the weapon of peace. American capitalists changed less than American diplomats between the first Five Year Plan and the summit meeting in May 1972. James Burnham is not without grounds when he reverses the usual interpretation and speaks of the suicidal tendencies of capitalists.

Some writers, like Magdoff, simply give up any idea of accounting in detail for diplomatic or military action by economic interest. This is reasonable enough, but leaves only the total interpretation which in turn explains nothing, since political purpose and economic purpose coincide in the objective of containment. An all-inclusive explanation is no explanation at all.

Other writers, such as Gabriel Kolko,[17] try to confer on the Vietnam War some sort of rationality in the absence of morality. But they manage to do so only by adopting the domino theory. The disproportion between the profits which the United States can derive from Vietnam and the cost of the war seems to make nonsense of the economic interpretation. The concurrence of views is, to my mind, instructive. There is only one way of reducing or eliminating the discrepancy, and both Walter Rostow and Gabriel Kolko resort to it—the domino theory.

Kolko is very free with the references to raw materials he can quote from official documents and politicians' statements. He also cites the following statement made by David Bruce, the United

---

[17] *The Roots of American Foreign Policy* (Boston: Beacon Press, 1969), pp. 88–131.

States ambassador to France, to an American Senate committee that "there is no question that if Indochina went, the fall of Burma and the fall of Thailand would be absolutely inevitable. No one can convince me, for what it is worth, that Malaya wouldn't follow shortly thereafter and India . . . would . . . also find the Communists making infiltrations."[18]

In the same vein, Eisenhower wrote in his memoirs:

> The loss of all Vietnam, together with Laos on the west and Cambodia on the southwest, would have meant the surrender to Communist enslavement of millions. On the material side, it would have spelled the loss of valuable deposits of tin and prodigious supplies of rubber and rice. It would have meant that Thailand, enjoying buffer territory between itself and Red China, would be exposed on its entire eastern border to infiltration or attack. And if Indochina fell, not only Thailand but Burma and Malaya would be threatened, with added risk to East Pakistan and South Asia as well as to all Indonesia.[19]

Anyone can find dozens, hundreds of similar quotations to illustrate the economic motives and aims of American diplomacy. Unfortunately for the "paramarxist" case, this kind of demonstration suffers from two weaknesses. Some of these arguments are so absurd at times and bear evidence of such a misreading of the facts that they look like obvious justifications designed for consumption by an ill-informed public. When John Foster Dulles denounced Ho Chi Minh at the time of the Geneva Conference in May 1954 as "a Moscow-trained Communist . . . who would deprive Japan of important markets and sources of food and raw materials," he was expressing himself in the terms which he considered best suited to his audience. Similarly, Jules Ferry did not shrink from an economic defense of colonial conquests, even though capital was being invested elsewhere than in the French empire. American politicians at times used crusading language—defense against Communism— and at times the language of the dollar—markets and raw materials. Both languages expressed their users' true thoughts.

Similarly, the "paramarxist" interpretation not only misses dis-

---

[18] *Ibid.*, p. 99.
[19] Dwight Eisenhower, *Mandate for Change* (Garden City, N.Y.: Doubleday & Company, 1963), quoted by Kolko, *Roots of Foreign Policy*, p. 100.

covering the secret which those engaged in the action fail to perceive, the "hidden element" characteristic of scientific truth, but confines itself to taking statements by diplomats and the domino theory at face value. The "bitter-enders" of the Vietnam War and the opponents of the war trying to find a "rationalization of the absurd" or, to paraphrase the title of a now forgotten book (*Sinngebung der Sinnlosen*), to make sense of the senseless, miraculously agree in finding a plausible reason for a particular decision, one side in order to justify it, the other to censure the system from which it issues. Which of them is telling the truth? Or is neither of them doing so?

No one will seriously contend that the loss of resources in the markets and raw materials of South Vietnam would deal a deathblow or even serious damage American prosperity or the world market (or, if the reader prefers, the United States' economic and commercial system). The United States has manifestly invested more money (to say nothing of men) in South Vietnam than it will ever get out of it. The question remains, therefore, whether the domino theory is true and whether, even if it is, it makes American diplomacy economically rational.

In the absence of experience the answer to the first question can only be conjectural and provisional, that Cambodia and Laos would probably have been drawn into the North Vietnamese (or Chinese) sphere of influence and have been subjected to Communist (or Communist-dominated) governments. The infection might have spread to Thailand, though that country might have fended off the danger (if "communization" is held to be a danger); after all, Indonesia managed to do so without help from the United States. Indonesia's intrinsic importance is greater than that of South Vietnam; Washington was resigned to its "loss," that is to say to the Communists' taking power, but benefited from the failure of a Communist *coup d'état,* and simply by its abstention, won a success which no one for once ascribes to the CIA. As to India,[20] one would really need to stretch the point to conceive of that country's becoming a victim of the reunification of Vietnam under a Marxist-Leninist regime.

---

[20] India signed a treaty with the Soviet Union in 1971 for reasons of power politics.

I find the political argument put forward both by the supporters of American diplomacy and by its "paramarxist" critics more convincing: that a super-power *must not* accept defeat because it cannot lose a battle without losing the war, cannot abandon an ally without jeopardizing the credibility of its commitments. Imperial logic makes ubiquity imperative and cannot tolerate retreat—a Pyrrhic logic which has more often led empires to disaster than to triumph.

Was such reasoning imperative in the case of Vietnam? I refer the reader back to Part I, Chapter 3 of this book. After the phase of relatively active hostility to the return of colonial power, a hostility which Roosevelt did not trouble to conceal, Truman and Acheson deliberately decided to side wholeheartedly with the French expeditionary force combating the Vietminh. The combat became an integral part of the defense of the free world against Communism.

This commitment appeared justified and confirmed by the North Korean aggression. It led to an uneasy cooperation between the United States, which furnished the money and arms, and France (and its empire), which supplied the men. In the field the French officers were defending the empire, the American mission the "free world." To the former a war against Communism made no sense, to the latter a war to defend a colonial order that was doomed in any case was even less meaningful.

The United States renewed its commitment after 1954 and the Geneva agreements in the hope that, purged of the taint of French colonialism, it could at least preserve a non-Communist regime in the South—a non-Communist regime which with Ngo Dinh Diem became anti-Communist by a process that was probably inevitable; for since the Vietminh had been the embodiment of nationalism, any other nationalism needed an ideology, and what other ideology could it have save anti-Communism?

Thereafter, but only thereafter, the United States was caught up in the machinery; the commitment created the stake. While Kennedy wished for better relations with the Soviet Union and a limitation of the armaments race, he was a "doer." His team was, as we have seen, composed mainly of academics, some of them enthusiastic advocates of the theory of counterinsurgency. After the Bay of Pigs fiasco he was looking for opportunities to regain Khrushchev's respect which he (rightly) feared he had lost—hence the stepping-up of intervention in Laos, the commando raids on North Vietnam, the ever-growing numbers of American advisers in South Vietnam, and the authorization of the generals' plot against Diem. Increased United States involvement was a result of failure. If Kennedy, Johnson, and Nixon were defending the United States world economic system in Vietnam without their knowledge or volition, it has to be assumed that this system, based as it was on political and military prestige, would collapse at the slightest tremor. The economic explanation of the United States' diplomatico-strategic behavior takes on a semblance of truth only in an indirect way that deprives it of credibility. How could this interpretation ever be refuted if the privileges of a dominant economy are imputed not to strength, but to a reputation for military force?

Once again setting aside a stage-by-stage account and resorting to the ultimate purpose by way of the domino theory, is the external action of the United States in various parts of the world governed by economic logic? The answer is dubious, to say the least.

In no region in the world is the United States' stake so high as in the Middle East, where the richest oil fields and largest known oil reserves still lie. Is American diplomacy there governed by an anxiety to keep access to these fields and to avoid alienating the governments of these countries? Yes and no.

The United States backs Israel, against which all the Arab states are leagued, though not with equal enthusiasm. It is probable that quite a number of professional diplomats in the United States (like their counterparts at the Quai d'Orsay) regret the existence of the state of Israel. The policy-makers in Washington do their best to maintain good relations with the Arab states; care is taken to avoid assigning soldiers of the Jewish persuasion to the American bases in Saudi Arabia, and the big oil companies drilling the subsoil there follow suit. In 1956 President Eisenhower finally persuaded Ben Gurion to evacuate the territory occupied during the Sinai campaign. During the Six Day War the United States deterred Soviet thoughts of intervention. American diplomacy has been backing the Israelis' arguments since 1967 and has supplied Israel with arms in spite of its oil interests.

Two traits or trends in American diplomacy therefore clearly emerge in the Middle East: Support for conservative governments in the Arab countries to protect American investments on the one hand, and military support for Israel on the other. American diplomacy contributed to the creation of the state of Israel, and so did Soviet diplomacy. At the time, the target of the Soviet diplomacy was the British Empire, with its illustrious past and its still impressive façade. Since then the Soviet Union has in crisis after crisis gained seemingly solid positions in Syria and positions in Egypt that are strong from the military standpoint but politically precarious.[21] The United States, though the policy-makers did not specifically think out a course of action designed to this end, has become Israel's protector and ally and has been compelled, too, to be its sole supplier of arms since the breach between France and Israel in 1967.

Is this alignment attributable to the influence of the Jewish community in America? Partly, without the slightest doubt; decisions on the external action of the American republic are always subject to pressures. The management of British diplomacy has always enjoyed the advantages of the secrecy and independence which are rightful adjuncts of the aristocratic tradition. In exceptional circumstances, as in the Thirties when the policy of appeasing Hitler went beyond a certain point and immediately after the Franco-British Suez expedition in 1956, public opinion encouraged by a section of the ruling class has grown restive and has enforced the revision or even the abandonment of a policy. On a daily basis, the British Cabinet and the Secretary of State for Foreign Affairs are not subjected to the constant harassment which so many American secretaries of state are compelled to undergo day in and day out in the United States. Where the Middle East and Israel are concerned, the representatives of the American Jewish Committee lobby the secretary of state, as do the representatives of the big oil companies. In the case in point the latter have not prevailed.

To take another part of the world, Latin America, Central America, and the Caribbean in particular: At the very birth of the republic some of the Founding Fathers looked toward Cuba, an island close to the shores of Florida, as if it belonged by decree of geog-

---

[21] It lost them in 1972, though whether temporarily or permanently remains to be seen.

raphy or history to the new commonwealth. The establishment of a hostile regime in Havana undoubtedly meant the transfer of allegiance of a state integrated from the very beginning in the republic's sphere of influence or responsibility. Santo Domingo and Guatemala are cases that resemble that of Cuba; it seems to me that their proximity and the feeling that such countries are part of the Western Hemisphere dictate the policy-makers' and the public's reaction. In the Caribbean and Central America, Washington has conducted a great power policy, even an imperialist policy in the ordinary sense of the term, asserting the de facto right to restrict these states' sovereignty and to forbid certain parties' access to power. Neither in Santo Domingo nor in Guatemala nor even in Cuba does the magnitude of the economic interests involved seem proportionate to the will to power. A sense of geography and memories of the past are at the root of these feelings and this behavior.

Since the Monroe Doctrine the Americans, conveniently forgetting that it was originally a British suggestion, have evolved for themselves a twofold myth: first, a geographical myth, that both the Americas belong in the Western Hemisphere, where the United States legitimately holds a special place of its own and by virtue of a special destiny it assumes special responsibilities; and second, a political myth, that the ban conveyed to the Holy Alliance more than a century ago against intervening in the colonies which had rebelled against Spain has become, without changing its nature, the assertion of a private preserve, the right to act in place of the Latin American states or assist them in defense against any foreign influences which the United States decides for itself are inimical to the prosperity or security of the area as a whole. Latin America has no exceptional or irreplaceable value either as a reserve of natural resources or as a market for manufactured goods or as a particularly promising field for direct investment. Canada, as we have seen, absorbs far more American capital, and so does Western Europe. For ten years the United States has been disinvesting from Latin America and repatriating from it more profits than it has been investing new capital. Indeed, in the past few years, following the frustration or meager returns from the Alliance for Progress, launched with such a flourish by Kennedy, Nixon has tended rather to a benign (or not so benign) neglect of Latin America.

The Yankees are well aware that public opinion in most Latin

American countries has manifested little liking for them, and they have drawn their conclusions. This negative attitude may well be due to the growing resentment aroused by a comparison between the relative progress achieved by the North Americans as against the South Americans in the past century and a half. The Yankees are inevitably rewarded for their success by unpopularity. Moreover, the life style and values characteristic of Hispano-Americanism do not inspire the offspring of affluence and efficiency with either liking or respect; and they are repaid in their own coin— they do not receive what they refuse.

The Vietnam War may perhaps incline the American government to greater tolerance or disinterest. Washington has maintained a virtually neutral attitude toward the Popular Front experiment in Chile. It demanded compensation from the nationalist Junta in Peru for the nationalization of subsidiaries of American firms. Though Nixon's policy in word and deed toward Latin America does not mark a turning point and still tends to withhold from the states in the Western Hemisphere exactly the same right to choose their system of government as it allows to states elsewhere, it leans in word and deed toward omission rather than commission. It shows an unreserved reluctance to recognize any distinction between a domestic regime and a diplomatic orientation. It does acknowledge that a socialist regime in Latin America, or even a regime which professes allegiance to Marxism-Leninism, imperils neither the world equilibrium nor the security of the Western Hemisphere. It doles out its aid parsimoniously and usually proportionately to the ideas of the government of the day.

Cuba's readmission to the Organization of American States has become at least a plausible possibility, since this would be substantively in consonance with Nixon's and Kissinger's philosophy. Would not putting an end to the blockade and dissociating the regime's diplomatic allegiance from its ideology be the best way to reduce the Soviet influence on Cuba?

To sum up the findings based on what has been discussed so far: The United States is henceforth bound to the outside world by its need to import raw materials, the magnitude of its direct external investments, and the profits it draws from them. The economic and the political aspects of the general purpose of American diplomacy are inseparable because this purpose is by definition freedom of access, a notion which encompasses the exchange of ideas, investments, and goods. The American economy's place in the world market, nevertheless, has no more governed the course of American diplomacy since 1945 than the republic's prosperity has depended solely on power politics.

There remains, however, over and above these definite conclusions, a question which will come up again later. Is not the capitalist world market a necessary element in the political and military equilibrium of the inter-state system, and has not the United States assumed the essential responsibility for the preservation of this equilibrium? Or are we to follow the proponents of the doctrine of a new isolationism and accept the notion that the United States took upon itself an unreasonable and disproportionate task which culminated tragically in the Vietnam War, in setting itself the goal of the stability of the inter-state system, the ban on resort to force, and the preservation of a global environment consonant with its ideology and open to its influence? Will the United States be able to enjoy its prosperity if it reverts to the tradition crystallized in George Washington's warning against "entangling alliances?"

Chapter Two

THE TWO MARSHALL PLANS:
THE ROUND TRIP OF THE DOLLARS

No one looking at the twenty-five year period 1947–72 in its entirety, the period running from the end of the Second World War to the beginning of the end of the postwar economic and monetary system, can withhold his admiration—admiration in the dual sense of approval and surprise.[1] It is hardly possible to refrain from admiring and approving of the success of the worldwide system which the Marxist-Leninists call capitalist: There was no serious or protracted depression, cyclical fluctuations were relatively slight, and the annual growth rate of international trade was higher than that of the national product. In Europe and Japan the national product grew about twice as rapidly as it had in the past. It looked as if Europe and the United States together, plus Japan and some of the other Asian countries, after the interlude of two wars and the vain attempts to restore the pre-1914 system between 1918 and 1938, had succeeded to the world economy of the previous century, with the United States replacing Great Britain as the dynamic center and dominant entity in finance and industry.

Nor is it possible to refrain from admiration and surprise at the irony of history and the hazards of prediction. After 1918 statesmen and students of history had expected a return to normal, to the familiar world of the nineteenth century; and it had been precisely that notion which had led to disaster. During the Second World War, however, policy-makers prepared for the postwar period, obsessed as they were by memories of mass unemployment

---

[1] I deal in this chapter with the American economy's effects on the developed countries and in the next with its effects on the developing countries.

and by fear of the breakdown of capitalism. Even the first stage, the reconversion of a war economy to a peace economy, filled them with forebodings which some of them publicly avowed. An economist in a neutral country,[2] for example, openly declared that accord with the Soviet Union would be preferable to dependence on the vast but unstable economy of the United States. Reconversion proved painless; capitalism got its second wind, and it met and defeated the Soviet challenge.

The irony of history was, however, to be carried further: Would the devaluation of the dollar in 1971 rock the international economy to its foundations? Do Americans, Japanese, and Europeans now regret their success? Will they want to halt the race for growth?

1.

The United States cannot, of course, be credited with the sole merit for what the Europeans and Japanese have accomplished. It is a fact, however, that their progress was due to the liberalization of trade within the setting of the capitalist world market and that the predominant economy partly determined that setting and the rules for competition within it. At first sight, the facts would seem to show that American predominance profited *the countries which had already advanced well down the road to industrialization* more than it cost them.

To this preliminary observation must be applied the distinction I drew earlier between the two meanings, or two aspects, of the *external action* of the United States. This action in the economic field is governed primarily by the decisions of the policy-makers and their subordinates, by decisions of state so to speak, but it also operates apart from any intention on the part of the governing parties and even without their knowledge, simply because of what the United States is or what it does at home. To take the most ordinary example: The factor which has contributed most to the world's prosperity in the past quarter of a century has been the absence of any major crisis in the United States. Another, and increasingly important, factor is the action of the nominally multinational corporations and the American bankers and investors. As

---

[2] Sweden, in this particular case.

a transnational cross-frontier society grows up, the behavior of private persons, too, plays its part, and its effects on domestic and foreign affairs become inseparable. It is not so much the action of the Federal government that is our main concern here as the strategies of corporations, as well as the behavior of such sections of the public as investors and even tourists.

The Marshall Plan in Europe and certain reforms in Japan (such as the agrarian reform) may legitimately be credited to American diplomacy. The United States' behavior as a benevolent ally in the one case and as a generous victor in the other contrasted all the more brutally with that of the Soviet Union, because the Soviet Union had emerged devastated from its trials and could not have rivaled the United States in liberality or generosity even if it had so wished.

In requiring Great Britain to restore the convertibility of the pound prematurely, American diplomacy committed an abuse of power and an error, which it repaired with the Marshall Plan. The Plan at the very least speeded up the reconstruction of the European economies. To prevent a recurrence of the wrangles over the repayment of war debts which had exacerbated transatlantic relations, the United States executive and legislature called the major part of the sums transferred unilaterally to the Europeans "grants"; ten years later the deficit in the United States balance of payments (or what is commonly implied by this term) made Americans regret that the Europeans did not have more to repay.

At the same time, the International Monetary Fund (IMF) and the General Agreement on Tariffs and Trade (GATT) came into being. The IMF voting rules gave the British and Americans a power which reflected their superiority at that time. The American negotiators rejected the far-reaching projects devised by Maynard Keynes and put forward by the British, for fear that the United States might be compelled to finance the weaker countries' balance of payments deficits. Fixed exchange rates and narrow margins for fluctuations were intended to prevent unauthorized devaluations at the expense of competitors and a repetition of the monetary disturbances of the Thirties, when each state had tried to shift its unemployment to others by devaluing its currency. In a letter to the IMF the American secretary of state supplemented the Fund's rules by pledging dollar convertibility into gold, a pledge which was to embarrass the Americans as much as their partners twenty years later.

In GATT the American negotiators obtained recognition for the principle to which they were most attached, the most-favored-nation clause. But they also agreed to exclude an eventual common market or free trade area from its application. They also permitted de facto discriminatory practice by Europeans with respect to American goods during the period of the "dollar gap"—that is, in the years during which dollars were in short supply in Europe.

As I see it, the following were paramount elements in American diplomacy's virtually indisputable contribution to the economic miracle in the West and Japan: the speeding up of European reconstruction through the Marshall Plan, the acceleration of Japanese reconstruction through direct aid, reforms, and the consequences of the Korean War, and the promulgation of rules of good monetary and commercial conduct, which, however imperfectly they were obeyed and however much they suited American preferences, promoted both the common prosperity and the restoration of a capitalist world market.

To this voluntary contribution I would add the way in which the Americans continuously and almost as a matter of course supplied examples of know-how, in respect to productivity, for instance. The American propensity to consider their own system exemplary, though it may lead to the direst havoc in politics or morals, proved most fortunate for the European and Japanese economies; the productivity missions which toured the United States, and the closely knit relationships which sprang up on both sides of the Atlantic, had beneficial repercussions on the Old Continent. After 1945 the Europeans had more to learn than to teach. The Americans, by very virtue of their philosophy, considered it a matter of course to teach others the secret of their own success. As the predominant economy, the United States had the advantage, from its partners' point of view, of believing in freedom and communication rather than secrecy and bureaucracy.

Was the United States not acting with a view to its own interests and in accordance with its own doctrines? Who doubts it and why should one doubt it?—though the American taxpayer was also swayed by idealistic sentiments at the time of the Marshall Plan. To discuss the motives of statesmen or states is fruitless. What I am examining here are actions and their effects, not intentions or ulterior motives.

It may seem paradoxical, but I believe it is true, that these governmental contributions were supplemented by private contributions, from the mid-Fifties onward, in the form of the massive exports of American capital to Europe and the abundance of dollars this engendered. In the early stages the European and Japanese economies advanced more rapidly than that of the United States precisely because they had lagged behind it and were renovating their manufacturing plants, technology, and management.[3] As the Common Market began to develop in the mid-Fifties, American capital began to flow into a rapid growth area; the American currency, by virtue of its transnational function, became plentiful. In some science-based branches of industry the American firms brought with them a knowledge and advanced technology that provided both a model for imitation and a competitive element. Direct American investment in Europe—though this is a very controversial matter—does incontrovertibly promote growth, since it enlarges the volume of domestic investment and normally yields a rate of profit higher than that earned by domestic firms. I shall leave aside for the moment the arguments about the respective advantages to direct investors abroad and to the recipients of these investments, and shall confine myself to stating the trite but frequently misconstrued proposition that, despite the allegations about "the imperialism of liberalism" often found in the "paramarxist" literature, the predominating economy does not invariably accentuate its superiority in the long run by means of free trade.

Industry in the United States and Germany overtook and outstripped that in Great Britain in the last quarter of the nineteenth century, when goods were freely admitted into that country and the City invested its capital in every direction. Even though these investments yielded a higher rate of profit abroad than they would have earned at home, it is still at least doubtful whether direct British investment abroad served the national economy as well as it served private investors.

To identify liberalism and free trade with a devious form of imperialism seems to me, therefore, too broad a generalization. It all

---

[3] As well as because they had an abundant supply of labor.

depends on the stage of development of the economies with which the predominant economy enters into relations. It all depends on the ability of the less-developed economies to choose the sectors in which the investments are to be placed and to supplement the capital coming in from abroad with their own. No underdeveloped country would risk complete free trade without any tariffs at all. The GATT rules do not in themselves bar the protection of industries or a skillful use of trade liberalization. The industrial countries of Europe and Asia have caught up somewhat under the postwar trade and monetary system in per capita product or industrial production.

Has the price of this progress been a greater degree of subordination or the alienation of a part of their industrial capital? Again, let us shelve the question for the moment. The first thing to do is to stress what seems to me obvious indeed, the fact that the United States, voluntarily or involuntarily, whether by the action of its government or by the action of its businessmen, whether by the supremacy of its policy or by the attraction of its example, has fulfilled the function of a predominant economy in such a fashion that it is wondering, twenty-five years after putting the Marshall Plan into effect, whether the outcome represents a failure of success or a success carried to excess. By helping its partners to catch up with it and to unite and thereby equip themselves with a vast market, was not the United States paving the way for its own downfall? Did not the devaluation of the dollar in 1971, when Richard Nixon was seeking a way out of the Vietnam War by the meetings in Peking and Moscow, symbolize the coincidence of *political* rapprochement with the enemy and *economic* disputes with allies? The disputes of political enemies are not economic in a world divided into two world markets. Conversely, such economic disputes generally affect relations between politically allied states which are members of the same transnational economic system. Yet the disputes must not become so embittered as to call in question the economic system or the political alliance.

2.

It was in the late Fifties that the last books dealing with the problem of the dollar gap were published and the earliest articles were written on precisely the opposite topic—the persisting deficit in the

United States balance of payments. The Fifties had, indeed, been notable mainly for the continuing progress of Europe and Japan, the gradual disappearance of monetary nonconvertibility, trade liberalization, the persisting annual deficit in the United States balance of payments, and the increasing flow of long-term capital investment, especially to Europe, precisely at a time when discriminatory measures against American exports were becoming fewer and fewer.

There had been a slight deficit in the American balance of payments during the Marshall Plan years, but that had been consistent with the American policy-makers' aims when the gold reserves at Fort Knox had amounted to well over $20 billion, rather more than one-half of the entire world reserves in gold. At the time, a redistribution of world reserves was a more frequent topic of discussion than the deficit in the American balance of payments. The United States' reserves had risen from $14.6 billion in 1938 to $22.9 billion in 1947 and $24.6 billion in 1949, but had declined to $20.6 billion in 1958. Ten years later they were about $10 billion.

Early in this period, in 1962 to be exact, E. M. Bernstein, one of the best American economic analysts, wrote about the basic data of the problem as follows:

The United States payment problem can be understood only as part of a long postwar adjustment designed to restore a pattern of international payments under which the world economy can prosper and grow. This has involved the rebuilding of the production capacity of Western Europe and Japan, the strengthening of their competitive position, the resumption of their important role in world trade, and the establishment of convertibility of their currencies. The international economic policies of the United States have been directed to the attainment of these objectives since 1945. They have been remarkably successful, as indicated by the high level of production and trade, the balance of payment surplus, and the greatly increased monetary reserves of Western Europe and Japan. . . . The postwar adjustment is apparently coming to an end. In the meantime, the long-run strength of the United States economic position is asserting itself. An analysis of three important sectors of the United States balance of payments shows that there are forces acting on United States trade, United States capital outflow, and United States government expenditures which may be expected to eliminate the payments deficit within the next two years.[4]

At that date American exports had remained practically stable as a percentage of total world exports—at 17.8 percent in 1950 and 17.1 percent in 1961, ranging between a maximum of 19.6 in 1957 (an exceptional year because of the events of 1956 and the closure of the Suez Canal) and a minimum of 17.1. True, the share of American exports of manufactured goods in total world exports had fallen from 27.3 percent in 1950 to 21.3 percent in 1959; but it had remained stable from 1959 to 1962. Imports had fallen as a percentage of the national product (from 3.2 percent in 1950 to 2.8 percent in 1961), but the American surplus in trade with Western Europe remained on an average about the same; Bernstein drew the conclusion that the American economy's competitive capacity had not deteriorated. Long-term capital outflows had resumed; toward Canada they had become stable in volume, and toward Latin America they had risen until around 1956, but had fallen to almost nil by about 1960; toward Western Europe they had increased substantially after 1955. In the aggregate, the volume of long-term capital outflows amounted at that date to between $2 and $3 billion. Bernstein did not foresee the likelihood of an increase; the reinvestment of profits and the call for foreign capital owned by nationals of the countries in which subsidiaries were established would be likely to reduce capital outflows.

Bernstein did not, of course, consider this result inevitable. "The fact is," he wrote, "that the payment deficit of the United States is still quite large, and may exceed $1.8 billion in 1962. Even under favorable conditions and with persistent effort, the payment deficit is not likely to be eliminated before 1964. Meanwhile foreign holdings of short-term and liquid dollar assets are enormous and the drain on United States gold reserves may continue even after the balance of payments is in surplus."[5]

---

[4] *Quarterly Review and Investment Survey,* 4th quarter (New York: Model, Roland & Co., 1962), p. 2.

[5] *Ibid.,* p. 9. Ten years later the same analyst wrote in the same review: "There is the risk that a resumption of the convertibility of the dollar into reserve assets would encourage a reduction in outstanding dollar holdings. An attempt by foreign monetary authorities to shift the com-

As everyone now knows, the restoration of the balance predicted by Bernstein for 1964 did not take place. The American doctrine (that the cost of foreign policy and investment abroad should be financed from a surplus on current account) remained unchanged. On the other hand, analyses became more refined, because over the previous ten years the United States balance of payments was at first grouped under two subheads (official reserve transactions balance and net liquidity balance), and subsequently, under four subheads in the Economic Report of the President transmitted to the Congress (January 1972) instead of in the simplified form used by Bernstein in the study quoted above. The response to the different methods of calculating the United States balance of payments has been a discussion on the nature and cause of the deficit, waged partly in economic and partly in political terms.

The distinction drawn between the official reserve transactions balance and the net liquidity balance[6] is due to the partial unification of the capital markets and the transnational overlap between national accounts and corporation accounts. Without going into details which would be of interest only to specialists, it is easy to see that the dollars generated by the American deficit may be held by private persons, corporations, or banks, or else may be deposited in the central banks. If the dollars are deposited in the central banks, the deficit shown in the official reserve transactions balance grows larger. If, however, the dollars are held by private persons, the deficit in the official reserve transactions balance (or in other words, the United States liquid dollar liabilities to foreign official agencies) grows smaller, or at any rate does not increase. Since there may be wide differences in interest rates between countries and on either side of the Atlantic, and since large masses of short-term capital respond to variations in the rates of interest or prospects of change in monetary parities by moving from one market to another, it becomes impossible to tell which of the two methods of calculating the deficit has more significance. A surplus on the official reserve transactions balance has no more economic significance in itself than a deficit in

---

position of their reserves away from dollars on a large scale could quickly deplete United States reserves or compel a renewed suspension of convertibility of the dollar as a reserve asset." *Quarterly Review,* 1st quarter, 1972, p. 7.
[6] See note at end of chapter, page 219.

the net liquidity balance (as was the case in 1969); the two figures arise both from short-term capital movements and from the transfer of dollars from the central banks to private persons, or vice versa. In the 1972 Report to the Congress the figures for 1969, 1970, and 1971 were given as follows: Net liquidity balance, deficits of $6.084 billion, $3.821 billion, and $23.439 billion; official reserve transactions balance, surplus of $2.704 billion in 1969 and deficits of $9.821 billion and $31.810 billion in 1970 and 1971. Let us leave these figures aside, for in themselves they need interpreting and do not furnish significant data.

Let us first take the balance for goods, services, and remittances.[7] It showed a surplus of $7.8 billion in 1964, but deteriorated progressively from year to year (except in 1970, when the United States adopted a deflationary policy). In the first three quarters of 1971 the surplus (at adjusted annual rate) had fallen to $.1 billion. The merchandise trade balance, which had been in surplus by $6.8 billion in 1964, had become a deficit of $1.7 billion in the first three quarters of 1971. From 1964 to 1971 imports had risen by 147 percent (14 percent yearly), but exports by only 74 percent; and there is the additional consideration that a portion of American exports were in the form of loans which the borrowers had to spend in the United States (tied loans).

The aggravation of the deficit (despite the increased income from American investment abroad) is obviously connected with the inflationary process, which started, or grew worse, in 1965, and with the massive intervention in Vietnam (between 1960 and 1964 exports rose from $19.650 to $26.478 billion, imports from $14.744 to $18.647 billion). Cost per man-hour had fallen in the United States between 1960 and 1965, and had risen in the other industrial countries. The statistics show the same rate of increase from 1966 to 1970 in the United States and among its main competitors, while the price of merchandise exports from the United States rose more than that of foreign merchandise exports.

Military transactions accounted for between $2.5 and $3.5 billion, and the services item was continuously in deficit, as were the items for private remittances and government grants. Hence only two

---

[7] Presentation in the February 1972 Report to the Congress by the President's Council of Economic Advisers.

items—merchandise trade balance and investment income—showed a favorable balance in the Sixties. The surplus balance for the latter increased by $1.2 billion on an average (1960–64) to $5.2 billion in 1970 (this is the net figure, the gross is $11.4 billion).

The deterioration in the balance on current account did not affect long-term investment flows, which rose from an average of 2.2 between 1960 and 1964 to 4.4 in 1970. The deterioration in the essential items in the balance on current account grew more rapid after 1970, a year in which the monetary authorities adopted an expansionist monetary policy to promote economic recovery, when interest rates remained higher in Europe owing to the recession. The official deficit in 1970 had been close to $10 billion. The continued outflow of dollars from the United States in 1971 increased the deficit until it at length became intolerable to the European central banks and faced them with the alternative of either absorbing dollars indefinitely or letting the dollar float on a free market (a single market or a two-tier financial and commercial market).

In the first half of the Sixties the debates and charges and countercharges between the Europeans (especially the French) and the Americans turned on two points, the choice of the item to which the "responsibility" (in the twofold meaning of causality and fault) for the American deficit should be ascribed, and the relationship between the value of gold and the value of the dollar. So long as the apparent trading surplus lay between $4.5 and $6 billion, the deficit could easily be ascribed to the United States' international role, its share in the "defense of the free world." The aggregate deficit, no matter in which of the two ways it was calculated, approximated the United States government's military expenditures abroad. To interpret the situation in this fashion was tantamount to failing to grasp the interrelation of the items in a balance sheet; the surplus on the merchandise trade balance was due in part to the abundance of dollars generated by government expenditures abroad and the tied loans. Moreover, even from the political standpoint, this sort of argument implied European concurrence in the United States diplomacy—a concurrence which, after 1965 at any rate, no longer held true.

The level of the debate on the relationship between gold and the dollar remained fairly low. To say that the value of gold is based on the value of the dollar, as one of the President's economic advisers maintained to me in frequent conversations, has no precise meaning. Supposing that all states jointly decided to divest gold of its monetary function; quite obviously, its price, once gold had become a raw material like any other, would fall, at any rate to start with,[8] but no single state, however powerful, can take such a decision unilaterally. It is generally agreed that the United States government will not let its gold reserves fall below a certain level (estimated at roughly $10 billion). Consequently, the value of gold is in no way based on the value of the dollar, but may rise above it if there is a twofold demand for it, industrial and monetary.

The demonetization of gold is likewise liable to be misconstrued. Since all the central banks hold a large part of their reserves in gold, they will not consent to an official demonetization comparable to the demonetization of silver in the past. No central bank, not even the Federal Reserve Board, is powerful enough to impose demonetization unilaterally. It is difficult to abandon gold as a standard of value entirely, since all currencies tend to fluctuate relative to other currencies.[9] It is not impossible to try to restrict the monetary use of gold to exchanges between central banks and to separate the two markets[10]—techniques which change, but do not abolish, the monetary use of gold.

Once these journalistic and political controversies were out of the way, the economists put forward or worked out one simple explanation and two more sophisticated theories. The simple explanation, which Professor Paul Samuelson adopted in the late Fifties but did not make public until several years later, cast the blame on the overvaluation of the dollar. The exchange parities established in 1948–49, after the pound had been devalued, had been wrongly calculated and were the response to an abnormal situation; once the ruins of Europe and Japan had been rebuilt and their industries reconstructed and modernized, the exchange rate between the dollar and the currencies of the major industrial countries became "un-

---

[8] If the central banks put part of their stocks on the market.

[9] It is possible in theory to relate to special drawing rights and to express their value in terms of half a dozen main currencies.

[10] In the long run, the viability of the two-tier system may be dubious if the disparity between exchange rates widens excessively. In any case, when the disparity becomes substantial, no central bank will part with its gold at the official rate; hence gold temporarily loses its monetary function.

realistic." The argument always seemed credible, but American economists, out of political caution or scientific scruple, seldom, so far as I know, tried to demonstrate it. During the Fifties the share of American exports in total world exports had not fallen appreciably; the share of American exports of manufactured goods in the world total was appreciably reduced, but this was a normal development, counterbalancing the increase in the shares of the Federal Republic of Germany and Japan. A calculation of the ratios of purchasing power should have identified the articles best suited to export. Besides, in view of the high level of American wages, a number of manufactured articles requiring simple processing, for which American industry does not have a sufficient advantage in productivity, would normally be more expensive in the United States than in Europe or Japan. In retrospect, I am inclined, like most of the economists, to say that Professor Samuelson was right and to regret that he failed to state his thesis publicly and convince the American policy-makers of the need for a dollar devaluation (in relation to gold or in relation to other currencies) before the period of accelerated inflation in 1965–70. The European governments might perhaps have protested against such a devaluation, which, indeed, they reluctantly accepted in 1971.

Of the two more refined theories, one, that of Jacques Rueff, declared that the crisis was inevitable and a permanent deficit abnormal; the other, that of Professor Charles P. Kindleberger, suggested, without perhaps categorically asserting so, that some American deficit was normal as an expression of the role the United States plays as a transnational banker by virtue of the size of the American capital market and the consequent lower rates of long-term interest.

The United States was able to treat the deficit in its balance of payments with "benign neglect" because the European central banks bought Federal bonds with the surplus dollars flowing into their coffers as a result of the deficit.

Did the deficit grow by what it fed on? Was it *determined* by the shifting to the United States of the dollars representing the deficit? The American deficits do not seem to me to have been the *major* cause of either the American or the European inflation before the period of accelerated inflation in 1965–70. There was a basic and essential weakness inherent in the gold-exchange standard, or in other words, on the use of a single currency, the American, as a reserve currency and the increase in international liquidities due to the deficit in the United States balance of payments. In the long run the United States deficit must necessarily give rise to uneasiness about the exchange parity, for the central banks would not be willing to accumulate dollars indefinitely. That is to say, the system was bound to "crash" some day, though this crisis would have nothing in common with the crisis of 1929. The foreseeable crisis would take the form of the nonconvertibility of the dollar into gold or into any other form of assets—a nonconvertibility which poses problems for the Europeans no less difficult than those in the preceding period.

The argument that the American deficit is "normal" was based on a comparison between the capital market in the United States and the capital market in all other countries. The American deficit was broken down into long-term investments abroad by American corporations and short-term investments on the New York market by foreign central banks. In this sense, at the macro-economic level of national accounts, the United States acts like a banker who borrows short and invests long, and thus takes advantage of the difference between interest rates and profit rates. The London market had practiced this sort of "conversion" for many years. But this means that the parity of the currency must not be open to doubt and that the banker function performed at the macro-economic level of national accounts shall be identical with the similar function within national entities.

That private persons in Europe should find it to their interest to convert their capital into cash[11] and sell to American corporations, and that Americans in turn should find it to their advantage to make long-term investments in Europe is indubitable. But this does not mean that there are always private persons or central banks prepared to hold on to dollars or that this transnational banker function satisfies everyone. Even when European private persons buy securities on the New York stock exchange, purchases which represent the counterpart of the dollars sunk in long-term investments in Europe, not all governments allow themselves to be convinced by Professor Kindleberger's theoretical arguments whereby, in the last analysis,

---

[11] The owner of a firm sells his capital and converts it into francs procured by the American investor for dollars. The owner's capital has been converted into cash; the American investor has acquired an asset.

the investments suit everyone's interests and the investor's nationality is irrelevant.

The events of 1971 furnished conclusive proof that the United States cannot go on fulfilling the function of a transnational banker indefinitely, at any rate once its rate of inflation (the rise in cost per man-hour) becomes as high as, or higher than, it is in the European countries. The European central banks have for many years been amassing more dollars than they wanted. The Americans stress the constraints of the banking function, whereas the Europeans perceive its advantages to the banker (without, however, denying the benefits accruing to his clients). Why did the Europeans tolerate this accumulation of dollars and what were the American arguments for forcing it upon them?

3.

Was the international monetary system, in the form in which it developed, with the dollar functioning as a transnational currency, concocted in advance and deliberately planned by the decision-makers in the United States with a view both to enabling the American corporations to make direct investments abroad despite the persisting deficit in the balance of payments, and to compel the central banks indefinitely to amass dollars which would ultimately become nonconvertible? No one would seriously make that assertion. At the time of the Bretton Woods negotiations the American representatives had opposed Maynard Keynes's far-reaching proposals put forward by the British, fearing that the burden of their partners' deficits would fall on the United States if they consented to the creation of a central world quasi-bank for the whole of the free economy. Similarly, the obligation to maintain fixed exchange parities had been intended to prevent a resumption of the practices of the Thirties, the recurrent devaluations set off by each other, as each state tried to get an advantage for its exports, being concerned less with increasing its reserves than with finding jobs for its unemployed, and to that end, with selling its goods abroad. In point of fact, the Europeans and Japanese did bring down their rate of unemployment lower than the United States, though the monetary system was probably only one of several causes of this difference.

Nevertheless, the discussion cannot be settled simply by discarding the mythology or demonology of "capitalism" or an omniscient and omnipotent American "imperialism." We may accept—and it seems to me probable—that those responsible for United States policy in the early Fifties did not foresee the consequences of the role of the dollar when the central banks considered it equivalent to gold. We may further accept that when President Kennedy entered the White House in the early Sixties, he was disturbed by the American balance of payments deficit and sincerely wished to reduce or eliminate it. The fact remains that the Europeans and Japanese today hold tens of billions (around 60 billion) of nonconvertible dollars[12] in their central banks' reserves. In late September 1971 the foreign monetary authorities' short-term claims on the United States amounted to around $45 billion, whereas the United States' net creditor position vis-à-vis the rest of the world had improved from year to year. From a net creditor for $44.7 billion in 1960, the United States had become a net creditor for $69 billion in 1970;[13] direct investment abroad had risen from $31.8 billion to $78 billion,[14] while direct investments by foreigners in the United States had risen only from $6.9 billion to $13.2 billion. The Europeans were repaying the Marshall Plan grants in the form of short-term loans, with which the American corporations were buying up European firms or setting up subsidiaries. During the Marshall Plan period dollars crossed the Atlantic to supply the European countries with the foreign exchange they required to purchase abroad more goods than they could have paid for with their exports. During the Sixties dollars crossed the Atlantic in both directions, eastward for long-term investment and westward to acquire Federal bonds or securities on the New York stock exchange.

This presentation of the facts is not politically or ideologically neutral; no presentation can be. It does nevertheless throw light on one of the aspects of the international monetary system and one of the dimensions of the transatlantic dialogue. I believe, therefore, that the question can legitimately be raised: Did the Europeans willingly or unwillingly accept this species of exchange between the

---

[12] Nonconvertible into assets (gold, special drawing rights). The dollar is still convertible into any other currency *on the foreign exchange market.*

[13] *Survey of Current Business*, LI No. 10, October 1971, p. 21.

[14] In terms of their book value, which is far lower than their real value.

short and the long term, the transnational banking function fulfilled by the United States? Did they do so because they felt it would be to their advantage or because they were compelled to accept it by the stronger power? Were the arguments used by the United States decision-makers military or economic?

The question I raised at the end of the last chapter arises again: In ensuring a general equilibrium within the inter-state system did not the United States acquire a moral or political claim on its European and Japanese partners for which they are paying by resigning themselves to amassing nonconvertible dollars? Or, to put it differently, is not the cost of foreign policy in foreign currency practically the same as the deficit in the United States balance of international transactions? The United States' partners lent it the amount in foreign currency it needed for policing the world. Moreover, the Federal Republic of Germany, acutely aware as it was of its vulnerability, its geopolitical weakness, did not oppose the Washington policy-makers' demands; thus, finance ministers in Bonn, Schiller in particular, unprotestingly accepted the various expedients devised in Washington, such as the two-tier gold market, the swap agreements, the Roosa bonds, and the like. In this perspective, the United States made use of its military predominance to impose a monetary system and, in particular, privileges for the dollar, to which its partners, had they enjoyed full freedom of movement and had they been capable of defending themselves on their own, would never have consented.

No one can either prove or disprove this proposition, though it does have a fair degree of probability. Although the framers of American monetary policy never threatened, even in private, to withdraw the American troops from Europe in order to put pressure on the leading politicians in Bonn, the Germans were well aware of the weakness of their position and considered it a matter of course that the price of their protection by the United States military presence must be economic or monetary concessions.

They acceded all the more readily in that the balance sheet of the system carried an item that was an asset even for those who were none too eager to tolerate it. The composition of the reserves, for example: Why, ask some supporters of Jacques Rueff's argument, would the central banks accept dollars instead of demanding gold unless pressures other than economic were being exerted on them?

This line of reasoning is far from foolproof, for as long as dollars appeared "as good as gold," they were in fact better than gold because they earned interest. Even if a dollar devaluation ultimately involves book losses, these would have been more than offset in advance by the interest collected. The economic objections have acquired irresistible force only in the past few years, when the rate of domestic inflation in the United States has exceeded the European rate of inflation and has led to deficits incommensurate with the average deficits in the previous years. As long as the deficits amounted to $2 or $3 billion, an amount roughly equivalent to the cost of American foreign policy or the value of American direct investment abroad, the governor of a central bank might well of his own accord prefer dollars to gold as the medium in which to hold his reserves of foreign exchange.

European finance ministers and governors of central banks feared the consequences of a crisis. After 1964 or 1965 they all knew perfectly well how the long-heralded crisis would work out. One day or another, the stock exchanges and foreign exchange offices would shut and the President of the United States would proclaim the dollar nonconvertible, at any rate into gold. None of them imagined that the decision-makers in Washington would accept the orthodox solution of revaluing gold. If the foreign central banks refused to continue accumulating dollars, the only way out was to declare the dollar nonconvertible, if the indispensable stock of gold was to be preserved.

Those who endorsed Kindleberger's thesis, such as Robert Mossé in France, did not, of course, feel that they had been refuted by events. The crisis leading to the nonconvertibility of the dollar resembled in every respect the run on a bank which does not have enough ready cash on hand, but possesses assets far in excess of its liabilities. The transnational banker which is the United States obviously cannot convert overnight the tens of billions of dollars held by its foreign creditors. No one knows, however, what proportion of these dollars is in fact owned by American corporations or American private persons, as either or both of them may well have bought foreign currencies with their dollars. Besides the dollar balances due to the United States deficits, billions more dollars arise and vanish, surge on to the markets and are converted into marks or Swiss francs as the case may be, depending on where the holders of capital expect a profit, either from a change in the value of a currency (devaluation or revaluation) or from a higher rate of interest.

Did the 1971 crisis *prove* that the dollar had been overvalued for twenty years? It did show that the contention was tenable, to say the least. Did it refute the theses argued by Kindleberger and S. C. Kolm about the "monetization" of French capital and the role of the United States as a transnational banker at the macro-economic level? Most certainly not. The United States continued to act as a transnational banker even after the dollar became nonconvertible. On the other hand, what the crisis did demonstrate was that this banker, like any other banker, is not proof against the risks of becoming insolvent because of the gap between his short-term liabilities and his liquid assets. It likewise demonstrated the drawbacks of using as a transnational currency a national currency managed in accordance with the requirements of the domestic economic situation rather than the needs of the international system. As long as the rate of inflation in the United States was lower than that in Europe, the American deficit of two to three billion dollars did not impair its credit as a banker; the inflation due to the Vietnam War after 1965, coming as it did at the same time as the accumulation of dollars which in reality were no longer convertible into gold, forced matters to a head, if only temporarily. The debate suddenly changed its tone, and the debaters—ministers and government or private experts— turned to different arguments, some of them exactly the reverse of those they had just been using.

On one point the American spokesmen, from president down to professor in the remotest backwoods university, displayed impeccable consistency; they continued to scorn gold as a relic of barbarism and to reject any thought of a drastic revaluation of the official price of gold, though in 1971 its price on the free market was approximately double the long-time official price ($35 the ounce), a figure which had trebled by 1973. The change in the Federal government's doctrine mainly concerned the dollar parity. For ten years the orthodox view, even among economists with no public responsibilities, had been expressed in the notion that "the dollar is as good as gold" or even that "the value of gold is based on the value of the dollar." Henceforth the orthodox attitude would be to count on the effects of devaluation to redress the balance of payments or, at the policy-making level, to dismiss all concern about the parity of the dollar and to leave it entirely to others to maintain it as best they can.

The Europeans begrudged the Americans the privileges accruing to them from their currency's transnational function. The United States was the only country to manage its economy without concern for its balance of payments. It was the only country to assume the right (contrary to the IMF statutes) not to suspend direct investment abroad when its balance of payments was in deficit. It was the only country to settle its deficit in its own currency, the foreign central banks having to resign themselves to holding their reserves in dollars. In the international monetary system all currencies were equal, but, as in *Animal Farm*, one was more equal than others.

To this the Americans now reply that there were constraints attached to these privileges. For ten, or even twenty, years they had denied themselves the tool which is most effective and least painful when a balance has to be restored—a change in monetary parity. Had not American corporations set up subsidiaries abroad? Certainly, but in return they had provided European, and to an even greater extent Japanese, goods with a market whose closure would have damaged their partners' prosperity far more than their own. In the future the policy-makers in Washington will no longer part with their monetary freedom, that is to say, the freedom to let the value of the dollar fall in relation to other currencies. They exercise this freedom by leaving no choice between a devaluation of the dollar, which the Europeans dread for commercial reasons, and the accumulation of nonconvertible dollars, which the Europeans often consider preferable, when all is said and done, to a further fall in the dollar's parity, though they hope it will be only temporary.

Besides, the policy-makers in Washington continue to demand the same privileges as they previously enjoyed, but no longer accompanied by the constraints formerly self-imposed. They had made long-term investments abroad with the dollars held in the reserves of the foreign central banks. President Nixon and his advisers do not conceal their determination to continue the expansion of capital investment abroad and claim that their surplus on current account finances both their expenditure of foreign policy and their direct investment abroad. Europeans are therefore coming to look back with regret to a position which they only recently deplored. What right have the Americans to demand a surplus on current account in order to finance their foreign investments? Why should they not cover the deficit in their trading balance in the same way as the British had covered, and more than covered, theirs in the nineteenth century, with the income from foreign investment? In 1971 foreign investment produced some dozen billion dollars in repatriated earnings; taking into account the earnings from foreign investments in the United States, the net income amounted to between $6 and $7 billion, a sum sufficient to cover the cost of foreign policy or the balance of trade deficit—always provided that the outward flow of investment capital dries up.

In short, the crisis of August 1971 settled none of the problems disputed among Americans, Japanese, and Europeans; the dollar remained the monetary standard by which prices are calculated and the currency in which market transactions are conducted. Europeans still feared a further devaluation and Americans left the responsibility for the value of their own currencies to the Europeans and Japanese with "benign neglect." The Americans did not desist from investing abroad even before the restoration of a balance of trade surplus. Is this the arrogance of power? If so, is the power economic or military?

4.

To sum up the findings from the foregoing analyses in the most neutral economic terms possible: The dollar became the monetary standard, the measure of value, the currency for intervening on the exchange market and for foreign currency reserves not because the decision-makers in Washington imposed it on their partners, but because immediately after the war it appeared to be a stable value, based as it was on the most developed economy and a huge stockpile of gold. When the American balance of payments deficit became permanent in the late Fifties, neither the Europeans nor the Japanese called for a devaluation of the dollar against the other currencies, nor did the Americans contemplate such a measure. While some economists called the gold-exchange standard unfair (because of the privileges of the predominant economy or transnational currency), there were practically no American economists who recommended a revaluation of gold; and the policy-makers and experts in Washington tried partial measures as stopgaps: they imposed an interest equalization tax to make access to the American capital market harder for foreigners (though with special exemptions for Canadians), tried to reduce the drain on foreign currency caused by maintaining American troops abroad, and reluctantly decided to put a ceiling on capital outflows from the banks and big corporations. From 1960 to 1964 prices rose more slowly in the United States than in Europe and the deficit continued at the same level (slightly more than $2 billion on the official reserve transactions balance). The Europeans urged the Americans to set their house in order, but they accommodated themselves to the various expedients devised in Washington. The European finance ministers differed in their approach to the monetary problem; while some wished to curb the American hegemony, others were concerned primarily with security and the military presence of the United States in Europe. Nor did they agree on the economic analysis of the crisis and the possible solution. None of them dared suggest a dollar devaluation; and General de Gaulle and his ministers probably did not realize that if they did carry their point, it would simply lead to nonconvertibility of the dollar and a worse period of uncertainty until the monetary system was reorganized.

The action, or rather inaction, of the Europeans (except the French) and Japanese was not due solely, or even mainly, to the preponderance of the United States. Japan was selling one-third of its exports to the United States and feared a revaluation of the yen; the Europeans had no wish to see a dollar devaluation, since their balance of trade with the United States was still in deficit, and they failed either to work out a joint stand toward United States direct investment or to reconcile their words with deeds. It took the inflation produced by the Vietnam War in 1965 and the consequent deficits which were incommensurate with the United States function as transnational banker to break the system; the central banks of the countries whose currency had to be revalued were no longer either able or willing to accumulate dollars; and the disproportion between the American reserves and the volume of short-term indebtedness eliminated the possibility of even theoretical convertibility. The transatlantic dialogue entered upon a new stage; in the previous ten years it had been concentrated on the privileges of the reserve currency and American direct investment abroad; now, as Washington saw it, the subjects for negotiation were to be the Europeans' trade policies, in particular the consequences of the enlarged Common Market.

What does the record of the preceding period look like on balance? The United States had undoubtedly benefited from some of the privileges inseparable from a reserve currency; it had managed its domestic affairs—budget and credit—without much concern for its balance of payments. The privileges did not in fact amount to much in practice; the alternations of rapid growth and stagnation (or decelerated growth) were no less marked in the United States than in the European countries. Since the American deficit was not wiped out during the period of deflationary policy, it must be attributed to causes[15] different in kind from those of the other countries' deficits, such as the overvaluation of the dollar, the advantages accruing to American investors from the size of their capital market, or both. The Europeans and Japanese profited from the overvaluation of the American currency throughout the postwar period. In return, the expansion of American capital was no longer merely continental, but became global.

The theoretical enumeration of the advantages and disadvantages of foreign investment is familiar enough: In the initial stage its advantages are that it creates additional employment, often introduces little-known manufacturing and management techniques, fosters a climate favorable to competition, produces a higher rate of profit than most domestic firms, and provides substitutes for imports. Its disadvantages lie in the fact that the subsidiary of a conglomerate may wipe out local firms by cutthroat competition and establish its own virtual monopoly in science-based branches of industry, and at a second stage may repatriate a large proportion of its profits and finance its investments out of local capital, thus ultimately creating such problems as the aggravation of balance of payments. Everyone agrees, of course, with such trite notions as: It would be better if IBM were a French company; it is better that computers should be made by IBM than that there should be no computers; and IBM earns foreign currency for France, even if most of the materials imported by its subsidiary are American.

---

[15] Until about 1965 at any rate; thereafter, the domestic inflation in the United States was not unlike that in some of the European countries.

Leaving aside such platitudes, is there any theory which can serve as a guide to choosing between desirable and undesirable investments, investments which on balance are good and investments which on balance are bad? I do not believe so. A simple example will throw light on the difficulty inherent in such a choice. To put it in strictly economic terms, what types of production should be reserved for national producers alone? Supersonic aircraft? Definitely not; for research and development are very costly, and there is no profit to be had until a large number of the craft are sold; involving, as it does, a maximum of capital investment and a minimum of profit (almost certainly a loss), is this not a case in point of a branch of industry which medium-sized countries should leave to larger economies?

Does a similar kind of reasoning apply to computers? If the criterion is the volume of capital investment and the rate of profit, perhaps so. Some large American corporations have made profits from computer manufacture, mainly owing to innovations. But the rapid technological advances and the indispensable cost of research and development call for corporations with vast capital resources; American predominance in this branch of industry is therefore, if not desirable or acceptable, at least understandable.

Lionel Stoleru writes in his book, *L'Impératif industriel:*

> The United States is getting hold of more and more of the computer market, 50 percent of the production of semiconductors, 80 percent of the production of calculators, and almost the entire market for integrated circuits. This being so, "the community will not be able to permit itself to neglect this vital sector if it does not wish to have to depend on the advances achieved outside the community and thereby risk imperilling the competitive capacity of this industry and the future development of its entire industry," as the committee on medium-term policy notes in its report.[16]

The administrative report he quotes is quite as vague in its phrasing as is usually true of such administrative prose.

"Depend on the advances achieved outside"? Indeed, none of the European economies can avoid such dependence; none of them can

---

[16] *L'Impératif industriel* (Paris: Le Seuil, 1969), p. 273.

hope to be independent in this area. What is the consequent danger to the future development of the economy? The American corporation will keep for itself the profits from innovation, but not the products; for it will have to supply its foreign customers with the models it has put on its domestic market. So long as the integrative structures (*structures d'accueil*) exist, that is to say, so long as French firms and technicians are able to work the "innovations" brought in from outside, the notion of "danger to development" will have no significant meaning.

When Stoleru is reasoning for himself instead of quoting bureaucratic jargon, he prefers to take competitive capacity rather than independence as a criterion. He lists three criteria for the choice of foreign investments:[17] *the criterion of economic effects,* namely the creation of added value and employment, the input of capital, and the sale of licenses and manufacturing processes; *the criterion of the effect on the industrial sector,* namely the establishment of new firms or the purchase of existing ones and the relative share of the foreign corporation in the total capital of the branch of industry; and *the criterion of the effect on the balance of payments,* namely the flows of imports or exports and goods or capital connected with the investment. Unfortunately, these criteria do not always coincide, and none of them provides decisive guidance. Indeed, the French government has swung between two opposing attitudes; it was bound ultimately to open up the country to American capital, since any investment it refused was likely to move to the other side of the frontier because of the Common Market (as happened with a Ford factory). Although officially reluctant to accept the inflow of American investment, if not positively hostile to it, the French government nevertheless offers foreign investors the same incentives as domestic investors. The success of Chaban-Delmas, the prime minister of France, in attracting a Ford factory to the city of which he is mayor provides an ironical illustration of the contrast between high policy and microdecision.

Should the criterion for appraising United States' direct investments differ with the method by which they are financed? The economic effect of an American investment on the economy of a par-

---

17 *Ibid.,* p. 225.

ticular country would depend on the origin of the capital invested. If borrowed locally, it would not add to the volume of investment. But in point of fact, total American direct investment abroad, as given in the *Survey of Current Business,* covers only outflows of funds from the United States. At the macro-economic accounting level the origin of the funds is largely irrelevant to the economic effect of the investments. If in any year Europeans buy several billion dollars' worth of securities on the New York stock market and Americans invest directly in Europe to an equivalent amount, the Europeans as individuals will have acquired part-ownership of American corporations—ownership which does not carry any say in their management—while the American corporations will have acquired the ownership, including managerial control, of the European firms purchased by them in Europe. If these operations are placed side by side, this will undoubtedly arouse anger; the Europeans will rightly feel that they are the losers in an exchange of this sort. There is nothing, however, to prevent such American investments from bringing them the same sort of advantages as would arise from investments financed by a surplus on the American balance of trade or on current account.

United States direct investment arouses protests when it persists in a period of protracted balance of payments deficit. The protests are justified in relation to a given criterion, that of the rules of international fair practice as laid down in the IMF statutes. In this case, it is as if the central banks lend the American monetary authorities the dollars arising from the deficit in the United States balance of payments by investing them on the New York market, the counterpart of these dollars having been made available to American corporations in marks, pounds, lire, florins, or francs for investment in the Federal Republic, the United Kingdom, Italy, the Netherlands, or France. Once again the European is furious; but what does he want? What can he do? Does he want a deflationary policy in the United States? Does he want a devaluation of the dollar? Does he want a stop on American direct investment until the balance of payments has been redressed? In point of fact, he *cannot* impose the solution he prefers on the American government, and he probably wants neither further devaluation nor the suspension of investment; and though he may tentatively recommend the first solution—which is a stricter management of the budget and credit—he cannot be sure that this will redress the balance so long as the dollar's transnational function enables the United States to spend more abroad than it receives from abroad.

In trying to draw up a balance for these two Marshall Plans, this round trip of dollars, three considerations seem to me to be decisive: 1. the respective advantages to the United States and to its partners, as shown by a quarter of a century's experience; 2. the countries' degree of dependence on the United States; 3. the prospects or likelihood of an exponential increase in American investment.

Of all the countries in the capitalist world market there is obviously one which has profited from all the advantages of the system without suffering any of its disadvantages—Japan. Its door is barely ajar to American capital, its currency has been undervalued for years, and in 1971 the American market was absorbing about a third of its foreign sales. No other system would have given it comparable opportunities for growth—at an average annual rate of over 10 percent. Western Europe has caught up somewhat in per capita production and per capita productivity; the six countries of the Community export more than the United States (excluding intra-Community trade). In 1953 United States exports accounted for 21.3 percent of world trade, the Community of Six for 13.6 percent; in 1970 the percentages were 14.0 and 14.6. It was inevitable, of course, that Germany should recover the place it had formerly held and that Japanese exports should reduce the percentage share of some other countries. The fact remains that the share of American imports fell only slightly between 1959 and 1970, from 14.4 to 13.7 percent, whereas its share of exports fell from 21.3 to 14.0 percent.

Are these solely the consequences of an overvaluation of the dollar which acted both as an incentive to investment abroad and a brake on the sale of goods? Are the wage differentials in a number of branches of production greater than the productivity differentials? Does the numerical growth of subsidiaries—which import from the United States, but also sell outside their host country goods which the parent corporations could have exported—ultimately affect the United States balance of payments positively or negatively? To these questions, crucial as they are for the future, no one is at present giving a categorical and convincing answer. In the United States, spokesmen for the big corporations maintain that subsidiaries earn more foreign currency than they cost, while spokesmen for the labor unions claim precisely the reverse.

In other words, as long as the advantages and disadvantages are defined in strictly economic terms—by growth rate of GNP or growth rate of productivity—it has not really been demonstrated that the United States' privileges—incontrovertible where the privileges are monetary—have decisively benefited it. Without alienating any of its capital, Japan has sold more to the United States than it has bought from it. The Europeans have alienated part of their capital, but the influx of investment has probably accelerated growth, whereas Japan was easily able to do without an external stimulus to acceleration. The first question, therefore, leads into the second: What does "dependence" mean in relation to the dominant economy? What imminent or future peril lurks within this dependence? The various entities within the Western economy, as it has developed in the past quarter-century, are interdependent. From 1953 to 1970 international trade progressed at an annual rate of 8.3 percent by value and 7.55 percent by volume; no economy, not even the American economy, would escape the repercussions of a monetary crisis that entailed a reduction in trade among nations. This reciprocal and traditional interdependence of trading entities is now supplemented by a society which may well be called transnational because it crosses frontiers and lies outside the control and laws of national states. When the American Congress enacted the interest equalization tax to restrict foreigners' access to the American capital market, the market in Eurodollars came into being and prospered, with its center in London and the subsidiaries of American banks providing its incentives and dynamics. All the nominally multinational corporations do, of course, have a nationality, most often American, but occasionally Swiss (Nestlé), Royal Dutch (Philips), or British (B.P.); strategy is worked out and decisions are taken at the headquarters of the parent corporation; and the decisions appropriate to the corporation as a whole or the parent corporation itself are not necessarily compatible with the national interest of each country which hosts a subsidiary. The fact remains that it is the corporations' decision-makers who survey the economic field as a whole and arrange transactions between one subsidiary and another in accordance with their overall policy; and even if there is no deficit in the American balance of payments, they have huge liquid assets available, which can cross frontiers to pursue the profits arising from a devaluation or a higher interest rate. The former picture of purchases and sales between companies, each of them belonging to a different national state, is becoming less and less applicable to these multinational corporations and the Eurodollar market. Sovereignty in the classic sense still exists juridically intact, but it is in danger of becoming inoperative; the regulation of the national economy by interest rate becomes impossible when raising the bank rate to slow down a rise in prices results in an influx of billions of dollars. Budgetary manipulation is perhaps the only instrument[18] which is not subject to the interdependence of the money markets.

This dependence on the world market does, it is true, leave each national entity a varying margin of autonomy. The United States made use of its partners' fear of the dollar's severance from gold to keep the gold-exchange standard in being for some years longer. Since August 1971 and the agreement of December 1971 the world has been living under a pure dollar-standard system, in spite or because of the nonconvertibility of the American currency, with the Washington monetary authorities definitely adopting an attitude of "benign neglect" and, whenever the question arises, implicitly facing the market with the following choice: either you accumulate dollars or—and we see no objection—you let the dollar parity fall. (The dollar did in fact fall in 1973 after a second official devaluation.) This is a position of strength, to be sure, and only a united Europe would be able to counter it.

In more general terms, it may be said that the unequal stature of national entities leads to the dissymmetry of their influence upon each other. Some key sectors fall under the domination of foreign capital. The dominant economy exports its inflation and its technology, both of which contribute to a takeover of certain branches of industry. Once again, the question is whether IBM's and Honeywell's position in computers, Singer's in sewing machines, Eastman Kodak's in photographic materials, or ITT subsidiaries' in telephone and telegraph equipment is to be regarded as a danger. And once again the answer is uncertain, for the same reasons.

---

[18] This is also, perhaps, true of the volume of the monetary supply if the influx from outside can be "neutralized."

Is it military independence that is in danger? To the extent that this independence still exists, it is preserved by every country which manufactures nuclear and conventional weapons or keeps its freedom to acquire them—hence France and Britain, but not Germany. When the State Department, objecting to the French nuclear deterrence force, barred the sale of a large computer to the French government, IBM seems to have circumvented the ban with the semi-surreptitious consent of the diplomats themselves. The conduct of France's or Germany's economic policies is subject to external constraints created mainly by the dominating economy and its extensions abroad. But I cannot see either the State Department or IBM or the ensemble of the conglomerates established in France imposing any constraints on the conduct of French diplomacy beyond those inherent in the realities of life.

To take the extreme case, Canada, which may be called an economic colony of the United States: The Canadians benefit from their situation by a standard of living approaching that of the United States (75 to 80 percent). The monetary authorities in Ottawa have recovered a margin of freedom by adopting a flexible exchange rate. Canada's diplomacy does not, of course, enjoy complete freedom; as a famous saying goes: Like Mexico, Canada is too far from God and too near the United States. In return, however, American capital investments serve as hostages and mitigate the disparity in power; the American conglomerates have an interest in Canadian affluence and find it to their advantage to set up processing plants across the border. While I am not suggesting that the European countries should complacently contemplate a fate comparable to that of Canada, the Canadian example does contradict the argument about the peril to economic development mentioned in the administrative report quoted by Stoleru.

The Western European countries are not, therefore, in danger of being brought into the same sort of subjection as the small Central American republics, crushed beneath the weight of a corporation more powerful than each of them, nor need they fear underdevelopment as a result of economic colonization; the real danger lies in a further expansion of the wave of United States direct investments in Europe, the reinvestment of profits, and additional outflows of capital to swell the "industrial America" established on the Old Continent, to such a degree that the Atlantic may become as easily spanned and as little visible as the border between the United States and Canada.

In short, apart from certain national defense industries, I do not see how those industries which should be barred to American investment for the sake of independence can be identified with any certainty. I do, however, believe that it is reasonable to hold that though the accumulation of American capital in Europe might equalize the standards of living on both sides of the Atlantic, its indefinite accumulation would impose American-made decisions on so many branches of industry, would subject so many managers to orders from foreign directors, and would deprive so many research workers of the chance to provide their native countries with the benefits of the patents produced by their labors, that dependence would, for the elite rather than the masses at any rate, become an experiment *in vivo* and a source of bitterness and resentment.

During the quarter-century of American paramountcy, trade and monetary controversies were marginal to "high policy," the policy that captures the attention of heads of state or heads of governments. Presidents Truman and Eisenhower acted as godfathers to the Common Market; in their eyes the *political* value of a united Europe as a barrier to Communism prevailed over the *economic* drawbacks of a European community with an external tariff, especially as it was fixed at a level lower than the tariffs of several individual European countries. The Kennedy Round further lowered the tariff, on an average below United States tariffs. General de Gaulle's veto on Great Britain's admission created an uproar, but it all turned out to be a tempest in a teacup. Trade liberalization had progressed by virtue of the Kennedy Round. Despite the common agricultural policy, United States farm exports have continued to grow (though they would have been even larger without it). The responsibility for the new asperity evident in transatlantic dealings seems to me to lie less with the enlargement of the Common Market than with the devaluation of the dollar and the deficit in the United States balance of trade.

Direct investment was abruptly relegated to the background, and now the debate turned on the monetary system and the conditions of trade alike. In 1972 the policy-makers in Washington refused to contemplate any reform whatever, at any rate before the elections, and the Europeans had to accumulate dollars to prevent the devaluation of the American currency. In 1973, after a second devaluation, they pressed for the restoration of a trading surplus before a new monetary system was established. The American policy-makers also accused their partners of infringing the GATT rules, with which no one was in fact complying any longer; the real question was who was the worst offender. Behind the controversies there lay concealed a basic question: By what right does the United States claim the privilege of permanently investing abroad and of selling more abroad than it buys in order to finance that investment? In default of a crusade, will dollar diplomacy prevail over the strategy of containment?

Note to page 196: The Report of the President's Council of Economic Advisers on the United States balance of payments was presented to the Congress in 1972 in the following form (in billions of dollars):

merchandise trade balance + military transactions, net + investment income + services = balance of goods and services (+ 3.6 in 1970; seasonally adjusted annual rate 1972, + 1.6, average of the first three quarters);

balance on goods and services + private remittances + government grants (excluding military grants) = balance on current account (− 0.4 in 1970; − 1.8 in 1971);

balance on current account and long-term capital (− 3.0 in 1970; − 10.2 in 1971).

In order to obtain the net liquidity balance, there must be added to this last item nonliquid short-term capital flows, errors and unrecorded transactions, and allocations of special drawing rights, so that the result is: − 3.5 in 1970 and − 28.4 in 1971. The official reserve transactions balance is obtained by adding to the previous balance transactions relating to liquid short-term assets and United States short-term liabilities to foreign official agencies other than official reserve agencies; this item showed a deficit of 6.0 in 1970 and 7.7 in 1971; it had shown a surplus of 8.8 in 1969, reflecting the conjunction of a deflationary policy with a reflux of short-term investment capital to the United States.

Chapter Three

AID OR COUNTERREVOLUTION: THE UNITED STATES AND THE THIRD WORLD

The economic and political relations between the United States and what has come to be called the Third World of the underdeveloped countries call for examination separately from the relations between the United States and Europe, for a number of reasons. In both cases the deliberate or explicit aim of Washington's diplomacy has been containment, a limitation of the areas over which Soviet power might be extended or of countries in which a Marxist-Leninist regime might come to power. In both cases aid was considered as one of the most effective means to this end. In fact, however, when American action and its effects in various geographical areas are examined in detail, a completely different picture emerges.

The contrast between the brilliant success of the Marshall Plan and the universally decried bankruptcy of the Alliance for Progress has some value as a symbol of an attempt by American policy-makers once again to live their "finest hour" and put into effect a national dream still cherished in the depths of their hearts, the dream of enabling other nations to share their own prosperity and civilization. It also symbolizes faith in the dollar as a weapon against both poverty and revolution, and points up the very real difference between the United States' behavior in Latin America and its behavior in Europe and between the capacity of differing economies to profit from the transfer of capital. There is no common denominator for the *rehabilitation of developed economies,* weakened by war but richly endowed with all the human and social resources essential for growth, and the *modernization of economies* lacking technical expertise or petrified in traditional molds. Europe used American aid to help itself. Elsewhere, not even the volume of the aid supplied by the United States was comparable to what it furnished the Old Continent. In any case, the basic factors involved had nothing in common.

1.

I shall start by giving a few facts and figures to emphasize the United States' attitude toward the developed countries as compared with its attitude toward the developing countries.

Between July 1, 1945, and June 30, 1967,[1] total aid to foreign countries was $117 billion; 39 percent of this went to developed countries accounting for 19 percent of the world's population; a second category of countries regarded as militarily important or politically threatened which provided bases or troops on the periphery of the Soviet sphere (Greece, Iran, Turkey, Vietnam, Formosa, Korea, Philippines, Thailand, Spain, and Portugal) received 31 percent for 11 percent of the world's population; the rest of the developing countries, accounting for 70 percent of the world's population, got 30 percent.

This period of reference includes the years of the Marshall Plan; the figures once again reveal American diplomacy's exceptional generosity to Western Europe—exceptional in both meanings of the word, a rare case in the whole of history, and one unprecedented and never repeated in United States practice. Another set of statistics from the same source, relating to 1957–67, points up the disproportionate share of economic and military aid received by countries in the second category (which the writer calls "clients," but for which I would use a less invidious term such as allied countries or "defenders of the frontierlands")—37 percent of the total as against 50 percent for the rest of the world. And between July 1, 1945, and June 30, 1967, the proportion of grants in economic and military aid amounted to 73 percent to developed countries, 87 percent to countries in the second category, and 42 percent to the rest of the world. In 1957–67 the proportion of grants was 82 percent to countries in the second category and 40 percent to those in the third.

This presentation of the statistics, which I have borrowed from a

---

[1] Figures from Harry Magdoff, *The Age of Imperialism: The Economics of United States Foreign Policy* (New York: Monthly Review Press, 1969), p. 124.

"paramarxist" writer, will necessarily appear partial or slanted, for it suggests the least favorable interpretation of the external action of the United States. The figures do not take into account the American contributions to the World Bank and other organizations for multi-lateral assistance. For the period as a whole, however, these contribu-tions account for only 10 percent of total American aid, although they have increased in recent years.

I shall therefore turn to another, ideologically neutral, analysis, by Robert E. Asher[2] and begin by distinguishing four periods. The first, 1946–48, is the period in which the assistance went to the war-devastated countries; the total economic aid at that time amounted to $14,044 million (45 percent in grants); the developing countries' share was $3,052 million. The distribution is accounted for by the needs of Europe and Japan on emerging from the devastation of war. The total aid in the second period, that of the Marshall Plan (1949–52), was $19,541 million in economic assistance (82 percent in grants); the underdeveloped countries' share was 4,601 million (73 percent in grants). The distinction between the two following peri-ods, 1953–61 and 1962–68, is emphasized by the titles of the legisla-tion passed by Congress, the Mutual Security Act and the Foreign Assistance Act. During these two periods the major proportion of the aid went to the developing countries, $23,991 million out of $27,404, and $31,685 million out of $33,138. The share of grants, however, fell from 82 percent during the Marshall Plan period to 66 percent in 1953–61 and 46 percent in 1962–68. Total grants by the Agency for International Development (AID) to the underde-veloped countries fell from $11,572 million in 1953–61 to $7,290 million in 1962–68. In the course of 1968 AID loans amounted to $929 million and grants to $963 million ($659 million, excluding Vietnam). The proportion of grants in AID assistance in 1966–68 fell below 40 percent.

In 1953–61 gifts and loans by AID and its predecessors accounted for over one-half of the total ($13,053 million, excluding Vietnam, out of $23,991 million). The program called Food for Freedom, that is, gifts of food surpluses, received $5,542 million. In the follow-ing period the Food for Freedom program accounted for $9,772

---

[2] First published in *Monthly Labor Review*, XCII, No. 11, November 1969; Brookings Institution Reprint 174.

million as against $13,700 million for AID grants and loans. A growing proportion of the loans in the Sixties fell into the category of "tied loans." On the other hand, the American contribution to the international organizations increased to $1,869 million during the latter period, as against $189 million in the previous period. In mid-1969 the volume of aid to the underdeveloped countries supplied by the World Bank as a group was equal to that of AID (or its predecessors). Lastly, of all the countries it was Vietnam that, with $400 million, received the largest share of the AID budget ($1,892 million). Aid to development was inseparable from United States foreign policy.

In absolute volume American aid (with or without grants of farm surpluses) far exceeded that of all other countries, none of whose contributions reached the amount of a billion dollars yearly. As a percentage of the national product American aid was less than .5 percent in 1968.

I have no intention of leveling any accusation against the United States or of bringing any moral judgment to bear on this aspect of its external behavior. It should simply be noted that the developed countries, Japan and Europe, received the larger share of the American generosity (or of the grants whereby the Americans enriched their partners without impoverishing themselves). Contrary to a common view, safeguarding the developed countries was more important to the American economy and American diplomacy than safeguarding the Third World. A further point to be noted is that over the years the economic aid program became more and more closely tied to strategic and political considerations and less and less governed by the intrinsic needs of the countries concerned. And it should also be noted that economic aid was reduced in volume and in percentage of the national product and that the proportion of grants to total aid fell off as well. I should like to conclude with the seemingly ironical observation that in order to avoid repeating its mistake in the period after the First World War, the United States preferred grants to loans at the time of the Marshall Plan. The Europeans repaid these grants in some sort by consenting to lend yen or marks converted by the central banks into nonconvertible dollars. On this occasion the dispute which arose between Europeans and Americans was not about debts, but about the international monetary system and the nonconvertibility of the dollar. On the other hand, it was the Third World that had to bear the burden of paying the interest or reimbursing the principal of the loans granted in the form of aid and finding the foreign currency required for repatriating the profits of direct investments by American firms. In this way AID loans and direct investments become curiously akin, both of them originating, in one view, from aid or, in another, from the expansion of American capitalism. Underdeveloped countries which receive a loan from an international organization or direct investment by a large corporation one year have to spend the next year and the ensuing years earning the foreign currency to pay off the interest and amortize the loan or to repatriate part of the profits earned by the foreign corporation's subsidiary. In theory, in macro-economic analysis the additional expansion triggered by the influx of outside capital can procure the requisite foreign currency directly or indirectly. In many countries, however, this clearinghouse device has tended to break down in the past quarter-century for a number of reasons, which have also operated to brake the growth that foreign capital investment should have set in motion and to make it harder to procure foreign exchange.

The underdeveloped countries' main exports are primary commodities and raw materials. But the international trade in manufactured goods has increased faster than the trade in foodstuffs and raw materials. The volume of exports of manufactures (1963 = 100) rose from 28 in 1938 to 136 in 1966. The figures for foodstuffs and raw materials for the same years were 61 and 113.[3] The volume of international trade has risen by over 100 percent every ten years since the Second World War. It rose from $54 billion to $95 billion between 1954 and 1959; ten years later it had reached $272 billion. But while exports from developed countries rose by over 200 percent, exports from developing countries rose by only 100 percent. The latter's share in world trade declined from 30 percent to 20 percent.[4] To take some other figures (from the United Nations monthly statistical bulletin for March 1971): If the 1963 level =

---

[3] The reason for this is not necessarily, or solely, that technology brings a saving of raw materials per unit of manufactured product. Trade liberalization and the Common Market have contributed to this remarkable expansion of the trade in manufactured goods.

[4] Jerome Fried, "How Trade Can Aid," Foreign Policy, No. 4, Autumn 1971, pp. 53–54.

100, the index for world exports in the second quarter of 1970 was 184 and for the volume of manufactured goods in that quarter 210; it had been 201 throughout 1970.

A comparison of the price indices for 1960–70 does not give a clear picture of the terms of trade. The price index (1963 = 100) for all foodstuffs, nonfood agricultural products, and minerals was 107 in 1970. But there were appreciable differences between the indices for one product and another: 138 for tea, coffee, and cocoa in 1970, 99 for grains, 109 for fats and oilseeds, 84 for all textiles, 64 for wool and cotton, 122 for metalliferous ores. For all manufactured goods the unit price index was 117 in 1970—which meant a deterioration in the terms of trade for exporters of grains, fats, wool, and cotton, but not for exporters of metalliferous ores or tea, coffee, and cocoa.

Should it be said that there was a long-term deterioration in the terms of trade as between exporters of primary commodities and exporters of manufactured goods? The statistical demonstration depends on the year taken as the year of reference. Magdoff calculates on the basis of a paper prepared for the second United Nations Conference on Trade and Development at New Delhi in 1968 that the loss of purchasing power as a result of the deterioration in the terms of trade (relative to the average for 1953–57) represents 36.5 percent of the aid received in 1961 ($1,824 million), 40 percent in 1962, 35.7 percent in 1963, 34.1 percent in 1964, 40.1 percent in 1965, and 42.8 percent in 1966.[5] The long-term terms of trade are affected by conflicting factors; in some cases savings on the consumption of raw materials must reduce the demand for them in spite of the aggregate increase in industrial production. Advances in agriculture in the developed countries lead to a reduction in their imports of certain primary commodities, such as sugar and tobacco. Man-made fibers depress the cost of raw materials for textiles such as wool and cotton. Conversely, the industrialization of the Third World may well require the working of deposits of poorer quality or may bring better prices for some minerals.

Irrespective of the long-term movement of the terms of trade, countries which earn their foreign currency by exporting a few raw materials are liable to the repercussions of the economic situa-

---

[5] Magdoff, *Age of Imperialism,* p. 158.

tion in the developed countries, particularly in the United States. Violent fluctuations in the terms of trade may lead to a massive reduction in the unit value of copper or lead from one year to the next and consequently to a deficit in the exporting country's balance of payments for which it is in no way responsible. In any event, the countries exporting primary commodities are quite rightly convinced that they are getting the rawest deal in a fluid situation and that only those economies which include a large labor component in the goods they sell abroad have a chance for genuine development.

The developed countries' tariffs do not, on the whole, work in favor of local processing of the Third World countries' raw materials. All that the industries which do the processing, those in the United States, for example, need for protection is that crude raw materials be admitted free of duty and no more than a small duty be charged on the first processing stage. Where mines are worked by subsidiaries of multinational corporations, the decision whether to process locally or to import the raw commodity depends not only on the customs tariff but on the firm's general strategy, whose rationale does not necessarily coincide with the national interest of the country in which the subsidiary is located.

Is all exploitation (in the neutral sense in which we speak of a deposit which is exploited or nonexploited) of all natural resources by foreign capital to be construed in the same way as "exploitation" in the Marxist sense of the word? If a case is taken in isolation and if it is assumed that a mine would have been "exploited" just as efficiently by national capital in the absence of foreign capital, then indeed intervention by foreign capital implies a levy on the national income. But if the national capital had had the same capability and the same initiative as the foreign capital, the foreign capital would not have been able to set up in that country. Moreover, even if the national capital had been able to cope with a particular deposit, the question remains whether the remainder of the economy would have been unchanged if there had been no foreign capital investment in it.

The theoretical justification of foreign investments seems to me just as far removed from what actually happens. Foreign capital, it is said, always supplements the capital available locally and tends to create, directly or indirectly, production which, when sold abroad, either replaces imports or brings in the foreign currency required for paying the interest or repatriating the profits. This macro-economic clearinghouse device works effectually only in a favorable context where direct investment in dollars or marks affects the aggregate value of investment or labor productivity in the recipient country.

Any theory condemning or justifying foreign investments as such in the Third World seems to me to be devoid of political or historical relevance, so greatly does the effect of these investments vary with the recipient country and the investors' strategy. The repatriation or nonrepatriation of profits is not a satisfactory criterion. The repatriation of some part of the profits is inevitable. Furthermore, local reinvestment of all profits would equally lay itself open to "paramarxist" criticism. For would not the result be an indefinite growth of the value of the capital invested instead of the indefinite growth of the burden of indebtedness due to both repatriation of the interest and to amortization? Take an annual influx of $1,000 at 5 percent interest with repayment in twenty years: After twenty years the servicing of the debt would amount to $1,525 ($525 interest plus $1,000 amortization) while the annual influx would remain, by definition, $1,000. I take this artificial and rather meaningless example from Magdoff[6] solely for the purpose of illustrating the possible dangers of foreign loans.

In Europe pessimists see an Americanized economy, ranking second in world industrial power, looming on the horizon and crushing the old nations of Europe beneath its weight. Observers of the Third World, for their part, find that debt servicing or the repatriation of profits are already absorbing a large proportion of the flow of capital—whether in aid or investment—toward the developing countries. Carried to the extreme, interest, amortization, and profits would absorb all the aid and more. Neither of these two projections of disaster is inconceivable; neither has been demonstrated. It all depends on the recipient country's reaction to the influx of investments from outside, that is, whether these investments trigger the development of the weak economy or reinforce the domination of the strong economy.

For the time being, the influx of American capital is not creating any balance of payments problem for Europe, but it does contribute

---

[6] *Ibid.*, p. 153.

to a deficit in the United States balance of payments, a deficit which many people regard as a subtle means of acquiring the ownership of European firms. On the other hand, most of the Third World countries do not earn the foreign currency they need to repay their debts and devote the bulk of new aid to development. Europeans fear the alienation of their industrial capital, the Third World countries fear insolvency. Since the latter nations do not form a cohesive group, it will be more rewarding to carry this examination further by taking different regions separately.

2.

The external action of the United States in the Third World includes the economic, political, and military decisions of the Federal state, the strategies of corporations, and the consequences, unwelcome to the governments or even to the corporations' own directors, of the clash between widely differing societies and unevenly developed or industrialized economies. The overthrow in Guatemala of the Arbenz government, suspect of progressive tendencies, falls into the first category, as does the increase or reduction in American aid to Brazil depending on who is in power there (a reduction when Goulart was president, an increase after he was overthrown). The massive reduction in the flow of American capital to Latin America falls into the second category, decisions taken by the corporations, not by the Federal government. The "brain drain" falls into the third category, decisions taken by individuals, often encouraged by corporations, sometimes by the Federal government.

To take Africa first. If Africa is understood to include Egypt and the North African countries, certain key events symbolize American diplomacy there, such as the United States' refusal to finance the Aswan Dam in 1956 (which triggered off the nationalization of the Suez Canal), its attitude toward the war in Algeria, and its intervention, through the United Nations, in the Congo in order to prevent the Soviet Union from gaining a hold there or prevent the breakup of the country as a unit.

John Foster Dulles' strategy in 1955–56 was still part of the primary phase of the cold war and the containment policy. Until Stalin's death Soviet propaganda and even Soviet diplomacy were directed against the concept of neutrality or nonalignment as preached and practiced by politicians like Nehru. After 1955 Stalin's successors gave a place in their conceptual system and view of the world to national bourgeoisies and to the new states which, without joining either the socialist world or the imperialist camp, were engaged in a transitional and necessary task. Soviet diplomacy was in fact reviving an old tradition of the Bolsheviks. Lenin had not hesitated to conclude an agreement with Atatürk even while he was persecuting the Turkish Communists. The agreements whereby the Kremlin sold arms to Nasser in 1955 despite the harsh treatment he was meting out to the Egyptian Communists testified to a return to its customary realism. The American secretary of state would probably personally have consented to the financing of the Aswan Dam even so; but the President's indifference and the hostility of Congress, which banned the use of the funds provided for the Egyptian project under the Mutual Security Act, drove him to the brusque and offensive refusal to which Nasser retorted even more spectacularly. From that date on, the dialectic of the conflict between Egypt and Israel drew Nasser inexorably toward Moscow, while the United States became the ally of Israel. Today the Egyptians are irritated by the Soviet military presence[7] and Washington has not given up hopes of renewing normal relations with Cairo. The fact remains that between 1955 and 1972, owing to the successive crises in 1956, 1967, and 1970, the Soviet Union has gained possession of military bases in Egypt, Syria, and Yemen and has a treaty with Iraq. Containment has not been much of a success, even though Soviet expansion has been an expansion of Soviet power rather than of Communism.

Throughout the Algerian war American opinion displayed sufficient indulgence or sympathy for the rebels' cause to alienate French opinion, while the policy-makers in Washington were too solicitous of French susceptibilities to entirely satisfy the revolutionaries of the Third World. Kennedy and Johnson must ultimately have preferred the Fifth Republic to the Fourth in this respect, since General de Gaulle finally settled on an Algerian policy in conformity with American anticolonialism, though parading an uncompromising determination to be independent of the United States, an allied power, but one too strong for the good of the world and for the best interests of the American people.

---

[7] To which they put an end in July 1972. Temporarily?

The Congo crisis falls within the activist phase of American diplomacy and remains a unique episode in the cold war in Africa and an ambitious venture by the United Nations. It cost the Secretary-General his life, and the organization its illusions. Dag Hammarskjöld was succeeded by a Burmese diplomat lacking the Swede's charisma and resolution; and American diplomacy finally gained its ends. The Congo was reunified and the progressive leaders, the maquis, and the Katanga secession vanished without leaving any visible trace. After the deaths of the earlier leaders, Lumumba, Gizenga, Tshombe, and Kasavubu, a former noncommissioned officer succeeded to the supreme power and has been exercising it for years, entrenched behind an army which the Americans are helping him to train and maintain.

In the years that followed, the policy-makers in Washington were not greatly concerned about the innumerable *coups d'état* in the African states south of the Sahara. They backed the cause of a unified Nigeria even though the central government received arms from the Soviets, whereas French diplomacy sided with, but did not go so far as to recognize, Biafra and probably encouraged gunrunning to it. This was an instance of rivalry among Western states, the issue perhaps being oil or oil field concessions. To all appearances, the American diplomats remained indifferent (or almost indifferent) to the conversion of one or another of these states to Marxist-Leninist phraseology rather than to the reality of Marxism-Leninism.

Investments in Africa as a whole (excluding South Africa, but including the United Arab Republic) amounted at the end of 1970 to $2,012 million, including $1,009 million in Libya and $200 million in Liberia, leaving about $800 million for all the rest of the countries in North Africa and Africa south of the Sahara. Total repatriated profits were $119 million (excluding Libya and Liberia, the two major recipients of American capital). American diplomacy hoped to concentrate its activities and aid on the major states, Congo-Kinshasa (or Zaire) and Nigeria. It did not, however, consent to sever relations with South Ãfrica; it did participate in the sanctions against Rhodesia voted by the United Nations, but without much enthusiasm. Progressive or Marxist African leaders denounced the United States as a bulwark of world imperialism; when they assailed neocolonialism, they found themselves at issue with France more often than with Britain. "Africa has made a bad start," wrote Réné Dumont, one of the most eminent international experts on agriculture. To which another, even more pessimistic, observer retorted, "Can Africa get started at all?" In any event, American diplomacy does not seem responsible for either Africa's underdevelopment or the tardiness of that development. Since the Congo crisis the great powers have tended to leave the Africans to themselves, save for "exploiting" a few deposits of raw materials. There has been no equivalent to the Alliance for Progress. It is with respect to Latin America that American diplomacy provides a target for "paramarxist" criticism.

A distinction must be drawn at the outset between two areas in Latin America, the Caribbean together with Central America, and the rest of Latin America. I shall not attempt even a quick historical sketch of the relations between the Colossus of the North and the dwarfs of Central America or the nations of South America, but simply recall the fact that ever since the Founding Fathers, Jefferson and John Quincy Adams, United States leaders have always claimed or acknowledged a special responsibility in the first of these two areas. In the second they have not used the same methods nor as a rule has it been granted similar attention.

From 1898 to the presidency of Franklin Roosevelt and his proclamation of the Good Neighbor Policy, United States policy-makers resorted to gunboat diplomacy without the slightest hesitation or restraint, and even expressed it in legal terms in the famous Platt Amendment embodied in the Cuban Constitution of 1900, when American troops were occupying the island—an amendment giving the United States the right to intervene in case of prolonged economic or political disorder. (In return, Cuban exports on entry into the United States enjoyed a 25 percent reduction on the ordinary tariff.) The United States invoked the Platt Amendment on several occasions in order to send in the Marines, in 1900 (the occupation lasted three years) at the request of President Estrada Palma, and again in 1917 and 1920. It cooperated with Machado's dictatorship from 1925 to 1933. Roosevelt managed in 1934 to induce Congress to repeal the Platt Amendment, the model formulation of limited sovereignty.

It was in Central America, too, that the United States employed the procedures of subversion that were thereafter to become conventional by instigating a revolt against the Colombian government and creating the state of Panama in 1903, then obtaining its permission to build the Panama Canal and garrison it permanently. In accordance with the previous century's tradition—first to conquer and then to purchase—the United States paid Colombia an indemnity of $21 million in 1921.

In Nicaragua, too, the United States used subversion to overthrow President Zelaya in 1909 and replace him with a pro-American president, Díaz, who appealed for American troops two years later to crush the rebels. By virtue of the occupation, which lasted until 1925, American diplomacy acquired strategic privileges and a military base. The United States troops did not withdraw finally until 1934, under Roosevelt's Good Neighbor Policy. Similarly, Santo Domingo was occupied from 1916 to 1924 and Haiti from 1915 to 1933. Incidentally, Santo Domingo enjoyed forty-three presidents and thirty-nine *coups d'état* between 1844 and 1916. An independence which permitted the rule of President Duvalier and his Tontons Macoutes was hardly an unmixed blessing; American diplomacy can live with any situation provided that it does not result in an uncongenial government or provide an external power with an opportunity to interfere.

United States diplomacy with respect to this area is not readily accounted for by economic motives. Neither Santo Domingo, Nicaragua, Panama, nor Haiti possesses mineral wealth or commercial importance. An American writer[8] has even noted that trade between the United States and the occupied countries did not increase more than trade with the other Latin American countries. It is possible that in some cases the occupation actually impaired trade.

The gunboat diplomacy of 1898–1934 coincided with practices of a similar kind which the European powers did not hesitate to use where needed. Policy-makers in the United States carried these diplomatic methods further, because the whole area, in accordance with an offensive interpretation of the Monroe Doctrine, in some sort belonged to it; as Theodore Roosevelt put it, the United States had to assume "the exercise of an international police power on the hemisphere." The Monroe Doctrine prohibiting interference

---

[8] D. M. Dozer, *Are We Good Neighbors? Three Decades of Inter-American Relations* (Gainesville: University of Florida Press, 1959).

by European states in the affairs of the newly independent nations became a justification for the United States to intervene to prevent distant states from finding a situation favorable to their intervention.

Even Woodrow Wilson was brought to the point of sending an expeditionary force to Mexico as late as 1917, but was soon able to withdraw it. This brief campaign was in fact the result of an interplay of actions and reactions, rather than of any desire to impose an authoritarian government. Wilson had, on the contrary, refused to recognize Victoriano Huerta, a Mexican president who did not owe his power to elections and an elected Assembly. Nevertheless, Wilson occupied Veracruz on April 22, 1914, after failing to obtain the apology he demanded for the arrest of a group of American seamen. Two years later he sent a punitive expedition against Pancho Villa, a bandit chief who had risen against President Carranza, who favored constitutional procedures and was also an uncompromising nationalist. The punitive expedition under General Pershing nearly started a general war between Mexico and the United States. In the end, the pacifist movement within the United States, mediation by other Latin American states, and concern about affairs in Europe prevented matters from going to extremes. In January 1917 Wilson decided to withdraw the expeditionary force and in March he recognized Carranza and secured certain safeguards for American investments.

It was not until Franklin Roosevelt's presidency that military nonintervention became a matter of principle. The New Deal President refused to intervene in Cuba when Machado, the United States protégé, was overthrown by an army revolt, and in Mexico when the American oil companies were nationalized. At the same time, Cordell Hull was concluding commercial agreements to promote trade with all the Latin American countries. The American forces withdrew from Nicaragua in 1933, from Cuba in 1934, and from Haiti and Santo Domingo in 1940.

United States diplomacy with regard to the two above-mentioned areas in Latin America since 1945 has to be viewed in the context of a continuous tradition. The major South American countries, Argentina, Brazil, Chile, and Peru, had never been treated by the Colossus of the North in anything like the same way as the little nations in the Caribbean and Central America; and as they had no common frontier with the American republic, they were spared the experiences of Mexico. In both culture and trade they had closer ties with the Old Continent than with the New World until the Second World War. It was owing to the war that the United States purchased, in exchange for moral support and strategic advantages, the commodities which Europe could no longer buy. The Organization of American States (OAS) fits into the general concept of a network of alliances whose proclaimed intention was to guarantee the security of all its members and to prevent Communist aggression and infiltration, but which was regarded by some of its members as an instrument for the domination or hegemony of the Yankee republic, since the disparity in strength between it and its partners is so great as to be incompatible with the principle of equality or to render that principle impossible of application.

Latin America is a case in point for many reasons. In the first place, no military aggression from outside threatens any Caribbean or South American country; the Monroe Doctrine is so construed in an offensive sense as to forbid the establishment of any regime which professes the ideas of a state external to the Western Hemisphere on the assumption that any such regime would be the result of infiltration or subversion. Indirectly, therefore, the United States is likely to revert to the practice of limited sovereignty in spite of its ideology, and perhaps in spite of itself. By concluding more and more agreements for reciprocal military assistance when no great power can possibly invade the Western Hemisphere, the United States is liable, voluntarily or involuntarily, to exert a conservative or counterrevolutionary influence on the domestic politics of every state concerned. As the main supplier of capital it arouses nationalistic reactions against the alienation of the national wealth. The strength of the anti-Yankee sentiment was harshly illuminated at the end of Eisenhower's second term, when Vice-President Nixon made a tour of Latin America. The strength of these feelings was undiminished ten years later when Nixon, who had meanwhile become president, sent Nelson Rockefeller on a study tour after the failure of the Alliance for Progress. Does the United States owe its unpopularity to what it *does?* To what it *is?* To its intentional diplomacy or the behavior of its large corporations?

If one looks at the entire period from the independence of the Latin American states to the end of the Second World War and if one thinks back to 1945, it is hard to see why the United States should bear the responsibility for the relative underdevelopment of the Western Hemisphere. The diplomacy of the American republic, apart from the Caribbean and Central America, was concerned with trade and investment opportunities. It played no active part in domestic politics and it did not impose the free trade which checked industrialization and kept most countries confined to their role as suppliers of raw materials. While the United States has not urged Brazil, Argentina, or Chile to industrialize, neither has it prevented them from doing so, and it has not contrived to set up compliant regimes by subversion. Before 1945, indeed, no one attributed to the developed countries the duty to aid development. States or corporations that invested capital abroad did so solely for profit or strategic advantage, and made no bones about it.

The contrast between the United States' affluence and expansion in the nineteenth century and Latin America's lag in development during that period accounts in part for the anti-Yankee sentiment in Latin America that dates back a quarter of a century. A further factor is the cultural clash between Hispanic and Anglo-American values. Does the last quarter-century supply good grounds for the counts in the indictment?

3.

The Latin Americans harbor three grounds of complaint against the United States: The *cultural* grounds are that the influence of American civilization permeates their society with quite different traditions and corrupts or destroys its values; the *economic* grounds are that the Americans "loot" their natural resources and that corporations often acquire ownership of them and retain the profits derived from exploiting them; and the *political* grounds are that the United States Federal government, military assistance missions, and conglomerates interfere in domestic affairs to procure favors or to support men or parties devoted or sold to the cause of what is called the "free world" but is in fact the United States itself.

Let us leave aside the cultural grounds of complaint, important though they are in Latin America, as indeed everywhere in the world, for the subject would require a whole book to itself. Intellectuals and the traditional upper classes alike, though for opposite reasons, detest a civilization which claims to serve the interests of the common man and spreads the cult of efficiency. Landowners feel that they are condemned morally—and politically too in the long run—by the very power that protects them or on which they rely to prolong their rule. Intellectuals, with their European background, humiliated in their national pride and too numerous to attain the positions of prestige to which they aspire, ascribe the survival of unworthy rulers to the Yankees alone, for the ruling classes within the nation make common cause with the ruler of the world. The former are betraying their native country and the latter its own ideals in order to maintain together a common despotism.

Examining the factors behind the two other grounds of complaint, the economic and the political, we find them to be the same as those heard throughout the world: the exploitation of other people's wealth through direct foreign investment; the "brain drain," that is, the emigration of a large number of scientists and technicians to the United States; and interference by the directors of subsidiaries and even the directors of the parent corporations themselves in domestic affairs. Without exposing any of these subjects to exhaustive investigation or controversy, let us briefly examine the data with particular reference to Latin America.

Six or seven years ago Europeans were talking and writing a great deal about the "brain drain," the losses sustained by countries which had paid for educating highly qualified manpower who did not repay them in services rendered. Indeed it seemed as if the poor or the less wealthy countries were assuming the burden of training doctors, engineers, physicists, and chemists for the benefit of the wealthiest country in the world. Two facts seem to have struck public opinion and to have given rise to the controversy. First is the special case of doctors attracted by the industrialized countries, particularly Britain and the United States. One source estimated that 4,000 physicians had crossed the Channel and 20,000 the Atlantic.[9] According to this source, 1,400 doctors qualified abroad yearly (of whom only 300 to 400 were Americans) and became legally entitled to hang out their shingles. Everyone went about saying that

---

[9] Alain Murcier in *Le Monde*, April 24, 1967.

there were more Indian doctors in the United Kingdom than British doctors in India. Was not this "brain drain" tantamount to aid by the poor to the rich, even though the latter had trained the Indian doctors in its own universities and at its own expense?

This drain was due to a sort of suction and discharge mechanism. The deliberate Malthusianism of the American Medical Association, the *numerus clausus* for American medical students (some 8,000 yearly were being university-trained in the Sixties), created a vacuum which doctors in the developing countries were eager to fill, not merely from a wish for higher income or better living conditions; for a doctor trained in Western procedures does not always find back in his own country the technical and social conditions which will enable him to practice his profession as he has learned it. Those who argue not exactly in favor of the "brain drain," but against dramatizing it exaggeratedly, stress the discharge aspect of the system. In some cases they even suggest that these emigrants would in any case choose to practice in the cities with their ample facilities rather than in the countryside with its lack of them.

Regardless whether the responsibility lies with the country that causes them to leave or the country that attracts them, it is hard not to regard this immigration, *in certain cases at least,* as a nationally deplorable consequence of the freedom of persons. In 1964 it was estimated that there were 3,773 doctors of Latin American origin in the United States, including an exceptional quota of Cubans—a figure of historical or symbolic significance; the Castro revolution cost Cuba a large proportion of its educated class. A few years later a military *coup d'état* in Argentina caused several hundred professors to emigrate to the United States and decimated the staffs of some of the best Argentinian universities. It was the discharge mechanism which was at work in this case.

The second fact which gave rise to controversy was the passage of legislation in 1965 amending the conditions for immigration into the United States, lifting certain geographical restrictions on entry and facilitating the admission of persons with exceptional qualifications in the liberal professions, the arts, and the sciences. Foreigners, especially Europeans, viewed this as likely to cause increased emigration. As things turned out, the reduction in the NASA budget a few years later and the crisis in the universities led to unemployment of scientists and technicians. In some cases emigration in the reverse direction or the émigrés' return to their countries of origin seems probable.

The Europeans also profit from this migration. Britain and Canada receive qualified manpower from the developing countries. In some cases they serve as countries of transit and supply the United States with professionals just as they receive them from India or Malaysia. Of the developed countries in Europe, France suffers least from the "brain drain" in proportion to its population (the absolute figures are much the same as those for Greece) and retains some of the students from Africa who attend its universities.

Whatever may be thought of this phenomenon, its main cause is the encounter with other societies at different levels of development. Periodic recruiting by some American corporations supplements the attraction of the dominant economy with the most and best-equipped laboratories and the greatest diversity of jobs. The United States will not close its doors to engineers and scientists from abroad, and it is not always within a foreign country's power to prevent students who have attended the universities of Britain, the United States, and France from failing to return, or to hinder the departure of doctors, engineers, or technicians in search of better working and living conditions even more than better pay.

According to some statistics, Latin America supplies about 10 percent of the scientific and technical brains received by the United States from the rest of the world. The following figures are worthy of note. In 1962–66 the United States and Canada received 774 persons (skilled technicians) from Costa Rica, 3,005 from Mexico, 1,137 from Peru, 402 from Venezuela, 1,475 from Brazil, 823 from Chile, 3,572 from Colombia, 1,495 from Ecuador, and 1,122 from Paraguay. These figures are taken from an article by S. Watanabe in *International Labor Review*, April 1969.[10] But the true significance of these figures obviously depends on the needs of the countries from which the emigrants come and the stock of qualified manpower from which they are drawn. Statisticians have therefore computed an index (Harbison-Myers) to measure a country's ability to produce qualified manpower. This index, inevitably crude,

---

[10] See also Walter Adams, ed., *The Brain Drain* (New York: The Macmillan Company, 1968).

is the arithmetical sum of: 1. enrollments in secondary education as a percentage of the 15–19 age group, 2. enrollments in higher education as a percentage of the adult age group multiplied by a weighting coefficient of 5.[11] The index does not, of course, show the qualification of the qualified manpower or the qualification of those who leave and those who stay. But though the index is as high as 50 or 60 for the developed countries, it seems probable that at 20 or 30 the developing countries have the qualified manpower requisite for economic development. Several Latin American countries do reach fairly elevated levels in this index. Reverting to the list of countries above, Costa Rica has an index of 47.3, Mexico 33.0, Peru 30.2, Venezuela 47.7, Brazil 21.0, Chile 51.2, Colombia 22.6, Ecuador 24.4, and Paraguay 22.7. Figures for two additional Latin American countries, Uruguay and Argentina, reach the heights of 69.8 and 82.0 respectively.

This index seems to me to point up the virtually undisputed fact that most Latin American countries (though not Brazil) educate more graduates than they can employ in jobs for which they think they are suited. Is it to be concluded, as the Indian economist Deena R. Khatkhate does in an article in *Finances et développement* (March 1970), that the emigration of surplus graduates provides a sort of safety valve, reduces the pressure of graduates in search of jobs, and increases the fluidity of the labor market? To answer this, one would have to know more about the selection of the emigrants and the nature of the surplus graduates.

We will confine ourselves here to two observations, one about Latin America as country of emigration, the other about the United States as country of immigration. Taken in aggregate, Latin America educates enough graduates to tolerate the emigration of a portion of them without damage so long as the aggregate statistics alone are taken. It is to be feared, however, that a statistical breakdown might lead to a quite different conclusion. Furthermore, the amendment of the United States immigration legislation has changed the geographical distribution of qualified manpower settling in the United States. The number of qualified immigrants rose from 1,369 to 6,046 yearly between 1949 and 1957. After a

---

[11] E. Harbison and C. Myers, *Education, Manpower and Economic Growth: Strategies of Human Resource Development* (New York: McGraw-Hill Book Company, 1964).

four years' decline, the rise was resumed. From 6,000 in 1963–65 the figure rose to 7,205 in 1966, 12,523 in 1967, and to a peak of 12,128 by June 30, 1968. Thus, in the late Sixties the number of scientists and engineers entering the United States rose by 100 percent and of doctors by 50 percent as compared with the late Fifties and early Sixties. The increase was due to the influx of Asians, whose numbers rose from 360 to 4,160; in point of fact these were mainly students who were enabled to change their legal status from temporary visitors to permanent residents.[12] Whatever these emigrants' residual contribution to their countries of origin and whatever the surplus of graduates in these countries in relation to current demand, I find it hard to conclude that "all is for the best in the best of all possible worlds." It seems more fitting to end on an ironic note by noting that the attraction exerted by the United States is reflected in the degree of anti-Americanism diffused throughout the world at large. Only the surplus of qualified manpower in the United States—if it lasts—will curb an emigration more consonant with the logic of international relations than with the humanly desirable distribution of talents and burdens.

Turning to direct United States investments, what contribution do they make to development? What influence do they give the investors on the economy or government of the recipient country? Let us discard stereotypes, the notion that the directors of large companies such as United Fruit, as masters of the small countries whose governments they manipulate, bribe and corrupt officials and overthrow hostile ministries or organize plots against them. In Chile ITT did at least contemplate a preventive plot against the Allende government, which did in fact nationalize the conglomerate's subsidiary (but President Nixon did not follow up the suggestion). On the whole, the relations between governments and the subsidiaries of the large corporations no longer resemble these stereotypes, which nowadays are closer to myth than reality. The political and social influence of American corporations varies, of course, in inverse proportion to the stability of governments and the cohesion of nations; and almost everywhere in Latin America it seems to be on the decline, since any and all regimes can readily appeal to anti-Yankee feeling to muster public opinion in their favor.

---

[12] Figures are from an article by George W. Baldwin "Brain Drain or Overflow," *Foreign Affairs*, January 1970.

The size of the profits and repatriated profits is one of the major counts in the indictment. At a lower level, this count is expressed in crude terms; Christian Goux and Jean-François Landeau call the ratio between the volume of American capital investment and the value of repatriated profits "the racket rate." The numerator derived from American statistics for the balance of payments[13] relates only to the book value of investments. Probably this is undervalued and the ratio overvalued accordingly. The ratio for the whole of Latin America and the Western Hemisphere[14] was around 10 percent in 1970, ranging from 9 to 10 percent to over 10 percent. In 1970 the value of interest, dividends, and repatriated profits of subsidiaries was $1,081 million, while the value of investments was $14,683 million; the percentage therefore was under 9 percent. It was higher in 1969, with $1,277 million repatriated as against a capital value of $13,841 million, or 9.3 percent. Actually, the aggregate percentage conceals far more significant differences. In the cases of Mexico, Panama and the other Central American republics, Argentina, Brazil, and Colombia, the ratio of repatriated funds to the book value of investments is much lower than 9 or 10 percent. In Mexico it is just over 5 percent ($90 million to $1,774 million), in Argentina around 8 percent ($92 million to $1,288), and in Brazil under 5 percent ($89 million to $1,843 million). The aggregate percentage is higher owing to the special case of Venezuela; but the growing power of the Organization of Petroleum-Exporting Countries is rapidly changing the distribution of profits between these countries and the oil companies. In any event, to call the ratio of repatriated profits to capital investment a "racket rate" smacks of demogogic pamphleteering rather than a genuinely scientific study. For either all foreign investment, in a developing country at least, is held to be a kind of "racket" or neo-colonialism inconsistent with the interests of the recipient country—in which case this should be stated explicitly and a case should be made out for a national development without foreign trade or even without a place in the world market—or foreign investments, most but not all of them American, must be admitted to contribute

---

[13] *Survey of Current Business,* XV, No. 10, October 1971.

[14] The figures for the nineteen Latin American republics and the other countries in the Western Hemisphere are given separately in the statistics. Goux and Landrau use a figure for the Western Hemisphere as a whole.

or to be likely to contribute to the recipient country's growth, even if in themselves they constitute a levy by the developed countries on the profits (or surplus value) of the underdeveloped countries—in which case the repatriation of a portion of the profits is an integral part of the system.

As we have seen, both repatriation and nonrepatriation are attacked. The book value of American investments in the Western Hemisphere rose from $9,271 million to $14,683 million between 1960 and 1970. The amount of profits repatriated was much higher, therefore, than the net capital outflow in the same period. In the eight-year period 1963–70 the total United States net capital outflow was $2,833 million and the total of interest, dividends, and repatriated profits $8,841 million.

This comparison appears in all Latin American indictments of the United States, so much so that Professor Charles Kindleberger pays particular attention to the Latin American tendency to compare debt service on outstanding investment with new capital inflows. When new investment falls below current debt service, the Latin Americans claim that foreign investors are taking more out of Latin America than they are putting in. Implicitly, they would approve of continuous reinvestment of dividends, a pyramiding technique to which Australia and E. T. Penrose object.[15] To which the reply might be that Australia with its diversified economy does in fact fear the alienation of national capital and that Latin America with its still virtually nonindustrial economic structure legitimately fears the effect of repatriating profits on its balance of payments.

Be that as it may, Professor Kindleberger considers the Latin American reasoning "totally unacceptable." The correct comparison should be between the repatriation of interest, dividends, and profits, and gross investment rather than new net investment. I am inclined to side with Professor Kindleberger so far as the economic analysis is concerned; but the controversy seems to me primarily academic. A little further on in his study, Kindleberger reverts to the decisive point, that every loan leads to increased aggregate pro-

---

[15] C. P. Kindleberger, *American Business Abroad* (New Haven and London: Yale University Press, 1969), p. 171. For Mrs. Penrose, an Australian economist, see "Foreign Investment and the Growth of the Firm," *Economic Journal*, LXVI, June 1956.

ductivity through which the debt can be repaid. "The Latin American comparison makes sense only where past investment has been used unproductively or where the productivity has not been accompanied by the appropriate reallocation of resources so as to produce exports or economize on exports sufficiently to produce the foreign exchange needed for debt service."[16] He concedes that "this may well be the case"; but it is not the case with investment in Venezuelan oil. This example encouraging an optimistic view can easily be countered by examples illustrating precisely the contrary.

The efforts of the underdeveloped countries, and sometimes even of the developed countries, to attract American capital show that either the governments are betraying their countries or that the latter derive some advantages from such investment, at any rate in the short term.[17] The second assumption is the more acceptable, even where immediate advantage and advantage to certain branches of industry do not necessarily imply aggregate and long-term advantage. The recipient country and its government can easily be saddled with the responsibility for failing to spread the immediate advantage and the advantage to certain branches of industry to other branches in due course. But this sort of reasoning, though suited to pure economic analysis, disregards the manifold links between the foreign investor, development strategy, the distribution of social forces, and executive policy.

Depending on the country concerned, different socio-economic models approximate the true situation. Let us examine the case of Brazil, for instance, using a study by Celso Furtado, the Brazilian economist.[18] I shall not attempt to reproduce his line of argument in detail here, nor do I want to set up Brazil as an illustrative example; I should simply like to show how the transition from economic analysis to socio-political analysis can come about. The American economist can simply say that "this may well be the case," that is, that the increased productivity due to foreign investment may not have led to a growth and reallocation of productive capacity such as to produce the requisite foreign exchange. An econ-

---

[16] Kindleberger, *American Business Abroad,* p. 173.
[17] This does not mean that foreign investment is necessarily the best possible means of development.
[18] *Obstacles to Development in Latin America,* trans. Charles Ekker (Garden City, N.Y.: Anchor Books, 1970).

omist who is also a sociologist or historian will try to grasp the interplay of the social and political variables which impede this process or bring it to a standstill.

Celso Furtado's argument, reduced to essentials even if this reduces it to a caricature of itself, stresses two points: that the function of local industry has been to produce import substitutes, and that industrialization in this form tends to come to a standstill of its own accord if purchasing power becomes inadequate owing to uneven income allocation. Industrialization in Brazil has passed through two phases of rapid progress, the boom in consumer goods industries (the prime example being textiles) and the boom in durable and capital goods industries. Neither of them, however, was geared to export, so that the process tended to slow down as soon as the domestic market was saturated.[19]

In Brazil's case the effects of economic causality and social causality have operated in conjunction. Two agricultural sectors exist side by side: pre-capitalist agriculture, dominated by the great landowners, with an unlimited supply of labor and land; and an export agriculture (coffee) with an advanced technology which absorbs part of the manpower supply and whose prosperity depends on external demand. When that demand collapsed during the 1929 crisis, the government, supported by the privileged classes, tried to maintain the exporters' earnings and managed to do so only by destroying a large part of the surplus coffee. Since export earnings fell, they had to promote a noncompetitive substitute industry and then enable it to survive by protecting it through manipulation of the exchange rates or by means of customs tariffs. A similar process again occurred with durable consumer goods (cars) and capital goods in the Fifties. Celso Furtado believed that the process was once again on the verge of breakdown. In the Forties the average annual growth rate of industrial production had been over 7 percent; it was nearly 9 percent in the following decade and exceeded 11 percent between 1956 and 1961. But it fell to below 2 percent between 1962 and 1968.[20] In recent years, however, from 1968 to 1972, industrial growth has picked up again. Furtado, while accounting for this revival by increased public investment and the

---

[19] *Ibid.*, pp. 141–45.
[20] *Ibid.*, p. 129.

diversification of exports, considers (or considered at the time of his writing) that the structural factors which lead to a self-induced standstill of growth by its own process are still latent and will start operating again after the present phase is over.

The cause of the blocked development in Brazil is probably the curve for aggregate demand,[21] or in other terms, the allocation of the national income. This determines the goods for which there will be an increased demand if the national income increases and is allocated in a certain way. But this demand curve is determined both by the structure of the traditional agriculture and by the type of industrialization, which, under governmental protection, is geared to import substitution. The foreign corporations aggravate the consequences of these twin domestic causes. Industrialization must participate in the export flow if it is to break down the barriers to development and spread its profits.

How far is participation in industrialization by foreign corporations responsible for the structural distortions of the Brazilian economy which are liable to block growth and slow down the dissemination of technological advances? On the basis of Furtado's analysis, the authorities seem to me to be quite as responsible as the foreign corporations. The corporations in Latin America have in fact produced mainly for the local markets. The manufacturing industries established in Latin America with American capital sold 92.5 percent of their production on the local market and exported only 1.8 percent to the United States and 5.7 percent to other countries.[22] Their decisions, while rational within the corporations' total strategies, did not necessarily coincide with the host countries' national interest; but those countries did not contemplate or desire industrialization for export and both protected the incipient industries, whether domestic or foreign, by manipulating the exchange

---

[21] *Ibid.*, p. 153. The curve is as follows:

Percent of the Population	Population (1,000)	Income per Capita (U.S. $)	Total income (U.S. $1 million)
50	45,000	130	5,850
40	36,000	350	12,600
9	8,100	880	7,128
1	900	6,500	5,850
100%	90,000	350	31,428

[22] Figures (for 1965) from Magdoff, *Age of Imperialism*, pp. 159–62.

rates, by inflation, and by subsidies, and sheltered them from competition. By allowing them to charge noncompetitive prices, they thereby excluded them from the world market.

Industrialization by subsidiaries of foreign corporations everywhere suffers from well-known drawbacks. These include a tendency to import the most recent technology and consequently to adopt a capital-labor ratio consonant with the situation in the developed rather than the developing countries, and the transfer of decision-making to authorities outside the country concerned. In the latter instance the reasoning of those involved is determined by their total strategy and is rational for the corporation, rather than for each of its subsidiaries, and even less so for each country in which there is a subsidiary. Furtado supplements these trite accusations with another objection, at once economic and political. Large corporations, although officially juridical persons in private law, in fact perform a public function. Adopting the argument popularized by John Kenneth Galbraith, that the prices fixed by corporations no longer have anything to do with the market and are calculated in such a way that a percentage for the profit recognized to be normal is added to the cost, Furtado contends that a power of decision of this sort is politically unacceptable and that the fact that the conglomerates appropriate all their subsidiaries' profits is unfair, even, or especially, if these profits are reinvested. "Through the mechanism of internally generated financing, such enterprises are in a condition to appropriate an ever-growing part of the wealth created in the country. There arises, then, the double problem of the denationalization of the domestically accumulating capital and of the dearticulation of the national system of decisions."[23]

Thus in Latin America what "may well be the case," according to the American economist, is the case, according to the Brazilian economist. The accumulation of capital through self-financing leads to the denationalization of national capital. The servicing of foreign capital investment absorbs a growing proportion of the foreign currency produced by exports: 49.7 percent in Brazil, 44.3 percent in Mexico, 43.3 percent in Chile (figures for 1967, from Furtado).[24]

Confronting Kindleberger's economic analysis with Furtado's eco-

[23] Furtado, *Obstacles to Development,* p. 133.
[24] *Ibid.,* p. 64.

nomico-socio-political analysis facilitates the transition from the economic to the political indictment.

4.

There are two counts in the real indictment; the arguments are both economic and political. In the first place it is argued that direct investments in Latin America by the large corporations have most of the drawbacks and only some of the advantages generally attributed to them. Investments in the primary sector do not act as growth incentives and the corporations collect the largest profits they can as fast as they can for fear of nationalization, even if this means sacrificing future benefits. The disparity between net capital flow and profits repatriation illustrates the risks to a system if foreign capital investment stops coming in before the economies concerned have reached the threshold from which growth continues of its own momentum. In the manufacturing industries the foreign corporations' subsidiaries are liable to absorb part of the best-qualified management executives and they are far from willing to disseminate their skills and know-how. They work for the domestic market and supply import substitutes, but do not break down the dependence of these countries on the world market, to which their exports are mainly primary commodities or raw materials. In some cases these subsidiaries work for a narrow market and produce at a high cost and by virtue of tariff protection. Furthermore, the managements of foreign subsidiaries cannot and will not exercise any influence to assist a system that promotes industrialization. The country's policy-makers are all the less inclined to carry out an industrialization policy when it appears that its profits, at least in the initial stage, would go to foreign firms.[25]

In other words, the major argument of the proponents of foreign investment—what would happen if there were no such investment? —may go into reverse when the political variables and the influence of the American corporations on the national group of businessmen and members of the government are taken into account. The economists themselves have taught us the virtue of competition and the propensity of each and all of us to laziness; the national

---

[25] See Joseph Grunwald, "Foreign Private Investment," *Virginia Journal of International Law*, II, No. 2, March 1971; Brookings Institution Reprint 204. A bibliography is attached to the article.

elements are liable, in certain circumstances, to leave to others what they could do themselves. It is the withdrawal of the American corporations that would be the challenge.

We need only take the argument one stage further to arrive at the second, and capital, count in the indictment, namely that for fear of Communism American diplomacy tends to keep in power governments which in fact, whatever the intentions of the policy-makers in Washington, will not take the measures, such as fiscal and tariff measures, income redistribution, and reforms in the agri-cultural structure, which the structure of Latin American econo-mies needs if development is to be accelerated. The aim of Ameri-can diplomacy is both to prevent Communists from coming to power, for political reasons, and at the same time to promote de-velopment, for ideological or humanitarian reasons. Even if it is assumed that the policy-makers in Washington in their heart of hearts sincerely wish to achieve both aims, how can the impartial observer deny that they give the first aim priority over the second and accept too complacently the virtue of investments, most cer-tainly a source of profits but only conjecturally an impetus to industrialization? It is on the basis of this argument that critics, even American critics, denounce the counterrevolutionary role now played by the United States in Latin America, and in some cases in other parts of the world as well.

During the cold war era Britain's Sir Denis Brogan published an article on the myth of American omnipotence which aroused a great deal of interest. Public opinion blamed the Democrats for the "loss" of China, as if the United States had ever possessed it and as if the President were responsible for the Communists' vic-tory in the Chinese civil war. In exactly the same way, the Latin Americans and their friends tend to argue as if the United States reigned omnipotent over the major Latin American countries through the intermediacy of client governments.

For twenty-five years American diplomacy indifferently tolerated despotic and inefficient regimes (such as Duvalier's in Haiti) so long as they did not profess Marxism-Leninism. On the other hand, the possibility of a shift toward a Soviet regime led to intervention in Santo Domingo. Anti-Communism took precedence over all other considerations in dictating the American policy-makers' behavior in the Caribbean and Central America.

American diplomacy with regard to the rest of Latin America may well have been dictated by the same order of priorities; but there is a major difference, in that sending in the marines was not one of the "normal" means of exerting American influence. Neither Argentina, Brazil, Chile, nor Uruguay, nor even Venezuela or Colombia, is so dependent on the CIA and American capital that the vicissitudes of their domestic conflicts must be attributed purely to the Colossus of the North. American diplomacy displayed hostility to President Goulart of Brazil and hastened to recognize the military junta which overthrew him; but the army's seizure of power was also and principally accounted for by the fact that a conflict between various sections of the privileged classes had reached a deadlock. Perón in Argentina had never concealed his hostility to the United States. The Institutional Revolutionary Party which has governed Mexico for decades parades an uncompromising nationalism. In Chile free elections brought to power a Popular Unity government with Communist participation; but the armed forces overthrew it only three years later.

For twenty-five years the United States army trained, and is still training, a number of Latin American officers, and for over a decade it has been teaching them the techniques of counterinsurgency. The Americans' "guilt" is enhanced if the conduct of the entire Latin American military is blamed on Washington; but in fact, Washington is no more the sole factor that determines the role of the armed forces in Latin America than Moscow, Peking, or Havana solely determines the role of the intellectuals there. It is officers drawn from the anti-Yankee bourgeoisie or petty-bourgeoisie who are likely to supply the teams which will enforce policies of modernization or will set up such socialistic and nationalistic regimes as those in Peru and elsewhere. It is a combination of local conditions and external influences that is responsible for situations which vary from country to country.

Fidel Castro has involuntarily supplied ammunition to those who reject authoritarian planning and political despotism as the means for solving the problems of underdevelopment. With all due allowance for the consequences of the United States' unilateral quarantining of Cuba (comparable with the quarantining of Yugoslavia after Tito's schism in 1948), the socialism which Fidel Castro represented as liberal in his early conversations with Jean-Paul Sartre has taken a course similar to that of the socialism in Eastern Europe, not as a result of Moscow's influence but by a sort of internal fatality. To restore the sugar crop to its prerevolution level, Castro had to "militarize" the workers and even the entire population.

Castro's bad management seems all the more extraordinary in that local circumstances were relatively favorable despite the American quarantine; there was no overpopulation, there were abundant agricultural resources relative to the size of the population, and there was a fairly large middle class; diversification of agriculture and the establishment of light industries made an improvement in general living conditions perfectly feasible.[26]

This does not apply to Latin America as a whole, which must industrialize and wishes to do so, three-quarters of a century or a century after Western Europe. The proportionate share of industry in the whole of Latin America's national product is comparable with that for the United Kingdom, France, or Germany eighty years ago (an exception is Argentina, where industry accounts for one-third of the national product).[27] Industry absorbs only a small proportion of the surplus manpower created by population growth. The service sector is becoming overinflated, and huge cities which provide industrial employment are proliferating like cancerous growths. The most socially and intellectually developed countries— Chile, Uruguay, and Argentina—are incapable of trying for an industrialization of the Asian type (like that in Hong Kong and Taiwan), with light industries geared to export by virtue of high labor productivity and low wages; labor and the labor unions in Latin America would not tolerate any such policy and there are no entrepreneurs, either national or foreign, of the required type. The Latin Americans, therefore, are right in feeling that the international economy to which they belong does not create the conditions they need. Some of them imagine that their true interest would lie in seceding from this framework and adopting the political institutions they would require for introducing compulsory saving and accelerated industrialization.

They are not wrong in appreciating the difficulties inherent in

---

26 The bulk of the middle class chose to emigrate after 1960–61. A democratic or liberal socialism would have been preferable.

27 Joseph Grunwald, "Some Reflections on Latin American Industrialization Policy," *Journal of Political Economy*, LXXVIII, No. 4; Brookings Institution Reprint 203, p. 833.

closing the industrial gap in countries which are advanced in many other respects. Where their error lies is in failing to see that the growth rate of their national product[28] is not very different from that of the now-developed countries at a comparable stage in their development; they are wrong, too, in saddling the Colossus of the North with the responsibility for the situation instead of trying to turn evils (or dangerous remedies for evils) to good use, or in other words, making good use of American investment.

As long as the Europeans had colonial empires, both American politicians and the American public sided with national liberation movements and remained faithful to their tradition and national ideology. South Africa with its apartheid, Rhodesia with its incipient apartheid, and the Portuguese colonies, which are, in theory at least, integral parts of Portugal, still survive. Despite these enclaves of European paleo-imperialism,[29] the United States is now the decisive influence. By virtue of its ideology of the "common man," its tradition as the "first new nation," its optimism, its lack of interest in the past, and its confidence in the future, the American nation claims to be in the vanguard of history. Europeans curious about their own future, from Alexis de Tocqueville to Jean-François Revel, if one may venture to couple two such dissimilar names, have been seeking a clue to it beyond the Atlantic. Yet the economy which dominates the capitalistic world market, the only state capable of counterbalancing the Soviet Union, the major supplier of capital and technology, is now the main target of the "para-marxist" critics who ask whether the anti-Communism of American diplomacy does not necessarily cast it in the role of the mainstay of counterrevolution.

Is the state which twenty-five years ago took the lead in the defense of the free world open to charges, like the British, of founding an empire in a fit of absentmindedness?

---

[28] Though it varies from country to country, the national product is increasing at a far higher rate than that of population growth. The rates are highest in Mexico and Brazil; in Argentina and Uruguay, however, they seem to be virtually at a standstill.

[29] Chinese propaganda may come to propagate the notion that the Soviet Union is the last paleo-empire, a continuous land mass comprising an empire with an imperial citizenship and with non-Russian races whose population is growing faster than that of the Russian homeland.

Chapter Four

THE CHANGING FORMS OF IMPERIALISM

In 1969 the United States had eighty treaties with forty-two states and 302 major and 2,000 secondary military bases abroad covering an area twice the size of the state of Delaware; three and a half million men in arms, one-third of them serving abroad; and a defense budget of some $75 billion. In the Mediterranean the Sixth Fleet was protecting the security of Israel and perhaps, too, the security of Europe—and its oil supplies; the Seventh Fleet, stationed between the Sea of Japan and the Gulf of Tonkin, ensured the mastery of the Pacific. On the thirty-eighth parallel and on the Potsdamerplatz American troops mounted guard in mid-Korea and mid-Berlin. In Western Europe, for twenty years now one of the great centers of the affluent world and once more an integral and active member of the capitalist world market, were garrisoned 300,000 American soldiers together with 7,000 nuclear warheads to counterbalance the nuclear power and conventional forces of the countries of the Warsaw Pact.

By 1972 the armed forces had been reduced from three and a half to two and a half million,[1] the defense budget had fallen from $65.4 billion to $50.8 billion (in 1964 dollars), yet the major basic assumptions of United States strategy—or defense policy, if the reader prefers—had nevertheless remained unchanged. The area to be defended seemed to encompass the entire globe; in 1972 the United States' military frontiers were still the demarcation lines traced in Europe in 1945, in Korea in 1945 (revised in 1953), and in Vietnam in 1954. Under its multilateral military alliances

---

[1] See Note A, page 282.

(SEATO and ANZUS in Southeast Asia, and the North Atlantic Treaty), its mutual security treaties (with Japan, the Philippines, and Taiwan), its organizations under American command (NATO), and its programs of assistance to Latin America, the United States was filling a global role visibly different from the diplomacy of a state "like any other" or a national state. With military bases scattered all over the globe and investments distributed throughout the rich countries of Europe and the poor countries of Asia and Africa alike, this expansion, in some respects unprecedented though succeeding to and replacing the naval and financial predominance of Great Britain in the previous century, almost irresistibly attracted those ancient terms fraught with associations of glory or resentment, "empire," "imperial," and "imperialism." So far I have avoided these terms as far as possible because I should like to define them before employing them.

1.

The word "empire" has two meanings in common usage, the one abstract, the other concrete, and each of them includes further shades of meaning and ambiguities.

Empire—*imperium*—connotes either supreme power or the historical entity within which such power is exercised domestically or which itself exerts this power externally. Napoleon acceded to the Empire, and France, no longer republican but imperial under the constitution he gave it, subjected part of Europe to its rule, although the frontiers of empire were never identical with those of the territories annexed by it.

Empire in the abstract connotes the supreme or unconditional nature of power. In practice, the empire of the seas, as an equivalent to the mastery of the seas, does not rule out degrees of mastery or the means of enforcing it. It is not embodied in law, since the high seas are owned by all nations or none. What we have here is not a recognized authority nor even always a supreme power, but the virtually irresistible ability of a state to impose its will whenever it needs to. The empire enforced by the British navy from 1815 to 1914 owed a great deal to a reputation for invincibility which deterred competitors from putting it to the test.

Where the term "empire" designates a political or historical entity, it denotes characteristics which differ in each particular case. The first of these, the most continuous in Europe, is derived from the Roman example and consists in a *plurality of peoples* subjected to a single empire or, in other words, to a single supreme power. The contrast between a plurality of peoples constituting an "empire" and the homogeneity or national unity of the population within a "kingdom" has never gone unnoticed in ordinary and political parlance in France, all the less so in that the Kingdom of France was constantly opposed to the "imperial" pretensions of the Holy Roman Empire of the German nation or the House of Hapsburg. But in its third edition in 1719 the *Dictionnaire de l'Académie*[2] stated that provided a kingdom was large enough, it deserved to be called an empire. The Founding Fathers of the Republic of the United States envisioned an American Empire or an English-speaking empire in the New World.

As contrasted with kingdom or nation, the term "empire" therefore places the emphasis either on territorial extent or moral dimension or else on the diversity of the persons or groups of persons subject to one and the same rule. The distinction was of little moment in the past, for how could territorial extent or moral dimension have effect without conquest in an area which included no large or coherent ethnic groups? Kingdoms seldom attained imperial dimension without expanding their frontiers.

The contrast between empire and republic lies in the *nature of the domestic system*. Owing to the example of Rome, the classical historians and philosophers tended to identify the enslavement of peoples abroad with the loss of liberties at home. Montesquieu follows an ancient tradition in his chapter on the incompatibility of the republic with conquest. Historically, no regime is proof against the temptation of empire, in the sense of the domination of a weak entity by a strong one. At the time of the Peloponnesian War the Greek cities considered Athens more imperialistic than Sparta, although Athens enjoyed a splendor of culture and intellectual freedom, whereas Sparta trained its citizens as hoplites, not so much with a view to conquest as to keep its conquered populations in subjection. Athens had progressively converted the alliance of the

---

[2] Quoted by George Lichtheim in an essay, "Imperialism," in *Commentary*, April 1970.

independent cities which it had led out against the Persian Empire into a virtual empire, or at least a system in which they were no longer its equals, and the tribute it levied went to adorning Athens with monuments and satisfying the demands of the poorer citizens rather than to preserving peace and fulfilling its responsibilities for the common defense.

This illustrates the difference between the term in the strict sense of the Roman Empire and in the looser sense of the Athenian empire and the diverse forms of empire or virtual empire, the degree of empire depending on whether the supreme power is formal or informal, unconditional or conditional; in some cases sovereignty is openly asserted, in others it is concealed beneath some ideological or juridical form of words which on the surface seem to mean precisely the opposite, such as the reference to the sovereign equality of states in the United Nations Charter.

The dual meaning of the adjectives "imperial" and "imperialist" flows from a similar source. Some historians and politicians would use the term "imperial" for a diplomacy which intervenes all over the world without aiming at constructing an "empire" in the legal or practical sense of the term, and "imperialist" for a diplomacy which they wish to condemn and whose intent to dominate or exploit they wish to unmask.

The American literature on the subject has revived the use of the adjectives "imperial" and "imperialist" in recent years, the isolationist criticism in order to bring United States diplomacy back to a "new isolationism"[3] or at any rate a national diplomacy, and the "paramarxist" criticism to find some form of economic interpretation of American "imperialism"; midway between these two schools various commentators with a traditional European background have at times defended and at times even applauded the United States' imperial rather than imperialist role.

How is a national state to be distinguished from an imperial state in its external action rather than its internal structure (its political system or the unity or heterogeneity of its population)? Even where states are equals in accordance with the juridical principle of sovereignty, the part they play within an inter-state system

---

[3] Robert W. Tucker, *Nation or Empire: The Debate Over American Foreign Policy* (Baltimore: The Johns Hopkins Press, 1966); and Tucker, *A New Isolationism: Threat or Promise?* (Washington: Universe Books, 1972).

will always differ. Although the concept of a "great power" did not gain legal recognition in the concert of Europe in the nineteenth century, diplomats had a fairly precise notion of what it implied in the way of a body of rights and obligations, or, in point of fact, privileges rather than obligations. No international "question" was to be handled or solved without the participation of all the "great powers." Any advantage acquired by one of them gave the others a legitimate claim to compensation. In any inter-state system a small power usually tends to identify its "national interest" with its physical or political and moral survival, or both; consequently, depending on various geographical or military considerations, it seeks refuge in neutrality, abstention, or alliance with the great powers. The great powers, however, construct alignments and foster oppositions instead of adapting themselves to the situation as a conjunction of constraints and opportunities. Whatever the structure of the system may be, they therefore try to influence the external action of the other powers.

I can, therefore, perceive only a difference of degree between an "imperial" diplomacy and a great power diplomacy. If an imperial diplomacy is characterized by its "magnitude of power, scope, and nature of purpose and the character of its relationships with other states,"[4] do not these expressions apply as they stand to any great power? At most it may be said that a great power becomes increasingly imperial as the disparity grows between it and its allies when it has to assume the defense of or responsibility for broad areas of the diplomatic field. In this sense, a bipolar system inevitably requires an imperial diplomacy on the part of each of two superpowers designed to limit its rival's expansion.

If a bipolar system is also open to the operation of revolutionary forces, diplomacy becomes still more imperial through ideological propaganda and interference in the domestic affairs of other states, each great power trying to uphold, safeguard, or extend regimes professing loyalty to its ideas or institutions. "An Imperial State," Tucker says, "by definition, must have as its purpose the creation and maintenance of order. For the relationship of control maintained with the other, and weaker, states is constitutive of order."[5]

---

[4] Tucker, *Nation or Empire,* p. 50.
[5] *Ibid.*

Does American diplomacy from 1947 to 1972 deserve to be qualified as "imperialist"? It all depends on the meaning assigned to the term. In practice the term "imperialist" has pejorative associations, the term "imperial" has not. "Imperial" even preserves something of inherited memories of historical glory. The imperial state makes use of its strength, if need be, to defend its protégés rather than to enslave its clients or dictate its will to the weak. Insofar as the analysis is situated within the inter-state system, every great power tends toward an imperial diplomacy, and it in turn toward imperialism, because the nature of the system is a nonegalitarian relationship in which the great power dictates to its allies how they shall behave abroad, if not at home.

I do, however, believe that a distinction can be drawn between imperial and imperialist diplomacy without going outside the inter-state system, on the basis of the sentiments of the peoples and governments pro ected, whether as clients or allies. To take Western Europe: It was governments freely elected by universal suffrage which wished for the North Atlantic pact and it was they who asked for the presence of American troops on the Old Continent and the pact's military organization under American command. The French government had no difficulty in obtaining the evacuation of the bases on French territory occupied by NATO detachments; the relationships within the North Atlantic pact nevertheless remain nonegalitarian. The nuclear weapons, both strategic and tactical, are not part of the integrated command system; the President of the United States, and he alone, can order them to be launched. The American policy-makers devise the strategy, moving from "massive retaliation" to "flexible or graduated response"; and although they discuss it with their allies and allow them to participate in various ways in formulating the doctrine and putting it into practice, they retain the *imperium,* the supreme power of decision. Great Britain has reserved the right to use its strategic nuclear force apart from the NATO authorities in an emergency affecting its national interest—though this right is more theoretical than real—while France, although it has equipped itself with a strictly national strategic nuclear force, possesses very little autonomy as regards its deterrence capability. In my opinion, the term "military protectorate" ("protectorate" in its original sense of an "exercise of protection") or "hegemony" (a term which originally meant simply military leadership) may legitimately be used to denote the *political* action of the United States in Europe. During the cold war period the United States mustered its friends or financed its clients within countries threatened by a large Communist Party. Its action, whether political or ideological, could not be called imperialist without misuse of the term, since it was in practice helping nations to defend themselves against "outside pressures or attempted subjugation by (unarmed) minorities," to adopt the wording of the Truman Doctrine.

It is scarcely more difficult to appreciate the position in the Caribbean with respect to Cuba and Santo Domingo; the diplomacy was definitely "imperialist." It is true that an "armed minority" seized power in Havana, and nobody can affirm that Fidel Castro would have received an absolute majority in free elections in 1960. Reasoning of this sort does not excuse the attempt on the Bay of Pigs and would entail intervention in any country whatsoever on the pretext of overthrowing or preventing a socialist revolution. Only one further step is required to reach the intervention in Santo Domingo, which was designed to frustrate a revolution which *might have become* socialist.

The ambiguity of the adjectives "imperial" and "imperialist" as applied to diplomacy is not due only to the multiplicity of cases midway between the *protection* of Europeans at their own request and the *interventions* in the Caribbean to set up or uphold pro-American regimes and to overthrow or frustrate the establishment of hostile regimes; imperialism of the classic style *seems* to have disappeared in our time. A few years ago I defined imperialism as "the diplomatico-strategic behavior of a political unit which constructs an empire, that is, subjects foreign populations to its rule."[6] The Romans, the Mongols, and the Arabs were empire-builders. But I stressed two ambiguous or uncertain factors: What populations are to be considered as foreign? And is an official respect for the sovereignty of a state enough to exempt the other state concerned from the charge of imperialism? Where is the dividing line between an influence of great powers acknowledged to be legitimate and an imperialism denounced as culpable? I did not overlook the

---

[6] Raymond Aron, *Peace and War, A Theory of International Relations,* trans. from the French by Richard Howard and Annette Baker Fox (Garden City, N.Y.: Doubleday & Company, 1967), p. 259.

quite obvious fact that any leading power in a heterogeneous system is compelled to exert an influence on the domestic affairs of secondary states, to the extent, at least, required to prevent the triumph of a party linked with the rival camp—which does not rule out "discrimination between degrees of interference, influence, or domination."[7] In other words, imperialism in the form of behavior calculated to construct an empire in the classic and political sense has receded from the foreground, while imperialism in the form of a nonegalitarian relationship between states and a great power's will to influence the domestic life and foreign conduct of a small power has, like Descartes' common sense, never been so widespread as it is in our own time.

Europeans nowadays readily identify three kinds of empire: the *Roman Empire*, a nostalgia for which lasted for centuries; the *multinational* empires of the Hapsburgs, the Romanovs, and the Sublime Porte, all three victims of the First World War, set in motion by the two first-named; and the *colonial empires* of the British, French, Dutch, and Belgians, victims, in turn, by delayed action of World War II. Of the great powers in the present system only the Soviet Union still retains the typical features of the multinational empires engendered by history and conquest, the dominant role of one of its peoples (the people of Great Russia), and an urge toward revolt harbored by some nationalities (or peoples or ethnic groups), as evidenced by the frequent denunciations of "bourgeois nationalisms." The cultural autonomy of the diverse nationalities is not illusory, but as soon as it seems likely to transgress the bounds laid down for it by the authorities in Moscow, it becomes criminal. The Union of Soviet Socialist Republics even today is still more like a traditional empire—based on force and maintained by central power—than like a federation.[8]

The oppression of peoples or ethnic groups by a government regarded as alien, the sense of discrimination against them by minorities even within relatively homogeneous nations, and multinational states like the Soviet Union which have taken over from military empires are little noticed phenomena which are relegated to com-

---

[7] *Ibid.*, p. 260.
[8] The very nature of this multinational state seems to me a more insuperable obstacle to democratization (in the Western sense) than the economic system itself.

paratively unimportant news items, but they do serve as a reminder that imperialism in the political and classic sense of the domination of a people or state over ethnic groups conscious of their subjection to an alien power has not disappeared. What have disappeared are colonial empires of the European type and the will to "imperialism" in the sense of an official appropriation of sovereignty. The European nations compelled to divest themselves of political and military sovereignty have discovered, sometimes to their surprise, that their prosperity and standard of living did not depend on "imperial greatness."

2.

I have shown in an earlier chapter that it is not possible to explain the changes in American diplomacy stage by stage by the needs or interests of the American economy, and I have gone on to acknowledge that its economic motives cannot readily be distinguished from its political motives in a survey of its general aim— to prevent prohibition of access. The course of events, too, suggests that a notification that foreign investment will not be permitted access certainly does not lead to a suspension of commercial intercourse unless Washington itself decrees a quarantine or prohibits trading. I will now carry the investigation further to see whether the outward expansion of American capitalism in the form of trade and capital investment which has been going on for the past twenty-five years is due to an internal imperative, or what may be called "contradictions" within the domestic system.

Are the American corporations trying to ensure their supplies of raw materials, control the prices of them, and prevent their European competitors from gaining the advantages in price which they would enjoy if the American corporations had to make use of more expensive domestic raw materials? All these interpretations are to be found in passages in various paramarxist works. The volume of the capital invested and the question of price confer on a single raw material, oil,[9] the importance of an affair of state. The repatriated profits from *all* American investments in mining were $664 million in 1969 and $609 million in 1970, of which $439 million

---

[9] Prices for calculating taxes charged by producer countries, real cost price, price delivered Gulf of Mexico, and price ex-Middle East.

and $322 million came from developing countries. To attribute the wealth of the United States to the exploitation of the mines of South America and Asia calls for a good deal of imagination or ignorance. The figures for oil are of a wholly different dimension: $2,638 million and $2,603 million, mainly from the Middle East and Venezuela. These are certainly very large earnings, though the producer countries' claims will probably reduce them; but they are accounted for in part by the very large sums required to ensure the maintenance of production capacity.

The volume of interest, dividends, and repatriated profits ($6,026 million in 1970, to which must be added $1,880 million on account of fees and royalties) constitutes, as we have seen, a quite appreciable proportion of the American economy's profits. Still, like figures must be compared with like. Total profits from manufacturing industry in the United States amounted to $29.5 billion in 1970,[10] while *repatriated* profits from manufacturing industries abroad totaled $1,838 million and total profits $3,324 million; hence repatriated profits were less than 10 percent and total profits about 12 percent. United States income from investments abroad as compared with a national product in excess of $1,000 billion simply bear no comparison with British investments in 1914, whose capital value was larger than the national product.[11] The American corporations' rate of profit before taxes varies from year to year from 9 to 13 percent (9.3 percent in 1970); it is usually lower than that for investments abroad—which is not surprising, for if it were not, why would American businesses accept the headaches and risks of investing abroad? Excluding the oil industry, the domestic rate of profit was, however, higher than the rate for foreign investment from 1963 to 1968 (for aggregate investment, not for investment in manufacturing industry alone).

Do these figures lead to the conclusion that American capitalism would be brought to a standstill if it no longer received the interest, dividends, and profits from investment abroad? Or if it could no longer continue to invest abroad? The figures prove nothing of the sort. To show that the economy could not do without this ex-

---

[10] The figure for 1970 was exceptionally low; it had been $36.0 billion in 1969, and was $34.1 billion in 1971 and $37.6 billion in 1972.

[11] The same was true of France, whose investments abroad in 1914 are estimated at some 45 billion gold francs, whereas the national product was probably somewhere around 35 billion.

pansion would call for either an empirical study or a theoretical analysis. Historians would once again have to fall back either on the Keynesian theory of a scarcity of profitable investment opportunities or the Marxist or paramarxist theory of diminishing return as applied to profits. So far as I know, neither of these two theses has been demonstrated conclusively.

Both theory and common sense suggest, I think, that American corporations hold that the general prerequisite for direct investments is their ability to offset, and more than offset, the drawbacks of working abroad by greater efficacy and the fact that the return on the investment is generally higher than the yield from most national firms in the host countries. The American tax authorities at first encouraged investment abroad because they regarded it as a form of aid to development. When the rate of tax was higher in the United States than abroad, the corporations deferred paying their taxes by reinvesting their profits locally—a device not always available to them in the United States. Tax liability could be halved when accumulated profits were assessed as capital gains rather than dividends. The Revenue Act of 1962 made any final repatriation liable to corporate income tax, but deferred payment was still permitted. Generally speaking, the American government officially subscribes to the theory of tax neutrality, that is to say, the principle of laying down rules which neither penalize nor favor the foreign investor in relation to the domestic investor.

Balance of payments considerations induced the Johnson administration to issue new rules based on a distinction between three categories of country: 1. Developed countries with hard currencies (the Europe of the Common Market), 2. Developed countries with soft currencies, and 3. Underdeveloped countries. Repatriation was permitted for the 3 respective categories of "all but 35 percent, 65 percent, and 105 percent of 1965–66 (base year) profits."[12] President Nixon rescinded these restrictions; and in practice a complex system of insuring American investments was established by agreement between the United States authorities and the authorities of the host countries. Even in Europe it seemed as if, despite public pronouncements, the governments were competing to attract foreign

---

[12] Kindleberger, *American Business Abroad* (New Haven and London: Yale University Press, 1969), p. 59.

businesses, whereas the first thing they should have done was jointly to draw up a code to prevent overbidding, which was costly to Europeans and profitable to the conglomerates on the other side of the Atlantic.

Must we revert to Lenin's monopoly capitalism and the law of diminishing return as applied to profits? There are at least two major differences between the monopoly capitalism that Lenin examined, following Hobson and Hilferding, and the modern American conglomerates, in that banking no longer controls industry and the Americans do not collect the interest on their loans, as the British did at the turn of the century, but repatriate only a fraction of the profits and reinvest a large proportion of them. Would not the distribution of investment remain the same if the conglomerates ceased expanding and if the Federal government did not spend $70 or $80 billion on national defense? Certainly not; but the fashionable criticism of a society becoming wealthy while the state remains poor and consequently provides inadequate community services shows that the government would probably not find it too hard to maintain full employment if it allocated its resources in some other way.

Three-quarters of a century ago there were two conflicting theories about Great Britain, one of them (Hobson's) historical, which explained imperialism, colonial conquests, and the profits derived from foreign investment by the activities of a few privileged groups; the other sociological or theoretical, which postulated a necessary connection between the internal structure of the capitalist economy at a particular stage in its development and the vast increase in foreign investment and colonial conquest. Similarly, as regards the United States, the paramarxists place the emphasis on the profits derived from its economic and diplomatic activities abroad,[13] while the other school seeks, like Hobson, to identify the *decision-makers*, whose interests are not those of the community and, in extreme cases, to represent the United States as a victim exploited by its empire rather than, conversely, postulating an empire exploited by the United States.[14]

---

[13] See Note B, page 283.
[14] Ronald Steel, *Pax Americana* (New York: the Viking Press, 1967), p. 13: "Unlike Rome, we have not exploited our empire. On the contrary, our empire has exploited us, making enormous drains on our resources and energies."

I have already discussed the first argument; the second will require greater attention, all the more so because in the course of examining it we shall find some of the arguments on which the first argument relies. The works of which I am thinking deal with "Pentagonism," the "military-industrial complex," and the major organizations of the bureaucracy, or, in short, the pressure groups which have developed within American society and the Federal government over the years owing to the external behavior of the United States and the real or fictitious need for armaments. The phrase "military-industrial complex" as before-mentioned owes its popularity to President Eisenhower's use of it in his farewell address. It also designates somewhat imprecisely certain traits of American reality, accentuated by the effects of United States' diplomatic activities all over the world. The major organizations, the allegedly private corporations and the public agencies, control industry and government alike. The conglomerates contribute the major portion of American investment abroad and receive the bulk of the orders for armaments. An exchange of personnel between the corporations and the Pentagon has grown common; the corporations' executives or lobbyists establish close relations with acting officers, and when the latter retire, they find lucrative jobs in these same corporations, an old-boy network that creates or symbolizes the military-industrial complex.

To counter the argument about the Pentagon's predominating influence Gabriel Kolko,[15] a proponent of the contrary argument which I have called "paramarxist," advances statistics relating to the occupational origins of those who have held key positions in government; 65.8 percent of them had made their careers as lawyers or with financial or industrial corporations, or in other words, in careers closely bound up with the upper levels of American capitalism. The minority in power tends, he says, to deliver the instructions of big business, big finance, or big law in the corridors of the Capitol or the White House. Kolko employs many arguments which do not invalidate the theory of the military-industrial complex, but attribute a predominating influence within it to the corporations rather than

---

[15] *The Roots of American Foreign Policy* (Boston: Beacon Press, 1969), p. 20. The study covers the years 1944–60. The number of persons examined was 234, of positions 678.

the Pentagon. The aircraft industry lobbies in favor of the air force rather than conversely. It is the industry that proposes and imposes its plans, the cost of which regularly, and by far, exceeds the appropriations first accepted. Retired generals and admirals are hired as public relations consultants by firms working for the Pentagon; but after they have retired do they still have any authority over their former colleagues?

I am perfectly prepared to endorse Kolko's arguments on all these points; it seems to me inconsistent with the facts to assert that the Pentagon has gradually acquired the ascendancy or authority over United States diplomacy or domestic politics which by tradition normally belongs to civilians. Never have civilians controlled the conduct of military affairs so closely. While Truman and Acheson let a national hero, MacArthur, perpetrate errors which provoked Chinese intervention, they did not hesitate to recall him when, by his statements rather than his acts, he came close to insubordination. President Truman forbade the bombing of the Chinese bases in Manchuria and obstinately rejected MacArthur's doctrine that "there is no substitute for victory," or in other words, acquiesced in a draw.

Similarly, it was first Johnson and then Nixon who conducted the war in Vietnam, authorized the commando operations in the North, drew up the list of bombing targets for the heads of the air force, and set the limits to the bombing areas. The commitment was due far more to the political leaders than to the chiefs of staff. At the time of Dienbienphu only Admiral Radford recommended intervention, while General Ridgway opposed it even more resolutely than the senators.

Over the past twenty-five years the influence of civilians, especially of academics since 1960, on defense policy has, I think, been far more striking than any influence the other way around. Civilians from universities or research institutes devised the concepts which later permeated Pentagon thinking. Civilian supremacy was never asserted so strongly as it was in McNamara's time. Similarly, the massive increases in defense appropriations were the result of political judgments made by politicians, by Truman and Acheson during the Korean War and by Kennedy in 1961, when he speeded up the program for 1,000 Minuteman missiles and forty-one nuclear submarines, each equipped with sixteen Polaris missiles.

It was civilians again, together with a general summoned back from retirement, Maxwell Taylor, who worked out the concept of a military apparatus capable of waging two and a half wars, who replaced the notion of massive retaliation with that of flexible response and created the special units for counterinsurgency and nonconventional warfare. Though the obvious fact that corporations used lobbyists to obtain defense contracts is undeniable, the initiative throughout the period lay with the politicians, civilians, and academics rather than the generals. When the mood in the White House and in the country changed, the cuts in the budgets for the space and defense programs threw thousands of specialist experts out of work and put some large businesses in financial difficulties without arousing any strong reactions either in the Pentagon or on Wall Street. It was a Republican president, theoretically the representative of big business, who accepted Soviet superiority in megatonnage and number of missiles.

An argument which does not run contrary to that of the supremacy of the armed forces, but differs from it in positing a militarization of the civilians or, more precisely, a military type of thinking of the civilian policy-makers, seems to me more likely to be correct. Nuclear weapons—the first weapons in history which are to achieve their political purpose without ever being actually used—give a new meaning to the old Clausewitzian doctrine of the instrument of force in the service of the state or of "intelligence personified." Only the head of state can order these weapons to be used. Moreover, the doctrine of use is transformed into a doctrine of nonuse, a political or psychological doctrine in no way military in the traditional sense of the word. In the analysis of deterrence the man in uniform does not, as such, have a professional skill unavailable to the amateur; he is no longer the superior of the man in the business suit. In other words, neither disarmament in 1946 nor rearmament in 1950, neither the doctrines of nuclear strategy nor the waging of limited wars in Korea and Vietnam, nor the agreements on arms limitation, from the Moscow agreement of 1963 to SALT in 1972, are evidence of the supremacy of the chiefs of staff. All the events of the last quarter-century point to, if they do not prove, the contrary. It is certainly true that corporations largely specializing in arms manufacture have put pressure on the Pentagon and Congress in order to procure orders. The personal relations between generals or admirals and corporation representatives may well have led in certain circumstances to preferential consideration to one program over another. The key to the situation, however, the cardinal fact which engendered the notion of the military-industrial complex, its actual existence and the mythology with which it is surrounded in the public mind, is the armaments race itself, so closely linked with the rivalry with the Soviet Union. The armaments race itself, however, is, I believe, determined by the interrelation of technology and politics, in which the armed forces have in no way had the initiative.

Those who look upon the Pentagon as a kind of octopus sucking in personal incomes and plunging them into an abyss of increasingly sophisticated and expensive armaments in response to a fictitious threat bring up the theory of "overkill" in one form or another. What need is there, they ask, for 1,000 Minutemen and 600 Polaris or Poseidon submarine-borne missiles when a single hydrogen bomb of even one or two megatons is powerful enough to devastate a great city? Beyond a certain threshold it is not a matter of indifference whether one of the super-powers has the greater megatonnage? Would not the Soviet-American crisis in October–November 1962 have developed in exactly the same way if the United States had not possessed many times more ballistic missiles than the Soviet Union? Personally, I believe that the outcome of the crisis was determined mainly by the superiority of the United States' conventional forces in what would have been the theater of operations; but no one can definitely rule out the supposition that the decision-makers in Washington may have derived confidence and an assurance of their strength from a comparison between the two thermonuclear arsenals. The test of will in the absence of a test of strength takes place in the recesses of diplomats' minds. The armchair theoretician may safely say that beyond a given level of destruction—20 million, 50 million corpses?—differences vanish; there is nothing to show that diplomats think like this, or even that they are wrong to think otherwise. If there are wide disparities between destructive capabilities, the first strike by the stronger side would cause such damage to the resources and nuclear forces of the weaker that the latter might well forgo what would simply amount to posthumous retaliation.

Be this point of disputed theory as it may, the qualitative armaments race was started, almost irresistibly in all probability, by technology itself. The Soviets *could* not accept the Baruch plan (for how could they thrust the motives of someone whom they felt to be an enemy in the class struggle?) proposed by the United States soon after the war to prevent the proliferation of nuclear weapons and competition among states to discover the secrets of that all too lethal weapon. After the Soviets exploded an atomic bomb in 1949, President Truman could not fail to give the signal to go ahead with research with a view to producing a hydrogen bomb. The Russians and Americans had the first model ready in the same year, 1954. In 1957 the first sputnik shattered the American leaders' complacency with one blow, so assured had they been of their superiority in science and technology. The armed forces hastily asked their allies, Great Britain, Turkey, and Italy, for permission to install medium-range missiles, as if they feared that the American means of deterrence were inadequate and dreaded that the Soviets would possess a superiority in the number of missiles within a few years. This was an excessive reaction, as also perhaps was the Kennedy–McNamara program of 1961–62. Nevertheless, bomber aircraft were gradually replaced with missiles and the conquest of space followed the conquest of the air. Is it conceivable that a nation aspiring to world leadership would not have committed its resources, its genius, and its prestige to the race to the moon, which was hardly distinguishable from the race for superiority in the thermonuclear arsenal of hydrogen warheads and ballistic missiles buried in silos or mounted on submarines?

The official aim of the Kennedy–McNamara program was to maintain for some years not only a numerical superiority in ballistic missiles, but also a first-strike capability (elimination of a portion of the Soviet retaliation forces). Yet in the final analysis it would certainly appear that McNamara never quite believed in the subtleties of his entourage of whiz-kids who refused to accept the simple theory of balance by second-strike reciprocal destruction capability.[16] When McNamara advised the Russians to be careful to protect their ballistic missiles in silos, he was obviously discarding first-strike capability and fending off the danger as conceived by the

---

[16] In France, General Gallois expressed this theory in its simplest and crudest terms.

analysts, of a hasty Soviet reaction in a crisis if their weapons of retaliation were vulnerable.

Thereafter, the American policy-makers combined the armaments race with efforts at negotiation to halt that race and to stabilize the nuclear forces available to both sides. Kennedy achieved the Partial Test-Ban Treaty, Johnson the nonproliferation treaty, and Nixon the SALT agreements.

I shall not discuss here the question whether the United States could have negotiated an agreement of this sort several years earlier, before the Soviets had their present superiority in number of missiles and megatonnage. Nor shall I discuss the Americans' success in persuading the Soviets to abandon both the ABM idea, that is to say technical antimissile defense, and their traditional contention that a means of defense differs in kind from a means of attack. It seemed as if the Russians had finally endorsed the American doctrine which Donald Brennan of the Hudson Institute calls MAD, the acronym for Mutual Assured Destruction.

This chronology seems to me to support the axiom that research teams find what they are looking for. Unprecedented tools for destruction, computation, communication, and transport have been developed in the past quarter-century. With or without the competition between Russians and Americans, engineers would have produced hydrogen bombs and ballistic missiles and would have developed electronics. The armaments race was launched by science and teams of scientists rather than by the armed forces. When scientists and engineers were mobilized during the Second World War, the customary conservatism of general staffs was swept away in a flash by the real revolutionaries, the physicists, without a hope of return to the good old days. Between the two World Wars a general officer commanding the Saumur Cavalry School uttered the immortal sentence: "As war grows distant, the horse is recovering all its due importance." Perhaps it is more appropriate to recall a maxim of Auguste Comte's which I have quoted elsewhere, to the effect that the best proof of the fundamental pacifism of the industrial society is the disproportion between existing armaments and the armaments which could be manufactured if a temporary aberration created the occasion and the need for them.

The acceptance by a Republican president, Congress, and the Pentagon of some form of Soviet superiority clearly shows the decisive part played by opinion in the United States, in the long run at any rate, as well as the limitations of the military-industrial complex. The major organs of administration, such as the State Department, the CIA, and the Pentagon, do in fact tend to develop a will of their own, a certain autonomy; the loyalties of individual officers do tend to go to their department as well as the nation, perhaps primarily to the department. If he is to act, and above all to act rationally, the President must stand above the disputes between departments (and between his advisers too). To liken the United States (or the Soviet Union) to *a single* actor, as is inevitable in a simplified historical narrative, creates a gulf between representation and reality. Every department or organ is prone to empire-building and to assuming broader and broader responsibilities.[17] After 1947–48 all of them, despite their rivalry, kept their activities within the bounds of a definite historical and political world view, adopting an outlook whose concrete form was marked by opposition to the enemy, Communism, or the Soviet Union, one and the same in Europe but less of a single entity in the rest of the world.

This historical and political outlook slowly changed as a result of the Sino-Soviet conflict, the Vietnam War, the moral crisis within the United States, and the changes within the Soviet Union and the new face it is showing the world. The Soviet Union remains a rival, Communist China continues to be the embodiment of an economic and ideological system opposed to that of the United States; in proportion as the view of the other party changes, hostility softens into rivalry, and the defense budget, exposed to adverse senatorial criticism, is presented under three headings, strength, partnership, and negotiation, all three of which are components of a foreign policy aimed at creating a lasting peace and freedom by means of a *strategy of national security contingent on a realistic deterrence and a diplomacy of active negotiation.*

What remains of the mythology of the military-industrial complex? We are left with the reality of the major organs of administration in symbiosis, with a transfer or staff from one to another, with the permanent danger that each of them may take its own interests, that is to say its own expansion, for the national interest, with a

---

17 Even during the Cuban missile crisis there were disputes between the CIA and the air force about which of them was to be responsible for a particular observation or intelligence operation.

permanent need for supervision by Congress and stimulus from the presidency—parliamentary supervision to set bounds to the autonomy of the bureaucracies and presidential initiative to prevent their sinking into mere routine.

The mobilization for the cold war of a number of liberal (in the American sense) intellectuals and the traffic in academics between the universities and the Pentagon deserves perhaps more attention than the hiring of retired generals by General Dynamics. Some of the intellectuals at Kennedy's court may have disapproved beforehand of the landing in the Bay of Pigs (as Arthur Schlesinger did) or may have averted their gaze from the commando operations in North Vietnam or regretted the intervention in Santo Domingo. Contrary to a long-standing tradition, the republic's external action had become the overriding concern of the President and his advisers. The younger generation rejected this order of priorities; it rejected both the paramountcy of the United States and the subordination of domestic problems to preserving a non-Communist government in Saigon. It does not believe that the republic's prosperity and the survival of capitalism require the kind of action which has been carried on within the inter-state system for a quarter of a century or even the role of dominant economy in the capitalist world market.

3.

If executive power is weaker in America than in France, the reason for this lies perhaps more in circumstances than in the laws. It is generally in its relations with foreign powers that the executive power of a nation has the chance to display skill and strength. If the Union's existence were constantly menaced, and if its great interests were continually interwoven with those of other powerful nations, one would see the prestige of the executive growing, because of what was expected from it and of what it did.[18]

This was the view of Alexis de Tocqueville nearly a century and a half ago; for thirty years—since 1941—the great interests of the Union have been interwoven with those of other powerful nations.

---

[18] Alexis de Tocqueville, *On Democracy in America*, I, 8 (section entitled "Accidental Causes That May Increase the Influence of the Executive Power").

Circumstances have led to the consequences foreseen by an observer from the Old World, though it did not necessarily require genius to foresee it. The President of the United States has used "the almost royal prerogatives" he already possessed when Tocqueville was writing *On Democracy in America*. Is it to be said that now that the republic has become imperial, it has been transformed into an empire at home and that the President acts as a sovereign? Or that the Constitution, drafted by men more anxious to limit than to fortify the executive, hamstrings the external action of the United States or renders it unstable and excessive now in one direction, now in another?

The Constitution did not strictly specify the respective prerogatives of the executive and the Congress (the Senate in particular) with regard to foreign policy. The Senate enjoyed and still enjoys two rights: It declares war and ratifies treaties, and it votes appropriations. In theory, Congress would reduce to impotence a president to whom it refused the funds to conduct his diplomacy. In the past few years the Senate has made use of this weapon to compel President Nixon to reduce the intervention of American troops in Southeast Asia and to prohibit his sending troops into certain countries, notably Cambodia.

The President, in turn, still possesses prerogatives, whose limits no one, jurist or layman, can precisely determine, as commander-in-chief of the armed forces. It is in this capacity that he acts as needed, without a declaration of war, to protect the property and persons of American citizens in foreign countries. No wars have been declared for twenty-five years; the President, for good or ill, had no difficulty in sending an expeditionary force first to Korea and later to Vietnam without a declaration of war. Nonetheless, he secured the support of both parties and of influential senators in each case. The resolution passed by the Senate in 1964 following incidents in the Gulf of Tonkin gave the President virtually a blank check; a few years later the drafters and signatories of this resolution regretted the trust they had placed in Johnson on the strength of information which, in retrospect, seems dubious or slanted.[19]

Moreover, even the need for congressional ratification of a treaty

---

[19] The Southeast Asia Treaty Organization (SEATO), due to Dulles, had been approved by the Senate. The intervention in Vietnam could be founded on that treaty.

can be circumvented. Two examples are to be found in all textbooks on constitutional law. A joint resolution of the two houses was needed to obtain congressional agreement to the official admission of Texas to the Union owing to the lack of a two-thirds majority in the Senate. Arrangements with foreign governments comparable with treaties may be signed by the President in the form of executive agreements, such as the Roosevelt–Churchill agreement in 1940 on the transfer of fifty destroyers to Great Britain in exchange for American bases in the British West Indies. The principal treaties in the past quarter-century, the North Atlantic Treaty and the peace treaty with Japan, were negotiated by presidential advisers in cooperation with the most influential senators. The Senate did not have to pass upon all the President's commitments to dozens of foreign states. On the other hand, the vote on appropriations for foreign economic assistance and defense enables the Congress not so much substantially to modify the President's actions as to express its feelings about the executive or particular countries.

Since the earliest days of the Union, President and Senate have exerted a reciprocal influence upon one another with regard to the external behavior of the United States, though observers agree that the President's influence has usually prevailed over the Senate's. Of the wars waged since independence, only two, the War of 1812 against England and the war with Spain in 1898, resulted from initiative by members of Congress or pressure groups rather than the President's intentions or acts. Action by the President had more weight than Congress in starting the four major wars, the Mexican War, the Civil War, and the interventions in 1917 and 1941. While the President has made wide use of his "almost royal prerogatives" since 1945, he has introduced no innovations, but has simply gone further down a road that had long been open.

In the nineteenth century President and Senate were usually in agreement where the aim of executive action was continental expansion. Texas was an exception; the Senate's opposition to its annexation was due in part to disputes between Whigs and Democrats and personal quarrels (Clay, Van Buren, Polk). Polk, who was in favor of annexation, obtained congressional consent by joint resolution after he was elected President, ratification having been rejected by the Senate before the presidential election. On the other hand, the Senate on many occasions, indeed almost systematically,

opposed ventures that too closely resembled those of European im-
perialists. The unification of the American continent, including
even Canada, was the republic's manifest destiny; the possession or
annexation of territories which could not become an integral part
of the Union and constitute new states was incompatible with that
destiny. Hence the Senate's resistance, already mentioned in the
prologue to this book, with regard to Hawaii, Samoa, what are now
the Virgin Islands, and even the Philippines, the annexation of
which the Senate ratified only in the process of ratifying the treaty
as a whole. Similarly, once the imperial fervor inflamed by propaganda died down, opinion became uneasy about the legitimacy of the
war with Spain and even more uneasy about the annexations subsequent upon victory; and when the crusading fever cooled down
after Germany's defeat in the First World War, the Democratic
president was faced with a Republican majority in Congress. There
is no point in repeating an oft-told tale; the United States rejected
the treaty negotiated by its president and his grand concept, the
League of Nations. Furthermore, the "revisionism" which attributed
the responsibility for American intervention to the banks and the
merchants of death[20] created a climate in which Congress assumed
greater responsibility for the conduct of American diplomacy and
influenced the course of events; the enactment of the neutrality
legislation in the Thirties reduced the deterrent effect which the
likelihood of American intervention might have had upon Hitler.
Roosevelt's obsessive desire to induce Stalin to join the United
Nations and his remark at Yalta that the American troops would
probably not stay in Europe more than two years provide illus-
trations of Paul Valéry's remark that man has to be dragged back-
ward into the future.

Thirty years later Americans—journalists, academics, politicians,
and ordinary citizens—are no longer asking whether diplomacy can
be conducted properly under the Constitution as it stands, but
whether an imperial diplomacy is compatible with the republican
system and whether the Senate has not divested itself of its prerogatives and so become derelict in its duties.

---

[20] A Senate committee with Senator Nye of North Dakota as chairman conducted a far from impartial investigation of the activities of the banks
which had granted loans to the Allies and the arms manufacturers and
their share in taking the United States into the war.

The diplomacy of the immediate postwar period was "bipartisan." It was a Republican senator, Arthur Vandenberg, a repentant isolationist, who took the decisive role in preparing the North Atlantic Treaty and getting it through the Senate. Before the latter half of the Sixties and the Vietnam War no president, neither Truman, Eisenhower, Kennedy, nor Johnson, was at any time at odds with Congress about fundamentals. Is it therefore to be concluded that Congress and opinion, the parties and the press, allowed the executive complete freedom of action and continuously supported it? Obviously not.

The active diplomacy of a containment encompassing the entire globe enjoyed massive support *in the main* from both parties, from the press, and to judge by the results of opinion polls, from the bulk of public opinion. On two occasions, however, the President, first Truman and then Johnson, was bitterly criticized by the press and Congress for his conduct of two wars, those in Korea and Vietnam. The criticism was, indeed, perfectly intelligible: The right to dissent is sacred in the eyes of American citizens; it symbolizes, so to speak, the individual's freedom in relation to the authorities. The people are sovereign and judge those to whom they have delegated the governance of the republic. The two wars, moreover— imperial wars to uphold the inter-state order, to defend the frontierlands of the area for which the United States was responsible, to bar the crossing of a demarcation line, undeclared wars with no evident justification, clear purpose, nor prospect of decisive victory—had every feature calculated to render them unpopular. Nevertheless they were accepted by public opinion, at any rate as expressed in answers to questions from public opinion institutes or in elections.

Truman and Acheson were assailed by Republican senators, by a section of the press, and by Senator McCarthy, but they were never compelled by any irresistible mass movement of opinion to abandon the Korean battlefield or to seek a decisive victory as far north as the Yalu. On the other hand, the revolt against Lyndon Johnson and the Vietnam War was extraordinarily violent and probably forced his decision not to stand for reelection in 1968. His successor had to repatriate most of the expeditionary force. When Nixon sent troops into Cambodia after the overthrow of Prince Sihanouk, the campuses exploded; the guerrilla warfare in the Senate, waged especially by the Foreign Relations Committee and its chairman,

Senator Fulbright, grew fiercer. The President was forced to promise not to commit ground troops in Cambodia and Laos (although he continued to send in advisers and the air force was simply transferred to Thailand). Yet when faced with the North Vietnamese offensive in 1972, Nixon took the decision to mine the harbors of North Vietnam, reinforce the fleet in the Gulf of Tonkin, and bomb North Vietnam even more savagely, the degree of public outcry was in no way comparable to that in 1968 and 1969. It seemed as if once operations were confined to the professionals of the air force and the navy, moral outrage, even among students and their professors, tended to slacken. A republic can wage imperial war only with a professional army.

Which of the two theses, the fear that congressional interference with the conduct of foreign affairs may jeopardize its continuity and efficacy or the claim that the nature of diplomacy is incompatible with the essence of democracy, has been confirmed by a quarter of a century's experience?

Do Congress and public opinion bear the responsibility for some of the mistakes widely acknowledged today, such as the too-speedy repatriation of the American troops after 1945, demobilization and the relatively low defense appropriations in the crucial years between the alliance against the Third Reich and the outbreak of the cold war? There is no reason to think so. The President wished to meet what he assumed to be the wishes of the majority by bringing home the GIs; if he himself had been convinced that the national interest required the deferment of their repatriation or a slower rate of demobilization, he would in all probability have managed to convince the public so. In 1945 the republic's leaders were acting in this respect consistently with the traditional American custom of returning to the jobs of peace as soon as possible after the country has finished up its job of war.

President Truman may have resorted to the language of crusade at the time of Korea because he thought it was needed to mobilize Congress and the country. Here, too, the policy-makers may have conjured up constraints of their own making engendered by their dread of a wholly imaginary wave of protest. The conduct of the campaign—the crossing of the thirty-eighth parallel, the offensive toward the Yalu, defeat, retreat, and negotiations for armistice— was seemingly governed mainly by differences of opinion among those responsible for the running of the war and their decisions and indecisions and by the tense relations between the President and General MacArthur and between Acheson and a section of the Senate. As compared with the British Secretary of State for Foreign Affairs, the head of the American State Department has a hard time of it, perpetually harassed as he is by Senate committees and pressure groups. This does not mean, however, that the President himself does not enjoy wide freedom of action.

This freedom is not, however, unrestricted, to judge by the evidence. The statistics drawn from public opinion polls with which Dr. Kenneth Waltz[21] buttresses his contention can be variously construed. They do show that there is always a substantial section of opinion (a large percentage of those who answer the questions) which in times of crisis approves of the presidential action. During the Korean campaign those who replied to the questions fell into three groups, their size varying with the circumstances: a minority favoring withdrawal, a larger group favoring a vigorous strategy (a strategy for victory), and a third group favoring a limited war and negotiation. These reactions were normal reflections of the divisions within the political element, who made the mistake of combining extremist language with moderate action. This error was shared by members of the executive.

Perhaps the influence of opinion and a Congress who reacted to the supposed trends in this opinion contributed to the apparent extremism of a diplomacy of the status quo. Nixon was applauded when he took the risk of going to Peking. Had opinion changed in the meantime? It undoubtedly had; but would it have raised an insuperable obstacle some years earlier? McCarthyism and the anti-Communist obsession in the country colored the external action of the United States, induced policy-makers to refrain from certain kinds of forward action, and accentuated the contrast between cold war rhetoric and the behavior toward the Soviet Union. For some years now the reaction against past excesses has been aggravating the apparent instability of both American diplomacy and the country

---

[21] Kenneth Waltz, "Electoral Punishment and Foreign Policy Crisis," in James N. Rosenau, ed., *Domestic Sources of Foreign Policy* (New York: Free Press, 1967). See also J. E. Muller, "Trends in Popular Support for the War in Korea and Vietnam," *The American Political Science Review*, LXV, No. 2, June 1971.

itself. In the early Sixties the Senate often voted larger defense appropriations than the executive had asked for. Senate committees were dubious about the first Partial Test-Ban treaty in 1963; the President would have found it hard to get an appropriation for ABM in 1972. He may have consented to an apparent Soviet superiority because he despaired in any case of obtaining the funds for some other program.

Opinion and Congress jointly contributed to the second thoughts Johnson shared with the new secretary of defense regarding the request by the chiefs-of-staff for 200,000 more men. It was not that a majority in the opinion polls declared themselves in favor of withdrawal, but the methods of public protest and the senators in the Foreign Relations Committee exerted a pressure which morally, if not constitutionally, hamstrung the President. The Vietnam War, indeed, supplied critics and countercritics with arguments; it showed up the almost royal prerogatives of the executive, the undemocratic nature of foreign policy, and the President's ability to create *faits accomplis,* to present incomplete and partial information, and to act as the commander-in-chief of the armed forces and the person solely responsible for the activities of the CIA. The man in the street knows nothing about the major part of the diplomacy conducted in the name of the Union, and the members of Congress themselves know only what appears on the surface. Has the republic henceforth an *imperator* and has the Senate no functions save to perform a ritual and preserve an illusion?

The republic has not in this sense become an empire. The most influential newspaper in the United States published an investigation of the CIA and disclosed the manifold activities of the secret services. In what European country would such indiscretions have been permitted? Whether a majority of the persons questioned do or do not state that they are against the president in office or his policy little matters; opinion is not measured solely, or even mainly, by numbers. The press, the intellectuals, and the universities create the climate in which the president and his advisers live. How can they fail to be sensitive to that climate? To student riots? To the disintegration of the universities? To the number of deserters? To the violence of demonstrations? To the alienation of artists?

I do not mean to say that the United States has followed a course midway between the uneasiness of the Democrats and the uneasiness of the diplomats, with effective external action and without sacrificing control by the representatives elected by the people. This is not the case. The American republic's experience has been similar to that of the imperial powers which preceded it; the president has the vast and almost terrifying power to commit the nation to ventures which he does not believe he can then abandon without losing face. The external action of the United States to some extent lies beyond the scope of checks and balances. The president concludes de facto alliances by executive agreement; in his capacity as commander-in-chief he sends troops to Santo Domingo and advisers to Vietnam. He covers the CIA when it trains Cuban emigrés (and *The New York Times* tells Fidel Castro all about it). The Senate discusses the amount and distribution of aid and refuses it to states which nationalize American corporations without compensation. Basically, foreign policy is the preserve of the president, his private advisers (who do not testify before Senate committees), and the vast civilian and military organizations in charge of immense interests closely interrelated with those of other nations.

What does seem to me untrue, however, is that in a country in which the freedom to dissent still exists and in which departments vainly try to impose their mania for secrecy on the most talkative ruling class and the most inquisitive press in the world, there are no longer any restrictions on the president's power. There is no more an *imperator* internally than an empire externally. Only a *quasi-imperator of a quasi-empire.*

All those who use the term "American empire" promptly qualify it by adding that this empire does not in any way resemble any other empire, that it does not involve either military conquest, as did that of the Romans and Mongols, or direct administration of native peoples in the manner of the Europeans in Africa toward the end of the last century. It is an empire with neither frontiers nor sovereignty, invisible and ubiquitous.

I shall leave to others the game and pleasures of historical comparison made so fashionable by the Spenglers and Toynbees—Greece and Rome, Europe and the United States, for example; anyone is at liberty to stress the similarities or differences according to taste. Personally, I am far more interested in what gives the present situation its singularity, such as nuclear weapons, instant communications, rapid transport, the prodigious increase in the means of production and destruction, the conjunction of a scientific and technological civilization with a democratic ideal, the global extension of the field of diplomacy, the constant dialogue, despite interruptions by the authorities, between Russians, Chinese, Indians, Europeans, and Americans.

All inter-state systems throughout history have been oligarchical, dominated by a few states, the most populous and the best armed. The relationship between strong and weak is in essence dissymmetrical. The strong impose their will upon the weak where there are no laws to determine the rights and obligations of each. They do so even in civil societies subject to the rule of law.

The international economic system also involves in essence nonegalitarian and dissymmetrical relationships. All trade is nonegalitarian when evaluated by labor component. A high-productivity country takes a larger labor component than it gives. United States monetary policy preserves a relative autonomy; the policy-makers in the European countries to a large extent have to adjust their policies to decisions taken on the other side of the Atlantic. Last but not least, the developed countries in general, and the United States in particular, "exploit" the Third World's resources regardless whether they have or have not acquired ownership of mines or oil fields.

Only one further step is needed to arrive at a new *theory of imperialism* which preserves something of the literature of the late nineteenth century as well as of Lenin's pamphlet. This theory rejects any identification of *colonialism* or the European state's appropriation of sovereignty in the African and Asian countries with the *imperialism* characteristic of capitalism. It matters little whether sovereignty is or is not appropriated; what counts is the economic, commercial, and monetary system whereby capitalist states skim off part of the surplus value in the underdeveloped countries and restrict their role there to that of suppliers of raw materials and buyers of manufactures, thereby maintaining a state of underdevelopment. It is this system itself which, it can be said, deserves to be qualified as imperialist.

Some caution is called for, however. If the fact that the developed countries buy raw materials and convert them into manufactured goods is designated exploitation, the great powers do exploit the world, but the European countries are far greater pillagers than the United States. In 1970 the six countries of the European Community imported raw materials to the value of around $9 billion and the countries of the smaller European Free Trade Area $4 billion, while the United States imported $3.425 billions' worth; the Six imported energy worth $7.784 million, the Free Trade Area about $4 billion, the United States about $3 billion; the value of food-stuffs, beverages, and tobacco imported by the Six was $7.5 billion, by the other Europeans over $6 billion, while the United States imported $6.2 billion and exported $5.2 billion. Among the developed countries it is obviously those poorest in raw materials, Japan and Europe, which are "consuming" other countries' reserves. The developed countries obviously come off best in this international division of labor; I do not think, however, that to identify this as "exploitation" in its dual sense is a felicitous use of terms. The identification is arguable in only three cases:

1. Where a country which absorbs a large proportion of an exported raw material makes use of its purchasing power or its political weapons to keep prices below the market price; the United States has been accused of using its strategic stockpiles to prevent a rise in the price of certain minerals. This first case illustrates "exploitation" as defined by the economists, the difference above or below the market price obtained by achieving a monopoly or virtual monopoly or a monopsony or virtual monopsony of some commodity, that is to say, by becoming its sole seller or sole buyer.

2. Where, as the Latin Americans argue, a foreign corporation which owns raw material deposits carries out a strategy of investment and trade with the parent corporation which may perhaps maximize *its* profits, but not the earnings of the host country. The structure of the system may be said here to be "imperialist" or "colonialist" in the "paramarxist" sense, because it is more profitable—other things being equal, of course—for a country to exploit its wealth itself than to have it exploited by a foreign corporation, and to process raw materials locally than to sell them in bulk. It is self-evident that these first two propositions—trite at best—do not give any guidance in deciding where and when it is best to resort to foreign capital.

3. Where the system itself as it operates seems bound to perpetuate the poverty of some and the wealth of others or even to widen the gulf between them. Not that, in the abstract, the wealth of the de-

veloped countries requires the poverty of the Third World or is
contingent upon it. But the operation of the system, or the capitalist
world market, is found to favor the already industrialized countries
so greatly that most of the others are doomed to a future of underdevelopment unless there is a socialist revolution (whether it is in
the name of Marxism or anti-Marxism is irrelevant).

Of these three cases it is the third which suggests the decisive question: Does the context created by the industrialized economies at
their present stage promote or hamper the retarded countries' takeoff? Experience over the past twenty-five years does not provide an
answer one way or another. It does suggest, rather, a piece of advice
that for once reconciles morality with prudence: Let the great powers
leave it to the small to choose freely the regime they wish.

Note A to page 252   The Defense Report on President Nixon's strategy for peace[22] is entitled "Toward a National Security Strategy of Realistic Deterrence." The tables appended to the report are divided into
three periods: 1953–60, subheaded "Massive Retaliation, Umbrella for
Allies" (credibility contingent on nuclear superiority); 1961–68 (the
Kennedy-Johnson period), subheaded "Strategic Deterrence" (credibility
contingent on assured destruction); and the Nixon period, also subheaded "Strategic Deterrence," but interpreted differently as "credibility contingent on sufficiency and/or SALT." Between the second
and third periods manpower in the armed forces fell from 3.5 million in
1968 to 2.5 million in 1972. Expenditure (in 1972 dollars) dropped from
$99.9 billion in 1968 to $76 billion in 1972, reverting to the 1964 level.
In percentage of gross national product defense expenditure was 9.5 in
1968, but declined to 6.8 in 1972, as against 8.3 in 1964.

According to the booklet entitled "Military Balance" published by the
Institute of Strategic Studies, Soviet defense expenditure (excluding reserves) amounted to $72 billion (in American dollars and at American
prices) or $84 billion (including reserves) in 1971 and $77 billion or $91
billion in 1972, or 5 and 10 percent more than the American expenditure.

According to this source, the Soviet Union probably maintains thirty-
one divisions in central and eastern Europe; twenty (including ten
armored divisions) are in East Germany, two in Hungary, and five (two

---

[22] Defense Report and 1972 Defense Budget: Statement of Secretary of
Defense Melvin R. Laird on the Fiscal Years 1972–76 before the Armed
Services Committee, March 9, 1971.

of them armored) in Czechoslovakia. There are probably forty-four divisions in the Far East. The divisions in Europe are at mobilization strength or close to it, as are half the divisions on the Chinese frontier. There are said to be sixty divisions in European Russia, eight between the Volga and Lake Baikal and twenty-one in southern USSR. Most of the divisions in the central area and half the divisions in the southern area are probably not up to combat strength and would need substantial reinforcement in case of war. These figures in conjunction with the figures for nuclear forces (1,520 intercontinental missiles and 61 missile-carrying submarines) and naval forces (231 surface vessels, 244 offensive submarines, 34 of them nuclear-powered, 26 nuclear-powered and 25 conventionally powered submarines armed with four to eight JS N-3 missiles with a range of 450 miles) give some idea of the Soviet Union's armament drive in recent years.

Kennedy may have speeded up the armaments race in the early Sixties, but the Soviets have been speeding it up for several years. The SALT agreement is not visibly slowing it down.

Note B to page 263 What is the position of the multinational companies in the world economy?[23] The published statistics and studies provide only an order of magnitude. American publications, such as the *Survey of Current Business,* regularly report the book value of direct United States investments abroad. This was around $67 billion in 1970. If it is assumed that the value of sales is roughly double that of the capital investment, production by subsidiaries accounts for $134 billion yearly—to which Behrman would add $75 billion for companies in which Americans own stock (on the basis of one dollar of sales to one dollar of capital) and $10 billion for royalties from patents and miscellaneous fees, making $219 billion in all. The total for non-American multinational companies is some $231 billion (130 + 95 + 6).

The total, $450 billion, exceeds the total volume of world exports, $300 billion. The transnational economy of these companies producing in a number of countries through their subsidiaries is therefore larger than the international economy arising from trade in goods.

Multinational firms are not an American invention; Unilever, and the before-mentioned Nestlé, Royal Dutch, and B.P., show that even small countries (such as Switzerland and the Netherlands) may be the headquarters of multinational companies.

---

[23] Articles by Jack N. Behrman and Lawrence G. Franko in Pierre Uri, ed. in *Policies for the Seventies: New Challenges for the Atlantic Area & Japan* (New York: Frederick A. Praeger, Inc., 1971).

The European tendency to identify multinational companies with American corporations is due to the rapid expansion of American multinational companies in the past quarter-century and the contrast between European investments in the United States and American investments in Europe; it is estimated that 15 percent of production in the nonsocialist world is under American control and 10 percent of American production under foreign control; but direct investments in the United States amount to only $9 billion, the remainder of foreign investment in the United States being only in stocks which do not entitle their holders to any say in management.

If the multinational companies' share of total production goes on growing at the same rate as in recent years, it will rise from 22 percent today to 35 percent in 1980 and 50 percent in 1990. These figures in themselves tend to suggest that the development in recent years will not continue at a similar rate.

The prerequisite for this expansion has been and still is the multinational company's possession of an advantage in technology or organization, or both, over companies in the host country. Even while it distributes its product or disseminates its know-how, the multinational company must perpetually be on the alert to find further advantages it can monopolize. It brings about an unprecedented mobility of the means of production. Its choice of one country rather than another in which to produce a particular type of article depends on a great many different considerations, the local wage level clearly being one of the most important.

There is not, of course, only one type of multinational company, but a great variety, some of them concentrating on a particular kind of production, others going in for the widest possible diversification, and others again with composite strategies. As I see it, the multinational companies have a positive effect on technological and economic progress, because they promote the rapid spread of advanced techniques and transfers of technology. They pose, as well, a challenge to national states, because if these states are to secure an adequate share of world industrial production they must bargain with the multinational firms and commit themselves to a policy of industrialization.

This means that the traditional theory of international trade and its comparative advantages no longer holds good. Monetary problems, too, are undoubtedly affected, because, quite apart from the deficit on the American balance of payments, the transfer of funds from one subsidiary to another is bound to set off cross-frontier movements of capital.

As concerns the future, a great many questions arise. Will the non-American multinational companies develop faster than the American? Will the United States lose the advantages it secured by greater direct foreign investment in the past? Or, conversely, will an unduly rapid expansion of its direct investments lead to action to curtail it?

My own view is that the multinational companies will retain an appreciable share of the world market, but that their recent rate of growth will not be protracted indefinitely. I believe, too, that the non-American multinational companies are likely to fight back and that the American superiority will gradually diminish, except in a few areas which require intensive and expensive technology. I also believe that the transnational economy brought into being by these companies is likely to last. As to attempts to draft a code of ethics for multinational companies—a code which would enable national states to recover some part of the sovereignty they have lost—they too are likely to be protracted, because of the newness and complexity of the problems involved, and because so little is known about them either empirically or theoretically and so little has as yet been done to investigate them.

Conclusion

THE END OF ECONOMIC SOVEREIGNTIES

In the conclusion to the first part of this essay I managed to compile a balance sheet of the success and failure of American diplomacy without unduly straining the facts—or perhaps of its success through failure and failure through success—in that within the inter-state system its aim was fairly consistent, but was not confined to ensuring the security, or even power, of the United States. A study of the preceding chapters reveals that no *single* aim could be identified as demonstrably governing the economic and monetary policies of the American government, much less those of the largely American-controlled multinational companies which have become an essential element in the world market and the transnational society. Nor could the aims or interests of these companies be construed as the inner secret of inter-state diplomacy.

The aggregate measure of American success is the growth of the world economy, that is, if it is assumed that the American policymakers really believed that their primary task was to prosper through their generosity to others or to ensure the greatest happiness of the greatest number simply by sharing their own affluence with others. By this criterion the American diplomats were strikingly successful in the countries at an advanced stage of development, but decidedly less so in the others. I shall, of course, take care not to imitate the critics who invariably put to the United States' discredit the despotism and poverty of countries which are all too manifestly poor and oppressed, even though they lie to some degree within the United States' sphere of influence. I shall merely point out once again that a dominant economy has, for good or ill, a dissymmetrical effect on other economies. The rules of GATT and the International Monetary Fund, and even perhaps the substitution of the dollar standard for the Bretton Woods monetary system, have contributed to an unprecedented growth rate in production and trade.

Between 1960 and 1969 the annual growth rate of the gross national product (GNP) was 5.1 percent for developed countries and 5 percent for developing countries.[1] Since the rate of population growth during the same period was 1.2 percent for the developed countries and 2.6 percent for the developing countries, the per capita product rose by 3.9 percent in the former and 2.4 percent in the latter. From these figures some will conclude that the disparity is increasing—which is true enough—and others that the growth rate in the developing countries would have looked quite respectable in other periods.

Moreover, exports from the underdeveloped countries rose by 6.7 percent yearly in value and by 6.4 percent in volume, and imports by 5.2 percent and 5.8 percent respectively in the same period. The rates for the developed countries were higher—8.4 percent and 9.5 percent for exports (volume and value) and 9.0 percent and 9.7 percent for imports. For imports, too, the figures for the developing countries, though lower, are impressive as compared with the past, but do, of course, show a reduction in their share of world trade.

Of the four regions in which statisticians group the developing countries, Asia—Southeast Asia in particular—has an abnormally small share of world trade.[2] With 59.5 percent of the developing countries' population, Asia exports only 26 percent of their total exports (average 1965–66). Latin America, with 15.9 percent of their population, accounts for 34.5 percent of their total exports. In India, Pakistan, and Indonesia neither the United States nor the other developed countries have enough influence to either cause or prevent the revolution which alone, according to many American and European intellectuals, can clear the way to development and modernization. Neither the United States government nor any of its agencies has any overriding position in India or Pakistan. It is the "Green Revolution" and technical progress in agriculture that have accounted for the hopes aroused in the past ten years. Even if Commu-

---

[1] Figures from a report to the third United Nations Conference on Trade and Development, Santiago, Chile, 1972 (TD/113/Supp. 2, p. 2, Table 1).
[2] Figures from an IMF-IBRD report on the stabilization of primary commodity prices (1967–68).

nist China's performance is better than India's, as seems probable from the information available, there is nothing to show that anyone, even the United States, can bring into being on the Indian subcontinent a party comparable to that of Mao Tse-tung.

In Latin America the Castro experiment has shown that planning and Marxist professions of faith do not suffice to ensure an economy's takeoff. It may well be true that Fidel Castro, especially in his earlier days, gave millions a sense of participation, for he taught them to read and prepared them for citizenship; the Cubans may benefit some day from their present trials. At the moment, the entire population has to be "militarized" to harvest a sugar crop even as large as it was before the revolution. With all due allowance for the American blockade, which I hope will be raised in the near future, there remains the trite and virtually self-evident fact that not all the Communist Parties display the "efficiency" in modernizing expected of them, though some of them do show signs of it, at a considerable cost to the suffering generations, but with comparatively bright prospects for the future generations who will witness their triumph.

If only Washington's diplomacy were to advance beyond nonintervention and assert a genuine neutrality toward governments motivated by nationalism or socialism (though all governments, not only that of the United States, generally meet hostility with hostility), Latin Americans would no longer be tempted to saddle the United States with a responsibility in which they themselves have at least some share. Even if they nationalize all the subsidiaries of American corporations exploiting the mines, the profits they would, in the most optimistic perspective, derive from them would still be paltry in comparison with their needs. They would very often lose by such a move unless they acquired a position of strength as well as the ownership.[3]

In the developed countries in which American diplomacy has succeeded—assuming that its ultimate aim was freedom of trade and

---

[3] Theodore H. Moran has shown in an interesting article in *Foreign Policy* (No. 5, Winter 1971–72), "New Deal or Raw Deal in Raw Materials," that all depends on the decisive level in a multinational corporation's vertical integration system. The oil-producing countries have succeeded in considerably increasing their share of the profits. They will continue doing so by demanding and getting part ownership and a share in exploitation and distribution at all levels, always provided that they do not imperil the security of supplies. The Shah of Iran has grasped this point.

the propagation of prosperity and technology—its success brings with it two possible factors which may well lead to failure. Is not the United States *in the long run impoverished rather than enriched by its grants?* Just as Germany and the United States borrowed from and outstripped the British in technical skills and knowledge at the end of the last century, are not Japan and Western Europe likely to catch up with and outstrip the United States owing to a higher rate of per capita production? Do not the devaluation of the dollar and the high proportion of earnings in foreign currencies from receipts from direct investments abroad foreshadow an American decline like that of the British? A second factor might be, conversely, *failure through excess of success.* The dominant economy has imposed a monetary system in which a national currency performs a transnational function; the transactions of the nominally multinational companies in capital, services, and liquid assets between one subsidiary and another disregard frontiers to such an extent that no accounting method can register them with any accuracy. The Eurodollar symbolizes the issue of a quasi-currency which cannot be controlled by states, though traditionally they are vested with the sole power to issue money. The revolt against the commercial and monetary system may be ascribed to national—not necessarily nationalistic—sentiment which regards economic sovereignty as a component of national sovereignty and is not disposed to countenance encroachments upon it. From Brazil to France economists and politicians alike are agreed that the seat of decisions on the distribution of resources and the shape of the economy ought to be the nation itself. But is this really the case in the transnational system created by the big corporations and the Eurodollar?

Let us take the first count in the indictment directed to a verdict of failure. In one sense, it is incontrovertible;[4] however inexact the figures may be, the growth rate of the national product in the Western European countries (except Britain), and especially in Japan, has been higher than in the United States, although in the United States it has not fallen below its past levels. The reduction in the share of American production in world production (from 40 to 30 percent between 1950 and 1970) and the narrowing of the gap between the per capita product in the United States and Western

---

4 See note on p. 295.

Europe and Japan, however, simply reflect the logic of the modern economy. There are no good grounds for regarding it as an early warning of decline. The true lesson to be drawn from a quarter-century of economic miracle is that the pessimistic axiom that the rich are growing richer and the poor growing poorer does not apply to developed countries. Though the poor countries have grown richer more slowly than the rich countries, the semi-rich among them have prospered more than the very rich. In this respect a comparison of countries and a comparison of classes suggest similar conclusions.

The unequal rate of development threatens American superiority only in the case of Japan. If Japan keeps up the rate that it has maintained for the past twenty years, it will overtake the United States in per capita product before the end of the century. Even now the growth rate of the Japanese national product[5]—more than 10 percent yearly—is endangering the balance of the trading system. Even if the proportion of the national product which is exported does not rise, Japanese industry's capacity to sell in the United States and Europe gives rise to defensive reactions and agreements for "voluntary restriction,"[6] which are hardly compatible with the official GATT rules.

Japan apart, the narrowing of the gap between the economies on both sides of the Atlantic is not yet jeopardizing United States superiority at decisive points and does not involve a structural imbalance in the United States balance of payments (if this notion has any meaning). In his report President Nixon's economic adviser, Peter G. Peterson, quoted statistics which are both true and "slanted." In the Sixties, he wrote, American exports of manufactured goods rose by 110 percent, Germany's doubled, and Japan's increased by 400 percent. Japan's share of world trade has increased from 1 percent to 6 percent in twenty years. But the aggregate figures for the European countries' trade conceal the fundamental distinction between intra-Community and extra-Community trade. If EEC's extra-Community trade alone is considered, the disparity between its share and the United States' share of the world total has been far smaller

---

[5] The growth rate of the Japanese GNP was 11.4, 12.9, 14.3, 14.2, and 12.0 in 1966, 1967, 1968, 1969, and 1970. Japanese exports rose from $828 million in 1950 to $4,055 million in 1960 and $12,922 million in 1970. The percentage ratio of imports to the national product is decreasing.

[6] The term seems somewhat ironic.

than the aggregate figures suggest. The EEC's share rose from 13.6 percent to 14.6 percent between 1953 and 1970, the United States' fell from 21.3 to 14.0, but its percentages for 1953 and 1954 (21.3 and 19.5) were above the average. In any event, the reduction in the United States' share was due to the increase in Japan's share far more than to Europe's (intra-Community trade excluded). In 1970 the value of extra-Community exports by the Six was $45 billion, that of United States exports $43 billion. The difference in imports is scarcely larger, $45,621 million as against $39,953 million. The countries which buy the most primary commodities and raw materials in relation to their population are, of course, the two insular developed countries with little space and few local resources, Great Britain and Japan.[7]

Has the United States lost its outlets because the prices of its exported goods have risen more rapidly than those of its competitors? The dollar may well have been overvalued since 1947–48, as I have already said, and inflation in 1965–70 probably slowed down exports; it certainly swelled imports. As regards the prices of exported manufactured goods, the index (1963 = 100) would suggest a slight loss in competitive capacity, but this was no longer so in 1970 and 1971.[8] In point of fact, the United States does not differ in this respect from other countries. While it is suffering from stronger inflationary pressures than its competitors, the deficits in its balance of payments will be similar to those of any other country. The relative decline in exports of American manufactured goods or, to put it more precisely, the reduction of the share of American manufactured goods in total exports of manufactures (from 20.5 percent in 1961 to 18.5 in 1970 and 17.1 in 1971) is not in itself a symptom of decline. The country which pays its workers the highest wages must, in a free trade system, be exposed to successful competition from its trading partners with respect to a number of articles which do not require complex processing.

Using the official statistics published in the *Survey of Current*

---

[7] Raw materials account for about 70 percent of Japanese imports. Forty-three percent of Japan's direct investments abroad are in raw materials.

[8] According to the United Nations monthly statistical bulletin for March 1971, the unit index figure for exports by value rose from 100 in 1960 to 110, 113, and 118 in 1967, 1968, and 1969, as against 104, 102, and 107 for the Federal Republic of Germany; 107, 109, and 110 for France; 101, 101, and 106 for Japan; and 110, 104, and 107 for the United Kingdom.

Business, Professor Raymond Vernon[9] has calculated the rest of the world's indebtedness to the United States and the United States' indebtedness to the rest of the world. He has no difficulty in showing that at the end of 1969 American assets amounted to $146 billion ($19 billion liquid, $56 billion semiliquid, and $71 billion in long-term investments) as against liabilities of $91 billion ($42, $37 and $12 billion for the same items). In 1970 the difference, i.e., the balance of assets over liabilities, was approximately $70 billion. But the United States is not like a banker who in the course of his business converts savings into investments within a single monetary area. The United States may of course repay if it wishes. But liquid liabilities which pass from one country to another, accumulating in the coffers of the central banks, lead to a monetary turmoil which is totally different from the liabilities of a banker to his depositors, who have no reason to fear that they may not be able to draw out their deposits.

Professor Vernon attributes its creditors' run on the United States as banker in part to the very way in which the deficit in the American balance of payments has been presented, and observes that "as long as a nation has command over assets located overseas, there is always some possibility for its government to turn these assets into a liquid form. Governments as a rule have the constitutional authority to take over the foreign bank accounts and securities of their nationals."[10] The earnings of mechanical engineers and other technicians working in the United States for subsidiaries of multinational corporations are the equivalent of an export of brain power or know-how, normal enough in countries in which 60 percent of manpower is now employed in the service sector.

The events of August 1971, it is generally agreed, marked the ending of the postwar monetary system, just as President Nixon's visit to Peking marked the ending of the postwar inter-state system. In a sense, both were in fact a yielding to reality. Communist China existed; the dollar "as good as gold" was not convertible into gold for lack of sufficient reserves. What is paradoxical is that this surrender strengthened the United States' position in both cases, at least in the short run. The dialogue between Washington and Peking

---

9 In *Foreign Policy,* No. 5, Winter 1971–72. "A Skeptic Looks at the Balance of Payments."
10 *Ibid.,* p. 56.

had induced Moscow to be moderate; for as soon as the Chinese and Russians came to consider each other public enemy number one, each of them tried to prevent the United States from favoring its rival. American diplomacy could even afford the luxury of nonalignment after the ending of the Vietnam War.

The devaluation and nonconvertibility of the dollar, regardless of the loss of prestige they at least temporarily occasioned, for the first time created a dollar standard. Before August 1971 it had been the dollar which, far more than gold, had served as a transnational currency and standard of value. It was still, in theory at least, convertible into gold and was in practice convertible into other assets. The American financial authorities had accepted the exchange rate resulting from the devaluations and revaluations of other currencies, putting on pressure from time to time to persuade the Germans and Japanese to revalue their currency. Nonconvertibility presented the United States' partners with the alternative between accumulating dollars indefinitely to prevent a further devaluation of the American currency, or consenting to devaluation with all its consequent commercial disadvantages to them.

The Americans accused the Europeans, and in particular the European Community, shortly to be enlarged, of violating the most-favored-nation clause and making more and more exceptions to the rule. They accused the Japanese of profiting by the liberalization of the other countries' trade while preserving the advantages from a virtual shutout by means of arrangements which were quite as covert or surreptitious as they were legal. The Europeans retorted that the Community had in no way impaired American exports, even exports of primary commodities, and that it bought more from the United States than it sold to it (the Community's trading deficit varied between $1 and $2 billion yearly, $2.4 billion in 1970); it was not until 1972 that the Community had a slight surplus. The United States' deficit arose in its trade with Canada and Japan;[11] the American market took one-third of Japanese exports. The Americans argued that without the common agricultural policy United States farm ex-

---

[11] The deficit in trade with Japan arises to some degree from action by the Europeans. The United States, as noted above, buys about one-third of Japanese exports. The Community of the Six accounted for 5 to 6 perecnt and Europe as a whole about 15 percent in 1969, or $2,070 million of a total of $15,990 million.

ports would have been far larger than they were, especially to third countries. The fact remains, however, that the value of Community purchases of American farm products doubled between 1958 and 1970 (rising from $885 million to $1,882 million). The spokesmen for the Community produced arguments in favor of the preference agreements with the countries of the European Free Trade Area and the Mediterranean countries, while the spokesmen for Washington claimed that these were repeated failures to respect the GATT rules. To go into the details of the alleged wrongs of each side is more or less irrelevant to this general conspectus. What concerns us here is the logical, yet paradoxical, conclusion of American diplomacy's "success" with respect to Europe, together with the "success" of the policy of European unification.

Monetarily, Europe has been more dependent on the dollar since the dollar fell from its pedestal than it was in the days when a president of the United States took a legitimate pride in keeping gold to the official price. Commercially, the Europeans are extending their network of preference agreements around the core of the Community and are manifestly becoming the leading trading unit in the world. Herein lies a contradiction between the Europeans' commercial potential and their monetary impotence, as well as between the United States' success in its desire for a united Europe as a barrier against Communism and its recent discovery that a unified Europe is a lively competitor and that the most-favored-nation clause, which it regards as sacrosanct, is falling into disuse. Washington's diplomacy toward Europe and even Japan over the past twenty-five years was dictated more by political considerations than by narrow economic interests. Accommodation with the Soviet Union has led to a reversal of its priorities and the relative importance it attached to the two spheres in which the external action of the United States is carried on, the inter-state system and the world market.[12]

---

[12] Is there any reason to fear that Nixon's United States may go further and find in Moscow its major partner when it is trying both to slow down the arms race and speed up trade? Will the Americans try to obtain additional energy resources from Siberia and will they grant their rival massive financial facilities for the purpose? To judge by past experience, this conjecture cannot be ruled out; capitalists have not yet lost the propensity to suicide attributed to them by James Burnham. In any case, it is mainly to the free economies that the American economy will continue to be bound, for better or worse.

The transatlantic controversy appears to turn on the antithesis between regionalism and universalism; the Americans blame the Community's trade policy for establishing a Community unit surrounded by a free trade area of preference agreements. Apart from the direct disadvantages of this policy to the United States, it denounces it bitterly because the policy conflicts with the universalism it traditionally professes. On the other hand, monetary regionalism, which would seem at first sight the logical complement of commercial regionalism, remains a fugitive concept, because in Europe it would require a de facto supranational authority which theoretically sovereign national states do not accept even verbally.

The widespread anti-Americanism seems to me due in part to the responsibility (in the sense of causality) of the American economy and in particular, the responsibility of the multinational companies and the Eurodollar market for the erosion of sovereignties and the increasing inability of states to retain effectual mastery of the economies entrusted to them. Celso Furtado, quoted earlier, and François Perroux[18]—the former asserting that any development project must always be national, the latter pondering the meaning of the independence of nations—share a common concern about the subordination of a political entity, so far as its economic projects are concerned, to a world market which is not so much the result of a balance of forces as dictated by the dominant economy and the strategies of the big corporations. If they had to choose between nationalism and economic internationalism, the developed countries, at any rate, would find the choice easy enough. But is it still possible to talk of internationalism when a national currency serves as a transnational currency and the dominant economy continues to invest all over the world, if only by borrowing the requisite capital in the host countries? Some day there will be a revolt against this sort of expansion, even if the economists were to prove irrefutably that the further the dollar spreads, the faster we all grow richer.

Note to page 288. The growth rates calculated by Angus Maddison (*Economic Growth in the West,* London, 1964) are as follows:
In 1950–60 the annual growth rate of per capita production was:

---

[18] François Perroux, *Indépendance de la nation* (Paris: Obier, 1969).

France 3.5; Germany 6.5; Italy 5.3; United Kingdom 2.4; United States 1.6.

In 1913–50 the American annual rate (1.7) was higher than that for all European countries except Norway (1.9).

In 1950–60 the annual growth rate of production by hour of work was: France 3.9; Germany 6.0; Italy 4.1; United Kingdom 2.0; United States 2.4.

The growth rate in 1960–70 fell in the Federal Republic of Germany and rose in the United States.

At the end of 1970, according to OECD statistics (*OECD Observer,* No. 56, February 1972), GNP at market prices per capita in U.S. dollars (at current prices and exchange rates) were 3,040 in the Federal Republic of Germany, 2,920 in France, 4,760 in the United States, and 2,170 in the United Kingdom. The disparity between most European countries and the United States decidedly narrowed in the postwar period, although the national product of the 250 million Europeans is still only about two-thirds that of the 215 million Americans.

The United States invests less proportionately than the European countries. Gross fixed capital formation accounts for 16.5 percent of the national product in the United States, 25.6 percent in France, 26.5 percent in the Federal Republic of Germany, 21.2 percent in Italy, 17.6 percent in the United Kingdom, and 35 percent in Japan (1970 figures).

Postscript

BETWEEN IMPERIAL DIPLOMACY
AND ISOLATIONISM

As the final pages of the original French manuscript were being written in November 1972, the war was drawing to an end in Vietnam and specialists in international affairs were celebrating[1] the twenty-fifth anniversary of the famous *Foreign Affairs* article by "X" (George Kennan) entitled "The Sources of Soviet Conduct."[2] At that time, politicians all over the world were asking themselves, and asking those who might be expected to know, what the future of United States diplomacy would be after the pivotal year 1971, that is to say what it would be during Nixon's second term and what it might become after the Nixon-Kissinger team had gone.

Readers of Kennan's article, especially readers outside the United States, were interested primarily in the concept of "containment," against which some other Americans were soon afterward to oppose the notion of "rollback." The former implied a defensive strategy designed to contain the expansion of Communism, which at that time was hardly distinguished from the power of the Soviet Union itself. The latter implied an offensive strategy designed to recover the territories already controlled or in course of becoming controlled by Moscow. In the course of this essay I have accepted the notion that the *actual* behavior of the United States over the past twenty-five years was consistent with the concept of containment, with a single exception, the attempt forcibly to unify Korea after the defeat of the North Korean offensive and the landing at Inchon.

How far did Kennan's article *in fact* influence United States

---

[1] In *Foreign Policy*, No. 7, Summer 1972 in a series of articles entitled " 'X' plus 25."
[2] *Foreign Affairs*, Spring 1947.

policy? The " 'X' plus 25" article in the Summer 1972 issue of *Foreign Policy* quoted for the first time the following remarks made by Dean Acheson to newspaperman Bob Woodward in an interview dated March 26, 1970. "[Kennan's article] was a description of what was happening anyway." Acheson went on to say:

> The "X" article was a perfectly fine article. Then Walter Lippmann decided that he didn't like it; well, it was as if God had looked over at George's shoulder and said, "George, you shouldn't have written such a bad article." They thought that containment applied everywhere, but it was nothing of the kind.

Arthur Krock supplied further information in *The New York Times* of April 17, 1972. Kennan had contributed far more to the change in the thinking and action of Truman's team by his diplomatic dispatches from Moscow analyzing the nature of the Soviet regime and the thinking and consequent conduct of external affairs of the decision-makers in the Kremlin than by his *Foreign Affairs* article.

Walter Lippmann and Henry Morgenthau immediately raised two objections rooted in the European, or traditional, philosophy of the national interest: that such a containment-oriented doctrine had unlimited implications and that it would amount to replacing the diplomacy of a *single* state with defined interests and great, though not unlimited, resources by a virtually universal, indeed a gobal, mission, that of putting a stop to the expansion of Soviet power or influence.

More specifically, the doctrine—for a relatively succinct summary of the external action of the Soviet Union was in process of being transformed into a doctrine—was open to objections from both right and left (to use the current, if vague, terms). The objection from the right, taken up by Dulles and James Burnham, involved the question whether assigning to the United States—which had emerged from the war with its industry intact, incomparable prestige, and an overwhelming material superiority over any other state—the thankless and sterile task of "containing" the Soviet Union's expansionist aspirations was not simply to adhere to a "negative, futile and immoral notion."

Lippmann adopted a somewhat similar line, but one designed to prevent the paralysis of an American diplomacy stripped of all freedom of movement and self-doomed to reacting instead of acting, to mounting guard all over the world, and to countering every Communist or Soviet attempt at expansion with the application of force. American diplomacy's freedom of action should take the form first and foremost of a sense of priorities discriminating between areas of vital interest and secondary areas.

Morgenthau saw Kennan's article and Truman's and Acheson's actions as a rejection of diplomacy (in the traditional sense) and the abandonment of the practice of negotiation, and put to his readers the alternative between fighting and negotiating. But in point of fact, the cold war between 1947 and 1953 still looked like a third alternative, "neither war nor intercourse," for which there had been no place in the classic system of inter-state relations. Lippmann, for his part, besides criticizing "globalism," the potentially unlimited obligations self-imposed by the United States, rejected the deductions which Truman and Marshall were preparing to draw from the impossibility of coming to an agreement with the Soviet Union on Germany. In 1947 he saw the presence of Russian troops in the center of Europe as the major threat to equilibrium and peace and did not give up all hope of obtaining their withdrawal by negotiation. At the same time, he opposed the creation of a Western Germany bound to the British and Americans. In that same year he was still predicting that the rulers of one republic would hasten to negotiate with the rulers of the other republic. Simultaneously, however, he correctly foresaw that if the United States' military presence in Germany continued indefinitely, it would inevitably lead to the indefinite continuance of the Soviets' military presence on the other side of the demarcation line.

Neither Kennan nor Acheson at the time recognized his own thinking in the alleged doctrine which Dulles, Lippmann, and Morgenthau were so vigorously attacking. Dean Acheson replied that neither he nor Truman had ever conceived that containment required intervention, and military intervention if necessary, everywhere and at all times to check the advance of Communism or Soviet power. The most cogent proof of this is the fact that Truman refused in 1947–48 to intervene in the Chinese civil war and accepted the victory of the Chinese Communist Party.

Insofar as the United States set itself a goal or sought a mission for itself after the Second World War, what other policy save containment was open to it after cooperation with Stalin had proved impossible? The Soviet Union, weakened though it had been by its sacrifices for the common cause, had replaced the Third Reich as "the disturbing force," a threat to the European equilibrium and, indeed, the world equilibrium. It posed a challenge to the United States' military strength as well as its ideology by its very existence quite as much as by the suspicions it aroused. The United States had decided that domination of the Eurasian land mass by the German-Japanese alliance endangered the security of the United States, so why should it have allowed Stalin to fulfill Hitler's ambition for his own profit? If I myself have spoken of obsessive anti-Communism here and there, it must be remembered that this was at first the wholly normal and rational reaction to the ideology of the only state capable of opposing the American republic in all fields—military, political, and ideological. Containment in its original sense is less the result of the "Wilson syndrome," or the dream of peace through the universalization of democratic regimes, than its critics try to make out. It is rather due to the American style and the specific traits of the external behavior of a republic which has never accepted the *Realpolitik* or Machiavellianism of Old Europe; the concept, rather than the doctrine, of containment represented the defensive version of the inevitable rivalry with the Soviet Union.

How did this concept develop, without losing its defensive connotation, into "globalization" and "militarization"? Manifestly, the event that led to the historical consequences deplored by so many commentators was the Korean campaign. I would even be tempted to say that Dean Acheson's famous speech to the National Press Club in which he failed to include Korea as one of the positions in the American defense perimeter in Asia may have been interpreted in the Kremlin and at Pyongyang as a signal to go ahead in an attempt to unify Korea by armed force. When the North Korean troops crossed the demarcation line, Truman and Acheson together assessed, correctly in my opinion, the difficulty of the "discrimination" which Lippmann was examining from his armchair at the *New York Herald-Tribune*. The Europeans were anxiously awaiting the White House's response, regarding it as a test of the value and credibility of American commitments. The United States' intervention in a conflict which was at once a civil and a foreign war did not stem from the globalism of the Truman Doctrine, but from the political and psychological interrelation between American action in Europe and in Asia. The Germans, divided as they themselves were into occupation zones, felt directly concerned in the Korean crisis. Dean Acheson told me in private conversation in 1950 and several years later that he had had the feeling that the fate of the alliance between the Old Continent and the New World was at stake in late June 1950, when in forty-eight hours Truman and his advisers worked out their strategy in face of what they took to be a Soviet or Chinese aggression, probably an aggression decided on jointly during Mao Tsetung's lengthy visit to Moscow.

The extension of the doctrine of containment to Asia, the result of an event, or perhaps an accident, was precisely as reasonable as the United States' replacing of Great Britain as the power which guaranteed the balance in Europe and as the protector of the peripheral states (Turkey and Greece). Japan would not have tolerated the reconstitution of a unified Korea under a hostile government, and the United States, which had taken over the burdens of Japanese sovereignty, acted as any Japanese government would have acted; even if Truman and Acheson were not thoroughly conscious of their historical role, their action lay in a direction consistent with an objective logic which philosophers would ascribe to Hegel's Cunning of Reason. Intervention by the Chinese "volunteers" prevented them from recognizing Communist China, as they had been thinking of doing before June 20, 1950.

The militarization of containment in Europe was another consequence of the Korean campaign. It is true that some commentators (Hubert Beuve-Méry, for example) had drawn attention to the implications of the North Atlantic Treaty, stating that it contained the germ of German rearmament. Their predictions were justified by events, although that does not irrefutably demonstrate the truth of their contention. It was the climate created by the Korean campaign that induced Acheson to suggest to the Europeans in September 1950 both that they should make some effort to rearm and that the Germans should share in the attempt. Was the Korean campaign an opportunity rather than a cause? Even the American diplomats who had special knowledge of the Soviet Union and never believed in the likelihood of war between the two super-powers were undoubtedly in favor of strengthening the United States' military apparatus. Quite rightly, I believe. In its new role the American republic had to learn that the conduct of external action in peacetime requires not merely an economic potential, an "arsenal of the democracies," but an immediately available military force.

Were NATO, the stationing of an American army in Europe, and the rearmament of the Federal Republic of Germany no more than unnecessary precautions? Could the ideological, economic, and political competition have proceeded without any guarantee of security but the American commitment and the improbability of a full-dress Soviet invasion? Many commentators and historians nowadays would uphold this thesis. I myself am hesitant to do so. No one can reconstruct with any certainty the history of what did not happen. I still doubt that German unification on terms acceptable to the West would have been possible, even if the stimulus to a militarization of containment over and above the Korean crisis and Stalinism had not indefinitely protracted both the nuclear armaments race and the organization on both sides of the demarcation line of an integrated defense with conventional and tactical nuclear weapons. (The Soviet side boasted several hundred medium or intermediate-range ballistic missiles as well.) Some people today are pondering how to put an end to this armaments competition and asking whether it would not have been wiser to avoid it in the first place. In 1950 the governments and majority opinion in Europe wanted NATO. Once they were within the system, Europeans and Americans found it hard to get out. And not all Europeans want to get out.

Let us not forget either that after the phase of détente in 1953–58 Khrushchev created a fresh cold war climate by his truculence and adventurism (the Berlin ultimatum). It required the second Cuban crisis (the missile crisis) to eliminate the threat to Berlin and to bring about the signing of the first Partial Test-Ban Treaty. The extension of containment to Asia and its militarization owe less to the article by "X" or the terms of the Truman Declaration of March 1947 than to historical circumstances, some of them, like the Korean campaign, semi-accidental, others determined by technology (the armaments race), and yet others probably due to bureaucratic clumsiness, vested interests, and the results of unwise decisions.

Does this mean that there is no connection between the Truman Doctrine and American diplomacy's fulfillment of the imperial function during its period of paramountcy (approximately 1947–67)?

Certainly not; the connection exists; but to postulate the alternative of *nation* or *empire* is likely to draw the reader subtly and insidiously toward the conclusion that isolationism is the only way to discard the imperial role and return to a national diplomacy.

The Vietnam experience accounts for the excessive zeal displayed in querying the fundamentals of American diplomacy as conducted for twenty-five years. The proponents of a radical revision have a stake in stressing the connection between the thinking of the American decision-makers since 1947 and the Vietnam tragedy; the proponents of a moderate revisionism, however, place the emphasis on specific factors, such as bad luck, mistaken judgments, and inappropriate strategies, which determined the course from "zenith to descension," from ascent to descent.

In the chapter entitled "The Changing Forms of Imperialism" I drew attention to the varied meanings of the words "empire," "imperial," and "imperialism" and suggested that any great power in a bipolar and revolutionary system is irresistibly drawn toward an imperial diplomacy. George Liska and Robert Tucker agree on this point, although they express it somewhat differently.[3] I do not think I am misrepresenting their central theme in expressing it as follows: An imperial state (or a state which fulfills an imperial function) is characterized by a *worldwide* purpose. From which there follows a basic distinction between two aims, the physical security of a state and its inhabitants and the establishment of an international environment consonant with the imperial state's idea or purpose. Between these two aims stands the nation's economic well-being (or prosperity) and the preservation of its institutions.

In 1953 I myself wrote:

The West has not and does not need to have the equivalent of a secular religion with its church and theology, the interpreter

---

[3] Cf. George Liska, *Imperial America: The International Politics of Primacy* (Baltimore: Johns Hopkins Press, 1967), p. 10: "An empire or imperial state is, in the above sequence, a state that combines the characteristics of a great power, which, being a world power and a globally paramount state, becomes automatically a power primarily responsible for shaping and maintaining a necessary modicum of world order. . . . The key structural pattern of the imperial system is the identity and location of the dominant or leading power engaged in shifting conflicts with successive challenges and rivals."

—Pope and Emperor combined—of the prophets. But it must represent an idea of an international order. The national interest of the United States, even the collective interest of the Anglo-Saxon minority, will not win over any state or arouse any sentiment of loyalty unless it appears jointly liable for an international order, an order of power as well as law. . . . It is legitimate to regret the passing of the ages in which dispassionate and amoral diplomacy was merely a subtle exercise in influences and statecraft. In the twentieth century the strength of a great power is diminished if it ceases to serve an idea.[4]

The concept of containment was in fact expanded into a doctrine of international order, and this doctrine was calculated to lead to imperial, or even imperialist, intervention, or to put it another way, intervention in order to uphold a government favorable to the institutions and ideologies of the United States, even against its people's aspirations. The modern concept of containment combines with the ancient principle of American morality in inter-state relations, that of nonresort to force—a combination which tends to equate the right of peoples to self-determination, with the ban on choosing a Communist-type regime or the obligation to maintain a pro-American regime.

Here two debatable questions arise, interrelated to some degree, but not identical: What kind of environment has American diplomacy *in fact* contributed to establish? And to what extent has the external action of the American republic been governed by the traditional philosophy of peace under the law and the right of peoples to self-determination?

The imperial diplomacy of the United States does not in the least resemble,. except by way of rationalization or propaganda, the before mentioned "Wilson syndrome."

This imperial diplomacy has, it is true, retained its ideological characteristic of being *against* the Europeans' colonial empires by resorting to the plea, in many cases a valid one, that resistance to Communism requires the support of national sentiment. From 1945–46 to 1962, during the roughly fifteen-year era of "decolonization,"

---

[4] In an article, *"En quête d'une doctrine de politique étrangère,"* Revue française de science politique, 1953; reproduced in Raymond Aron, *Etudes politiques* (Paris: Gallimard, 1972), pp. 476–78.

the Americans exerted their influence in favor of national liberation movements. The decision-makers in Washington did not trouble about subtlety when the Netherlands showed that it had some mind to resist the Indonesian nationalists; they forced the government at The Hague to yield. They displayed slightly more restraint with regard to France because they needed her more. They made only one exception, although not without some hesitation; they refused to support Ho Chi Minh, because he was suspect of combining an indubitable nationalism with allegiance to Moscow. They put pressure on the French government to grant to other nationalists the independence of which the Vietminh was the embodied will. This exception was the source of the Vietnam tragedy. In the case of Algeria, American diplomacy did its best to accommodate both sides; nevertheless, from the French point of view, it seemed to side wholly with the "rebels."

Except in the areas where it directly confronted the Soviet Union or Communist China, United States imperial diplomacy therefore presents two faces, one of fidelity to the tradition of "the first new nation" and the right of peoples to self-determination, the other, a novel one, of resistance to "armed minorities." Is the second inconsistent with the first? Not necessarily. But it is becoming increasingly evident that the first is disappearing into the limbo of history along with the European colonial empires.

Did imperial diplomacy in Africa, Asia, and Latin America have any other objective, once the European empires had disappeared, than the preservation of the status quo? Its major, if not its sole, objective seems to me to have been to prevent parties professing Marxism-Leninism or likely to open the way to Marxism-Leninism from coming to power. Since revolutionary parties throughout the world nowadays use a socialist vocabulary more or less impregnated with Marxism, United States imperial diplomacy tends in fact to favor existing regimes for fear that revolutionary regimes may be worse, either in themselves or in relation to what the Americans would prefer.

Was it an ideological diplomacy? Yes and no. Certainly it was *negatively ideological,* in that it was against regimes presently or potentially Marxist-Leninist. But this negatively ideological diplomacy can just as legitimately be called realistic because it prefers a rightist authoritarian regime—even one that does nothing toward modernizing a country—to a leftist authoritarian regime. This negatively ideological diplomacy leads to pathetic or ridiculous attempts to swathe in a cloak of democracy the nakedness of an arbitrary power, regardless whether it is accepted by the masses and whether it is incapable of subjecting itself to the electoral processes which American policy-makers regard as the sole proof of legitimacy.

In short, if the aim of United States imperial diplomacy can be said to be a favorable environment, this is progressively and inevitably defined restrictively by the nonallegiance of states to Marxism-Leninism and therefore by the consequent freedom of access (in most cases) for persons, goods, and capital from the United States. As soon as containment comes to mean nothing but resistance to parties presently or potentially pro-Soviet, the diplomacy becomes imperial rather than ideological, or to put it another way, becomes essentially realistic. It still uses the expression "free world," but this world is free not because the people in it govern themselves freely, but because it is not closed to United States influence.

The uneasy conscience resulting from this degeneration of the crusading spirit into imperial realism has been displayed on many occasions in the past twenty-five years. The violence of Senator McGovern's attacks on President Thieu echoed the style of similar attacks on Syngman Rhee twenty-five years earlier, or those on the Greek colonels. United States diplomacy, like that of all great powers, accepts whatever allies offer themselves and integrates them at least nominally into the free world without caring too much about the democratic orthodoxy of the regimes for which it stands surety.

This uneasy conscience would not have exploded into a revulsion against American diplomacy as a whole had it not been for the Vietnam War. But the war does not seem to me to betoken the degeneration of a negatively ideological diplomacy into a realistic policy, but rather the notion of "the line which shall not be crossed" and the imperative of nonresort to force. I have already mentioned that the decision to subordinate anticolonialism to anti-Communism in Indochina was taken very early on by Truman and Acheson, and was confirmed not in spite of, but because of, the Communist Party's victory in China, with a view to containing the spread of Communism to Southeast Asia (without any distinction at the time between Russian, Chinese, and Vietnamese Communism). This decision was renewed by Dulles when he was negotiating the cease-fire in Korea in 1953 and after the Geneva agreement in 1954, by Kennedy in 1961, and by Johnson in 1965. Is this consistency to be seen as the logical sequel to the doctrine whose governing ideas were expounded by Truman or as an aberration explicable by a misconception of the specific conditions of the country and of the parties at odds with each other? The critics of imperial diplomacy naturally choose the first alternative. Even Robert Tucker prefers it in his defense of American diplomacy.

He first shows, as I myself have shown, that the contradiction between the imperative of nonresort to force and the requirements for containing Communism has been resolved on many occasions in the past twenty-five years by the United States' resorting to force (Santo Domingo) or the threat of force (Cuba, 1962). The contradiction also emerges between resistance to indirect aggression or action by "armed minorities" and the principle of noninterference in the domestic affairs of states or the right of peoples freely to choose their institutions once the fiction or dogma that people never voluntarily choose a Marxist-Leninist regime is discarded. But once the two contradictions are admitted, the imperial policy of containment—precisely because it bears no resemblance whatever to a moral crusade —not merely permits, but demands discrimination. Neither the White House nor the Elysée went into mourning when Sekou Touré rejected the French Community and took the road to Marxism.

Some spokesmen for Eisenhower and Johnson, for Dulles and Rusk have not hesitated, of course, to uphold the contentions in which Tucker's defense is grounded; Johnson himself brought up the possibility of the battlefield being transferred from Saigon to San Francisco if Vietnam were abandoned (Marshal de Lattre de Tassigny, indeed, saw the Communist wave rising as far as the Suez Canal). Should one believe in the sincerity of such discourse, the philosophy of indivisible peace and indivisible deterrence? To my mind, the philosophy implicit in American diplomacy appears as a synthesis of realism in deeds—the containment of Communism— and idealism in words—world order, nonresort to force, peoples' right to self-determination. In this synthesis lay the motive for a defensive strategy; the *faits accomplis* in Europe, North Korea (after 1951), China, and North Vietnam (after 1954) were never again called in question. The imperial policy of the United States has therefore tempered its potential universalism with respect for spheres of influence. This discrimination among spheres in turn rendered the "loss" of a particular country (by the victory of a Communist party) perfectly acceptable. Finally, this philosophy was defined by the purpose not merely of ensuring physical security, but of keeping as wide an area as possible open and favorable to American influence.

I do not deny that once the doctrine of containment was expanded to encompass the entire globe, it could some day end in disaster. What I do deny is that this disaster is *implicit* in the doctrine, that it *necessarily* results from it. On two points Tucker saddles the architects of American diplomacy with extreme views which they may perhaps have intoned ritually, but which did not express either their considered opinion or the logic of their action, the views that American interests and peace are inseparable and that world order and the security of the United States are interdependent. "It is, of course, the equation of world order and American security upon which the administration's defense of Vietnam must ultimately stand or fall."[5] Tucker goes on to add a passage to the effect that no one, of course, is unaware of the differences between the conditions for containment in Europe and in Asia or, today at any rate, of the split between Moscow and Peking and the relative independence of North Vietnam. Nevertheless, a victory by Hanoi would also be a victory for Hanoi's chief allies and would be likely to jeopardize all that has been achieved in the past twenty years. But the policy-makers reach this conclusion only by way of a self-fulfilling prophecy, arguing that it is precisely because they declared the Vietnam War a crucial test that it did in fact become one. It is precisely to the extent that each test of will between the United States and a Communist Party is viewed as a symbol of the test on a worldwide scale that it ultimately in some sort assumes that significance.

In other words, the *ideologically negative* diplomacy of containment should reasonably have been conceived of as a realistic diplomacy because it did not dispute the Soviet and Chinese possession of what they already possessed. Nor, unless it had lost all sense of reason, could it conceive of the sovietization of one-half of Vietnam as constituting a direct, a physical threat to the security of the United States. The territories lying between what each of the super-powers

---

[5] Robert W. Tucker, *Nation or Empire: The Debate over American Foreign Policy* (Baltimore: The Johns Hopkins Press, 1966), p. 77.

considers its own preserve are the theater of a confrontation which, depending on the area in which it occurs, becomes a primary or secondary issue either in itself or for its symbolic value. What led to the Vietnam tragedy was not the concept of containment nor perhaps the imperative of nonresort to force, but the *growing tendency to substitute symbol for reality in the discrimination of interests and issues.* The domino theory, though in itself implausible, was a clumsy reflection of the correct idea that the American commitment is devalued by any throwing in of the sponge.

I do not deny that nowadays, when nonmaterial issues are often given greater importance than material issues, and weapons gain their effect by the threat to use them rather than by their actual use, those responsible for an imperial diplomacy find it harder to avoid the temptation to transfigure any and all conflicts and to present them as the symbol of a determination which no one originally suspected. Thus, in the postwar era, from the Berlin blockade to the mining of the North Vietnam harbors, by way of the installation of missiles in Cuba, the policy-makers in Washington felt that the fate of the overall issue hung on the outcome of each crisis.

The North and South Vietnamese, whom the chess-players on the heights were only too prone to forget about, reminded the world and forced it to recognize that it was they who were the real issue at stake, in spite of and over and above the military maneuvers of high policy.

Tucker would perhaps reply that I am using slightly different terms to express the same idea. It is true that he too observes this substitution of symbol for reality, but he links it with the American philosophy of world order as inseparable from the security of the United States, whereas I see it as a corruption of the realistic diplomacy of containment, a commitment undertaken in specific circumstances and repeated in quite different circumstances, owing as much to the difficulty of maneuvering a retreat as to fidelity to a certain perception of the inter-state system.

The essence of the art of politics, as Tucker himself recognizes, is discrimination. The Vietnam War was the result of a failure to discriminate and of the implied axiom that any local conflict assumes a global value insofar as it involves a nonmaterial issue, the credibility of the American commitment, and insofar as this credibility remains the basis of world order and American security. It is the American diplomats themselves who create or tend to create these linked identifications. What is true is that by taking the place of Japan and the European nations the United States has made itself responsible for the military equilibrium within the Eurasian land mass. By taking on, over and above this task inherited from the Second World War, the effort to prevent Communists from coming to power in any country whatever[6] in Africa, the Middle East, and Latin America, the American policy-makers have taken the logic of imperial diplomacy to its extreme conclusion. Some commentators try to suggest, rather than to demonstrate, that if criticism of the Vietnam War is to remain consistent with its own logic, it must reject the very principle, not the ultimate applications, of imperial diplomacy. But they seem to me to be implicitly or intentionally committing the error for which they incidentally blame their country's diplomats, the failure to discriminate.

Only small powers restrict their ambitions to their physical survival and to preserving their legal independence and their institutions. The primary aim of a great power too is physical survival and preserving its domestic system intact; for ensuring its inhabitants' well-being and maintaining the foreign trade necessary for its prosperity and the growth of its national product are inseparable from its physical survival and the preservation of its institutions. Today, the industrial system of an economic entity, even an entity as vast as the United States, has become an integral part of a wider and more complex system. Over and above the first objective, physical security, the second objective, moral survival (or the preservation of the republic), and the third objective, its inhabitants' well-being, a great power, according to all historical experience, acts to achieve an ill-defined purpose which I will call the maintenance or creation of a favorable environment. The meaning and scope of the notion of a favorable environment change with circumstances.

In an international system such as the European system of the balance of power the potentially leading power, the Reich of Bismarck, for example, contents itself with the play of inter-state forces, diplomacy in the narrow sense, to prevent the formation of any

---

[6] But we must not exaggerate; the attempt at "containment" in Africa south of the Sahara and in Latin America varies from country to country with the means at hand or the importance of the material stake at issue.

coalition calculated to surpass it and its allies in resources and military strength. Between 1876 and 1914 neither Bismarck nor Wilhelm II and his ministers were governed by ideological considerations. The conservative outlook shared by the Prussian and Russian dynasties was displayed on several occasions, but did not stand in the way of the Franco-Russian alliance or the alignments in 1914, which, despite the bombardments of propaganda that echoed the guns, hardly depended at all on ideological affinities.

This discrepancy in the relations between states and the relations between regimes or societies is not a constant in European history; it was found necessary on two occasions, however: to put an end to the wars of religion in the seventeenth century and the wars of the French Revolution. On the first occasion citizens had to be members of their state church except where the state succeeded in excluding religion from the sphere of politics by declaring itself neutral and nonpartisan. On the second occasion, after 1815, the sovereigns at first tried for some years to strengthen the balance between states by joint action to keep the monster of revolution in fetters, but later reverted to greater moderation in practice, although the Russian army intervened on behalf of the Emperor of Austria in Hungary in 1848.

The fact that American diplomacy after 1947 was at least negatively ideological was no surprise to any observer with historical memories. What other course was open when the United States was confronting a Stalinist Russia and diplomatic alignments seemed to depend on the internal regimes of states? Inevitably the resistance to Soviet expansion took two forms, a defense of the lines of demarcation (which implied an acceptance of spheres of influence) and support for the established parties or powers at odds with a minority siding with Marxism-Leninism. In Europe the first form may be construed as a variation on the traditional diplomacy of the balance of power; in Asia it led, perhaps accidentally, to a war (Korea), and this war in turn continued in a confrontation between Communist China and a United States enmeshed in its system of military alliances with the insular states, including Nationalist China on Formosa. The second form included some spectacular episodes, such as the overthrow of Mosadeq in Iran, with aid from the CIA, and the military interventions in the Caribbean (Guatemala and Santo Domingo), an area which the diplomats even during the isolationist era traditionally regarded as a private American preserve; it also included constant semiclandestine activity in a number of countries. The Vietnam War lies, so to speak, at the point at which the two forms meet, for the defense of the demarcation line went hand in hand with the attempt to establish a regime in South Vietnam capable of surviving on its own.

The paramarxist critics—or some of them at least—assert that in order to preserve its imperialism of exploitation, the United States must mount guard all over the globe and that the entire system will crumble if a single one of its components is impaired. The critics born of the postwar Establishment, the liberals, and those who look back with pride to the Marshall Plan and the Truman Doctrine deplore the militarization or globalization (the transfer to Asia) of containment, the failure to take account of the changes within the Soviet world since 1947, and the disproportion between the stake and the cost in the Vietnam War. Tucker, while not denying the validity of the argument elaborated in the preceding pages, presents an extreme version of a thesis foreshadowed by a number of commentators, that nuclear weapons radically change the conditions of physical security. For a country like the United States security diminishes as external interests or commitments increase. With a thousand intercontinental ballistic missiles, forty-one nuclear submarines, each armed with sixteen Polaris or Poseidon missiles, to say nothing of long-range bombers and aircraft launched from carriers, has the United States anything to fear from any power, even one that was master of the Eurasian land mass from Brest to Vladivostock?

This thesis seems to me evident rather than paradoxical. No one has ever been able seriously to believe that the alliances with Australia and New Zealand, or even Formosa, the Philippines, and Japan, contribute to the security of the United States in a nuclear era; they in fact contribute to the security of the allied countries, increase the American republic's ability to intervene with armed force, if need be, and consolidate a form of order.

It is preferable, however, to avoid "escalation to extremes." *In theory*, deterrence would work just as effectively against a nuclear force installed in Cuba as against the Soviet missiles installed four or five thousand miles from New York or Washington. Even apart from the reduction of the time interval between the launching of a missile and its strike on the target, the United States must not, in a strategy based on deterrence, or in other words, on the presumed determination of the head of state, create the impression, however illusory, of a weakening of its will. With this reservation, I do not see how anyone could reject the proposition on which the new isolationism is based. The real question seems to me to lie elsewhere: to what degree is this situation as new as we are all prone to think? To what degree has the explanation for the United States' entry into war in 1917 and 1941 not confused justification with motive and rationalized a historical process due to the republic's involvement in the inter-state system? In short, would a German victory in 1917 (or a compromise peace) or even the victory of the Third Reich and Japan really have endangered the physical security of the United States?

The doctrinaires of the balance of power all answered these questions in the affirmative, because, since they were against crusading and in favor of intervention, they wished to defend intervention without transgressing the bounds of a realistic philosophy of inter-state relations. They never succeeded in fully convincing their fellow countrymen, because, to say the least, their thesis has never been evident and has never been demonstrated. If a revisionist school has arisen and contested the Establishment's conventional version following each of the wars, from that of 1898 through that of 1917, to that of 1941, the cause is not, or not solely, moralism or populism, the revolt against the bankers, the arms merchants, or the intellectuals of the eastern seaboard; as an insular power in relation to the Eurasian land mass, the United States has never been directly threatened by the breakdown of the continental balance, as Great Britain felt itself threatened for centuries. In 1916–17 it still had a choice between intervention and nonintervention and between intervention to impose a compromise peace on the Allies and intervention to impose a peace by defeat on the Germans. The "Wilson syndrome," on which so many commentators like to rely both to *characterize* and to *explain* the American style, results in part from the fact that the American republic always had too many choices available once its continental expansion had been completed. In the final accounting there is less difference than the realists suppose between Woodrow Wilson's slogan of "a world safe for democracy" and Walter Lippmann's requisites for equilibrium; what is involved here is simply an ideology designed to convince and commit a people separated by thousands of miles from the enemies its leaders designate for it.

If the Germany of Wilhelm II had won the war, would its ambitions have swelled beyond the Old Continent? Would it have posed so serious a threat of invasion as to compel the United States to militarize its civil life to an extent incompatible with the preservation of its institutions? I simply do not believe it. Because of the volume of its population, the abundance of its resources, its distance, and its geographical location, the United States had little to fear from a hegemony of the Wilhelmine Reich, at any rate for ten or twenty years to come.

Advances in military technology had somewhat impaired the American republic's insular advantages and invulnerability twenty years later; but neither Hitler's empire nor the Japanese empire directly endangered the country. It is true that having become an Asian power by annexing the Philippines, it would, if the Co-Prosperity Sphere had been established, have had to live with the possible loss of its possessions or with an order incompatible with its conception of the just and unjust—or in brief, in a hostile environment. Japan would have had enough to deal with in its Co-Prosperity Sphere for decades without launching an assault on the west coast of the United States or even its outer defense bases.

After his victory over France Hitler hoped to treat with Great Britain, for he admired its empire. He preferred to destroy the empire of the Czars which had become the Soviet Union. A totally unscrupulous and nonideological American diplomacy with complete freedom of movement, could such be conceived, was not irresistibly drawn by an evident military threat from Hitler or Japan into the choice which it progressively adopted. Drawing a distinction between physical security and the creation of an environment favorable to the expansion of the national values, though valid analytically, is somewhat hazardous, for no great power defines its national interest merely as its physical security. Diplomats think and act within a world already structured by enmities which cannot be reduced to calculations of strength or considerations of balance. The animosity against the Empire of the Rising Sun in that era of fascism and imperialism and against the Third Reich left the decision-makers no choice save futile protest or war. The United States diplomacy of the Thirties seems in retrospect execrable because it refused to choose. Most Americans knew that they could not tolerate the victory of Hitler or of Tojo's Japan; they also knew that they were not in the front line. In the course of the Thirties they came up with the least rational line of action: the enactment of legislation designed to *prevent* a recurrence of the events of 1914–17, and a hostile attitude toward the two states they fought after 1941. Isolationism emerged discredited, and rightly so, from this second test of the solidarity between the Old and the New World; since, when the moment of truth came, the United States did not in fact tolerate the hegemony or imperial domination of one state over the whole of the Old Continent, it would have been better to acknowledge and proclaim this solidarity beforehand and thus prevent a war in which the republic would inevitably be involved.

Was involvement inevitable because a comparison of the industrial potential of Europe and the United States revealed the danger of "fortress America"? The realists in 1941, as in 1946, defended war and subsequently containment on the grounds that a Germany or Russia ruling from the Atlantic to the Urals would ultimately be stronger than the United States. It was a facile defense in that it brought up the question of the requirements of the United States' physical security. Popular opinion, which never took these calculations of coal and steel quite seriously, came closer to the truth. Hitler's victory might some day have jeopardized the physical security of the United States, just as the extension of the Soviet sphere to Brest would; the American republic had twice contained an imperial expansion primarily because those responsible for its diplomacy had not identified the national interest solely with physical security. Twice it had wished to preserve an environment that would not be dominated by a hostile state.

Hence I do not attach much importance to the argument for a new isolationism based on the atomic revolution in weapons. Not that such argumentation is false; it is manifestly true.[7] But it has always been true that the less the United States concerned itself with the affairs of Europe and Asia, the better was its chance of escaping war and that it owed to its insular position and its size a security

---

[7] Intercontinental missiles do not change the situation; the United States needed bases abroad to defend others rather than to defend itself. After 1945, bombers and aircraft carriers gave the United States all the means of deterrence it needed before the latest nuclear revolution, missiles.

not directly or immediately threatened by European or Asian empires. The nuclear revolution forced the cities to discard statistical comparisons and to participate in the real debate, which had tended to be obscured by reference to the crusading spirit or the British navy's mastery of the seas;[8] the real question is whether the American republic is willing to play a part in the inter-state system similar to that of all great states in the past, not in order to ensure its physical security, which is taken for granted in any case, but in order to exert its power and influence in the inter-state sphere.

Although from the military point of view the change seems to me less than the theoreticians of a new isolationism claim, from the economic point of view, or with regard to the objective of the inhabitants' well-being, withdrawal has become far more difficult than it was thirty or fifty years ago. In this connection, I have discussed the United States' place in the inter-state system and the place of the American economy in the capitalist world market earlier in this essay.

The figures used by the doctrinaires of the new isolationism are precisely those on which Magdoff casts doubt. Not that the figures are wrong; the United States exports goods to the value of some $40 billion (at current prices), whereas the value of its GNP exceeds $1,000 billion. Net earnings from direct investments abroad amount to between $7 and $8 billion ($7.5 billion, according to the President's Economic Report to the Congress in January 1972), whereas total corporate profits before tax exceed $80 billion ($85 billion in 1971). Magdoff's observations[9] are worth repeating here, that the profits of the manufacturing (or processing) industries were only $34 billion in 1971; the profits of United States' manufacturing industry abroad account for an appreciable proportion of this total.

The link between the United States' role in the inter-state system and its place in the world economy is not, as I have conceded or rather have tried to demonstrate, as rigid as the paramarxist interpretations would have it. United States' direct investments in the Fifties and Sixties went to the industrialized countries. Canada and Western Europe hold two-thirds of United States' direct investment abroad,

---

[8] Tucker himself admits that such fears, though reasonable, were perhaps exaggerated.

[9] See pp. 165–66 above.

while the developing countries' share has fallen from 40 percent to 30 percent. A change in diplomacy would not lead overnight either to the loss of these investments or to a radically different attitude on the part of the Europeans. (I am leaving aside the Canadians, for the strictest isolationism would not exclude them from the American republic's defense sphere.)

The fact remains, however, that a secession from the inter-state system and the world market could not be brought off without risk and resistance. The military strength of the United States, the nuclear guarantee, and the presence of American troops on the frontierlands of the imperial zone have established the political and moral climate in which the Western economy has flourished for a quarter of a century. Does it still need an imperial republic present as well in certain subsystems, to guarantee the aggregate equilibrium of the system? The Japanese and Europeans tend to think so, and probably the directors of the American conglomerates, too.

Though I shall not adopt the paramarxist argument, it seems to me an incontrovertible fact that the establishment of subsidiaries is doubly useful to the American economy; first of all because the subsidiaries' rate of profit is normally higher—which makes an economy in which enterprises are managed with at least a partial view to profit-making, easier to operate—and, secondly because the manufacturing industry owned by American corporations abroad slows down the decline of this American-controlled sector of production in relation to the world total. It disseminates abroad the innovations first put on the market on the other side of the Atlantic. As a high-wage service economy, the American economy tends to transfer abroad some of its manufacturing industries. Would this transfer continue on the same terms if United States diplomacy no longer preserved the equilibrium of the inter-state system? Possibly, but this is doubtful.

It is certainly true that the Third World countries would not refuse to sell their raw materials to a republic which had withdrawn into itself. They could neither find a substitute purchaser overnight nor compel the United States (and the other developed countries) to modify the tariffs which discourage the first stage in processing raw materials in the producing country.

There happens to be one raw material, however, which is an exception and has quite a different significance, namely oil. If some experts are to be believed, by the 1980s the United States will have to import oil or natural gas to the value of about $25 billion. Dependence on foreign countries, which is now less in the United States than in any other developed country, would suddenly be substantially increased. Financing these imports would dictate a different export strategy. The oil embargo of October 1973 has changed the prospect by suggesting the use of national resources, but it has not made the new isolationism more popular.

The above observations do not refute the argument that the United States has no need of an imperial diplomacy to preserve its inhabitants' well-being, but do suggest that it needs to be somewhat more flexible and that it is not possible to state dogmatically that a change in the inter-state system would not affect the world market. But that is not the essential point, as I see it. Isolationism, *as defined by a refusal to take an explicit and resolute stand in European and Asian conflicts,* is discredited in the twentieth century, because at the moment of truth the decision-makers, opinion, and events have twice brought about intervention. The question is not so much whether, if American diplomacy were governed solely by considerations of physical security, it could and should stand aside from the turmoils of history; the real question is whether nonalignment and the refusal of "entangling alliances" would not give rise some day to such crises that once again, however much it wished to abstain, the American republic would be incapable of standing aside from them. If, as I think, American diplomacy was not *determined* by military danger or calculations of equilibrium either in 1917, in 1941, or in 1947, the security enjoyed by the American republic today in the shadow of the nuclear apocalypse is no guarantee whatever against the dialectic of politics or the waves of passion that were responsible for two interventions, which, had forewarning of them been given, might perhaps have prevented the wars.

To descend from the realms of abstraction to the world of history as it unfolded before our eyes in 1972, the rejection of an imperial role could basically take three different concrete forms: 1. an attempt to establish an autonomous equilibrium at either end of the Eurasian land mass without the United States' giving any guarantee or undertaking any prior commitment; 2. a growing lack of interest in local conflicts in the Middle East (Israel and the Arab countries) and Southeast Asia; **3.** an indifference to political disturbances within states, even if they enabled or were likely to enable a Marxist-Leninist party to accede to power. In other words, should the United States in its own interest, in its allies' interest, or in the world's interest maintain its two major alliances, those with Western Europe and Japan? Should it abdicate from its exorbitant pretension to crush revolutionary movements?

Isolationism in its narrowest definition entails the rupture or relaxation of the two alliances which shaped the structure of the postwar inter-state system, the American-Japanese alliance and the Atlantic alliance. A decision to this effect would probably involve nuclear proliferation in the short or the long run. If the United States were publicly to announce its refusal to ensure its allies' security in the future in the belt of islands girdling the Asian continent, the rulers of Japan would undoubtedly have no alternative but to reconsider the policy on which they have presently staked all, that of being a great economic power rather than a great military power, the possesssor of conventional weapons alone, with their air force and navy designed to protect the areas near the islands rather than to undertake distant expeditions. An isolationist United States would, as such, refrain from all intervention and would leave the three Asian great powers to work things out among themselves as they thought best.

Proliferation, in this particular case the nuclear armament of Japan, would not necessarily conflict with American interest, since this interest would be based on the assumption of a divisible peace and a fragmentary system. In the abstract the two arguments advanced by the isolationists are plausible, namely that the new nuclear states would not necessarily behave less rationally than the five, or the two, earlier nuclear states, and that conflicts in Asia, even nuclear conflicts, would not jeopardize the United States' physical security because the United States would not be involved. The attitude suggested in reasoning of this kind is not really compatible with historical experience. In the abstract, economic interdependence does not mean that peace is indivisible. Indeed, the relative isolation of a subsystem in which disputes do not entail a negotiated solution may well be seen to be the logical result of the reciprocal paralysis of the great powers. To suppose that regions or countries which play a leading part in the world market can be involved in hostilities which would throw trade relations into complete confusion without the slightest intervention by the paramount state or the dominant economy seems to me to be simply to concoct a scenario which any historian would on the face of it feel to be highly improbable.

Isolationism in Asia is the extreme reaction to an extreme "militancy." In northern Asia the Soviet Union, Japan, and Communist China already constitute a subsystem, the equilibrium of which would be upset by a complete withdrawal by the United States. Neither the Soviet Union nor China have any territorial claims on Japan.[10] Neither of them contemplates invading the islands. The wealth of Japan is not of the sort that can be seized by armed force. It is the two Communist states with common frontiers and alien populations on the frontierlands of their empires, that in fact have motives for fighting each other, according to historical experience. By taking the initiative in rapprochement with Peking, the United States has upset the system built up after the Korean War and has promoted the emergence of another system more consonant with the traditional logic of diplomacy. It both gains and loses thereby; it gains at least Sino-Soviet neutrality toward a negotiated settlement in Vietnam and the role of a *tertius* standing between Moscow and Peking; it loses to some extent the preponderant role it held for twenty-five years, for Japan will conduct a diplomacy of its own, concerned as much with opportunities in Siberia or China as with scowls in Washington. In the perspective of the next ten years the military alliance between Japan and the United States involves scarcely any risks to the latter and makes the formation and peaceful stabilization of the new system more probable. The real question is that of the psychological balance inside America between commercial rivalry and political-military alliance.

In Europe isolationism would take the form of the dissolution of the Atlantic Alliance, with the Europeans themselves assuming responsibility for their own defense. In choosing withdrawal after arguing in favor of nonproliferation for fifteen years, the American

---

[10] Japan has secondary territorial claims on the Soviet Union (some of the Kuriles) and on China (Peking or Taiwan) regarding some small islands to the north of Taiwan.

decision-makers would be giving a possibly unfortunate, but not un-precedented, example. By preaching nonproliferation, American presidents by implication undertook to guarantee the security of those of their allies who followed their instructions and obeyed their injunctions. If they suddenly lost interest in those who had put their faith in them, they would be playing false both to their com-mitment and to common sense.

Nobody, the isolationist will reply, proposes any such revision. What is unreasonable and ultimately unacceptable is that 250 million Europeans with a per capita income far higher than the Eastern European countries should confess themselves incapable of defend-ing themselves and rush to Uncle Sam like scared children to beg him not to withdraw a few thousand or a few tens of thousands of GIs—GIs who, according to Roosevelt, were not going to stay in Europe anyway after hostilities ended.

I must confess to some sympathy for this line of argument. I even happen to think that if the American diplomats followed the neo-isolationists' advice, they might perhaps render political Europe a service similar to that which they rendered economic Europe a quarter of a century ago. If the Europeans were confronted not with vague apprehensions about a possible withdrawal, but with the certainty that the last GI will have recrossed the Atlantic by a stated date, would they not find in themselves and in the smell of danger the initiative they need to rise above their status as protected states? In this case too, of course, proliferation would have to replace nonproliferation as the watchword of American diplomacy.

The obstacles are familiar. If there were an Anglo-French deter-rent force, what authority would decide its use? Would the Germans trust it as they trust the American force? Would they pay part of its cost without having their finger on the trigger? Do Europeans not prefer equality in dependence to the inequality which would be created by the possession by some of them of the weapons re-garded as decisive? And so on. Shock treatment—the announcement that the American army will withdraw by a stated date—confronts isolationists with a difficult choice: either the United States main-tains its guarantee without putting the seal on it by the presence of the GIs, in which case it is accepting the same responsibilities with augmented dangers, or it withdraws both troops and guarantee and trusts to the Europeans' instinct of self-preservation. In the second case the same contradiction would arise between economic interdependence and political-military dissociation as arises in Asia.

The world market as it has developed for twenty years has brought about an interpenetration of Europe and the United States (an interpenetration of which the book value of American investments provides only an inaccurate measure) so great that economic calculation suggests to any and all policy-makers in Washington that the present economic situation would best continue indefinitely. The cost in foreign currency of stationing the American troops in Europe amounts at the most to between $1 and $1.5 billion (taking German purchases of equipment into account). In budgetary terms American troops cost less in Europe than in the United States. Negotiators from beyond the Atlantic use the threat of withdrawal (a threat presented as due to pressure from the Senate) as a covert form of blackmail to extract commercial or monetary concessions. The position of strength ensured the United States by the military protection afforded the Europeans is undoubtedly worth, from its point of view, more than a billion dollars.

Even if American participation in the military balance at either end of the Eurasian land mass assumed a different character, and one closer to isolationist notions, by the end of the present decade, there remains one region where no one perceives on the historical horizon any force capable of taking the place of the United States— the Middle East. United States strength bars the Soviet Union from intervening with military force to compel Israel to evacuate the territories occupied during the 1967 war. Perhaps even more importantly than the Arab-Israel conflict, the oil reserves, of which not only the Japanese and Europeans, but probably the Americans themselves, will be in absolute need for the next twenty years, lie in the region stretching from Iraq to the Arabian Emirates in the Persian Gulf. If worst came to worst, the nation's well-being could survive the domination of the whole region by the Soviet Union, but it would be at the expense of a reorganization of the American economy and the world market, a reorganization theoretically feasible but one which would change the way in which the system works and require difficult readjustments. Of the two extreme lines of argument—Claude Julien's to the effect that the United States cannot renounce the "empire" to which it owes its wealth, and the isolationists' to the effect that the United States can preserve its prosperity if it withdraws into itself—the second is more easily arguable than the first; although this latter contention perhaps had some merit twenty-five years ago, it is less true today and will probably be even more questionable in 1980. It implies a moderation on the part of the Soviet Union which is more desirable than probable.

An isolationist who harbors no illusions—I refer here to R. W. Tucker—sees quite clearly the price to be paid for this stance, a reduction in the power and influence of the United States all over the world. But, as he expressly states, the decision-makers in Washington, if not the American people, have acquired a taste for power. Senators and journalists denounce the "arrogance of power" all the more bitterly in that the power is the appurtenance of the president and his entourage and of diplomats (in the narrow sense), the military, agents of the intelligence services or the CIA, and secretaries of the treasury. Anyone who has had much to do with ministers and their aides, no matter whether American or French, knows how greatly attached—professionally, so to speak—they are to power and how much they insist on being heard and obeyed. The senators have lost what the representatives of the executive have appropriated at home and abroad. The Vietnam War provided the legislature with a chance to recover some of its prerogatives which had fallen into abeyance. I can hardly see the president and his advisers and organizations surrendering the status they enjoy by virtue of their function in the inter-state system and their weight in the world market. According to Tucker, the best interpreter of a moderate isolationism, American anti-Communism is accounted for quite as much by the wish to retain an influence over other countries as by an ideological obsession.

Some will reply that an imperial state has never abdicated except under compulsion. This may be so, but to my mind it is dangerous to put one's faith in historical precedent and to draw reassurance from an act of faith. Public opinion has not been won over once and for all to imperial diplomacy; the political element which took up the challenge after the Second World War no longer exists and has not been replaced by another to which it can hand on the torch; the dual crisis, socio-moral and monetary, conventionally attributed to the Vietnam War leads to withdrawal or an aggressive dollar diplomacy—two attitudes equally unpropitious to a necessary, but not necessarily agonizing, reappraisal.

While the paramarxists in the United States and progressives the world over are writing thrillers about the globe's exploitation by the imperialist monster, some critics (like Ronald Steel) assert that the United States has been exploited by its empire more than the United States has exploited it. Each of these two ways of stating the problem is equally exaggerated and fallacious. If the two wars, in Korea and in Vietnam, are included, "empire," or rather imperial diplomacy, has cost the United States more than it has brought to it. In respect to the world market the balance sheet is difficult to establish; while the dollar was admittedly overvalued and the Europeans derived commercial advantage from this situation, they had to pay for it by monetary confusion and the expansion of subsidiaries of American corporations. Did this expansion in turn promote economic programs to a point at which the expropriation of national capital was compensated and more than compensated for? Did the absorption of a third of American exports by the subsidiaries of the conglomerates prevent a worse deterioration in the balance of trade? Or, conversely—as the labor unions claim—does the investment of capital abroad restrict the creation of more employment opportunities at home? No comprehensive study has yet been produced capable of serving as an adequate guide to choosing one rather than another among the varied propostions put forward. Two facts do, however, seem to me to be equally incontrovertible: that, according to the official figures, American corporations control the production abroad of manufactures worth $76.8 billion (two and a half times the total value of American exports of manufactures)[11] and that the surpluses in the balance of trade have declined to a point at which they have become deficits. These developments may, however, be regarded as economically logical, since the United States is still an exporter, mainly of primary commodities and articles requiring advanced manufacturing processes, but it shows deficits with respect to exports of nontechnology-intensive

---

[11] According to an estimate by another economist, Jack N. Behrman ("New Orientations in International Trade and Investment," in Pierre Uri, ed., *Trade and Investment Policies for the Seventies*), the total value of international production by subsidiaries of American corporations is $219 billion, as against $40 billion for exports.

goods manufactured by traditional processes (such as textiles, iron and steel products, and motor vehicles) and articles requiring fairly advanced technological processing but having a large labor-intensive component (such as tape recorders and television sets). In the case of a few articles (such as black-and-white and color television sets, radios, and cameras) imports account for a large proportion of the domestic market (52 percent, 70 percent, and 66 percent respectively). Although these figures are impressive in themselves, they should not obscure the fact that imported manufactures account for only about 10 percent of the total market for these products. Furthermore, in assessing the ultimate significance of the 1970 figures, conjunctural factors (dollar parity, domestic inflation) have to be taken into account.

It remains an indisputable fact, however, that the deficit in the United States balance of trade may become progressively larger as the share of services in the total product (about 42 percent, employing 60 percent of manpower) increases; but this is offset by the income from capital investments abroad and exports of services (inadequately measured by the item for fees and royalties). This crisis—if the term is to be applied to the culmination, however spectacular in the short term, of a logical transformation of economic relationships—coincided in 1971 with the agreements with Peking and Moscow, as if to symbolize the break with the postwar era; enemies became less inimical, allies less allied; economic agreements with enemies began to take shape, while economic disputes with allies became acuter.

To interpret events in this way is undoubtedly to oversimplify. Europeans had begun to make economic agreements with the Soviet Union and the Eastern countries long before the United States did; they had been the first to renew relations with Communist China. They would be guilty of the worst possible taste if they held against the United States the fact that it followed their own example and the advice they had lavished upon it. The fact remains, nevertheless, that United States diplomacy, liable as it always is to abrupt changes of direction, may perhaps, after subordinating economic considerations to strictly political imperatives, whatever the paramarxist interpretation, reverse its order of priorities from one day to the next; the European Community would then be regarded as an obstacle to American exports rather than to Communist expansion and Japan would in the future be considered a competitor—and an unscrupulous competitor at that, profiting from trade liberalization without opening up its own market to an equivalent extent— rather than as an integral part of the free world.

In the abstract, the proponents of a doctrine of moderate isolationism are quite right to argue that the United States has no need to guarantee the security of Japan and Western Europe in order to trade with these two partner-rivals. It remains to be seen whether its political and strategic withdrawal does not lead either to protectionism (the phenomenon typical of the Thirties) or, as is more likely, to an aggressive attitude toward its allies in trade and monetary negotiations. A majority of Europeans, especially the Germans, still consider the United States military presence necessary to their security. Not that they fear an aggression in the traditional sense; what they do fear is that in the event of a local disturbance of the equilibrium they may lose the freedom of action of which they feel assured by the reciprocal paralysis of the two super-powers. Isolationists beyond the Atlantic contend in reply that Americans will no longer fight for anyone in any event, not even to preserve the existence of Israel. This the Europeans simply do not believe, and they hold that the Soviets at any rate still have a healthy respect for the might of the American republic and distrust the giant's reactions which are still liable to be irrational or unpredictable.

Not only the cold war, but the entire postwar era came to an end with Nixon's first term, his visits to Peking and Moscow and the winding up of the Vietnam War. Two major uncertainties loom over the evolving new system, one depending on circumstances, the other historical in significance.

The first uncertainty lies in the mood of the American people and the extent to which the diplomats are dependent on that mood. It appears as if the intellectuals, academics, and journalists have not yet accepted the fact that it is entirely *normal* for the American republic to participate in the play of inter-state relations. In their revulsion from the horrors and absurdities of the Vietnam War they have conjured up, in order to rationalize their detachment from the outside world, an imaginary picture of spheres of influence stabilized once and for all, a Soviet Union permanently satisfied with the status quo, Japan and Europe already great powers, and an armed force never to be used again. Some of them reconstruct an imaginary history in which the United States is supposed to have provoked Stalin, while others attribute urban decay, crime, racial tension, and all the ills with which American society is manifestly afflicted to the cost of exercising power.

No one can tell what the money spent on Korea and Vietnam might otherwise have been used for. But to ascribe the cause of the urban crisis merely to lack of funds is to fall into the same error as that which was responsible in part for the Vietnam tragedy, the belief that the key to the solution of all human problems is simply economic or technological. The social processes which caused the crisis cannot be halted by the application of a few billion dollars more. America's black minority has made more progress in the past fifteen years than in the whole of the previous half-century despite all the expenditure lavished on the war in Vietnam. An injection of dollars will no more abolish the abject poverty of the socially alienated and the frustrations engendered or intensified by progress itself than it will wipe out the disorientation and crime spawned by the urban ghettos. The rejection by a section of young Americans —but not solely the young—of the values and virtues proper and propitious to a consumer society existed before the Vietnam War and will continue after it.

A phase of relative lack of interest in the world at large will therefore succeed the quarter-century of American paramountcy, a paramountcy which has now in any case been relegated to the past. Brezhnev's Soviet Union is a bore; the United States is still interesting, but as a laboratory rather than a model. The two super-powers have now genuinely accepted a status of equality; but when it comes down to bedrock, to the question of determination, does this equality still hold good? Is it true, as some commentators like to think, that armed force exercises less and less effect on inter-state relations? If so, why is the Soviet Union willing to go to such expense to enlarge and modernize its navy, air force, and army? Is this to be attributed to the military-industrial complex?

This brings me to the historical uncertainty. The Soviet Union has made use of its armed forces only twice; against its brother socialists, and the second time with some restraint and some care to ensure the minimum loss of human lives. The United States has waged two land wars in Asia, and it repeats—as it did after 1953, but this time with bitter determination—that it will never again wage a land war in Asia. In all probability the decision-makers will learn to live with revolutionary movements, even if their allegiance is Marxist-Leninist (purely in their jargon in most cases, provided that they are not adjacent to the Soviet Union). Of their own accord they will adopt the line advocated by the isolationists, but also recommended by the moderate critics of American "globalism."

By devising a multiplicity of schemata and models, the self-styled scientific study of inter-state relations has often contributed to the decline of the art of analysis rather than to the training of minds. None of the standard devices of historical experience, such as spheres of influence or the balance of power, can be applied as it stands to the system into which President Nixon is to fit the American republic; its breakup into two parts, the *horizontal* or geographical (the subsystems projected on the map of the world) and the *vertical* (the spheres of military, political, commercial, and ideological relations), the jungle of Nietzsche's saurians and the shaping of a transnational economic system, the contrast between the wealth of some and the poverty of others, the doubts of the wealthy about the road that led them to their wealth and their disillusion with it, even while the poor are just as eager to take the same road, are all factors making for a world of unprecedented complexity. The influence that the United States will exert on this world will be less than it has exercised in the past twenty-five years; this will perhaps enable it to avoid some of the frustration of impotent might.

It is for the historian to draw up the final balance sheet for this quarter-century, to compare the successes with the failures, to measure the cost and benefit to all concerned of American paramountcy. To it the Europeans owe, in part at least, both their progress and their security. They do not, however, feel bound by any sense of gratitude—a term and sentiment alike unrecognized by states—but henceforth they will have an opportunity to forge a future for themselves. The paradoxical situation of geographical proximity to the Soviet universe and moral kinship with the Atlantic world exists and will continue to exist as long as the Communist party of the Soviet Union continues to subject the economy to administrative planning and thought to a stifling discipline. According to Kennan, containment was to last until Soviet power was unsettled by its own contradictions or mitigated by the erosion of time The decay of ideology has divested Soviet power of its revolutionary intent and its force of attraction, but it has not divested the men in the Kremlin of the ambitions of a great power.

In match play the only way to become champion is to challenge the holder of the title. Not so in the inter-state tournament; here the titleholder must constantly put his title to the issue. The isolationist will prefer to sulk in his tent; the globalist will try to win every match. What tradition teaches is not cynicism but Aristotelian prudence—the supreme virtue in this world under the visited moon.

INDEX

Abgrenzung, 145
ABM (anti-ballistic missile), 278
Acheson, Dean, 33–34, 45, 54, 59, 67, 152
  backing of French in Indochina by,
    95–96, 182
  containment and, 298–99
  Korea and, 277
Adams, John Quincy, 231
Africa, 141, 163
  U.S. policies toward, 228–31
Agency for International Development
  (AID), 222–24
Agrarian reform, 248
  Japanese, 190
Albania, 43
Algeria, 55, 57, 82, 83, 101
  U.S. policies toward, 228–29
Allende, Salvador, 140, 156, 240
Alliance for Progress, 185, 220
Annam, 114, 126
Annexation of territory, U.S., 273–74
Anticolonialism, 176–77
ANZUS, 253
Appropriations, Senate, 272–73
Aqaba, Gulf of, 134
Arabs, 258
Arbenz Guzmán, Jacobo, 228
Ardahan, 52
Argentina, 233, 235, 249, 250
  repatriated profit ratio of, 241
Armistice Control Commission, 25
Asher, Robert E., 222
Associated States (Indochina), 95
Aswan Dam, 228–29
Atatürk (Mustafa Kemal), 229
Athens, 254–55
Attlee, Clement, 48
Australia, 60
Austria, 20, 29

Awami League, 135
Azerbaijan, 42, 44

B-36 (U.S. bomber), 77
Balance of payments, 194–202, 207–208
Ball, George, 106
Bangladesh, 108, 135
Banks, 169–70
Bao Dai (Emperor of Annam), 95, 96, 102
Baruch Plan (1946), 268
Bay of Pigs invasion (1961), 72, 182, 258
Belgian Congo, 73, 140, 228, 230
Ben Gurion, David, 183
Bengalis, 136–37
Beria, Lavrenti P., 53
Berlin, 20, 90
  1960 crisis in, 68, 78–79
  U.S. troops in, 252
Berlin blockade (1948), 39, 40, 57
Bernstein, E. M., 194–96
Beuve-Méry, Hubert, 301
Bevan, Aneurin, 57
Bevin, Ernest, 38, 95
Biafra, 230
Bidault, Georges, 30, 83, 95
Bipartisanship, 275
Bipolarity, 27, 134, 140
  of cold war, 9–11
  concept of, 4
Bismarck, Otto von, 130, 138
"Brain drain," 228, 236–40
Brandt, Willy, 132
Brazil, 228, 233, 235, 249
  brain drain of, 238–39
  industrialization and U.S. investment
    in, 243–47
  repatriated profit ratio of, 241
Brennan, Donald, 269
Brezhnev, Leonid, 110, 116, 119, 127
Brogan, Sir Denis, 248

Bruce, David, 179–80
Bulganin, Nikolai A., 67
Bulgaria, 15, 31, 43
Bundeswehr, 53
Bundy, McGeorge, 116
Burma, 180
Burnham, James, 179, 298
Byrnes, James F., 30

Cambodia, 93, 103, 117–18, 181, 276
Canada, 238
  U.S. investment in, 168, 185, 217
Capitalism, 163
  imperialist nature of, 260–71
Caribbean, 140, 184–86, 231, 258
Carranza, Venustiano, 233
Castro, Fidel, 74, 87, 89, 156–57, 249–50
Central Intelligence Agency (CIA), 73, 89,
    117, 140, 270, 278
  in Latin America, 249
  Vietnam activism of, 98, 102, 105
Chaban-Delmas, Jacques, 212
Chiang Kai-shek, 45, 46, 54, 65
  loss of mainland China and, 61–63
Chile, 186, 233, 235
  Allende and, 140, 156
  brain drain and, 238–39
  ITT and, 240
China, 45–46, 90
  admission to United Nations of, 65–66,
    110, 122
  India-Pakistan war and, 136
  Korea and, 69
  Nixon visit to (1972), 120–24, 131
  quarantining of, 48, 152
  Sino-American confrontations in Asia,
    53, 59–71
  Sino-Soviet split, 61, 64, 68, 71, 91–92,
    134, 138–39
  Soviet mutual assistance pact with, 69
Chou En-lai, 70, 110, 116, 127, 153
  Nixon and, 121–23, 131
Churchill, Winston, 20, 38, 41, 54
  on colonialism, 169
  Fulton speech of, 42
  at Teheran Conference (1943), 12–13
  on Yalta Conference, 14
Civil War (1861–65), 273
Clausewitz, Karl von, 88
Clay, Henry, 273
Clay, Lucius, 30
Clifford, Clark M., 104
Cochin China, 114, 126
Cold War, 9–12
  1941–45 period, 4, 12–28
    analysis of origins of, 24–28

Cold War (cont.)
  atomic bomb decision, 20–24
  Polish negotiations at Yalta, 13–20
  1945–47 period, 4–5, 28–42
    analysis of origins of, 35–42
    partition of Germany, 28–31
    Soviet rejection of Marshall Plan,
      31–35
  1947–53 period, 5, 43–53
    Korea and, 44–50
    rearmament of Germany and "thaw"
      after death of Stalin, 50–53
    Truman Doctrine (1947) and, 43–44
  1953–58 period, 5–6, 53–71
    German negotiation possibilities and,
      53–54
    Hungarian crisis (1956), 55, 56
    Suez crisis (1956), 54–57
  1958–63 period, 6, 59–91
    Cuban missile crisis (1962), 87–91
    nuclear strategy under Kennedy, 72–86
    Sino-American confrontations in
      Asia, 59–71
  1962–69 period, 67, 92–109
    French involvement in Vietnam, 94–97
    U.S. involvement in Vietnam, 98–107
  1969 and after, 110–47
    Nixon-Kissinger diplomacy and
      global system, 130–47
    Nixon visit to China (1972) and,
      120–22
    settlement of Vietnam War and, 111–
      20, 124–30
    success or failure of, 148–57
Colombia, 232, 238–39, 249
Colonial empires, 259
Colonialism, 164
  dissolution of empires of, 169, 176–77
Comecon, 142
Cominform, 31
Common Market, 85, 140, 144, 192, 218
  U.S. investment and, 178, 210
"Compellence," 88, 106
Comte, Auguste, 269
Conglomerates, 169–70, 264
  nationalization and, 174
Congress, foreign policy and, 271–83
Constitution of the U.S., 272
Containment, 44, 64–65, 140
  capitalist expansion and, 174
  economic, 169–70
  Kennan's Foreign Affairs article and,
    297–99
  Marshall Plan and, 178–79
  in Third World, 220
  Vietnam involvement and, 182–83

Control Council (Germany), 29, 30
Costa Rica, 238–39
Counterinsurgency, 79, 104, 249
Cuba, 72, 184–86, 233, 258
  Platt amendment and (1900), 231
  quarantining of, 249
Cuban missile crisis (1962), 72, 74, 79, 87–91, 108–109
Cultural Revolution, 92
Currency, see Dollar
Curzon Line, 13, 27–28
Czechoslovakia, 26, 36, 40, 144

de Gaulle, Charles, 14, 30, 57, 58–59, 133, 144
  Algerian settlement and, 229
  independent policies of, 82–86
  Indochina and, 96, 169
  nuclear strategy of, 80–82, 86
Deficit balance of payments, 194–202, 207–208
Democratic party, 273
Destroyer Deal (1940), 273
Deterrence, 88
Devaluation
  of dollar, 107, 189, 193, 200, 209, 216
  IMF rules regulating, 190
Díaz, Adolfo, 232
Dictionnaire de l'Académie, 254
Diem, Ngo Dinh, 97–98, 102, 182
Dienbienphu, battle of (1954), 59, 60, 66, 83, 97, 265
Djilas, Milovan, 28n, 61
Dollar
  devaluation of, 107, 189, 193, 200, 209, 216
  gold and, 198–99
  nonconvertability crisis and, 190–91, 204–206, 216
  as transnational currency, 202–19
Dollar gap, 191, 193–94
Domination, 4
Domino theory, 96–97, 103
  Kolko and, 179–81
"Dual hegemony," 56, 58
Duclos, Jacques, 37
Dulles, John Foster, 63, 68, 116
  "agonizing reappraisal" speech of, 53
  containment strategy of, 228–29, 298
  death of, 73
  on Ho Chi Minh, 180
  Indochina and, 65, 97, 153
  Suez crisis and, 55, 57
Dumont, René, 231
Duvalier, François, 232, 248

East Bengal, 135
Ecuador, 238–39
Eden, Anthony, 12, 15, 28, 55
Egypt, 55, 56, 67, 107, 184
  Six-day War (1967) and, 134–35
  U.S. policies toward, 228–29
Ehrenburg, Ilya, 52
Eisenhower, Dwight D., 50, 51, 54, 63, 72, 264
  China and, 65
  on domino theory, 180
  de Gaulle letter to (1958), 84
  Indochina policies of, 97
  Suez crisis and, 55–57, 183
Ellsberg, Daniel, 104
Erfurt, 20
Estrada Palma, Tomás, 231
Eurodollars, 145, 215, 226
Europe
  growth rate of, 188
  postwar recovery of, 191–96
  unification of, 144–47
  U.S. foreign aid to, 223
  U.S. investment in, 168
  U.S. troops in, 252
Executive agreements, 273
Exploitation, 4, 163
  of Third World, 172, 226, 236
Export-import ratio, U.S., 164–66

Federal Republic of Germany, 29, 31, 50, 145
  economic growth of, 171, 204
  See also Germany
Ferry, Jules, 180
Finland, 14, 40
First-strike capability, 268
Five Year Plans, 179
"Flexible response," 266
Fontaine, André, 9, 96, 107, 108
Food for Freedom, 222–23
Foreign aid, 220
  to developed countries, 221
  to underdeveloped countries, 221–23
Foreign Assistance Act, 222
Foreign investment, U.S., 166, 167–68, 218
  imperialism and, 260–71
  monetary ramifications of, 210–13
  in Third World, 226–28
Foreign markets, 165, 167
Foreign policy, U.S., 271–82
Formosa, 60, 221
Four-Power Conference (1947), 29, 30
Four-Power Conference (1955), 53

France, 26, 39, 76, 257
  Dulles threat on European army and, 53
  economic growth of, 171
  Indochina and, 45–46, 59, 93–97
  withdrawal from NATO of, 84–85
  partition of Germany and, 30, 66
  Suez crisis and, 55–57
  tactical nuclear weapons question and, 80–86
Free election principle, 38
French Union, 94–95
Fulbright, J. William, 173, 276
Furtado, Celso, 243

Galbraith, John Kenneth, 246
Gandhi, Indira, 135–37, 138
General Agreement on Tariffs and Trade (GATT), 190–91, 193, 219
Geneva Conference (1954), 59, 65, 95, 97
German Democratic Republic, 20, 53, 68, 145
Germany, 18, 53–54, 144
  atomic rearmament question of, 80
  Big Three breach in relations over, 28–31
  East Prussia ceded to Soviet Union from, 14, 20
  economic recovery of, 192
  entrance into NATO of, 53
  rearmament of, 48, 50, 53
Giap, Vo Nguyen, 79, 94, 124
Gizenga, Antoine, 230
Globalism, 140
  concept of, 3
Gold, dollar and, 198–99
Gomulka, Wladyslaw, 144
Good Neighbor Policy, 231
Goulart, João, 228, 249
Goux, Christian, 241
Great Britain, 24, 144, 263
  Anglo-Soviet treaty denounced, 53
  Common market bid rejected, 85, 140
  independence of India and, 169, 176
  Moscow agreement, 14–15, 16
  negotiations with Soviet Union on Poland by, 12–13, 27–28
  partition of Germany negotiations and, 28–31
  Suez Crisis, 55–57
  Truman Doctrine and, 43–44
  U.S. missile bases in, 76
Greater East Asia Co-Prosperity Sphere, 171–72
Greece, 12, 15, 24, 25, 28, 39
  foreign aid to, 221
  Truman Doctrine and, 43–44

Gromyko, Andrei A., 90
Grozea, Petru, 16
Guatemala, 74, 149, 185, 228
Guerrilla warfare, 65, 79, 101, 113

Haiphong, 94
Haiti, 232, 233
Hammarskjöld, Dag, 230
Hapsburgs, 254
Harbison-Myers Index, 238–39
Harriman, Averell, 33–34, 128
Hawaii, 274
Hegel, G. W. F., 176
Heterogeneity, 26, 64–65
  of cold war, 10–11
  concept of, 3
Hilferding, Rudolf, 163, 263
Hirohito (Emperor of Japan), 21
Ho Chi Minh, 46, 94, 96, 104, 113
  Dulles on, 180
Ho Chi Minh Trail, 94
Hobson, J. A., 163, 263
Holy Alliance (1815), 132–33
Holy Roman Empire, 254
Hopkins, Harry, 14, 20, 116
"Hot line," 90
Hué, 100
Huerta, Victoriano, 233
Hull, Cordell, 15, 116, 233
Hungary, 15, 26, 31, 36
  1956 crisis in, 55, 56, 144

Imperialism, 252–85
  classic works on, 163–64
  control of U.S. foreign policy and, 271–82
  expansive nature of capitalism, 260–64
  liberalism, free trade and, 192–93
  military-industrial complex and, 264–71
  nature of empires and, 252–60
Inchon landing (1950), 47
Income redistribution, 248
India, 90, 122, 176, 180, 181
  Pakistan War (1971), 107–108, 135–38
Indochina, 45, 59, 65, 83
Indonesia, 176, 181
Industrial-military complex, 50, 264–71
Inflation, 206, 209
Institutional Revolutionary Party, 249
Inter-Allied Advisory Council, 25
International Business Machines (IBM), 210, 217
International Control Commission (Vietnam), 99, 105
International Monetary Fund (IMF), 190, 206

International Telephone & Telegraph (ITT), 240
Iran, 42, 74, 221
Iraq, 229
Israel, 107, 134–35, 136–37
    U.S. support of, 183–84, 229
Italy, 25, 26, 39
    U.S. missile bases in, 76

Japan, 18, 66, 121, 171
    agrarian reform in, 190
    growth rate of, 188, 214–15, 290
    post-Vietnam global system and, 142–44
    rearming of, 60
    Truman atomic bomb decision and, 21–24
    U.S. foreign aid to, 223
    U.S. interests in, 168
    U.S. mutual security pact with, 253, 273
Jefferson, Thomas, 231
Johnson, Lyndon B., 65, 92, 107, 123
    foreign investment and, 262
    Vietnam War and, 101, 103–106, 113, 127, 275, 278
Jordan, 120, 134
Julien, Claude, 163–64, 167, 171, 173

Kars, 52
Kasavubu, Joseph, 230
Kashmir, 137
Katanga secession (1960), 73, 230
Katyn, 12, 16
Kemal, Mustafa (Atatürk), 229
Kennan, George F., 44, 51
    Foreign Affairs article of, 297–98
Kennedy, John F., 60, 68, 72–73, 115
    China and, 65
    Indochina involvement and, 153–54, 182–83
    nuclear strategy under, 72–86, 123
Keynes, John Maynard, 190, 202
Khatkhate, Deena R., 239
Khmers, 117
Khrushchev, Nikita S., 63–64, 67
    Cuban missile crisis and, 79, 87–91
    nuclear strategy beliefs of, 74–76
    U-2 incident and, 68
    visit to U.S. of (1960), 73
Kim, Jungwon Alexander, 70
Kim Il-song, 69–70
Kim Tu-bong, 70
Kindleberger, Charles P., 200, 205, 242–43
Kissinger, Henry, 110
    Nixon-Kissinger diplomacy and global system, 130–47
    Nixon visit to China and, 120–24

Vietnam War negotiations and, 115–20, 124–30
Kolko, Gabriel, 163–64, 264–65
    domino theory and, 179–80
Kolm, S. C., 206
Korea, 24, 40, 44–50, 59, 62
    Congress and, 275–77
    foreign aid to, 221
    Geneva Conference (1954) and, 65
    Nixon and, 111–12
    role of Soviet Union in Korean War, 69–71
Krock, Arthur, 298

Lamartine, Alphonse Marie Louis de, 52
Landeau, Jean-François, 241
Langer, W., 163
Lao Dong (Vietnamese Communist party), 98–99
Laos, 60, 79, 87, 93, 103, 118
    domino theory and, 181
    1971 crisis in, 117
    Nixon and, 276
Latin America, 140–41, 231–51
    U.S. interests in, 168, 184–86, 231–51
        brain drain, 236–40
        Brazil, 243–47
        investment and development, 240–43
        outline of U.S. relations, 231–36
        political, 247–51
League of Nations, 274
Lebensraum, 171–72
Leclerc de Hautecloque, Jacques Philippe, 94
Leipzig, 20
Lend-lease, 20, 33–35
Lenin, V. I., 163, 229, 263
Liberia, 230
Libya, 230
Liddell Hart, Sir Basil, 79
Lie, Trygvie, 52
Lin Piao, 104, 121, 133
Lippmann, Walter, 18, 81, 298–99
Liska, George, 303
List der Vernunft, 176
Lodge, Henry Cabot, 102
Lublin Committee (1944), 13, 15–16, 19
Lumumba, Patrice, 230

MacArthur, Douglas, 47–48, 66, 67, 152
    Truman and, 265, 277
McCarthy, Joseph, 275
McCarthyism, 60, 151, 277
McGovern, George, 68
Machado, Gerardo, 231, 233
Macmillan, Harold, 85–86

McNamara, Robert, 81, 106, 155
   civilian pressure on military and, 265–69
McNamara Doctrine, 74, 79
Magdoff, Harry, 169, 179, 225
Malaya, 65, 180
Malaysia, 104
Malenkov, Georgi M., 75
Malik, Jakob, 70, 104
Manchuria, 61, 101
Manifest Destiny, 274
Mao Tse-tung, 45–47, 65
   American attitudes toward, 66
   Korean War and, 61–63, 69–71, 111
   Nixon and, 121
Marshall Plan, 31–35, 177–78, 203
   aid statistics of, 222
   European recovery and, 190
Matsu, 53, 60, 63, 68, 91
Meir, Golda, 110, 137
Mendès-France, Pierre, 83
Metternich, Fürst von, 130, 132, 138
Mexican War (1846–48), 273
Mexico, 233, 238–39, 249
   repatriated profit ratio in, 241
Michael (King of Romania), 15–16
Mikolajczyk, Stanislaus, 19–20
Mikoyan, Anastas, 33
Military bases, 252–53
Military superiority, U.S., 169, 171
   capitalist expansion and, 174, 217
   U.S. foreign policy and, 264–71
Minuteman missile program (1961), 76, 265
Mirage IV missile, 82
MIRV, 123n, 148
Missile gap, 76
Modernization, 220
Mollet, Guy, 55
Molotov, Vyacheslav, 15, 28, 30, 37, 178
Monetary crisis, see Dollar
Mongols, 258
Monopoly capitalism, 263
Monroe Doctrine (1823), 232–33, 234
Montesquieu (Charles Louis de Secondat), 254
Montreux Convention, 52
Morgenthau, Hans, 10, 30
Morgenthau, Henry, 298–99
Morocco, 101
Moscow agreements (1944), 14–15, 16
Mossé, Robert, 205
Most-favored-nation clauses, 176, 191
Multinational empires, 259
Mutual Security Act (1959), 222, 229
My Lai affair (1968), 100

Nasser, Gamal Abdul, 57, 137, 229

"National interest," 256
National Liberation Front (NLF), 98–99
National Security Council, 116
Nationalization, 174
Navarre Plan (1953), 97
Nehru, Jawaharlal, 228
Neo-colonialism, 3–4
Net liquidity balance, 196–97
Netherlands, 171
New Frontier, 72
New Zealand, 60
Nicaragua, 74, 232, 233
Nigeria, 140, 231
Nixon, Richard M., 60, 68, 69, 272
   election of, 107
   foreign investment and, 262–63
   Latin American visit of, 234
   negotiated Vietnam settlement and, 114–20, 124–30
   Nixon-Kissinger diplomacy and global system, 130–47
   Peking visit of (1972), 110, 120–24
Nonconvertibility of dollar, 204–206, 216
North Atlantic Treaty Organization (NATO), 39, 50–51, 80, 253, 257, 273
   de Gaulle withdrawal from, 84–85
   German entrance into, 53
Nuclear deterrence, 80
Nuclear Nonproliferation Treaty, 123, 269
Nuclear strategy, 75, 266–70
Nuclear Test-Ban Treaty (1963), 74, 87, 90, 91, 123, 269, 278
Nye Committee hearings, 274n

Official reserve transaction balance, 196–97
Oil, 170, 183
On Democracy in America (Tocqueville), 272
Organization of American States (OAS), 186, 234
Organization of Petroleum Exporting Countries, 241
Osgood, Robert, 148–57

Pakistan, 107–108, 122, 135–38
Panama, 56, 74, 232
   repatriated profit ratio of, 241
Panmunjon, 59, 111
Pannikar, K. M., 47, 70
Paraguay, 238–39
Paris Economic Conference (1947), 28
"Peaceful coexistence," 3
Peloponnesian War, 254–55
Penrose, E. T., 242
Pentagon, 264–71
Pentagon Papers, 98, 102, 104–105

People's liberation movements, 83
People's Republic of China, 110
  See also China
People's Republic of North Vietnam, 98
  See also Vietnam War
Pershing, John J., 233
Persian Empire, 255
Peru, 140, 186, 233
  brain drain and, 238–39
Peterson, Peter G., 290
Philippines, 60, 65, 100, 221, 274
  U.S. mutual security pact with, 253
Pineau, Christian, 55
Platt Amendment (1900), 231
Plurality of peoples, 254
Poland, 31, 144
  Soviet takeover of, 27
  Teheran and Yalta negotiations on,
    12–20
Polaris missiles, 76, 265
Polk, James K., 273
Pompidou, Georges, 110, 132
Portugal, 221, 251
Potsdam Conference (1945), 20, 22
President, foreign policy and, 271–83
Pressure groups, military, 264–71
Protectorates, 257
Provisional Revolutionary Government
    (PRG), 124–26, 128
Pyongyang, 46, 47

Quang Tri, 119
Quemoy, 53, 60, 63, 68, 91

Radescu, Nicolae, 16
Radford, Arthur W., 69, 265
Rahman, Mujibur, 135
Rassemblement du peuple français, 83
Raw materials, U.S., 165, 167, 170
  access to, 171–73
Realpolitik, 130, 132–33, 138
Rearmament, 48–50
Reinvesting foreign profits, 168
Reparations, 29–30
Repatriated profits, 168, 172, 174, 227
  imperialism and, 260–61
  in Latin America, 241–43
Revel, Jean François, 251
Revenue Act (1962), 262
Revolutionary spirit 3–4
Rhee, Syngman, 112
Rhodesia, 251
  U.N. sanctions against, 230
Ridgway, Matthew, 69, 265
Rockefeller Nelson A., 234
"Rollback," 97
Roman Empire, 255, 259

Romania, 14, 15, 18, 31, 142
Roosevelt, Elliott, 17
Roosevelt, Franklin D., 12, 94, 115–16,
    130–31
  anti-colonialism of, 233
  Chinese interests at Yalta and, 61–62
  Japanese War agreements with Soviets
    of, 13–14, 21n
  Latin American policies of, 233
  Polish interests at Yalta and, 13–20
  postwar sentiment and, 275
  Stalin and, 40–42
Roosevelt, Theodore, 232
Rostow, Eugene V., 33–35
Rostow, Walter, 104, 116, 179
Rueff, Jacques, 200, 204

Saarland, 30
SAM missiles, 120
Samoa, 274
Samuelson, Paul, 199–200
Santo Domingo, 149, 185, 232, 233, 248,
    258
Sartre, Jean-Paul, 249
Sato, Eisaku, 143
Sato, Naotake, 21
Saudi Arabia, 183
Saxony, 20
Schelling, Thomas, 88
Schiller, Karl, 204
Schlesinger, Arthur, Jr., 271
Schumacher, Karl, 29
Search and destroy missions, 113
Secret Army (Poland), 13, 16
Senate, foreign policy and, 272
Senate Foreign Relations Committee,
    275, 278
Scoul, 62, 112
Seventh Fleet, 252
Sihanouk, Prince, 117–18, 120, 144, 275
Sinai Peninsula, 134
Six-day War (1967), 107, 134–35, 136–37
  U.S. and, 183
Sixth Fleet, 252
Skybolt missile program, 85–86
Soong, T. V., 61
South Africa, 230, 251
South Korea, 60
Southeast Asia Treaty Organization
    (SEATO), 60, 97, 253
Soviet Union, 24
  analysis of cold war and, 148–57
  atomic bomb decision and, 22–24
  Chinese mutual assistance pact of, 69
  India-Pakistan war and, 136
  Kennedy's nuclear strategy and, 74–76,
    79–81

Soviet Union (*cont.*)
  Kissinger-Nixon global system and, 130–47
  Moscow agreement, 14–15, 16
  as multinational empire, 259–60
  negotiations on German partition and, 28–31
  Nixon visit to (1971), 119–20
  nuclear weapons treaties of, 123–24
  postwar partition of Europe and, 25–28
  rejection of Marshall Plan by, 31–35
  role in Korean War of, 69–71
  secret Japanese war agreement with U.S., 13–14, 21n
  Sino-Soviet split, 61, 64, 68, 71, 91–92, 134, 138–39
  Six-day war and, 134–35
  Warsaw Pact established by, 53
Spain, 221
Spanish-American War (1898), 273
Sparta, 254
Spengler, Oswald, 279
Stalin, Joseph, 20, 49, 132
  death of, 52–53
  German partition and, 28
  Korea and, 46–47, 111
  occupation of Poland and, 18–19, 28
  origins of cold war and, 35–42
  rejection of Marshall Plan by, 31–32
  relations with China and, 61–63
  "Stalinism," 51–52
  at Teheran Conference, 12–13
  Truman Doctrine and, 43–44
  at Yalta Conference, 13–16
Stimson, Henry L., 23, 25
Stoleru, Lionel, 211–12, 217
Strategic Air Command (SAC), 76–77
Strategic Arms Limitation Treaty (SALT), 123–24, 148, 155, 266, 269
Strategic nuclear weapons, 77
Subsidiaries, 214–16
Subversion, 78, 79
Suez Canal nationalization (1956), 228
Suez crisis (1956), 53, 54–57
Summit Meeting (Vienna; 1963), 87
Survey of Current Business, 213
Syria, 120, 134, 184
  Soviet bases in, 229

Tachen Islands, 63
Tactical nuclear weapons, 77, 81–86
Taiwan, 60, 121, 253
Talleyrand, Charles M. de, 138
Tanaka, Kakuei, 143
Tariffs, 226

Tashkent, 137
Tax liabilities, foreign investments and, 262
Taylor, Maxwell, 155, 266
Technological superiority, U.S., 169
Teheran Conference (1943), 12–13, 15, 17
  Germany discussed at, 28
Têt offensive (1968), 100
Texas, 273
Thailand, 93, 103, 180, 181, 276
  foreign aid to, 221
Thieu, Nguyen Van, 97, 112, 117, 125–28
Third World, 140, 220–51
  foreign aid to, 221–24
  investment in, 226–28
  trade and, 224–26
  U.S. investment in Africa, 228–31
  U.S. investment in Latin America, 231–51
    brain drain, 236–40
    Brazil, 243–47
    investment and development, 240–43
    political, 247–51
Tho, Le Duc, 124–26, 129
Thuringia, 20
"Tied loans," 223
Tito, Joseph Broz, 40, 44
Tocqueville, Alexis de, 49–50, 251, 271–72
Tojo, Hideki, 21
Tonkin, 114, 126
Tonkin Gulf Resolution (1964), 272
Toynbee, Arnold, 279
Treaties, 252, 272–73
Truman, Harry S, 42, 65, 131–32
  atomic bomb decision of, 21–24
  Berlin blockade and, 57
  Indochina involvement and, 95–96, 152, 182
  Korea and, 45, 47–48, 59, 275–77
  MacArthur and, 265
  Polish negotiations and, 19–20, 27
Truman Doctrine (1947), 24–25, 28, 43–44, 134, 258
Tshombe, M., 230
Tucker, Robert W., 165, 256, 303
Tunisia, 101
Turkey, 12, 24, 28, 52
  foreign aid to, 221
  Truman Doctrine and, 43–44
  U.S. missile bases in, 76, 87

U-2 incident (1960), 68, 75
Ulam, A. B., 42
Underdeveloped countries, *see* Third World

United Fruit Company, 240
United Nations, 18, 37, 41, 52
  Bangladesh and, 136
  China question and, 65–66, 110, 122
  Congo intervention by, 230
  Korea and, 45–46, 59, 70–71
  negotiations on, 19–20
Uruguay, 249
Ussuri fighting (1969), 120, 122

Valéry, Paul, 274
Van Buren, Martin, 273
Vandenberg, Arthur, 275
Venezuela, 241, 249
  brain drain, 238–39
Veracruz occupation (1914), 233
Vernon, Raymond, 292
Vienna, 20
Vietcong, 100, 112
Vietminh, 94–95, 112, 182
Vietnam War, 68, 72, 79, 87, 92–109
  cold war and, 153–55
  domino theory and, 179–81
  French Indochina and, 94–97
  nature of, 111–15
  negotiations for settlement of, 115–20,
    124–30
  U.S. Congress and, 275–77
  U.S. involvement in, 98–107

"Vietnamization," 96, 117
Villa, Pancho, 233
Virgin Islands, 274
Vyshinsky, Andrei Y., 15–16

Waltz, Kenneth, 277
War debts, 190
War of 1812, 273
Warsaw Pact, 53, 252
Watanabe, S., 238
Weimar, 20
Westmoreland, William, 100, 106
Whigs, 273
Williams, W. A., 33, 163–64
Wilson, Woodrow, 233
Woodward, Bob, 298
World Bank, 222–23

Yahia Khan, Agha Mohammed, 108, 135,
  138
Yalta Conference (1945), 62
  German fate discussed at, 28, 30–31
  Poland negotiations at, 13–20, 27
Yalu River, 46, 47, 59, 69
Yemen, 229
Yugoslavia, 15, 31, 43, 249

Zaire, 230
Zelaya, José Santos, 232